Small Island States and International Law
The Challenge of Rising Seas

What happens under international law if a State perishes due to rising sea levels without a successor State being created? Will the State cease to exist? What would this mean for its population? Have international law and globalization progressed enough to protect the people thus affected, or does international law still depend on the territorial State when it comes to protecting entire populations?

Exploring these issues, this book provides answers to these pressing questions. Focusing on small island States as actors in the international community, it evaluates the challenges that the State as a subject of international law faces in general from globalization and humanization, and what this means for small island States threatened by rising seas. Highlighting the experience of the indigenous peoples of small island States as collectives, and to the individuals living in these States, the book addresses fundamental questions of general State theory and international law, drawing on an extensive body of source material.

As rising sea levels present an increasingly pressing threat to small island States, this book highlights the importance of international protection of the individual and the capacity of international organizations to act within existing international law. It identifies pressing problems where immediate action is required and argues that, in future, the responsibility for protecting individuals could shift to the international community, if a sinking island State can no longer protect its population on its own.

Carolin König works as a lawyer in a law firm specializing in energy law. Her personal focus is on international law and the climate policy aspects of energy law. She studied law at the Ludwig-Maximilians-University of Munich and the Katholieke Universiteit Leuven and holds a PhD in international law.

She was a research assistant at the Institute for International Law with a focus on International Human Rights Protection at the University of the German Armed Forces in Munich. She also gained professional experience at the German Foreign Office, in various law firms, including in the field of asylum law, and as legal advisor to the Permanent Mission of the Maldives to the United Nations.

Routledge Research in International Law

WTO Jurisprudence
Governments, Private Rights, and International Trade
Wenwei Guan

State Territory and International Law
Josephat Ezenwajiaku

Territorial Disputes and State Sovereignty
International Law and Politics
Jorge E. Núñez

Indigenous-Industry Agreements, Natural Resources and the Law
Edited by Ibironke T. Odumosu-Ayanu and Dwight Newman

Secession and Statehood
Lessons from Spain and Catalonia
Edited by Ana G Lopez and Jose Perea Unceta

The International Court of Justice and Municipal Courts: An Inter-Judicial Dialogue
Oktawian Kuc

Global Governance, Human Rights and International Law (2nd Edition)
Combating the Tragic Flaw
Errol P. Mendes

Small Island States and International Law
The Challenge of Rising Seas
Carolin König

Private International Law and Arbitral Jurisdiction
Faidon Varesis

Comparative and Transnational Dispute Resolution
Edited by Shahla Ali

For more information about this series, please visit www.routledge.com/Routledge-Research-in-International-Law/book-series/INTNLLAW

Small Island States and International Law

The Challenge of Rising Seas

Carolin König

Routledge
Taylor & Francis Group
LONDON AND NEW YORK

First published 2023
by Routledge
4 Park Square, Milton Park, Abingdon, Oxon OX14 4RN

and by Routledge
605 Third Avenue, New York, NY 10158

Routledge is an imprint of the Taylor & Francis Group, an informa business

British Library Cataloguing-in-Publication Data
A catalogue record for this book is available from the British Library

ISBN: 978-1-032-20442-0 (hbk)
ISBN: 978-1-032-20445-1 (pbk)
ISBN: 978-1-003-26359-3 (ebk)

DOI: 10.4324/9781003263593

Typeset in Times New Roman
by Deanta Global Publishing Services, Chennai, India

To my son Kilian,
in loving memory of my parents Monika and Wolfgang König.

Contents

Acknowledgments x

1 **Introduction** 1

A brief overview of the science behind climate change-induced rising sea levels 3
Small island States, the rising seas, and the international community 6
The rising seas and international law – open questions and how to find answers 12
Notes 15

2 **What does an entity need to qualify as a State? – or what it takes to be a State** 24

Notes 27

3 **When does a State cease to exist? – or what it takes not to be a State anymore** 31

Loss of territory 32
Criterion of "a defined territory" endangered by the rising seas? 33
Statehood endangered by the loss of "a defined territory"? 36
Examples of rights and duties associated with sovereignty 38
Examples of "statehood" without territory 46
States' considerations with regard to potential loss of territory 56
Conclusion 62

Loss of population 64
Concluding thoughts on what it takes not to be a State anymore 68
Notes 72

4 What it means to be a State – the emergence of the modern State and its significance today 99

Rights of a modern State 100
Challenges for the contemporary concept of a State 102
Humanization – the increasing importance of the individual 105
Globalization – the decreasing importance of territory? 114
Concluding thoughts on what it means to be a State 128
Notes 133

5 What it means not to be a State anymore – the consequences of the loss of statehood for the State's population and the international community 158

Loss of statehood and its effects on the respective populations – individual and collective dimension 159
Nationality and why having a State is (still) important for the protection of human rights 160
Emerging infringements on the human rights of (indigenous) peoples from small island States due to rising sea levels 165
Collective dimension of human rights infringements due to climate change 166
Conclusion 169
Loss of statehood – triggering a responsibility of the international community? 171
Human rights approach 172
Responsibility that comes with solidarity 175
Responsibility to protect 179
Causal responsibility 184
Responsibility of the one able to respond 191
Conclusion 198
Concluding thoughts on what it means not to be a State anymore 204
Notes 209

6 Closing remarks 243

Notes 252

Index 257

Acknowledgments

My sincere thanks go to Prof. Dr Bardo Fassbender for supervising the doctoral dissertation on which this book is based and to Prof. Dr Daniel-Erasmus Khan for his work and support as second reader. Also, the scholarship awarded by the Hanns-Seidel-Stiftung is gratefully acknowledged.

I am also indebted to the many people in New York who, during my time at the Maldivian Mission to the United Nations in 2012/2013, gave me insights into their work on behalf of small island States in the fight against climate change.

In addition, I would like to express my heartfelt gratitude to my family, colleagues, and friends who have supported me throughout the years in completing this book. I would especially like to thank Prof. Dr Lando Kirchmair, Christopher Kan, Thomas Streinz, and my sister Dr Stefanie König for their support. Without you, this book would not exist.

Carolin König
Munich, May 2022

1 Introduction

Climate change reshapes the global landscape: Lakes are drying up, rainforests become savannahs, and glaciers melt. In combination with the warming of the oceans, this leads to rising sea levels that make coastlines shrink and islands disappear.[1] In the end, the whole globe is affected.

> Perhaps the most important characteristic of climate change is that all people are locked together now and in the foreseeable future on planet Earth and will suffer together whatever changes in climate are triggered by human activities. The analogy is to a ship, which has a big hole in it.[2]

However,

> low-lying and other small island countries, countries with low-lying coastal, arid and semi-arid areas or areas liable to floods, drought and desertification, and developing countries with fragile mountainous ecosystems are particularly vulnerable to the adverse effects of climate change.[3]

Thus, some States are, so to say, *closer to the hole* and therefore more visibly affected, others are further away, but all are affected. With regard to Palau, a small island State in the Pacific Ocean, Toribiong, then president of Palau, said in 2012:

> If 20 years of climate change negotiations have taught us anything, it's that every state sees climate change differently. For some, it is mainly an economic issue … for others it's about geopolitics and their past or future place in the global economy, but for us it's about survival.[4]

The same year, the International Law Association established a special Committee on International Law and Sea Level Rise in order to study possible impacts of sea level rise and develop proposals for the progressive development of international law.[5] In 2019, the ILC also decided to include this topic ("Sea-level rise in relation to international law") in its program of work.[6] According to the recommendation of the working group, it aims to analyze "Law of the sea issues," "Statehood issues," and "Issues related to the protection of persons affected by sea-level

DOI: 10.4324/9781003263593-1

rise."[7] The decision to include the topic in the commission's long-term program of work points out:

> Sea-level rise has become in recent years a subject of increasing importance for a significant part of the international community – more than 70 States are or are likely to be directly affected by sea-level rise, a group which represents more than one third of the States of the international community. Indeed, as is well known, this phenomenon is already having an increasing impact upon many essential aspects of life for coastal areas, for low-lying coastal States and small island States, and especially for their populations. Another quite large number of States is likely to be indirectly affected (for instance, by the displacement of people or the lack of access to resources). Sea-level rise has become a global phenomenon and thus creates global problems, impacting on the international community as a whole.[8]

While discussing the matter at the UN General Assembly, Ms Chigiyal of the Federated States of Micronesia noted:

> [O]ver 100 States from all the major geographical regions of the world – including coastal States and landlocked countries, continental States and small island States, and developed and developing countries – had spoken in favour of the Commission's studying the topic. That was a testament to its relevance to the international community as a whole, not just to a small group of particularly vulnerable States.[9]

So, climate change is an enormous threat to the human rights of people all over the planet.[10] This, however, should not lead to resignation, but rather to action. Instead of endorsing and awaiting the *sinking of the ship*, possible adaptation and mitigation measures need to be considered *which could fix the hole*.[11] As such, climate change might be

> the ultimate test for the global community to unite and meet a challenge that respects no borders.[12]

This "ultimate test" poses a variety of pressing questions to international lawyers. In the following, the focus shall be laid on some questions related to climate change-induced rising sea levels and the international legal consequences of this phenomenon for small island States: What happens if a small island State gets submerged by the sea? Does it cease to exist? What happens to its nationals? Does the international community have an obligation to protect such a people that cannot be protected by its State?

This book aims to find answers on the basis of existing international law, even though international law in its traditional form remains rather vague with regard to these questions (sometimes, there are no answers given at all).[13] However, the concepts of international law are living concepts that are changing in the course of time. It is intended to point out where the particularly pressing problems lie, where immediate action is needed, where international law is already undergoing necessary changes, and where international law – particularly with regard to its primary subjects – the States – as well as its responsibility with regard to the protection of human rights needs to (further) adapt.

Thereby, the aim of this book is not to prescribe what the future of sinking island States should look like. It rather aims to raise awareness for the difficulties island States have faced and may eventually face in the future, and that these States may not be able to resolve on their own.

A brief overview of the science behind climate change-induced rising sea levels

When discussing the public international law consequences of climate change-induced rising sea levels, a short overview of the scientific findings with regard to this phenomenon seems appropriate.

Hence, what is climate change? Art. 1 para. 2 of the 1992 UN Framework Convention on Climate Change (UNFCCC) defines it as

> a change of climate which is attributed directly or indirectly to human activity that alters the composition of the global atmosphere and which is in addition to natural climate variability observed over comparable time periods.

The climate of the Earth is largely determined by the presence of naturally occurring gases in the atmosphere, including, in particular, water vapor, carbon dioxide (CO^2), methane (CH^4), chlorofluorocarbons (CFCs), nitrous oxide (N^2O), and tropospheric ozone (O^3).[14] These gases form, so to say, a greenhouse around the Earth. They are transparent to incoming shortwave solar radiation but absorb and trap longwave radiation emitted by the Earth's surface: 55 percent of incoming solar energy passes through the atmosphere. Four percent is reflected from the surface back to space, with the remaining 51 percent being absorbed by the Earth's surface and heating it up. This heating results in re-radiation of roughly one-third of this energy in the form of infrared radiation. Some of this outgoing infrared radiation is absorbed by the above-mentioned atmospheric gases. As a result, it stays within the "greenhouse." This is what is called the greenhouse effect.[15]

While the natural greenhouse effect is positive, keeping the Earth warm and habitable, scientific evidence suggests that continued increase in atmospheric concentrations of selected greenhouse gases due to anthropogenic (human-caused) activities is contributing to an "enhanced greenhouse effect."[16] The gases thereby act like a blanket surrounding the Earth. The thicker the "blanket" becomes, the warmer it gets underneath.[17] Less outgoing infrared radiation gets through – and more is absorbed. This subsequently leads to an increase in temperatures on the Earth's surface;[18] and a change of the Earth's climate: Prior to the Industrial Revolution, atmospheric concentration of naturally occurring greenhouse gases had been relatively stable for around 10,000 years.[19] Thus, there was always the same "blanket" around the Earth. When more and more fossil fuel-burning power plants were built to support industry and meet the ever-growing energy demands of modern consumers in the Industrial Age, humans began to interfere in the composition of the atmosphere. They emitted large amounts of additional greenhouse gases. Between 1970 and 2004 alone, global greenhouse gas emissions attributable to human activities increased by 70 percent. The "blanket" became thicker. Today, this poses great risks, not only to the environment, but also to human economy, and probably to the existence of some States.[20]

Why is a change in climate such a risk today? Globally, average temperatures are projected to increase by 2.9–3.4°C above pre-industrial levels (with a greater than 66 percent probability) over the course of the current century.[21] If one compares this rise in temperature to past temperature changes, one gets an impression of how much a few degrees actually matter: A look at the most recent era in which the Earth is believed to have experienced temperatures of 3°C above pre-industrial levels, makes the danger of today very clear: This era was the Pliocene Epoch – around three million years ago. According to Gavin Schmidt, director of NASA's Goddard Institute for Space Studies "[a]t that time, there was almost no ice anywhere. The sea level was 20 meters (65 feet) or so higher, and forests went to the edge of the Arctic Ocean where there is now tundra." Schmidt adds: "It takes a long time for those changes to manifest, but if we see 3°C … it pushes us in that direction."[22]

Thus, climate has always naturally changed, and it already had experienced great changes over geological timescales.[23] But the temperature changes in the last half century have led to an unprecedented rapid global warming trend.[24] This should be kept in mind: Adaptation[25] mechanisms by natural and human systems that were possible in the past might not be possible in the future. Such mechanisms will have (at least) extreme difficulties coping with the current pace of the warming. For instance, in the past, atoll islands seemed to be able to dynamically adapt to sea level changes through vertical growth in the coral reefs.[26] However, the average rate of warming at the end of the last glaciation when such adaptation was happening was about 5°C in some 10,000 years.[27] This comes close to the warming rate expected for the next century.[28] Prior to the nineteenth century, sea levels had not significantly changed for a few thousand years. It is estimated that during the twentieth century the global average sea level rose at a rate of approximately 1.7 mm/year. Sea levels are estimated to have risen since the 1990s by around 3 mm/year.[29] It is doubtful that natural adaptation is possible at such a quick rate. Thus, climate change and the associated rise in the sea level may cause significant and unpredictable coastline shifts.[30]

An increasing number of scientists now argue that a rise in sea levels could be well in excess of a meter by the year 2100 (up to 180 cm[31]), with potentially disastrous consequences for many coastal communities and millions of people.[32] The Intergovernmental Panel on Climate Change (IPCC) Special Report "The Ocean and Cryosphere in a Changing Climate" of September 2019 speaks of a likely range of sea level rise of 0.61–1.10 m by 2100, while expert elicitation studies show that even a global mean sea level rise of 2 m in 2100 cannot be ruled out.[33]

The reason for such a sea level rise is that seawater expands when it gets warmer and the volume of oceans increases globally (this is known as "thermal expansion" or "steric" sea level rise).[34] Additionally, increasing temperatures lead to the melting of polar ice and glaciers, which further contribute to sea level rise,[35] and an increased frequency of hot extremes and heatwaves, heavy precipitation events, and an increase in areas affected by drought, as well as an increased intensity of tropical cyclones (typhoons and hurricanes).[36]

The major cause of sea level rise in this century will be the melting of glaciers and grounded or land-based ice sheets (as opposed to the ones floating in the oceans). In this context it is worth noting that the Greenland ice sheet, were it to collapse and melt completely, would raise the global sea level by six to seven meters. Under the same premises, the West Antarctic ice sheet would raise that level by approximately five meters[37] – an alarming outlook considering that, for Greenland, the temperature threshold for breakdown of its ice is estimated to be at about 1.1–3.8°C above today's global average temperature.[38]

> Sustained mass loss by ice sheets would cause larger sea level rise, and part of the mass loss might be irreversible. There is high confidence that sustained global mean warming greater than a threshold would lead to the near-complete loss of the Greenland ice sheet over a millennium or more, causing a sea level rise of up to 7 m. Current estimates indicate that the threshold is greater than about 1°C (low confidence) but less than about 4°C (medium confidence) of global warming with respect to pre-industrial temperatures. Abrupt and irreversible ice loss from a potential instability of marine-based sectors of the Antarctic ice sheet in response to climate forcing is possible, but current evidence and understanding is insufficient to make a quantitative assessment.[39]

On top of that, the carbon currently caught in the ice could add to the thickness of the "blanket" when being released to the atmosphere. Hence, if at some point the Arctic permafrost releases more carbon than it absorbs, this would start a cycle: The extra carbon in the atmosphere would lead to increased warming which would cause more permafrost to thaw and more methane to release.[40]

Such changes clearly would have effects beyond mere environmental concerns. They raise geopolitical concerns due to their potential effect on the relationships among States. Such effects include changes of traditionally used shipping routes, access to resources previously considered beyond reach, as well as changes of agricultural production, water supply, and energy use. Moreover, much economic activity is concentrated at or near the coast that is in danger of getting submerged.[41] And above all, about 160 million people live less than one meter above sea level on land that could be submerged – or suffer chronic flooding – in this very century. Massive waves of migration and instability are to be expected:[42] A one-meter rise would flood 17 percent of Bangladesh, rendering at least 20 million people homeless.[43] Even under a conservative scenario of only a 0.4 meter increase in sea level by the end of the twenty-first century, the projected number of people flooded in coastal zones would be up to 94 million people.[44] The 2019 IPCC Special Report even speaks of "around 680 million people (nearly 10% of the 2010 global population), projected to reach more than one billion by 2050" living in the "low-lying coastal zone."[45] The latest Sixth Assessment Report speaks of "20% if global mean sea level rises by 0.15 m relative to 2020 levels; this exposed population doubles at a 0.75 m rise in mean sea level and triples at 1.4 m without population change and additional adaptation."[46] If global temperatures were to rise by 3–4°C, the UN Development Programme (UNDP) estimated that 330 million people could be permanently or temporarily displaced due to flooding.[47]

Small island States, the rising seas, and the international community

Small island States are island States that are small with regard to their populations and territories. They are often characterized by low income and heavy dependence on natural resources.[48] To the above-mentioned number of people in danger of being displaced, small island States, upon which this study focuses, contribute only a small percentage, due to the small size of the respective populations. However, they were

> among the first to grapple with the concept of climate change nearly 30 years ago, witnessing the alarming consequences of global warming firsthand. Living at sea level, they were impacted by worsening storms and floods, the loss of once vibrant fisheries, and the intrusion of salt water into land used to grow food.[49]

Today, they are disproportionately affected by such developments. Relative to their population sizes, between 2008 and 2014, they experienced levels of displacement that were three times higher than the global average.[50]

The total population of the four most threatened island States (Tuvalu, Kiribati, and the Marshall Islands in the Pacific, as well as the Maldives in the Indian Ocean) is only approximately half a million.[51] This number could be considered insignificant. In absolute terms, the challenge for small island States is considerable nonetheless: Their very nature[52] makes small island States particularly vulnerable to the effects of global warming[53] in a way that justifies and necessitates special treatment. In contrast to Bangladesh, the Netherlands, or other States with (heavily populated) low-lying coastal areas that will presumably be severely affected, small island States are threatened in their entirety – and as such their very existence as sovereign States. Hence, the main feature that makes a special discussion necessary is that some small island States could become extinct as sovereign States under international law due to the rising seas (without having any direct successors). They "face the real prospect of submergence and complete abandonment during the 21st century."[54] This could not only lead to statelessness of the respective affected populations,[55] but also to a phenomenon without precedent in international law. Ms Dunya Maumoon, Minister for Foreign Affairs of the Republic of Maldives, pointed out in 2015:

> For us in the Maldives, climate change is a security threat. It damages our economy, deprives us of our rights, our land and our way of life and threatens the very existence of our nation. When young children play by the beach, the waves lapping at their feet, when a fisherman looks to the sea for the day's catch and when we feel the cool breeze of the ocean caressing us, it seems inconceivable that those same waters may become our watery grave.[56]

Having recognized the problem, the 78th Conference of the International Law Association, held in Sydney, Australia, 19–24 August 2018, vividly recognized the need for an effective response to the urgent threats posed by sea level rise. It was concerned by the impacts that the sea level rise already has on low-lying islands and coastal areas, which are often densely populated; recognized that sea level rise will jeopardize further the habitability of such areas in the decades to come, creating a potentially large number of persons displaced from areas affected by sea level rise; and recognized further that that some of the affected populations may be forced to leave their homes to find assistance and protection abroad.[57]

Also, the discussion of the 2019 Berlin Climate Security Conference

> began with a stark reminder that, for some states, climate-induced displacement and migration represent an existential threat. In the Maldives, for example, sea level rise of 2 metres could submerge the entire country; many people had already lost property and had to rebuild their lives somewhere else due to the climate crisis.[58]

Then President of the Republic of Nauru, Baron Divavesi Waqa, reminded the audience that climate change also represented an "existential threat" for Nauru, which faced sea level rise, droughts, and record-breaking cyclones.[59]

Apart from the Maldives (highest point 2.4 meters; population 339,330) and Nauru (highest point 61 meters; population 12,809), the existentially threatened States are: Tuvalu (highest point 5 meters; population 11,468); Kiribati (highest point 81 meters; population 100,798); Marshall Islands (highest point 10 meters; population 72,191); and the Bahamas (highest point 63 meters; population 299,697),[60] particularly because the average altitude of the islands is far lower: For the Maldives and Tuvalu, it is reportedly about one meter, for other low-lying atoll States about two meters.[61] Sufficient natural adaptation is unlikely at the predicted speed, as pointed out above. Artificial adaptation to climate change (such as building new land or protecting existing land artificially)[62] is complex[63] and heavily dependent on resilience, access to resources, and the financial capacity of the communities involved. Thus, middle-income countries like the Maldives will probably be able to afford more expensive adaptation strategies than poorer countries such as Tuvalu in the Pacific.[64]

Moreover, there are regional differences: As such, the Pacific island region seems particularly vulnerable. Sea level rise in that region has been consistently higher, with consequently greater impact, than the global average in recent years, and the coastal communities are struck by frequent tropical cyclones.[65] Adaptation strategies must focus attention at the local scale.[66]

Tuvalu, to give an example of one of the most vulnerable States in this regard, is one of the smallest and remotest island States in the Pacific. It consists of four reef islands and five atolls scattered over 1.2 million square kilometers of the Pacific Ocean "halfway between Australia and Hawaii." The total land area of the country is roughly 25.6 square kilometers, which is relatively evenly distributed across the nine atolls. This geographical composition makes Tuvalu very vulnerable to coastal erosion and the rising sea level.[67] Because of the small size and the remoteness of the separate islands, dikes and sea walls are more difficult to install there than, for example, on the coast of the Netherlands. As such, Tuvalu's Fongafale Island, which is the largest island in Funafuti Atoll, would, according to scientists, become submerged by a sea level rise of only 0.6 meters, although it reaches an elevation of 1.2 meters.[68] Hence, following some estimates, Tuvalu could disappear within the next 50 years.[69]

Even without full disappearance, these States' populations can become existentially threatened. With the rising seas come inundation, soil salinization, sea water intrusion into freshwater lenses, and a decline in freshwater supply.[70] For instance, in Kiribati's Phoenix Islands group, all but one island, Kanton Island, can no longer support populations because of lack of potable water.[71] Also, for the Marshall Islands it is said that life on the islands could become untenable by the end of the twenty-first century if current trends in greenhouse gas emissions continue.[72]

For more than 20 years, scholars have been warning that low-lying island States are existentially threatened by global warming. And indeed, in 1998, the first uninhabited islands began disappearing. In 2006, the first inhabited island (India's Lohachara Island, home to 10,000 people) became submerged by the sea.[73] Residents of Papua New Guinea's Carteret Islands (a culturally unique Halia-speaking community) started abandoning their sinking islands in 2007. This evacuation is still ongoing,[74] and likely to become a forerunner of similar, albeit much larger, events to come.[75] The current evaluation of the project is devastating:

> In the twenty-first century, [...] a second attempt at resettlement began. That phase sought to relocate 50% of the island's population by 2020. Neither the government of [Papua New Guinea] nor that of the now Autonomous Province of Bougainville gave this priority or purchased land for resettlement, leaving the task to a local [Carteret Islands] organisation, Tulele Peisa ("Sailing the waves on our own") with some support from the Catholic church in Bougainville. Tulele Peisa regularly reported relocation being needed because of "rising sea levels." The lack of state-provided land meant that an "ideal opportunity for securing land for some of the world's first climate change displaced persons was lost" [...]. Obtaining any land beyond the 81 hectares donated by the church, let alone suitable land for

> successful relocation, was extremely difficult, and Tulele Peisa had no financial resources to secure land or develop a settlement [...]. By 2011 no more than ten households had relocated to Bougainville, and there were frequent disputes with nearby landowners. [...]. Despite frequent stresses, and several attempts, Carteret Islanders have been unable to establish multi-sited livelihoods.[76]

This is a bad outlook for future projects of this kind (Parry called the Carteret Islands "a portent of catastrophe to come,")[77] such as for people in Tuvalu, Vanuatu, and Kiribati who have already started to be displaced by the rising seas.[78] In this context, one must keep in mind that the rising seas are not an act of nature beyond our control. Global warming is caused by human activity.[79] Torres Camprubí argues therefore

> that the Earth may be leaving its most recent known, and currently official geological epoch, the Holocene, which began around 11,700 years ago and has been characterized by a relative environmental stability that has proved to be crucial for the development of human civilization as we know it today.

The (upcoming) Anthropocene, in contrast, is described as being "characterized by change, uncertainty and, probably, considerable instability in the behavior of the Earth system."[80]

Scientific conferences started to point to increased evidence of human interference with the climate at the end of the 1970s. The General Assembly first articulated this concern in 1988 in its Resolution 43/53:

> The General Assembly,
>
> Welcoming with appreciation the initiative taken by the Government of Malta in proposing for consideration by the Assembly the item entitled "Conservation of climate as part of the common heritage of mankind,"
>
> Concerned that certain human activities could change global climate patterns, threatening present and future generations with potentially severe economic and social consequences,
>
> Noting with concern that the emerging evidence indicates that continued growth in atmospheric concentrations of "greenhouse" gases could produce global warming with an eventual rise in sea levels, the effects of which could be disastrous for mankind if timely steps are not taken at all levels, [...]
>
> Convinced that climate change affects humanity as a whole and should be confronted within a global framework so as to take into account the vital interests of all mankind,
>
> 1. Recognizes that climate change is a *common concern of mankind*, since climate is an essential condition which sustains life on earth;
> 2. Determines that necessary and *timely action* should be taken to deal with climate change *within a global framework*;[81]

Such a global framework[82] was developed in the same year: The UN Environment Programme (UNEP) and the World Meteorological Organization (WMO) established the IPCC to provide scientific guidance on the threat of climate change. It published its First Assessment Report in August 1990, which predicted that global mean temperatures could rise by an average of about 0.3°C per decade during the next century, increasing a rise in the global mean sea level by 0.2 meters by 2030 and 0.65 meters (up to 1.01 meters according to the latest Sixth Assessment Report)[83] by the end of the twenty-first century.[84] Subsequent IPCC Reports published in 1995, 2001, 2007, 2013/2014, and 2022 have confirmed and elaborated upon these findings. The Fourth Assessment Report of 2007 concluded that "[w]arming of the climate system is unequivocal, as is now evident from observations of increases in global average air and ocean temperatures, widespread melting of snow and ice and rising global average sea level."[85] Seven years later, the Fifth Assessment Report found even stronger words:

> Warming of the climate system is unequivocal, and since the 1950s, many of the observed changes are unprecedented over decades to millennia. The atmosphere and ocean have warmed, the amounts of snow and ice have diminished, and sea level has risen.[86]

Thus, the "*common concern of mankind*" that was recognized by the General Assembly in 1988 became more and more precise over the years. The "*necessary and timely action [that] should be taken*" according to the General Assembly back then is not as clear though.

What is (still) clear is that "[i]f the changes are due to human activity, they are likely to continue and even accelerate unless we change our behavior."[87] Thus, action can and should be taken. But CO^2 that is currently spread in the atmosphere prevails there for 50–200 years.[88] The answer to the question "Can we fix climate change?" is therefore, as Proelß points out, "We don't know."[89]

Nevertheless, small island States are (understandably) quite active in the fight against climate change:[90] The first political manifestation of this can be found in a conference held in Malé (the capital of the Maldives) in November 1989,[91] where the countries that attended increased their awareness of their vulnerability to sea level rise. Back then, these countries called on the "world family of nations" to "immediately limit their greenhouse gas emissions."[92] In 1990, the Alliance of Small Island States (AOSIS) was created "as an ad hoc informal issue-specific mini-coalition of states' focused primarily on the issue of climate change."[93] This coalition now consists of 39 States and five observers that share the common characteristic of being constituted of small islands and low-lying communities. Its members all share a growing concern about the environment and the effects that climate change can have on the fragile ecosystems of their homelands.[94]

In 1992, the UNFCCC was adopted and entered into force on 21 March 1994. Its ultimate aim is the prevention of "dangerous" human interference with the climate system.[95] It has a near universal membership and provides the common international framework to address the causes and consequences of climate change.[96] It acts as a consensus-building exercise that lays the groundwork for succeeding agreements.[97]

Also in 1994, the developing countries declared in the Barbados declaration:

> While small island developing States are among those that contribute least to global climate change and sea-level rise, they are among those that would suffer most from the adverse effects of such phenomena and could in some cases become uninhabitable. [98]

The facts had thus been clear already throughout the negotiatory process of the 1997 Kyoto Protocol[99] where

> governmental Delegates themselves sought to reach a consensus, overcoming their individual divergent interests, and succeeding to adopt the Kyoto Protocol as a package deal, aware as they were of the importance of facing the challenge of climate change which affected ultimately humankind as a whole.[100]

The latest outcome in the UNFCCC field is the Paris Agreement[101] that was adopted on 12 December 2015 and has since been ratified by 193 of 197 Parties to the Convention.[102] In the preceding negotiations, small island States were actively involved. They held "the moral high-ground in the climate debate even if they have little actual economic or political clout."[103]

> They have drawn a baseline that has defined the meaning of dangerous climate, and this came to fruition in the 2015 Paris Agreement's target of limiting global warming to 2.0°C above pre-industrial levels and its recognition that the international community should aspire to limit the increase in global average temperature to 1.5°C above pre-industrial levels.[104]

Thus, due to their influence, the "1.5 goal" found its way into the Paris Agreement.[105] This was important because a 2°C warming could already be irreversibly dangerous:[106] The initiative of "1Point5 to stay alive" pointed out:

> With a 2°C increase, by the end of this century 1300 sq. kilometer of land will disappear in the Caribbean: an area comparable to the whole of Barbados, Saint-Vincent and the Grenadines, Anguilla, Antigua & Barbuda, combined. For a fair chance to stay alive, we want the world to agree on a 1.5°C max rise. 2 degrees not only invokes risks that could jeopardize the survival of nations, it also increases the chances of destabilizing feedback mechanisms that could carry warming even further.[107]

Hence, this target was "a victory [which 'may yet be a hollow victory'[108]] for small islands states that could be wiped out by rising sea levels well before we even get to 2 degrees warmer."[109] They "had won an acknowledgement of their right to remain habitable places to live."[110] The successful result was possible, because a "high ambition coalition" coalesced between different negotiating blocs, and members of AOSIS and the EU began to articulate common goals while meeting secretly for month before the Paris meeting.[111]

The convention entered into force (quicker than expected) on 4 November 2016 (30 days after the date on which at least 55 Parties to the Convention, accounting in total for at least an estimated 55 percent of the total global greenhouse gas emissions, had deposited their instruments of ratification, acceptance, approval, or accession with the Depositary).[112] It was thereby agreed that by 2100 they need to limit global warming to well below 2°C above pre-industrial times, with a 1.5°C increase as a scientific stretch goal. However, while it has already been doubted that even full implementation of the intended nationally determined contribution under the Paris Agreement would be enough to keep warming lower than 2°C,[113] it is clear that the "longer we wait to act, the greater the build-up in greenhouse gases, and the result will be a higher rate of warming."[114] Even if "we stopped emitting greenhouse gases tomorrow, the increase in atmospheric concentration of carbon dioxide, as a result of the burning of fossil fuels and destruction of forests since the industrial revolution, would persist for centuries."[115] In any case, scientists agree that "the extent to which countries work together to limit release of more greenhouse gases may have a significant impact on how quickly seas rise, and how much."[116]

Some effects will not be preventable though. Thus, while the "ideal solution to the disappearing-islands problem involves addressing the causes of global warming and preventing sea levels from rising any further,"[117] it is clear today that climate change will inevitably have significant impacts, impacts that go to the heart of international law: Some *States*, and thus some of international law's main subjects, are challenged. This has implications for traditional notions of international law, most notably those relating to the principle of territorial sovereignty and the presumption of liability for damages.[118] The functioning of the international community (in this regard) is contested.

The rising seas and international law – open questions and how to find answers

This book deals with the question of what happens under international law when a State sinks (due to the rising sea) without a successor State being created. Will the State lose its existence as a result? What would this mean for the affected population? While the personal fate of those affected is undoubtedly terrible, do international protection mechanisms at least provide a safety net to cushion the loss of the affected individuals? Is the humanization of international law and the globalization of the world already sufficiently advanced? Or does it (still) ultimately depend on the respective State when it comes to protecting entire population groups? If neither mitigation nor adaptation contribute to solving the human rights problems associated with climate change, does international law need to focus more on the individual who needs protection even without a State in the background? And must human rights law focus more on collective protection in the context of climate change?

The first part of the book (Chapters 2 and 3) aims to show what it formally "takes to be a State" (expression taken from Warbrick)[119] in the sense of what is necessary for an entity to qualify as a State, and at what point an entity loses its statehood by losing such qualifications. Thereby it forms the basis of analyzing the above-mentioned dangers for States that are threatened in their existence through the rising seas. However,

> [e]stablishing the criteria of statehood is only part of the exercise. What are the legal consequences of being a State – for any State and for all States? What are the rights and duties, the powers and immunities that attach to an entity simply because it is a State?[120]

The second part of the book turns to *what it means to be a State* for the State as such and its significance in the modern world. This is important, particularly from the point of view of the individual. This part again comprises two complementary chapters. It is intended to explore "what it means to be a State" and "what it means not to be a State anymore." Chapter 4 explores on the one hand the significance of States as such in the twenty-first century. On the other hand, it investigates what an entity gains from being a State. It aims to point out current changes of and challenges to the concept of the State. What is the purpose of a State in the contemporary world order? The traditional Westphalian notion of an independent State has greatly developed within the last century. National sovereignty became gradually modified by globalization on the one hand and humanization[121] on the other. Is the concept of the State as such outdated? The examination will show that neither humanization nor globalization has turned the State into an obsolete subject in international law, but rather that both trends had impacts on the concept of the State: the importance of the individual has increased, whereas (probably) the importance of territory has decreased. Moreover, individuals and international organizations can – to a certain degree – be seen as new derivative subjects of international law, additional to the States as international law's original subjects with their rights and duties. But despite the changes in the concept of the State, the status "State" with all its rights remains unique, crucial, gainful, and in demand. It will become clear that the status "State" does not differ too much from the traditional one. However, understanding the role of the State in the modern world might provide the possibility to rethink this role.

> By rethinking the role of the state as the central domain of moral concern and primary guarantor of human rights, it becomes possible to consider a range of alternative mechanisms for the fulfilment of rights for those who no longer have a state. In other words, by recognising a new "ought" – that those who are denied basic human rights as a result of climate change impacts should count as part of a global community of moral concern in which state

> boundaries no longer function as a constraint on the fulfilment of human rights – it is possible to pave the way for a new "is."[122]

Thus, possibly, as the protection of the individual becomes more important (internationally), and the ability of international organizations to act becomes more vital, the responsibility to protect individuals could go over to the international community, at least when the State in question can no longer protect its population sufficiently.

This is scrutinized in the next chapter. On the basis of the previous findings, the vacuum that arises when a State disappears (for the populations in question and the international community) is analyzed (Chapter 5). The analysis of the loss that the extinction of a State brings with it shall lay its focus on the populations in question and the challenges they face (individually and collectively) from the possible loss of their nation State. Seeing this, and on the basis of what the previous chapter showed regarding humanization and globalization, this chapter then synthesizes the role of the international community.

In the course of humanization, human rights-related obligations for the respective States were identified beforehand as increasingly important. Individuals claiming their rights in this context might very well fall on deaf ears though, because their primary protector of human rights, being their State, disappeared. But it has been shown that (the protection of) human rights became internationalized. Hence, a (subsidiary) responsibility of the international community shall be tested.

While the situation of the disappearance of entire States without successors has up to now not been regulated by any norms of international law, a development in this regard might be visible: The international community is – according to the UN's *R2P* (Responsibility to Protect) initiative[123] of 2005 – responsible for assisting States when it comes to human rights violations through mass atrocities. The concept confirms that a State has a responsibility to protect its population from genocide, war crimes, ethnic cleansing, and crimes against humanity. This does not come as a surprise. But if the State is unable or unwilling to fulfill this responsibility, it becomes, according to the concept, the responsibility of the international community to act in the State's place. That seems logical with a view to the previously examined trends of humanization and globalization. And the idea behind this concept could fit the current case of sinking island States which is explored in more detail below.

Moreover, it appears wrong if a *community* that perceives itself as more than just a loose collection of coexisting States does not get involved in a situation where one of its members faces extinction due to the rising seas. In particular, if there is a probability that sea level rise is caused jointly by all States together and even more so if there are human rights of individuals involved that are meant to be under a shared responsibility, there should be an obligation for the international community to act in place of a sinking State.

Notwithstanding the declining fate of the theory of fundamental rights and duties of States, it cannot be denied that international law rules such as the ones relating to independence, sovereignty, and equality of States still occupy a central role in the international legal order. This, however, cannot be justified on the basis of their hierarchical position, but, rather, has to be explained because of the peculiar content of the rights and duties under consideration. Such rights and duties, in fact, continue to be crucial to the functioning of the international legal order as they provide a set of basic obligations which support the peaceful coexistence of independent and sovereign States.[124]

In the end, a legal vacuum would remain where the rising seas lead to the extinction of a State. This is a vacuum that international law is currently not prepared to fill. Therefore, it is the primary responsibility of the international community today to prevent this legal vacuum from arising in the first place, and to protect the affected individuals who are not protected otherwise.

The conclusion, in Chapter 6, seeks more to persuade than to describe. The addressee is the international community, which has a crucial role to play in acting together with and supporting member States in their efforts to turn what the Secretary-General has called the "greatest collective challenge facing humankind today – climate change – into the greatest opportunity for common progress towards a sustainable future."[125]

Notes

1 K. Akasaka, "Guiding Principles Needed: Towards a global strategy for climate change," *2 UN Chronicle* (2007), p. 22.
2 E. Brown Weiss, "Strengthening Compliance with Climate Change Commitments" in H. Hestermeyer, R. Wolfrum (eds), *Coexistence, Cooperation and Solidarity: Liber Amicorum Rüdiger Wolfrum* (2012), p. 701.
3 UN Human Rights Council, *Human Rights and Climate Change*, 28 March 2008, p. 2.
4 Pacific Islands News Association, *Island nations want climate change in world court* (2012).
5 International Law Association, Committee on International Law and Sea Level Rise, "Establishment of the Committee and Its Mandate" in D. Vidas, D. Freestone, J. McAdam (eds), *Report of the International Law Association* (2019), p. 4.
6 ILC, *Report of the ILC Covering the Work of its seventy-first session,* 29 April–7 June and 8 July–9 August 2019, Official Records of the General Assembly, Seventy-fourth Session, Supplement No. 10, 2019, p. 340-341.
7 ILC, *Report of the ILC Covering the Work of its Seventieth Session*, 30 April–1 June and 2 July–10 August 2018, Official Records of the General Assembly, Seventy-third Session, Supplement No. 10, 2018, p. 328–9.
8 Ibid., p. 326, para. 1.
9 UNGA, *Sixth Committee – Summary record of the 22nd meeting*, 3 December 2018, para. 56.
10 Yale Center for Environmental Law & Policy, *Climate Change and the International Court of Justice: Seeking an Advisory Opinion on Transboundary Harm from the Court* (2014), p. 38.
11 "Ultimately, adaptation is an exercise in damage limitation. It deals with the symptoms of a problem that can be cured only through mitigation. However, failure to deal with the symptoms will lead to large-scale human development losses," K. Watkins et al., *UNDP Human Development Report 2007/2008 – Fighting Climate Change: Human Solidarity in a Divided World* (2007), p. 198.
12 UN Habitat, *How the UN System Supports Ambitious Action on Climate Change: UN System Chief Executives Board for Coordination* (2014), Foreword by the UN Secretary General.

13 Cf. C. Schaller, T.-S. Schrader, "Der Anstieg des Meeresspiegels als Thema für den VN-Sicherheitsrat," *SWP-Aktuell, Nr. 41, Juni 2020* (2020), p. 1.

14 P. J. Sands and I. Millar, "Climate, International Protection," (last updated March 2012) in R. Wolfrum (ed.), *The Max Planck Encyclopedia of Public International Law: opil.ouplaw.com.home/EPIL* (2012), para. 1.

15 M. C. MacCracken, "Climate Change and Global Warming" in J. E. Oliver (ed.), Encyclopedia of World Climatology (2005), p. 202 et seq.; J. Kerr Casper, *Greenhouse Gases: Worldwide Impacts* (2010), p. 6 et seq.; IPCC 2007: S. Solomon, D. Qin and M. Manning, *IPCC 2007 – The Physical Science Basis*, p. 96 et seq. See also with further references: W. C. G. Burns and H. M. Osofsky, "Overview: The Exigencies That Drive Potential Causes of Action for Climate Change" in W. C. G. Burns, H. M. Osofsky (eds), *Adjudicating Climate Change: State, National, and International Approaches* (2009), p. 2 et seq.; P. J. Sands and I. Millar, "Climate, International Protection," (last updated March 2012) in R. Wolfrum (ed.), *The Max Planck Encyclopedia of Public International Law: opil.ouplaw.com.home/EPIL* (2012), para. 1.

16 P. J. Sands and I. Millar, "Climate, International Protection," (last updated March 2012) in R. Wolfrum (ed.), *The Max Planck Encyclopedia of Public International Law: opil.ouplaw.com.home/EPIL* (2012), para. 1.

17 B. Pittock, "The science of climate change: knowledge, uncertainty and risk" in C. Lever-Tracy (ed.), *Routledge Handbook of Climate Change and Society* (2010), p. 20.

18 IPCC 2007: L. Bernstein et al., *IPCC 2007 – Synthesis Report*, p. 36; cf. N. Schrijver, "The Impact of Climate Change: Challenges for International Law" in U. Fastenrath, R. Geiger, D.-E. Khan, A. Paulus, S. von Schorlemer, C. Vedder (eds), *From Bilateralism to Community Interest: Essays in Honour of Judge Bruno Simma* (2011), p. 1278; B. Pittock, "The science of climate change: knowledge, uncertainty and risk" in C. Lever-Tracy (ed.), *Routledge Handbook of Climate Change and Society* (2010), p. 19; W. C. G. Burns and H. M. Osofsky, "Overview: The Exigencies That Drive Potential Causes of Action for Climate Change" in W. C. G. Burns, H. M. Osofsky (eds), *Adjudicating Climate Change: State, National, and International Approaches* (2009), p. 2 et seq. in much more detail with further references.

19 On the concentration: K. Pittel, D. Rübbelke, and M. Altemeyer-Bartscher, "International Efforts to Combat Global Warming" in W.-Y. Chen (ed.), *Handbook of Climate Change Mitigation* (2012), p. 95.

20 P. J. Sands and I. Millar, "Climate, International Protection," (last updated March 2012) in R. Wolfrum (ed.), *The Max Planck Encyclopedia of Public International Law: opil.ouplaw.com.home/EPIL* (2012), para. 1.

21 IPCC 2018: H. de Coninck; A. Revi et al., *IPCC 2018 – Global Warming of 1.5°C*, p. 357.

22 Cf. Aljazeera, *As UN says world to warm by 3 degrees, scientists explain what that means* (2015); M. A. Chandler, *The Climate of the Pliocene: Simulating Earth's Last Great Warm Period* (1997), p. 2.

23 Prehistoric global warming even led to a complete transformation of the Earth's surface, with the disappearance of massive ice sheets, continent-wide changes in vegetation cover, regional extinctions, and sea-level rise of about 120 meters (B. Pittock, "The science of climate change: knowledge, uncertainty, and risk" in C. Lever-Tracy (ed.), *Routledge Handbook of Climate Change and Society* (2010), p. 16).

24 Ibid., p. 14; D. A. Farber; C. A. Carlarne, *Climate Change Law* (2018), p. 212.

25 The IPCC defines adaptation as "The adjustment in natural or human systems in response to actual or expected climatic stimuli or their effects, which moderates harm or exploits beneficial opportunities." (IPCC 2007: M. Parry, O. Canziani and J. Palutikof, *IPCC 2007 - Impacts, Adaptation and Vulnerability*, p. 6).

26 L. Yamamoto and M. Esteban, *Atoll Island States and International Law: Climate Change Displacement and Sovereignty* (2014), p. 105; cf. S. Park, *Climate Change*

and the Risk of Statelessness: The Situation of Low-lying Island States (2011), p. 10–11; W. Zukerman, *Shape-Shifting Islands Defy Sea-Level Rise* (2010); D. H. Spennemann, "Water futures and their influence on sovereignty in the Marshall Islands" in D. Ghosh, H. Goodall, S. H. Donald (eds), *Water, Sovereignty and Borders in Asia and Oceania* (2009), p. 62.

27 Some 120,000 years ago, at the peak of the last interglacial period, the oceans were approximately 4 to 6 meters higher than today's level (D. D. Caron, "Climate Change, Sea Level Rise and the Coming Uncertainty in Oceanic Boundaries: A Proposal to Avoid Conflict" in S.-Y. Hong, J. M. van Dyke (eds), *Maritime Boundary Disputes, Settlement Processes, and the Law of the Sea* (2009), p. 7, citing J. F. Marshall and B. G. Thom, "The sea-level in the last interglacial," *263 Nature* (1976), p. 120).

28 B. Pittock, "The science of climate change: knowledge, uncertainty and risk" in C. Lever-Tracy (ed.), *Routledge Handbook of Climate Change and Society* (2010), p. 16.

29 L. Yamamoto and M. Esteban, *Atoll Island States and International Law: Climate Change Displacement and Sovereignty* (2014), p. 38; cf. B. Pittock, "The science of climate change: knowledge, uncertainty and risk" in C. Lever-Tracy (ed.), *Routledge Handbook of Climate Change and Society* (2010), p. 22.

30 J. Lisztwan, "Stability of Maritime Boundary Agreements," *37 Yale Journal of International Law* (2012), p. 155, with further references.

31 R. J. Nicholls and A. Cazenave, "Sea-Level Rise and its Impact on Coastal Zones," *328 Science, New Series 5985* (2010), p. 1518. M.-E. Carr, M. Rubenstein, A. Graff and D. Villarreal, "Sea Level Rise in a Changing Climate: What Do We Know?" in M. Gerrard, G. E. Wannier (eds), *Threatened Island Nations: Legal Implications of Rising Seas and a Changing Climate* (2013), p. 35–6 (0.75 to 1.90 meters) with further references. These numbers vary in different regions: for an overview over expected sea level rise in the Pacific region, see J. Aucan, "Effects of Climate Change on Sea Levels and Inundation Relevant to the Pacific Islands," *Pacific Marine Climate Change Report Card: Science Review 2018*, pp 43–9 (2018).

32 B. Pittock, "The science of climate change: knowledge, uncertainty and risk" in C. Lever-Tracy (ed.), *Routledge Handbook of Climate Change and Society* (2010), p. 29; cf. J. Barnett, "Adapting to Climate Change in Pacific Island Countries: The Problem of Uncertainty," *29 World Development* (2001), p. 977; S.-Y. Hong, J. M. van Dyke (eds), *Maritime Boundary Disputes, Settlement Processes, and the Law of the Sea* (2009), p. 7; M. Hayashi, "Sea-Level Risen and the Law of the Sea: Future Options" in D. Vidas, P. J. Schei (eds), *The World Ocean in Globalisation: Climate Change, Sustainable Fisheries, Biodiversity, Shipping, Regional Issues* (2011), p. 187; UN Secretary General, *Oceans and the law of the sea Report of the Secretary-General*, 10 March 2008, para. 354–7; M. Gerrard and G. E. Wannier, "Overview" in M. Gerrard, G. E. Wannier (eds), *Threatened Island Nations: Legal Implications of Rising Seas and a Changing Climate* (2013), p. 4.

33 IPCC 2019: M. Oppenheimer and B. Glavovic, "Chapter 4 – Sea Level Rise and Implications for Low Lying Islands, Coasts and Communities" in *IPCC Special Report: The Ocean and Cryosphere in a Changing Climate* (2019), p. 520 (4.1.2).

34 IPCC 2007: S. Solomon, D. Qin, and M. Manning, *IPCC 2007 – The Physical Science Basis*, p. 414.

35 L. Yamamoto and M. Esteban, *Atoll Island States and International Law: Climate Change Displacement and Sovereignty* (2014), p. 37–8; cf. I. Allison, *The Copenhagen diagnosis: Updating the world on the latest climate science* (2009), p. 37.

36 UN Human Rights Council, *Report of the Office of the UN High Commissioner for Human Rights on the relationship between climate change and human rights*, 15 January 2009, p. 5, para. 8–9; cf. J. Barnett and J. Campbell, *Climate Change and Small Island States: Power, Knowledge and the South Pacific* (2010), p. 9.

37 C. Schofield, "Rising Waters, Shrinking States: The Potential Impacts of Sea Level Rise on Claims to Maritime Jurisdiciton," *53 German Yearbook of International Law* (2010), p. 1945; cf. IPCC 2007: M. Parry, O. Canziani and J. Palutikof, *IPCC 2007 – Impacts, Adaptation and Vulnerability*, p. 834; A. Bojanowski, "Anstieg des Meeresspiegels: Grönlandeis könnte komplett verschwinden," 08.12.2016 *Der Spiegel* (2016); J. Leber, *The Paris Climate Deal Is A Good Start–But Probably Not Good Enough* (2015).

38 IPCC 2007: M. Parry, O. Canziani and J. Palutikof, *IPCC 2007 – Impacts, Adaptation and Vulnerability*, p. 41; cf. http://www.1point5.info/whatsup (last visited 30 June 2019); B. Pittock, "The science of climate change: knowledge, uncertainty and risk" in C. Lever-Tracy (ed.), *Routledge Handbook of Climate Change and Society* (2010), p. 24.

39 IPCC 2014: R. K. Pachauri and L. Meyer, *IPCC 2014 – Synthesis Report*, p. 74.

40 National Snow and Ice Data Center, *Methane and Frozen Ground* (2017): "Right now, the Earth's atmosphere contains about 850 gigatons of carbon. [...] We estimate that there are about 1,400 gigatons of carbon frozen in permafrost."

41 M.-E. Carr, M. Rubenstein, A. Graff, and D. Villarreal, "Sea Level Rise in a Changing Climate: What Do We Know?" in M. Gerrard, G. E. Wannier (eds), *Threatened Island Nations: Legal Implications of Rising Seas and a Changing Climate* (2013), p. 42.

42 http://unfccc.int/meetings/marrakech_nov_2016/items/10041.php (last visited 20 November 2019); I. Allison, *The Copenhagen diagnosis: Updating the world on the latest climate science* (2009), p. 37. A number of States presented climate change as an issue of global security before the UNSC for the first time in April 2007 (C. Di Leva and S. Morita, "Maritime Rights of Coastal States and Climate Change: Should States Adapt to Submerged Boundaries," *5 Law & Development Working paper Series* (2008), p. 1; cf. UN Human Rights Council, *Report of the Office of the UN High Commissioner for Human Rights on the relationship between climate change and human rights*, 15 January 2009, para. 61–4.).

43 J. Lisztwan, "Stability of Maritime Boundary Agreements," *37 Yale Journal of International Law* (2012), p. 155; cf. on Bangladesh: J. McAdam and B. Saul, "Displacement with Dignity: International Law and Policy Responses to Climate Change Migration and Security in Bangladesh," *53 German Yearbook of International Law* (2010), p. 234 et seq.; C. Toomey, *The Maldives: Trouble in paradise* (2009).

44 L. Yamamoto and M. Esteban, *Atoll Island States and International Law: Climate Change Displacement and Sovereignty* (2014), p. 39, with further references.

45 IPCC 2019: H.O. Pörtner, D.C. Roberts, V. Masson-Delmotte, P. Zhai, M. Tignor, E. Poloczanska, K. Mintenbeck, M. Nicolai, A. Okem, J. Petzold, B. Rama, N. Weyer (eds) "Summary for Policymakers," in: *IPCC Special Report: The Ocean and Cryosphere in a Changing Climate* (2019), p. 5.

46 IPCC 2022: Summary for Policymakers, IPCC WGII Sixth Assessment Report, SPM.B.4.5.

47 Cf. S. Park, *Climate Change and the Risk of Statelessness: The Situation of Low-lying Island States* (2011), p. 3.

48 J. Barnett, "Titanic states? Impacts and responses to climate change in the Pacific islands," *59 Journal of International Affairs* (2005), p. 206.

49 http://aosis.org/ (last visited 29 August 2019) (Why is AOSIS important? – posted by the admin on 10 July 2019).

50 J. McAdam, B. Burson, W. Kälin and S. Weerasinghe, "International Law and Sea-Level Rise: Forced Migration and Human Rights," *FNI Report 1/2016* (2016), p. 19.

51 M. Gerrard and G. E. Wannier, "Overview" in M. Gerrard, G. E. Wannier (eds), *Threatened Island Nations: Legal Implications of Rising Seas and a Changing Climate* (2013), p. 6; S. Park, *Climate Change and the Risk of Statelessness: The Situation of Low-lying Island States* (2011), p. 3; K. M. Wyman, "The National Immigration Policy Option: Limits and Potential" in M. Gerrard, G. E. Wannier (eds), *Threatened*

Island Nations: Legal Implications of Rising Seas and a Changing Climate (2013), p. 337 et seq.

52 The UNGA lists several factors that contribute to the vulnerability of small island States: (a) their small size; (b) remoteness; (c) vulnerability to external (demand and supply-side) shocks; (d) narrow resource base; (e) exposure to global environmental challenges (UNGA, *Five-year review of the Mauritius Strategy for the Further Implementation of the Programme of Action for the Sustainable Development of Small Island Developing States Report of the Secretary-General*, 6 July 2010, p. 8, para. 12; cf. S. Atapattu, *Human Rights Approaches to Climate Change: Challenges and Opportunities* (2015), p. 223).

53 Cf. E. Ronneberg, "Small Islands and the Big Issue: Climate Change and the Role of the Alliance of Small Island States" in C. P. Carlarne, K. R. Gray, R. G. Tarasofsky (eds), *The Oxford Handbook of International Climate Change Law* (2016), p. 774.

54 R. J. Nicholls and A. Cazenave, "Sea-Level Rise and its Impact on Coastal Zones," *328 Science, New Series 5985* (2010), p. 1519.

55 S. Park, *Climate Change and the Risk of Statelessness: The Situation of Low-lying Island States* (2011), p. 3.

56 UNGA, *Agenda item 8*, 3 October 2015, p. 14.

57 International Law Association, Committee on International Law and Sea Level Rise, Sydney, *Resolution 6/2018*, Australia, 19–24 August 2018, p. 1 (see Annex for the Sydney Declaration on the Protection of Persons displaced in the context of Sea Level Rise).

58 Berlin Climate and Security Conference, *Conference summary*, 4 June 2019 (https://berlin-climate-security-conference.de/sites/berlin-climate-security-conference.de/files/documents/summary_berlin_climate_and_security_conference.pdf) (last visited 29 August 2019).

59 Ibid.

60 UN Commission on Human Rights, *Expanded working paper by Françoise Hampson on the human rights situation of indigenous peoples in States and other territories threatened with extinction for environmental reasons*, 16 June 2005, para. 25; cf. C. Schofield, "Rising Waters, Shrinking States: The Potential Impacts of Sea Level Rise on Claims to Maritime Jurisdiciton," *53 German Yearbook of International Law* (2010), p. 204–5; D. Wong, "Sovereignty Sunk? The Position of 'Sinking States' at International Law," *14 Melbourne Journal of International Law* (2013), p. 349.

61 S. Park, *Climate Change and the Risk of Statelessness: The Situation of Low-lying Island States* (2011), p. 1, with further references.

62 To get an impression of past projects: J. Barnett and J. Campbell give an overview of projects in the Pacific region in J. Barnett and J. Campbell, *Climate Change and Small Island States: Power, Knowledge and the South Pacific* (2010), p. 116–18, table 6.2. Schenk mentions in this regard that adaptation as such will have to change. "It will require fundamental changes not only to how we design our infrastructure, but also how we fund and manage it over time and think of the various infrastructures as interconnected systems of systems." (T. Schenk, *Adapting Infrastructure to Climate Change: Advancing Decision-Making Under Conditions of Uncertainty* (2018), p. 1).

63 J. Barnett and J. Campbell, *Climate Change and Small Island States: Power, Knowledge and the South Pacific* (2010), p. 211 et seq., describing also the different levels on which adaptation measures are or should be planned.

64 L. Yamamoto and M. Esteban, *Atoll Island States and International Law: Climate Change Displacement and Sovereignty* (2014), p. 121; cf. K. Watkins et al., *UNDP Human Development Report 2007/2008 – Fighting Climate Change: Human Solidarity in a Divided World* (2007), p. 198.

65 S. Gruber, "Human Displacement and Climate Change in the Asia-Pacific" in B. Boer (ed.), *Environmental Law Dimensions of Human Rights* (2015), p. 184 with further references.

66 M. Edwards, "Parochialism and Empowerment: Responding to Ecocolonialsim and Globalisation in the Southwest Pacific" in A. Gillespie, W. C. G. Burns (eds), *Climate Change in the South Pacific: Impacts and Responses in Australia, New Zealand and Small Island States* (2000), p. 267.
67 International Human Rights Instruments, *Common core document forming part of the reports of States parties – Tuvalu*, 9 January 2013, p. 4, para. 4; cf. J. Grote-Stoutenburg, *Disappearing Island States in International Law* (2015), p. 2; IPCC 2007: N. Mimura and L. Nurse, *IPCC 2007 – Small islands: Chapter 16*, p. 698.
68 Cf. C. Schofield, "Rising Waters, Shrinking States: The Potential Impacts of Sea Level Rise on Claims to Maritime Jurisdiciton," *53 German Yearbook of International Law* (2010), p. 201; F. Thornton, *Climate Change and People on the Move* (2018), p. 26.
69 S. Park, *Climate Change and the Risk of Statelessness: The Situation of Low-lying Island States* (2011), p. 1.
70 K. L. Maharjan and N. P. Joshi, *Climate Change, Agriculture and Rural Livelihoods in Developing Countries* (2013), p. 2014.
71 C. Schofield and D. Freestone, "Options to Protect Coastlines and Secure Maritime Jurisdictional Claims in the Face of Global Sea Level Rise" in M. Gerrard, G. E. Wannier (eds), *Threatened Island Nations: Legal Implications of Rising Seas and a Changing Climate* (2013), p. 146 with further references.
72 M. Gerrard and G. E. Wannier, "Overview" in M. Gerrard, G. E. Wannier (eds), *Threatened Island Nations: Legal Implications of Rising Seas and a Changing Climate* (2013), p. 3; UNGA, Compilation prepared by the Office of the UN High Commissioner for Human Rights in accordance with paragraph 15 (b) of the annex to Human Rights Council resolution 5/1 and paragraph 5 of the annex to Council resolution 16/21 – Marshall Islands, 2 March 2015, p. 10, para. 37.
73 A. Powers and C. Stucko, "Introducing the Law of the Sea and the Legal Implications of Rising Sea Levels" in M. Gerrard, G. E. Wannier (eds), *Threatened Island Nations: Legal Implications of Rising Seas and a Changing Climate* (2013), p. 123 with further references.
74 By 2020 it was planned to have half of the population evacuated, however, up to 2018 only very few households were successfully evacuated at all. Cf. J. Connell, "Nothing There Atoll? 'Farewell to the Carteret Islands'" in T. Crook, P. Rudiak-Gould (eds), *Pacific Climate Cultures: Living Climate Change in Oceania* (2018), p. 82; S. Gruber, "Human Displacement and Climate Change in the Asia-Pacific" in B. Boer (ed.), *Environmental Law Dimensions of Human Rights* (2015), p. 184.
75 S. Gruber, "Human Displacement and Climate Change in the Asia-Pacific" in B. Boer (ed.), *Environmental Law Dimensions of Human Rights* (2015), p. 185.
76 J. Connell, "Nothing There Atoll? 'Farewell to the Carteret Islands'" in T. Crook, P. Rudiak-Gould (eds), *Pacific Climate Cultures: Living Climate Change in Oceania* (2018), p. 82 (footnotes omitted).
77 R. L. Parry, "The last tide could come at any time. Then these islands at the end of the Earth will simply vanish" in *The Times*, 21 December 2006, cited after J. Connell, "Nothing There Atoll? 'Farewell to the Carteret Islands'" in T. Crook, P. Rudiak-Gould (eds), *Pacific Climate Cultures: Living Climate Change in Oceania* (2018), p. 73.
78 E. Kwa, *Climate Change and Indigenous People in the South Pacific: Conference on "Climate Law in Developing Countries post-2012: North and South Perspectives" (26–28 September 2008, Faculty of Law, Ottawa, Canada)* (2008), p. 13.
79 IPCC 2014: R. K. Pachauri and L. Meyer, *IPCC 2014 – Synthesis Report*, p. 40.
80 A. Torres Camprubí, *Statehood under Water: Challenges of Sea-Level Rise to the Continuity of Pacific Island States* (2016), p. 9–10.
81 UNGA Res. 43/53 of 6 December 1988 (emphasis added).
82 On the UN regime on climate change in general: D. Wallace, "The UN regime on global climate change" in D. Wallace, D. Silander (eds), *Climate Change, Policy and Security: State and Human Impacts* (2018), p. 41 et seq.

83 Final Draft IPCC 2022: IPCC WGII Sixth Assessment Report, *Chapter 16*, 16.5.3.4.1 Hazard trends in deltas.
84 P. J. Sands and I. Millar, "Climate, International Protection," (last updated March 2012) in R. Wolfrum (ed.), *The Max Planck Encyclopedia of Public International Law: opil.ouplaw.com.home/EPIL* (2012), para. 2; IPCC 1990: J. T. Houghton, G. J. Jenkins and J. J. Ephraums, *IPCC 1990*, p. xi.
85 P. J. Sands and I. Millar, "Climate, International Protection," (last updated March 2012) in R. Wolfrum (ed.), *The Max Planck Encyclopedia of Public International Law: opil.ouplaw.com.home/EPIL* (2012), para. 2; citing IPCC 2007: L. Bernstein et al., *IPCC 2007 – Synthesis Report*, p. 30.
86 IPCC 2014: R. K. Pachauri and L. Meyer, *IPCC 2014 – Synthesis Report*, p. 40.
87 B. Pittock, "The science of climate change: knowledge, uncertainty and risk" in C. Lever-Tracy (ed.), *Routledge Handbook of Climate Change and Society* (2010), p. 21.
88 K. Pittel, D. Rübbelke, and M. Altemeyer-Bartscher, "International Efforts to Combat Global Warming" in W.-Y. Chen (ed.), *Handbook of Climate Change Mitigation* (2012), p. 95.
89 A. Proelß, "International Environmental Law and the Challenge of Climate Change," *53 German Yearbook of International Law* (2010), p. 67.
90 A. Torres Camprubí, *Statehood under Water: Challenges of Sea-Level Rise to the Continuity of Pacific Island States* (2016), p. 231–2: Despite their general reluctance with regard to international actions and the ratification of international agreements, all Pacific island States are Parties to the UNFCCC. On the role of AOSIS: E. Ronneberg, "Small Islands and the Big Issue: Climate Change and the Role of the Alliance of Small Island States" in C. P. Carlarne, K. R. Gray, R. G. Tarasofsky (eds), *The Oxford Handbook of International Climate Change Law* (2016), p. 761 et seq.
91 "Malé Declaration on Global Warming and Sea Level Rise" (1989).
92 L. Yamamoto and M. Esteban, *Atoll Island States and International Law: Climate Change Displacement and Sovereignty* (2014), p. 111 with further references; cf. J. Grote-Stoutenburg, *Disappearing Island States in International Law* (2015), p. 21.
93 K. V. Laatikainen, "The Alliance of Small Island States at the UN: the Promise and Pitfalls of Single-Issue Groups in Multilateral Negotiations" in K. V. Laatikainen, K. Smith (eds), *Group Politics in UN Multilateralism* (2020), p. 137.
94 http://aosis.org/ (last visited 29 August 2019); cf. E. Ronneberg, "Small Islands and the Big Issue: Climate Change and the Role of the Alliance of Small Island States" in C. P. Carlarne, K. R. Gray, R. G. Tarasofsky (eds), *The Oxford Handbook of International Climate Change Law* (2016), p. 762 et seq.
95 UNFCCC, *Introduction to the Convention* (2016).
96 https://unfccc.int/process/convention/what-united-nations-framework-convention-climate-change (last visited 21 May 2022).
97 P. J. Sands and I. Millar, "Climate, International Protection," (last updated March 2012) in R. Wolfrum (ed.), *The Max Planck Encyclopedia of Public International Law: opil.ouplaw.com.home/EPIL* (2012), para. 3; cf. W. C. G. Burns and H. M. Osofsky, "Overview: The Exigencies That Drive Potential Causes of Action for Climate Change" in W. C. G. Burns, H. M. Osofsky (eds), *Adjudicating Climate Change: State, National, and International Approaches* (2009), p. 10.
98 "Barbados Declaration" (1994), p. 3 III 2.
99 "Kyoto Protocol to the UNFCCC" 1997.
100 A. A. C. Trindade, "International Law for Humankind: Towards a New Jus Gentium," part 1, *316 Recueil Des Cours* (2005), p. 210 (footnotes omitted); on the Kyoto Protocol K. Pittel, D. Rübbelke, and M. Altemeyer-Bartscher, "International Efforts to Combat Global Warming" in W.-Y. Chen (ed.), *Handbook of Climate Change Mitigation* (2012), p. 93 et seq.; cf. C. P. Carlarne, K. R. Gray, and R. G. Tarasofsky, "International Climate Change Law: Mapping the Field" in C. P. Carlarne, K. R.

Gray, R. G. Tarasofsky (eds), *The Oxford Handbook of International Climate Change Law* (2016), giving an overview over international climate change law.

101 On the legal character of the Paris Agreement, D. Bodansky, "The Legal Character of the Paris Agreement," *25 Review of European Community & International Environmental Law 2* (2016), p. 142 et seq.

102 As of May 2022.

103 J. Leber, *How The Islands That Will Be Destroyed By Climate Change Won A Victory In Paris* (2015); cf. A. Torres Camprubí, *Statehood under Water: Challenges of Sea-Level Rise to the Continuity of Pacific Island States* (2016), p. 231–2: All Pacific Island States are Parties to the UNFCCC.

104 J. Barnett, "The dilemmas of normalising losses from climate change: Towards hope for Pacific atoll countries," *58 Asia Pacific Viewpoint* (2017), p. 3.

105 Art. 2 of the Paris Agreement ("Paris Agreement" (2016)).

106 J. Leber, *The Paris Climate Deal Is A Good Start–But Probably Not Good Enough* (2015). On the relevance of 1.5 temperature rise on Pacific islands, see P. Pringle, "Effects of Climate Change on 1.5° Temperature Rise Relevant to the Pacific Islands," *Pacific Marine Climate Change Report Card: Science Review 2018*, pp 189–-200 (2018).

107 http://www.1point5.info/whatsup (last visited 30 June 2019). On the (unlikely?) pathways to keep under 1.5, see M. Schaeffer, U. Fuentes Hutfilter, R. Brecha, C. Fyson, B, Hare, "Insights from the IPCC Special Report on 1.5°C for preparation of longterm strategies," *Climate Analytics Report, April 2019* (2019). If all governments achieved their Paris Agreement commitments the world will likely warm 3.0°C – twice the 1.5°C limit they agreed in Paris (Climate Action Tracker, "Some progress since Paris, but not enough, as governments amble towards 3°C of warming," *Report of December 2018*).

108 J. Barnett, "The dilemmas of normalising losses from climate change: Towards hope for Pacific atoll countries," *58 Asia Pacific Viewpoint* (2017), p. 3.

109 J. Leber, *The Paris Climate Deal Is A Good Start – But Probably Not Good Enough* (2015); cf. I. de Águeda Corneloup and A. P. J. Mol, "Small island developing states and international climate change negotiations: the power of moral 'leadership'," *14 International Environmental Agreements: Politics, Law and Economics* (2014), p. 282–3, 286 et seq. (analyzing the structure of AOSIS impact on past climate negotiations); cf. E. Ronneberg, "Small Islands and the Big Issue: Climate Change and the Role of the Alliance of Small Island States" in C. P. Carlarne, K. R. Gray, R. G. Tarasofsky (eds), *The Oxford Handbook of International Climate Change Law* (2016), p. 761 et seq.

110 J. Leber, *How The Islands That Will Be Destroyed By Climate Change Won A Victory In Paris* (2015).

111 K. V. Laatikainen, "The Alliance of Small Island States at the UN: the Promise and Pitfalls of Single-Issue Groups in Multilateral Negotiations" in K. V. Laatikainen, K. Smith (eds), *Group Politics in UN Multilateralism* (2020), p. 135.

112 https://unfccc.int/process-and-meetings/the-paris-agreement/the-paris-agreement (last visited 21 May 2022).

113 UN Human Rights Council, *Report of the Special Rapporteur on the issue of human rights obligations relating to the enjoyment of a safe, clean, healthy and sustainable environment*, 1 February 2016, para. 76. "Even assuming that every country achieves the emission reductions targets they have pledged, the result of these efforts will still be global average warming of at least 2.6°C above pre-industrial levels by the end of the century." (J. Barnett, "The dilemmas of normalising losses from climate change: Towards hope for Pacific atoll countries," *58 Asia Pacific Viewpoint* (2017), p. 3.)

114 K. Akasaka, "Guiding Principles Needed: Towards a global strategy for climate change," *2 UN Chronicle* (2007), p. 22.

115 B. Pittock, "The science of climate change: knowledge, uncertainty and risk" in C. Lever-Tracy (ed.), *Routledge Handbook of Climate Change and Society* (2010),

p. 22–3; K. Pittel, D. Rübbelke, and M. Altemeyer-Bartscher, "International Efforts to Combat Global Warming" in W.-Y. Chen (ed.), *Handbook of Climate Change Mitigation* (2012), p. 95.

116 C. Nunez, *Sea level rise, explained: Oceans are rising around the world, causing dangerous flooding. Why is this happening, and what can we do to stem the tide?* (19 February 2019) – https://www.nationalgeographic.com/environment/global-warming /sea-level-rise/ (last visited 4 September 2019).

117 J. Kittel, "Comment: The Global 'Disappearing Act:' How Island States Can Maintain Statehood in the Face of Disappearing Territory," *Michigan State Law Review* (2014), p. 1230.

118 N. Schrijver, "The Impact of Climate Change: Challenges for International Law" in U. Fastenrath, R. Geiger, D.-E. Khan, A. Paulus, S. von Schorlemer, C. Vedder (eds), *From Bilateralism to Community Interest: Essays in Honour of Judge Bruno Simma* (2011), p. 1278.

119 C. Warbrick, "States and Recognition in International Law" in M. D. Evans (ed.), *International Law* (2006), p. 219.

120 Ibid., p. 242.

121 Humanization is meant to describe the increasing influence of human rights and the increasing importance of individuals in international law.

122 S. Willcox, "A Rising Tide: The Implications of Climate Change Inundation for Human Rights and State Sovereignty," *9 Essex Human Rights Review 1* (2012), p. 16.

123 UNGA Res. 60/1 of 24 October 2005; cf. G. J. Evans and M. Sahnoun, *The Responsibility to Protect. Report of the International Commission on Intervention and State Sovereignty* (2001).

124 S. M. Carbone, L. S. di Pepe, 2States, Fundamental Rights and Duties," (last updated January 2009) in R. Wolfrum (ed.), *The Max Planck Encyclopedia of Public International Law: opil.ouplaw.com.home/EPIL* (2012), para. 36.

125 UN Habitat, *How the UN System Supports Ambitious Action on Climate Change: UN System Chief Executives Board for Coordination* (2014).

2 What does an entity need to qualify as a State? – or what it takes to be a State

One might have expected States (as the primary subjects of international law) to be precisely defined under international law. This is not the case. There is no commonly accepted definition of a State. Georges Scelle even said in 1950 that he "himself had been active in international law for more than fifty years, and still did not know what a State was; and he felt sure that he would not find out before he died."[1] If, however, international law did not determine what a State is, Kelsen argues, its norms, which obligate and empower the States, would not be applicable.[2]

Accordingly, when the Declaration on the Rights and Duties of States[3] was drafted in 1948, the United Kingdom suggested that a definition of "State" should be included.[4] In the end, it was merely possible to find agreement on the fact that "[t]he definition would be difficult to establish and highly controversial"[5] and even more remarkably that "no useful purpose would be served" by the definition of a *State*.[6]

During the discussions on the Vienna Convention on the Law of Treaties,[7] a new attempt to define a "State" was made by Sir Gerald Fitzmaurice as Special Rapporteur on the subject of the law of treaties: A State, he suggested, is "an entity consisting of a people inhabiting a defined territory, under an organised system of government, and having the capacity to enter into international relations binding the entity as such."[8] In the final draft article, his definition was excluded though.[9] It appears to be indeed an "almost impossible task."[10]

A State is

> an abstract entity which can be neither seen, nor heard, nor touched. This entity is not identical with either the rulers or the ruled; neither President Clinton, nor citizen Smith, nor even an assembly of all the citizens acting in common can claim that they are the state. On the other hand, it includes them both and claims to stand over them both.[11]

Thus, "State" describes both an apparatus of power, and a […] personal structure, as well as the relationship between these two.[12] Cohen argues that "the term 'state' has no absolute fixed meaning, but rather takes on varying implications in accordance with the claim for which it is being used."[13] Hence, it remains true that statehood has – according to Crawford – despite its importance, or perhaps because of it, never been defined as generally binding under international law.[14]

DOI: 10.4324/9781003263593-2

In "the lack of a better model,"[15] the Montevideo Convention on the Rights and Duties of States,[16] being a regional contract with only sixteen State parties (binding only those parties)[17] in force since 1933, gained much fame internationally. It offers a set of criteria that form today the most frequently cited statehood elements and are generally "accepted as law:"[18]

> The State as a person of international law should possess the following qualifications: (a) a permanent population; (b) a defined territory; (c) government; and (d) capacity to enter into relations with the other States.[19]

Yet, in preparation of this convention, there was minimal discussion concerning the definition. There was neither discussion on whether the requirements were to be satisfied on a continuing basis, nor on the consequence of a failure to satisfy them.[20] The criteria seemed "apparent" and "a long-established feature of international law."[21] It was not even "deemed necessary to comment on the stipulations regarding conditions which the State must meet as a party of International Law."[22]

Often, when statehood is approached, authors restrict their discussion nevertheless to quoting the Montevideo criteria.[23] Although they did not remain uncriticized,[24] and other attempts to define a State were made,[25] none proposed a profoundly different definition. As such, the American Law Institute defines the State nearly identically:

> Under international law, a state is an entity that has a defined territory and a permanent population, under the control of its own government, and that engages in, or has the capacity to engage in, formal relations with other such entities.[26]

In its comment a), the American Law Institute mentions, though, that "each of its elements may represent significant problems in unusual situations."[27] Indeed, the criteria are most likely neither final nor exhaustive. This can already be seen from the reading of the Montevideo Convention: "should possess" is used instead of "shall possess" which is customarily used when intended to be final and exhaustive. Thus, they must be seen as a benchmark.[28] In any case, those same elements are mentioned by almost any author defining the State.

Georg Jellinek's doctrine of three elements: People, territory, and power ("Drei-Elemente-Lehre")[29] served "as starting-point for definitions of the state especially in constitutional theory over the course of the 20th century."[30] It is an acknowledged achievement of this theory that it reopened to political, social, and historical realities and thus even fertilized neighboring sciences, especially the newly formed political and social sciences.[31]

Max Weber, a sociologist and economist, and contemporary and friend of Jellinek

> also noted that a formal characteristic of the state was an administrative order that 'claims binding authority, not only over members of the state, the

> citizens ... but also to a very large extent over all action taking place in the area of its jurisdiction'.[32]

For him, "a state is a human community that (successfully) claims the monopoly of the legitimate use of physical force within a given territory."[33]

Kelsen ties in with Jellinek's theoretical offer to nominally unite and methodically separate legal and social science studies under the umbrella of the concept of the State, by submitting the concept of the State to the concept of law.[34] He suggests that a community having a legal order, individuals on a clearly demarked territory applying and obeying this legal order, and legal independence with regard to other States is a State under international law,[35] holding State and legal order as equal.[36]

As with Jellinek, but expressly conceded, Carl Schmitt's concept of the State is a concept of legitimacy.[37] He argues that the State is the political status of a people organized in territorial cohesion.[38]

For "all purposes of International Law" Phillimore defines a State as

> a people permanently occupying a fixed territory (certam sedem), bound together by common laws, habits, and customs into one body politic, exercising, through the medium of an organized Government, independent sovereignty and control over all persons and things within its boundaries, capable of making war and peace, and of entering into all International relations with the other communities of the globe.[39]

Hence, the idea of statehood is essentially that it is a particular territorial community which is accepted as a separate entity with a sufficient degree of independence in international relations and is not subject to the government or authority of another State.[40]

However, while all of the definitions mentioned above bring up more or less all the criteria that are cited in the Montevideo Convention, some authors, for instance, do not explicitly mention *territory* but seem to lay their focus more on government and population.[41]

Regarding the two elements of a State that are most relevant to this study (territory and population), a State's territory is "some portion of the earth's surface which its people inhabit and over which its government exercises authority."[42] There is no rule that prescribes a minimum area to constitute a State territory.[43] A State's population shall be seen as comprising[44] all the inhabitants of the respective State's territory plus the State's nationals who stay abroad as long as they have some continuing effective linkage to their home State.[45] Thereby, there is again no minimum limit prescribed regarding the number of individuals forming a population entitled to be regarded as a State's population in the sense of international law.[46]

In the end, all the criteria for Statehood are flexible, uncertain, and open to manipulation and interpretation. Thereby, they allow a variety of entities with different circumstances to be classified as States.[47] There is no consistent custom in international law in applying the criteria.[48] "Statehood is [...] quite simply customary status under international law. It is not the statehood criteria which are customary, but statehood itself."[49] Particularly important in this regard is to keep in mind that the different criteria are all closely linked to each other and cannot be regarded in isolation. There is, rather, one element that constitutes a State instead of three (or four) separate elements: This one element comprises all the elements, though. A State is a *populated governed territory with relations to other States.*[50]

The acceptance of the conditions must be subject to two qualifications: Firstly, they can only be stated in general terms, and secondly, they must be attended by a reasonable degree of permanence.[51] The Montevideo criteria are, as Jain points out, the bare minimum required for effective control and thus define Statehood "based on the principle of effectiveness among territorial units."[52]

Notes

1 ILC, *Summary records of the second session 5 June–29 July 1950*, Yearbook of the ILC 1950 Volume I, 1950, p. 84, para. 22.

2 H. Kelsen, "Recognition in International Law: Theoretical Observations," *35 AJIL* (1941), p. 606; similar: T. D. Grant, "Defining Statehood: The Montevideo Convention and its Discontents," *37 Columbia Journal of Transnational Law* (1999), p. 404.

3 "Draft Declaration on Rights and Duties of States" (1949); see for the discussions: ILC, *Summary Records and Documents of the First Session including the report of the Commission to the General Assembly*, Yearbook of the ILC 1949 (1956), p. 6–128, 135–83, 208, 214, 240, 256.

4 UNGA, *Preparatory Study Concerning a Draft Declaration on the Rights and Duties of States – Memorandum submitted by the Secretary-·General*, 15 December 1948, p. 186 para. 4; ILC, *Summary Records and Documents of the First Session including the report of the Commission to the General Assembly*, Yearbook of the ILC 1949 (1956), p. 173 para. 29.

5 Ibid., p. 65, para. 21.

6 Ibid., p. 259, para. 21; American Society of International Law, "UN: Report of the ILC: Covering its first session, April 12– June 9, 1949," *44 AJIL* (1950), p. 19: "The Commission concluded that no useful purpose would be served by an effort to define the term 'State,' though this course had been suggested by the Governments of the United Kingdom and of India. In the Commission's draft, the term 'State' is used in the sense commonly accepted in international practice. Nor did the Commission think that it was called upon to set forth in this draft Declaration the qualifications to be possessed by a community in order that it may become a State."; cf. R. Cohen, "The Concept of Statehood in UN Practice," *109 University of Pennsylvania Law Review* (1961), p. 1129; A. G. Jain, "The 21st Century Atlantis: The International Law of Statehood and Climate Change-Induced Loss of Territory," *50 Stanford Journal of International Law* (2014), p. 24.

7 "Vienna Convention on the Law of Treaties" (1969).

8 ILC, *Documents of the eighth session including the report of the Commission to the General Assembly* – Report by G. G. Fitzmaurice, Special Rapporteur, Yearbook of the ILC 1956 Volume II, 1956, p. 107 (Art. 3. Certain related definitions).

9 ILC, *Documents of the second part of the seventeenth session and of the eighteenth session including the reports of the Commission to the General Assembly*, Yearbook of the ILC 1966 Volume II, 1966, p. 178, 192.

10 W. T. Worster, "Law, Politics and the Conception of the State in State Recognition Theory," *27 Boston University International Law Journal* (2009), p. 143.

11 M. L. van Creveld, *The Rise and Decline of the State* (1999), p. 1.

12 C. Möllers, "Staat" in W. Heun (ed.), *Evangelisches Staatslexikon* (2006), p. 2272; cf. A. Affolter, "Zur Lehre von der Persönlichkeit des Staates," *20 Archiv für öffentliches Recht* (1906), p. 409–10.
13 R. Cohen, "The Concept of Statehood in UN Practice," *109 University of Pennsylvania Law Review* (1961), p. 1156.
14 J. R. Crawford, "Islands as Sovereign Nations," *38 International & Comparative Law Quarterly* (1989), p. 280.
15 T. D. Grant, "Defining Statehood: The Montevideo Convention and its Discontents," *37 Columbia Journal of Transnational Law* (1999), p. 414.
16 "Convention on Rights and Duties of States: Montevideo Convention" (1933).
17 The Montevideo Convention was negotiated among and signed by [Argentina], Bolivia, Brazil, Chile, Colombia, Cuba, Dominican Republic, Ecuador, El Salvador, Guatemala, Haiti, Honduras, Mexico, Nicaragua, Panama, [Paraguay], [Peru], United States, [Uruguay], and Venezuela (those in square brackets have not ratified the convention); A. Alvarez, *El nuevo derecho internacional en sus relaciones con la vida actual de los pueblos* (1962), p. 92 et seq. with further explanations.
18 L. Henkin, *International Law: Politics and Values* (1995), p. 13; M. Gagain, "Climate Change, Sea Level Rise, and Artificial Islands: Saving the Maldives' Statehood and Maritime Claims Through the 'Constitution of the Oceans'," *23 Colorado Journal of International Environmental Law and Policy* (2012), p. 89; M. Schoiswohl, *Status and (Human Rights) Obligations of Non-Recognized De Facto Regimes in International Law: The Case of 'Somaliland': The Resurrection of Somaliland Against All International "Odds:" State Collapse, Secession, Non-Recognition and Human Rights* (2004), p. 12; T. D. Grant, "Between Diversity and Disorder: A Review of Jorri C. Duursma, Fragmentation and the International Relations of Micro-States: Self-Determination and Statehood," *12 American University Journal of International Law and Policy* (1997), p. 653 (calling it a "near-talismanic reference"); cf. "Declaration on the 'Guidelines on the Recognition of New States in Eastern Europe and in the Soviet Union" (1991), p. 165: "the State is commonly defined as a community which consists of a territory and a population subject to an organized political authority."
19 "Convention on Rights and Duties of States: Montevideo Convention" (1933), Art. 1. See in detail exploring the different criteria: ILC, *Sea-level rise in relation to international law, Second issues paper by Patrícia Galvão Teles and Juan José Ruda Santolaria* (73rd session of the ILC (2022)), # 75 et seq.
20 Cf. D. Wong, "Sovereignty Sunk? The Position of 'Sinking States' at International Law," *14 Melbourne Journal of International Law* (2013), p. 354; T. D. Grant, "Defining Statehood: The Montevideo Convention and its Discontents," *37 Columbia Journal of Transnational Law* (1999), p. 416; cf. A. de Mello Franco, "Minutes of the Fifth Session (December 19, 1933): Second Committee – Seventh International Conference of American States" in Second Committee (ed.), *Minutes and Antecedents: Seventh International Conference of American States* (1933), p. 103–29, where many articles of the Montevideo convention were discussed, yet not Art. 1
21 Cf. T. D. Grant, "Defining Statehood: The Montevideo Convention and its Discontents," *37 Columbia Journal of Transnational Law* (1999), p. 416, mentioning Jellinek's doctrine of three elements.
22 R. Rivas, "Report of the Second Sub-Committee: Rights and Duties of States" in Second Committee (ed.), *Minutes and Antecedents: Seventh International Conference of American States* (1933), p. 165; cf. D. Wong, "Sovereignty Sunk? The Position of 'Sinking States' at International Law," *14 Melbourne Journal of International Law* (2013), p. 354.
23 A. G. Jain, "The 21st Century Atlantis: The International Law of Statehood and Climate Change-Induced Loss of Territory," *50 Stanford Journal of International Law* (2014), fn. 84, with further references; cf. T. D. Grant, "Defining Statehood:

The Montevideo Convention and its Discontents," *37 Columbia Journal of Transnational Law* (1999), p. 415.

24 For example J. Duursma, *Fragmentation and the International Relations of Micro-States: Self-determination and Statehood* (1996), p. 112–13; T. D. Grant, "Defining Statehood: The Montevideo Convention and its Discontents," *37 Columbia Journal of Transnational Law* (1999), p. 434 et seq.; L. Henkin, *International Law: Politics and Values* (1995), p. 13; B. Finucane, "Fictitious States, Effective Control, and the Use of Force Against Non-State Actors," *30 Berkeley Journal of International Law* (2012), p. 36, 37; M. Craven, "Statehood, Self-determination, and Recognition" in M. D. Evans (ed.), *International Law* (2014), p. 217.

25 J. W. Garner, *Introduction to Political Science: A Treatise on the Origin, Nature, Functions, and Organization of the State* (1910), p. 38–41 for a large number of definitions; M. Weber, *Wirtschaft und Gesellschaft: Grundriss der verstehenden Soziologie* (originally from 1922, ed. by J. Winckelmann 2002), p. 822; J. A. Andrews, "The Concept of Statehood and the Acquisition of Territory in the Nineteenth Century," *94 The Law Quarterly Review* (1978), p. 410 et seq.

26 The American Law Institute, *Restatement of the law – Third: The foreign relations law of the United States* (1987), § 201, p. 72.

27 Ibid., § 201, cmt. (a), p. 72.

28 A. Abass, *Complete International Law: Text, Cases, and Materials* (2014), p. 124.

29 G. Jellinek and W. Jellinek, *Allgemeine Staatslehre* (1914), p. 396 et seq.

30 P. Minkkinen, "The Container and the Septic Tank: Statism, Life, and the Geopolitics of Territoriality," *23 Finnish Yearbook of International Law* (2012–2013), p. 395.

31 C. Möllers, *Staat als Argument* (2000), p. 33; P. Minkkinen, "The Container and the Septic Tank: Statism, Life, and the Geopolitics of Territoriality," *23 Finnish Yearbook of International Law* (2012–2013), p. 397.

32 P. Minkkinen, "The Container and the Septic Tank: Statism, Life, and the Geopolitics of Territoriality," *23 Finnish Yearbook of International Law* (2012–2013), p. 396, citing M. Weber, *Economy and Society: An Outline of Interpretive Sociology* (edition by G. Roth, C. Wittich (eds), translated by E. Fischoff, 1978 [originally from 1922]), p. 56.

33 M. Weber, *Politics as a Vocation (lecture originally delivered 28 January 1919)* (2003), p. 1; cf. J. Vidmar, "The Concept of the State and its Right of Existence," *4 Cambridge Journal of International and Comparative Law* (2015), p. 548.

34 C. Möllers, *Staat als Argument* (2000), p. 36.

35 H. Kelsen, *Hans Kelsen oder die Reinheit der Rechtslehre* (1988; ed. F. Koja), p. 76; H. Kelsen, *Allgemeine Staatslehre* (1925), p. 16.

36 H. Kelsen, „Recognition in International Law: Theoretical Observations," *35 AJIL* (1941), p. 608; cf. A. Gamper, *Staat und Verfassung: Einführung in die allgemeine Staatslehre* (2007), p. 43.

37 C. Möllers, *Staat als Argument* (2000), p. 81.

38 C. Schmitt, *Der Begriff des Politischen* [1932] (1963), p. 20: "Staat ist nach dem heutigen Sprachgebrauch der politische Status eines in territorialer Geschlossenheit organisierten Volkes."

39 R. Phillimore, *Commentaries upon International Law* (1879), p. 81.

40 J. R. Crawford, "Islands as Sovereign Nations," *38 International & Comparative Law Quarterly* (1989), p. 280, for other essentially similar definitions s.: Guggenheim. Paul, "Principes de droit international publique: Les etats comme sujets du droit des gens," *80 Recueil Des Cours* (1952), p. 96; W. W. Willoughby, *The Fundamental Concepts of Public Law* (1931), p. 63; M. v. Seydel, *Grundzüge einer allgemeinen Staatslehre* (1873), p. 1; J. C. Bluntschli, *The Theory of the State (1895, authorised English Translation from the Sixth German Edition*), p. 23; H. Ruiz-Fabri, "Genèse et disparition de l'État à l'époque contemporaine," *38 Annuaire Français de Droit International* (1992), p. 153; cf. A. G. Jain, "The 21st Century Atlantis: The International Law of

Statehood and Climate Change-Induced Loss of Territory," *50 Stanford Journal of International Law* (2014), fn. 85.

41 T. J. Lawrence, *The Principles of International Law* (1895), p. 56; H. Wheaton, *Elements of International Law: With a Sketch of the History of the Science: in Two Volumes* (1880), p. 62; E. D. Vattel, *The Law of Nations: Or, Principles of the Law of Nature Applied to the Conduct and Affairs of Nations and Sovereigns* (1797), p. 1.

42 UN Security Council, *Third Year, 383rd Meeting*, 2 December 1948, p. 11.

43 R. Y. Jennings and A. Watts, Oppenheim's International Law (1992), p. 121; the smallest State is the Vatican City with a total area of 0.44 km^2 (J. Duursma, *Fragmentation and the International Relations of Micro-States: Self-determination and Statehood* (1996), p. 374). Other diminutive States include Nauru (21 km^2), Liechtenstein (160 km^2), and Monaco (2 km^2); see: https://www.cia.gov/library/publications/the-world-factbook/rankorder/2147rank.html (last visited 30 June 2019); cf. Y. Abdullah, "The Holy See at the United Nations Conferences: State of Church?" *96 Columbia Law Review* (1996), p. 1863; fn. 230; cf. G. Ireland, "The State of the City of the Vatican," *27 The American Journal of International Law* (1933), p. 273; T. Darsow, *Zum Wandel des Staatsbegriffs: Unter besonderer Berücksichtigung der Lehre und Praxis internationaler Organisationen, der Mikrostaaten und der PLO* (1984), p. 24–5.

44 Cf. B. Vukas, "States, Peoples and Minorities," *231 Recueil Des Cours* (1991), p. 284.

45 Cf. International Court of Justice – The Hague, *Nottebohm case (Liechtenstein v. Guatemala)* – Dissenting opinion of Judge Read (6 April 1955), p. 44. This was, however, a dissenting opinion. The court ruled that Nottebohm's nationality was not based on a "genuine" and "effective" link to Liechtenstein.

46 J. R. Crawford, "State," (last updated March 2012) in R. Wolfrum (ed.), *The Max Planck Encyclopedia of Public International Law: opil.ouplaw.com.home/EPIL* (2012), para. 21; J. W. Garner, *Introduction to Political Science: A Treatise on the Origin, Nature, Functions, and Organization of the State* (1910), p. 67; J. C. Bluntschli, *The Theory of the State (1895, authorised English Translation from the Sixth German Edition)*, p. 16.

47 J. R. Crawford, The Creation of States in International Law (2006), p. 197; on "[t]he (ir)relevance of the statehood criteria," J. Vidmar, "The Concept of the State and its Right of Existence," *4 Cambridge Journal of International and Comparative Law* (2015), p. 549 et seq.

48 W. T. Worster, "Law, Politics and the Conception of the State in State Recognition Theory," *27 Boston University International Law Journal* (2009), p. 153.

49 J. Vidmar, "The Concept of the State and its Right of Existence," *4 Cambridge Journal of International and Comparative Law* (2015), p. 551.

50 Similarly, J. R. Crawford, "Islands as Sovereign Nations," *38 International & Comparative Law Quarterly* (1989), p. 280: "two essential elements to statehood: the existence of a separate territorial community with its own system of government, and the independence of that territorial community from all others." Cf. C. Ebert, *Die Beurteilung der Staatlichkeit politisch-sozialer Verbände* (1988), p. 15, 18–19.

51 T.-C. Chen, *The international law of recognition: With special reference to practice in Great Britain and the United States* (1951), p. 59.

52 A. G. Jain, "The 21st Century Atlantis: The International Law of Statehood and Climate Change-Induced Loss of Territory," *50 Stanford Journal of International Law* (2014), p. 16; citing; J. R. Crawford, The Creation of States in International Law (2006), p. 46; T. D. Grant, "Defining Statehood: The Montevideo Convention and its Discontents," *37 Columbia Journal of Transnational Law* (1999), p. 416–17.

3 When does a State cease to exist? – or what it takes not to be a State anymore

Climate change and particularly climate change-induced rising sea levels endanger some or all of the different elements of the affected island States and certainly the effectiveness of the respective entities. It will certainly affect the physical territory of States. In particular, small island States, being small States consisting of "a naturally formed area of land, surrounded by water, that is above water at high tide" (Art. 121(1) UNCLOS)[1] are endangered by the rising seas. By rendering some inhabited land incapable of sustaining human habitation, climate change will enforce migration of some or all of the people of a State's population from the respective State's territory.

At some threshold, climate change-induced migration, together with territorial degradation, might threaten the very existence of some States.[2] Such a situation has, up to now, never occurred, and will, if the forecast[3] is proved wrong, hopefully never occur. However, as early as 1993, scientists were mentioning the existential threat of climate change-induced rising seas:

> Slightly higher rises in sea level increase the areas of potential inundation, threaten the existence of certain island states (e.g., the Maldives) and pose problems for sustaining numerous coastal cities.[4]

As this becomes more and more likely, and the voices announcing such possibilities become louder and louder, this chapter aims at investigating at what point a State ceases to exist as a State, hence what it takes for an entity not to be a State anymore.

The traditional situations where a State ceases to exist are merger, the voluntary absorption of one State by another State, and the breaking up of one State into several.[5] These cases offer little insight into the situation of threatened island States, as there is never simply a void, but rather a replacement of one State by another.[6] Sinking island States, where there would not be a successor State, would be unprecedented, entirely novel, and unique in that sense.[7]

The question of whether or not a State ceases to exist as a State when losing State criteria is not regulated by international law. Although a State must, as stated by the American Law Institute's Draft Restatement "show[s] reasonable indications that the(se) requirements … will continue to be satisfied."[8] This, however, is

DOI: 10.4324/9781003263593-3

rather an argument concerning the question of the coming into existence of States, not their ceasing. As the Montevideo Convention was also originally concerned with what it takes to be a State, (customary) international law seems to be silent about what it takes not to be a State anymore (at least when there is no succeeding State).[9] While it is argued that there is an urgent need for a clear regulation on that,[10] it is "common to find pronouncements to the effect that international law has no real understanding of when a state ceases to exist."[11] In any case, once a State is firmly established, there is a strong presumption against its extinction.[12]

Accordingly, during an international expert meeting on climate change and displacement convened by the UN High Commissioner for Refugees, it was explicitly stated that "the legal presumption of continuity of Statehood needs to be emphasized and the notion and language that such states will 'disappear' (i.e., lose their international legal personality) or 'sink' ought to be avoided."[13]

Nevertheless, as Crawford pointed out, "where a state does not exist, rules treating it as existing are pointless, a denial of reality."[14] "[I]t would be legally unsound and historically untrue to affirm [a State's] immortality."[15] Thus, even though the demise of statehood is not specifically mentioned, logically "[s]ince customary international law provides for the criteria on which the existence of a State can be determined, extinction of States must be determined by reference to these same criteria."[16] As such, Craven argues that the general criteria for statehood should govern not merely the legal "creation" of States, but also their "extinction."[17] Similarly, Grotius, Pufendorf, Vattel, Bluntschli, Huber, Hall, and others emphasized throughout the centuries that the extinction of a State is determined by reference to the criteria of statehood.[18] Moreover, the criteria for statehood are interlinked, so in principle, the territory should be inhabited by the population being under the control of an independent government.[19]

> So where the territory of a state becomes submerged by the sea, or where the population of a state evacuates *en masse* to other territories, or where it falls into a state of extended anarchy, it should be possible to conclude that the state has ceased to exist.[20]

McAdam counters that "the law is not so clear-cut" though.[21] Changes affecting the criteria of statehood do not automatically jeopardize the continuity of a State.[22] "[P]resumably statehood would similarly not cease if such loss or exile were temporary. The implication is that where such a situation would be permanent, statehood could be questioned."[23] But up to now "[t]here is no precedent for loss of the entire territory or the exile of the entire population."[24] If, however, the entire population of a State were to perish or to emigrate, or if the whole of its territory were to disappear, most authors suggest, that a State would then cease to exist.[25]

Loss of territory

With regard to the identity of the State, territory is often seen as the most important element.[26] Therefore, many authors are of the opinion that a State without territory is not imaginable.[27] Yet, it is a customary rule (described by Anzilotti as one of the most certain of international law), that territorial changes do not affect the identity or continuity of States.[28] Arguing that any territorial change would lead to the extinction of a State is certainly "fully in contradiction with positive international law"[29] and contrary to State practice.[30] Thus, what is the threshold for changes in territory that would render a State endangered in its existence; and are rising seas leading to such point?

Criterion of "a defined territory" endangered by the rising seas?

Territory is affected by the rising sea. It might be the criterion most obviously affected out of the different State criteria.[31] But is it actually endangered? The territory of a State includes the territorial sea and its seabed and subsoil, as well as the airspace above it. The territorial sea is the strip of sea immediately adjacent to the land area and internal waters of a coastal State seaward of the baseline. If baselines, from where to measure the maritime zones to which States are entitled (in particular the territorial sea) were fixed, the area of the territory would not actually change at all. Only the State's landlines would change. However, changing landlines do not matter.[32]

However, (at least up to now), baselines are to follow landlines: If they move inland as a result of permanent flooding, the outer boundaries of maritime zones (territorial sea, contiguous zone, and exclusive economic zone) would have to shift accordingly.[33] The "normal baseline" as defined in Art. 5 UNCLOS is the low-water line along the coast (as marked on large-scale charts officially recognized by the coastal State).[34] According to Art. 7 UNCLOS, baselines may also be drawn along certain natural formations offshore (islands or reefs).

With the rising seas different scenarios are possible:

Once the entire land territory of a State is under water, the State will (most likely) not be able to claim "an adjacent belt of sea, described as the territorial sea," as this is, according to Art. 2 UNCLOS, only possible in *extension* of the "land territory." Moreover, it might become doubtful that the State is still a State, and according to Art. 3 UNCLOS only States have the right to establish the breadth of their territorial sea.

Even when there is some territory left at low tide, but no territory left above water at high tide, such land does not count as *island* anymore. It counts as a *low-tide elevation* within the meaning of Art. 13 UNCLOS. According to Art. 13(2) UNCLOS, a low-tide elevation that is wholly situated at a distance exceeding the breadth of the territorial sea from the (mainland or an) island, has no territorial sea of its own. Thus, land that is entirely below the water at high tide cannot qualify as the basis for territory surrounded by territorial waters at all.[35] Therefore, the respective island State loses its territorial sea, as soon as no land area is above water at high tide.

If an area remains above water (even at high tide), but the remaining land cannot sustain human habitation or economic life of its own, such land counts as a *rock* in the sense of Art. 121(3) UNCLOS. Rocks do not have an exclusive economic zone or continental shelf according to Art. 121(3) UNCLOS, but they do *not* automatically lose their territorial sea. Hence, there is still (a State's) territory.

If not the entire territory of the island State, but only an island off the coast becomes a low-water elevation, such development could also have a major impact on the baselines: According to Art. 7(4) UNCLOS, in principle, no straight baselines may be drawn to and from low-water elevations. Thus, not only islands and rocks off the coast that sink completely and permanently into the sea lose their ability to provide the basis for baselines and thus can no longer generate maritime zones. Also, land that rises out of the water only at low tide because of rising sea levels becomes a low-tide elevation and thus again loses its territorial sea, its contiguous zone, and its exclusive economic zone. The further the submerged elevation is from the closest running baseline (such as the baseline of another island or the normal baseline along the coast), the more area is lost.[36] Whereas it is conceivable that States could reinforce coastal sections and certain natural formations with artificial fortifications to protect them from permanent flooding, such an approach involves enormous costs and is therefore not feasible for all States.

For archipelagic States, this rule, that also applies to archipelagic baselines according to Art. 47(4) UNCLOS, can have particularly serious consequences: It is even possible that the demise of individual islands and drying reefs would cause the archipelagic State to no longer meet one or more of the requirements for drawing straight archipelagic baselines. For example, it is conceivable that the ratio of water area to land area will eventually exceed the critical 9 to 1 mark as a result of sea level rise. This would mean that the archipelagic State would completely forfeit its archipelagic waters and would now have to draw baselines around individual islands or island groups.[37]

However, those limitations were imposed to deny States the possibility to *construct* "islands" solely in order to "generate unfairly and inequitably huge maritime spaces."[38] Island States that are losing their proper territory teleologically can and should be treated more generously in this regard. While the mere presence of a rock in the sense of Art. 121 UNCLOS might rightly not be considered sufficient to justify the fulfillment of a State's territory,[39] for island States that used to possess territory which was originally fulfilling the requirements of being regarded as islands in the sense of Art. 121 UNCLOS, such limitations do not seem adequate. In addition, the international arbitral tribunal in the dispute between the Philippines and China (South China Sea Arbitration)[40] has emphasized, in 2016, that it makes a difference whether an island is unsuitable for human settlement of its own accord or because external influences have rendered the island unsuitable for settlement, for example as a result of war, pollution, or environmental damage. This could also argue that an island that has only become unsettled due to sea level rise is not downgraded to a rock according to Art. 121(3) UNCLOS.[41]

Generally, the purpose of the Law of the Sea Convention, according to its preamble, is the "strengthening of peace, security, cooperation and friendly relations among all nations."[42] While denying States the right to preserve their territorial outlines when the sea is rising would clearly lead to destabilization and uncertainty, a stabilizing interpretation of the convention, preserving the status quo would be in accordance with the purpose of the convention and the principle "that the state of things that actually exists and has existed for a long time should be changed as little as possible."[43] As such, "the 1982 Convention seems to have established once and for all, the parameters for establishing stable borders in the oceans which can no longer be switched easily or at all, on account of changing situations."[44] Against this background, one of the proposals in the debate on international law is to freeze baselines at the level of their registration in official nautical charts, as has been mentioned before.[45]

Australia, for example, is hoping to thereby "maximize the stability and clarity that the Convention brought to oceans governance and maritime jurisdiction."[46] Also the Maldives takes the view that,

> once a State has determined the extent of its maritime entitlements in accordance with UNCLOS and deposited the appropriate charts and/or geographic coordinates with the UN Secretary-General, [...] these entitlements are fixed and will not be altered by any subsequent physical changes to a States' geography as a result of sea-level rise.[47]

This is because "(a) this position is most consistent with the principles of stability and certainty of international law; and (b) the considerations of equity and fairness require that SIDS' maritime entitlements are protected, especially given the particular vulnerability of SIDS to climate change."[48] Stable maritime zones are also favored by the members of the Pacific Islands Forum.[49] And New Zealand recalls that "[a]ll States had an interest in preserving the balance of rights and responsibilities under the Convention. It was also in the interests of all States to ensure there was certainty regarding maritime zones, to avoid potential disputes."[50]

Yet, State practice is not consistent: As such, for instance, the United States,[51] the Netherlands,[52] and Romania[53] take the position that UNCLOS provides for *ambulatory* baselines.[54] Referring to this ambiguity, some States explicitly stress "the overriding importance of fully respecting the letter and spirit of the [UNCLOS] Convention" in conducting further study on "Sea level rise in relation to international law" and of ensuring that the content of any further study would fully comply with the Convention: "[a]ttempts to modify or undermine the Convention would have adverse consequences."[55] Thus, at this point, it is not clear whether baselines should be fixed or not.[56]

In the end, aquitorial sovereignty is seen as a derivative of territorial sovereignty. The State has sovereignty over the territorial sea only by virtue of its inseparable connection with the land territory.[57] As such, sovereignty over land territory is different from sovereignty over water. Aquitorial sovereignty is limited (for instance by the right of innocent passage in the territorial sea) according to Art. 17 UNCLOS.

What might in any case matter long beforehand (and irrespective of whether baselines are fixed) is the fact that a State's territory needs to be *habitable*. Loss of territory as a result of climate change will not take the form of rapid submergence as a result of rising sea levels. Instead it will take the form of gradual erosion of territory accompanied by degradation of the quality and inhabitability of the remaining territory.[58] Wong points out that population displacement due to extreme weather events, as well as food and groundwater scarcities will occur long before territory is completely inundated.[59] First of all, fresh water becomes salinized and agriculture becomes difficult.[60] As such, for low-lying island States such as Tuvalu and Kiribati, insufficient fresh water, as the water lens shrinks, has been cited as the most probable trigger for rendering these countries uninhabitable in the longer term.[61] As stated in the report of the Secretary-General for the World Humanitarian Summit from 2 January 2016: "For some people living in small island States, rising sea levels put them at risk of losing their entire homeland."[62] Thus, by rendering territory uninhabitable and eventually submerging it, the rising seas are clearly endangering territory, particularly because habitability is itself a characteristic of territory.[63] So, even though uninhabited territories can be *part* of an inhabited State's territory, completely uninhabitable and uninhabited territory is not able to qualify as a State's territory.[64]

Statehood endangered by the loss of "a defined territory"?

The physical disappearance of all the land territory of a State is unprecedented and not considered by international law.[65] Oppenheim's classic treatise distinguishes six modes of losing State territory: Cession, dereliction, subjugation, prescription, revolt, and operations of nature.[66] While, particularly, the last one could be seen as fitting the case of small island States, only merger, annexation, dissolution, and absorption are mentioned as possible scenarios leading to the extinction of a State.[67]

Marek uses the example of an island that becomes submerged in her book *Identity and Continuity of States in Public International Law* from 1968 and takes it for granted that a State in such a situation would cease to exist.[68] Others seem to follow her view.[69] Shaw adds that the necessity of having a territorial basis is self-evident[70] and commonly presumed.[71] Thus, "a State without a territory is not possible."[72] Crawford seems to agree by stating: "statehood is not simply a factual situation. It is a legally circumscribed claim of right, specifically to the competence to govern a certain territory."[73] Territory appears inseparable from concepts of the other State elements, namely population, government, and independence.[74] Indeed, without it, there is no government over this territory and no population populating this territory.

Historically, the Peace of Westphalia established a system of nation States exercising sovereignty over certain territories only in 1648. It aimed to establish a world order "on the basis of States exercising untrammeled sovereignty over certain territories and subordinated to no earthly authority."[75] The concept of personal allegiance as the foundation of political society disappeared and the modern international law which is *territorially* organized was established.[76] Thus, territory seems to be an essential element for the sovereignty of a society.[77] Based on this system it seems logical that statehood is conditioned on territory.[78] Territory became, as O'Connell has suggested, "perhaps the fundamental concept of international law."[79] Statehood nowadays "is the customary international legal status of a certain territory."[80] However, the fixation on territory is a rather recent phenomenon.[81] There were times when the concept of society was based primarily upon personal allegiance rather than upon territory.[82] As such, Cicero defined a State as "an assembly of men living according to law."[83] Thus, there was no focus on territory. For the ancient Greeks, a State was the *personal* union of citizens in a "politeia."[84] For instance, Thucydides wrote "it is men that make a State, not walls nor ships devoid of men."[85] Also in the post-Roman era, the focus rested, for many reasons, including religion, on personal allegiance rather than on territory.[86]

Even later, States' definitions did not always include the element of the territory: Lawrence says "[a] state may be defined as a political community, the members of which are bound together by the tie of common subjection to some central authority, whose commands the bulk of them habitually obey."[87] Wheaton defines a State as "any nation or people, whatever may be the form of its internal constitution, which governs itself independently of foreign powers."[88] And Vattel describes States as "political bodies, societies of men who have united together and combined their forces in order to procure their mutual welfare and security."[89] As such, the emphasis is laid more on population, collective will, and government than on territory.[90] Some authors even suggest that territory is not necessary to statehood at all and a State could live in-situ – without a territory – at least after statehood has been firmly established.[91] Does this mean that even if territory is endangered by the rising sea, statehood does not have to be seen as being endangered?

What might be most important under the current system is that a State loses the basis for (territorial) sovereignty by losing its territory. Sovereignty, however, is since Bodin, the essence [Wesensmerkmal] of the State.[92] It is usually conceived as a monopoly of authority in a particular territory.[93] It has thus been traditionally defined in reference to the principle of territoriality.[94]

> In order to become operational, sovereignty must be split up into freedom of action, which is mostly characterized as territorial sovereignty, and the protection of territory against outside interference, which is mainly considered in terms of territorial integrity.[95]

According to Shaw, "[t]he political/legal notion of sovereignty itself is founded upon the fact of territory."[96] It is "the bundling of rule-making authority within bounded territories,"[97] providing the "link between regulation and geography, or power and space, linking power and space in bounded sovereign state-territorial parcels. Sovereignty sets up a dichotomy of inside/outside: Inside is the domestic arena of politics and community; outside is characterized by anarchy and international relations."[98]

Traditionally, international law has its mission and purpose in the "delimitation of the exercise of sovereign power on a territorial basis."[99] Under international law, a sovereign State is empowered to exercise exclusive and total jurisdiction within its territorial borders, while any other States correspondingly must not intervene in the internal affairs of a sovereign state.[100] In this sense, the International Court of Justice (ICJ) stated in 1949: "By sovereignty, we understand the whole body of rights and attributes which a State possesses in its territory, to the exclusion of all other States, [...]."[101] It is therefore an essential attribute of the sovereignty that it should possess jurisdiction over all persons and things within its territorial limits.[102]

The development of sovereignty meant a formal demarcation of political authority on territorial grounds.[103] On the one hand, every person on the territory of a State is under this State's jurisdiction (positive aspect of the territorial jurisdiction); on the other hand, no sovereign action may be exercised on the territory of a State that is not coming from or authorized by this State (negative aspect).[104]

> In so far as "sovereignty comprises both elements, person and territorial,"[105] [...] a State would not be sovereign without a territory. And a State without sovereignty is a contradiction in terms.[106]

Examples of rights and duties associated with sovereignty

There are various rights associated with sovereignty.[107] First, there is the power exclusively to control its own domestic affairs, domestic affairs being the affairs concerning the State's *territory*. Second, there comes the exclusive jurisdiction over a *territory* and any person staying there. Third, there is the power to admit and expel aliens from State's *territory*. Fourth come the privileges of its diplomatic envoys in other countries.[108] Except for the last one, all of these rights seem to require territory. For the rights concerning diplomatic envoys, the necessity of territory is not as obvious. However, diplomacy is based on reciprocity and therefore these rights might wane as soon as the State loses its ability to grant the respective right to other States within its territory due to the loss of its territory.

The correlative duties or obligations binding the States make the dilemma of deterritorialized States even more clear: The duty not to intervene in the affairs of another State becomes difficult to carry out: Affairs of another State are the affairs in the area of exclusive jurisdiction of other States, namely the territory of the other State.[109] If the State in situ needs other States' territory within which it can act, generally any action will "interfere" with the sovereignty of the host State.

Similarly, the duty to abstain and prevent agents and subjects from committing acts constituting a violation of another State's independence or territorial supremacy cannot be followed by deterritorialized States either. Any sovereign act on the territory of another State (without its explicit consent which would put into question the sovereign character of the "guest" State's action) would be a violation of this other State's territorial supremacy.

As such there is a general duty not to perform acts of sovereignty on the territory of another State.[110] Acts of sovereignty in this sense include legislative acts like proclamations of laws and holding parliamentary sessions, executive acts such as adaptions and promulgations of regulations, as well as acts of the judiciary like judicial hearings and remission of sentences.[111] Thus, if all these actions cannot be performed, a State will no longer be able to act. Internal sovereignty (being sovereignty inside a territory) is by its very nature not possible without territory. External sovereignty is complicated too: Outside of the territorial limits of a State there seems to be no room for sovereign actions.

SOVEREIGN ACTION ON FOREIGN TERRITORY

It seems impossible for a State without territory to comply with its duties as any action necessarily would take place under the jurisdiction of another State. Thereby, this action would either be in violation of this other State's sovereignty, or – in case of the permission of the other State – not entirely sovereign anymore.

A) CASES OF INTERVENTIONIST ACTIONS ON FOREIGN TERRITORY

Prominently cited as a case where sovereign action of a State on foreign territory was seen as infringements is the case of the arrest of Adolf Eichmann, a Nazi war criminal, by Israel on Argentinian territory.[112] He was abducted in May 1960 from Argentina by Israeli nationals, brought to Israel for trial, and was sentenced to death (and eventually executed in 1962).[113] Argentina protested the Israeli infringement of its sovereignty.[114] After an intervention of the UN Security Council,[115] Israel and Argentina issued a joint statement acknowledging that "the incident [...] violated the basic rights of the State of Argentina."[116]

Likewise, the case of Antoine Argoud, an ex-colonel in the French army who had participated in a conspiracy to assassinate then President de Gaulle and who was abducted from Munich in 1963 was seen as an infringement of Germany's sovereignty.[117]

These cases[118] show that there is no room for personal jurisdiction without having a territory, because the territorial State will always have supreme jurisdiction.[119] In order to exercise personal jurisdiction over a person under the territorial jurisdiction of another State, a State will always need this other State's consent.

B) CASES OF TOLERATED ACTIONS ON FOREIGN TERRITORY

By consent of the State whose territory is encroached upon, a State that lacks authority over territory or population can be granted exceptions from the (territorial) jurisdiction of the State(s) where it acts.[120]

As such, the ICJ stated in its judgment on "Armed Activities on the Territory of the Congo" that the requirement of consent "to the crossing of the border by [here Ugandan] troops"[121] has to be rigorously observed and the instruments claimed to express such consent have to be strictly interpreted.[122]

In other cases, territory is leased to foreign States. One example is the Panama Canal Zone: The US was granted extensive rights over this area.[123] The Hay-Bunau Varilla treaty[124] reads: "The Republic of Panama grants to the United States all the rights [...] which the United States would possess and exercise if it were the sovereign of the territory [...]."[125] Even though there was some controversy about the issue of sovereignty,[126] in the end "Panama maintained a general, although nominal, sovereignty in the Canal Zone,"[127] which entitled it to conduct activities like imposing taxes on the incomes of all persons employed in the Canal Zone.[128] Also, the US Supreme Court held in the case *Coulson v. Government of the Canal Zone* that the United States is not the owner of the territory.[129] Concordant, the Supreme Court of Panama stated in *Re Cia. de Transportes des Gelabert,*[130] in Re *Burriel*[131] and in *Re Kenneth Robert Bartlett*[132] that the Canal Zone does *not* represent foreign territory for Panama.[133]

Another example is the lease of Guantanamo Bay from Cuba to the United States.[134] Here, the initial government of the new sovereign State of Cuba leased land to the United States for an indefinite period.[135] Similarly, but not indefinitely, the Soviets exercised authority over some military bases in Finland in 1955 and the United Kingdom over its military bases in Jordan from 1946 to 1957 and Libya from 1945 to 1969.[136]

In the end, the host State could theoretically evict the putative State from its territory.[137] Albeit this being in practice sometimes harder than it sounds in theory, as can be seen from the case of Guantanamo Bay,[138] where the United States refuses to give the territory back to Cuba, even the US Supreme Court has held that a lease over territory does not give rise to "sovereignty."[139] Similarly, Wang Tieya observes for the lease arrangements concerning Hong Kong that sovereignty was not transferred. It was, however, a "good example of the distinction between sovereignty and the exercise of rights stemming from sovereignty."[140] Thus, in all these cases, the sovereignty was at least not completely transferred, but is depending on the continuous consent of the host State.[141]

Another example of tolerated action on foreign territory is the case of governments in exile.[142]

> A government in exile is a government which has been forced to leave the territory of its State due to enemy occupation or civil war and which claims governmental powers with the consent of the State of residence [...] as long as there exists a genuine chance to return.[143]

It can exercise sovereign acts only as long as its functions are not constrained by its "host" government.[144]

Hence, principally, all subjects of international law "are such only when they are actually *superiorem non recognoscentes*."[145] For States without territory, the host State must, in the end, always be recognized as superior. Fundamentally, the host State will remain sovereign over the territory on which the putative State acts or resides. Consequently, the validity of the putative State's actions and legal order would rest on the host State, not on international law.[146] Thus, for "guest States" it is, so to say, "logically impossible [...] not to be subject to the power of the host state."[147]

Therefore, the extent of the entity's independence depends on the host State: Consequently, the criterion "independence," strictly applied, would not be met without a territory.[148] The State without territory "will have to rely on the cooperation of the executive organs of the host state."[149] Concepts of responsibility, equality, and the ability to bind and enforce obligations over territory require the State to be legally independent. If the guest State's existence derives from the host State, there would be, in truth, no separate State: The guest State would be a component legal order of the host State. Consequently, the host State would have ultimate legal control over – and be responsible for – the territory in question.[150]

C) LIMITATIONS ON ACTION ON FOREIGN TERRITORY AS A CONSEQUENCE

The previous sections can be summarized with Max Huber's classic definition of sovereignty: "Sovereignty in the relations between States signifies independence. Independence in regard to a portion of the globe is the right to exercise therein, to the exclusion of any other State, the functions of a State."[151] Whenever some other State exercises sovereignty over a territory, a "guest State" would not be able to "obey[s] no other authority."[152] Consequently, as there are, apart from Antarctica, no areas left that cannot be attributed to some State's territory (*terra nullius*) and would be open for appropriation,[153] there are no areas left where States that have lost their territory could act sovereignly.

The international community is not structured as a hierarchical society, but rather as a community of (formal) peers.[154] Modern international law and international relations are characterized through the ability of States "to assert that they are not subordinates to other authorities" or "not to recognize any superior within the international community."[155] This is comprehensively true on the State's own territory, but only there. "To claim territory is to deny it to others."[156] As such, "[n]o rule is clearer than the precept that no State may lawfully attempt to exercise its sovereignty within the territory of another."[157] Already in 1678, when Leibniz was evaluating what accounted for sovereignty for the Duke of Hanover, in whose service he then was, he wrote that the first condition for sovereignty was a minimum size of territory.[158] A majesty, being for Leibniz a ruler, who is not a sovereign because of the lack of territory, can enforce his authority or rights only by applying his own or other sovereigns' forces from the outside, "by means of war,"[159] or as shown above by infringing upon the sovereignty of the territorial State where it acts. During the 1940s, it was observed that "the sovereignty of any state is unrestricted on its own territory only, while on foreign territory it naturally yields to the sovereignty of the foreign state."[160] While this statement might have become qualified mainly due to a change with regard to the unrestricted sovereignty (due to the increasing importance of human rights), the fact that a State cannot act unrestrictedly sovereignly on the territory of another State has not changed. It remains a fundamental concept of the contemporary international legal system, or the "hallmark of the modern state."[161]

When a State plans to uphold its State quality by receiving new territory, as for example the Republic of the Maldives has planned,[162] a respective contract should rather be built similar to the cases, where the sovereignty was actually transferred, such as the cession of Louisiana or Alaska to the United States,[163] than to cases where territory was only leased and the transfer of sovereignty is open to debate.

Various forms of joint sovereignty have been proposed for disputed areas, as for example Jerusalem, or the Falkland Islands/Malvinas.[164] They have, however, not been (successfully) adopted. At times, sovereignty over a territory was temporarily held by more than one power in trust of the population of the territory, as for example in the pre-WWII case of the League of Nations control over the Saar before its return to Germany in 1935.[165] Historical examples of shared territorial sovereignty (for example Kuwait and Saudi Arabia until 1966 and Kuwait and Iraq until 1975) eventually ended up in territory getting divided.[166] Thus, sovereignty seems to be territorially exclusive.

OTHER FORMS OF SOVEREIGNTY

Duursma says: "The world today recognizes no form of sovereignty other than the territorial form."[167] Contrary to this view, Rayfuse points out that *functional* or non-territorial sovereignty is recognized under international law and brings the examples of "governments-in-exile" or communities either made diasporic by processes of invasion and colonization, or overrun and internally dislocated or formally deterritorialized.[168] As such, diasporas (being "migrant communities away from a real or imagined 'homeland'") have proliferated within the last 25 years.[169] People increasingly use the label "diaspora" for themselves also because of the realization of their growing influence on the world.[170] Hence, Rayfuse summarizes that

> international law [thereby] already recognizes that sovereignty and nation may be separated from territory. International law is thus fully capable of responding to the problem of disappearing states in a way that positively recognizes their sovereign rights without further victimizing them by the loss not only of their territory but of their sovereign existence as well.[171]

So, is it possible that a State could exist as a deterritorialized but still sovereign State?[172] Up to the sixteenth and seventeenth centuries, sovereignty was the exercise of authority within different domains (seigneurial, ecclesiastical, juridical, etc.). The different domains were not delineated precisely, but often overlapping with one another.[173] Hence, practically it is possible to imagine different forms of sovereignty existing next to one another. As such, the "functional sovereignty" of the Order of Malta,[174] for example, seems to coexist in parallel to the territorial sovereignty of States. Yet, the reason why they can coexist is that the sovereignty of the Order of Malta is "only" functional.

Could a State exist with functional sovereignty? Riphagen concluded in 1970 that "'functional sovereignty' has a hard time in trying to survive the attacks of 'territorial sovereignty' in the competition between the two concepts as models for the regulation of international relationships." A distribution of space among entities would just be the simplest way to do it.[175]

Another option would be that a State existed with *personal* sovereignty.[176] In the case of Western Sahara (a traditional State in contrast to a modern State as named by El Ouali), the tie of allegiance "was founded on personal allegiance between subjects and their governors, rather than on a precise territorial base."[177]

> That the Sherifian State at the time of the Spanish colonization of Western Sahara was a State of a special character is certain. Its special character consisted in the fact that it was founded on the common religious bond of Islam existing among the peoples and on the allegiance of various tribes to the Sultan, through their caids or sheikhs, rather than on the notion of territory.[178]

Similarly, in the case "Sovereignty over Pedra Branca/Pulau Batu Puteh, Middle Rocks and South Ledge," Singapore, in support of its assertion that the Sultan of Johor did not have sovereignty over Pedra Branca/Pulau Batu Puteh, advances an argument based on what it describes as "the traditional Malay concept of sovereignty." Thus, it contends: "Malaysia has glossed over [...] the traditional Malay concept of sovereignty. This concept undermines Malaysia's claim to an original title. It is based mainly on control over people, and not control over territory. Traditional Malay sovereignty is people-centric and not territory-centric."[179] The Court did not accept this argument and stated that sovereignty is both, territorial and personal.[180]

According to El Ouali, "[t]he territorial element was in fact at the origin of the distanciation between people and their leadership."[181] Thus, a mere sovereignty of the people is possible; but the territorial element brings clarity and peace.[182] In order to enable States with personal sovereignty and territorial sovereignty to coexist next to each other, international law would have to offer some sort of hierarchy for cases of conflict. "Sovereignty per definition consists of internal hierarchy and territorial demarcation."[183] Simultaneously, it provides an ordering principle for what is "internal" to States, meaning where they are sovereign, and what is "external" to them, meaning where other peer States are sovereign.[184] It is the basic constitutional doctrine of the law of nations, governing the world community which consists primarily of States having, in principle, a uniform legal personality.[185] The modern field of conflict of laws can be traced back to Joseph Story and Friedrich Carl von Savigny.[186] Both of them pointed out territory as the ordering element in cases of conflict of laws.[187]

Under these circumstances, no personal unit could exercise its State functions, because any territorial State had the sovereign right to exclude it from doing so within its territory. As long as international law does not "permit two states to be sovereign over the same territory – and it cannot do so given that sovereignty, as exclusive authority, is the organizing idea of international law,"[188] it will be difficult to have different forms of (unrestricted) sovereignty coexisting next to each other. Therefore, such other forms of sovereignty would most likely not be an option for deterritorialized States (yet).

Contrarily, in medieval times, jurisdiction was mainly personal, but neither discrete nor exclusive. It rather overlapped and different authorities claimed final jurisdiction on the same matter.[189] Bull describes this by saying:

> If modern States were to come to share their authority over their citizens, and their ability to command their loyalties, on the one hand with regional and world authorities, and on the other hand with sub-state and sub-national authorities, to such an extent that the concept of sovereignty ceased to be applicable, then a neo-medieval form of universal political order might be said to have emerged.[190]

In such a case, the conflict potential could only be contained by having clear personal or territorial rules on who will have the supreme authority. Carl Schmitt pointed out in this regard:

> If both parties in the conflict are unable to negotiate their right of co-determination in terms of a concordat, the conflict of competences must end in the same way as the confessional civil wars of the sixteenth and seventeenth century: either in a precise answer to the big question quis judicabit? ["who will decide?"] or in an equally precise itio in partes ["return to the region"] – that is, in a spatially clear territorial or regional demarcation, in accordance with the principle cuius region eius religio ["who rules defines the creed"].[191]

Bodin and Hobbes (both influenced by the experiences of religious wars) stated that in absence of clearly located sovereignty, polities would be doomed to the bloody consequences of religious strife.[192] While at least in Europe, after Westphalia, religion diminished in importance as a source of intra-European warfare,[193] the conflict potential of imprecise divisions of sovereignty is still existent. The "transnational character of Islam"[194] might globally become a challenge in this regard. In many conflicts, transnational religious ties have escalated and prolonged the conflicts.[195] Thus, a lesser focus on a State's territory and a greater focus on other forms of ordering principles like religion could be a positive step with regard to conflict prevention. This is also true, where States' territories came into existence rather out of the creativity of the mapmaker than out of political reasons, particularly in Africa.[196]

Taking into consideration the humanization of international law and the principle of popular sovereignty, that is self-determination, the State can also be seen as the body that is primarily meant to enable the people to determine itself, "politically, economically, socially and culturally in accordance with international law principles."[197] Also, when talking about the right of self-determination, both the International Covenant on Civil and Political Rights (ICCPR) and the International Covenant on Economic, Social, and Cultural Rights (ICESCR), as well as many UN General Assembly Resolutions, talk about the people. Thus, the main actor is the people and not the State.[198] However, as each people needs a body to determine itself, the (territorial) State is a necessary component for self-determination.

Schrijver asks whether rights and duties of the vanishing States under international agreements would vanish too when the State disappears, or if they would succeed to the people of the State. He notes in this regard that, interestingly, both the "Vienna Convention on Succession of States in Respect of Treaties" and the "Vienna Convention on Succession of States in Respect of States Property, Archives, and Debts" define "succession of States" as "the replacement of one State by another in the responsibility for the international relations of territory"[199] and not of its people.[200]

Hence, *de lege lata*, the international system is established for being a territorial system; but this system is currently challenged by the emerging importance of individuals. *Per se*, statehood is imaginable without a territory.[201] There are various examples in history that show the possibility of mere personal units. Thus, personal (rather than functional) sovereignty would probably be an option for sinking island States. Burkett argues that climate change requires "meaningful interpretations of the law and may sometimes justify significant departures from precedent or legal status quo." She argues that "deterritorialized statehood is an appropriate means for continued existence."[202] She further states that "if the deterritorialized experience of other international governance entities and the diasporic modifications of the current Westphalian system are not themselves convincing, a reasonable extension of existing law applied to the extraordinary circumstances that climate change introduces might suffice."[203] Nevertheless, this would need great changes in the international system, changes that would possibly lead to great uncertainties.

CONCLUSION

Thus, it would seem that today, sovereignty needs territory on which it is to be exercised,[204] because territory provides the basis for the State's sovereignty.[205] The rights of a State with regard to sovereignty did not arise by chance. Rather, they form the necessary basis for the association of all States and their coexistence.[206] The modern sovereign State confines itself territorially, meaning sovereigns claim hierarchy within borders where they enjoy "a mostly unrestricted sphere of free action within which they possess the power of sovereigns"[207] and do not recognize any higher authority.[208] On account of this sovereignty they are guaranteed equality outside their borders with the other States.[209] Hence, as Shaw argues: "[w]ithout territory, and more particularly territorial sovereignty, a legal person cannot be a state. It is the basic characteristic of a state and thus statehood."[210] Willoughby adds that "although the political jurisdiction of a State is not, in some aspects of its exercise, exclusively territorial in character, the existence of sovereignty itself, and therefore of a State, is dependent upon the claim upon the part of the State to a territory of its own."[211]

Any other form of jurisdiction needs to be limited in order to protect the independence and sovereign equality of States.[212] Consequently, no State can possibly have full jurisdiction over its nationals in a world that is fully covered by territorial jurisdictions of other States without having its own territory. International law, where territory has a central role itself,[213] is very strict in relation to action on the territory of a foreign State without the latter's consent. A general presumption in favor of territorial supremacy guides all areas where extraterritorial activities are conducted.[214] Jurisdiction over its nationals and full sovereignty over a certain territory seem to be essential tools of a State. Without a territory, the statehood of a deterritorialized entity must be questioned,[215] because, substantially, the entire land surface in the world is claimed by one State or another as its own territory over which it has exclusive territorial jurisdiction. Consequently, the members of a landless body would automatically be subject to the legal jurisdiction of the State within whose borders they were. Therefore, the body would not be sovereign and therefore it could not be regarded as a State.[216]

However, while sovereignty seems inseparable from the existence of a State,[217] "as a particular spatiality of power and authority [it] seems unsuitable for an increasingly globalized world."[218] Thus maybe, the Westphalian notion of State sovereignty (consolidating existing entities by dividing Europe into territorial States and thereby establishing an international order where nation States were exercising sovereignty over certain territories)[219] is currently transforming or in need of being reformed (see in more detail Chapter 4).

As for now,

> [t]he rules of modern International Law are so permeated from end to end with the idea of territorial sovereignty that they would be entirely inapplicable to any body politic that was not permanently settled upon a portion of the Earth's surface which in its collective capacity it owned.[220]

Examples of "statehood" without territory

Direct rule presupposes not only extensive authority, but also territoriality.[221] The following section shall explore some counterexamples of "statehood" without territory.

NON-TERRITORIAL UNIONS

If island States would lose their territory and continue to exist next to territorial States, a situation would arise where different ordering systems would coexist. This is not entirely unrealistic. The sovereign territorial system altogether was not the inevitable outcome of underlying processes.[222] There were alternatives and some of them may in the future alter or even transform the State system.[223] In the time of the Holy Roman Empire, there were different non-territorial unions existing next to each other: Feudalism, the church, and the Holy Roman Empire all lacked territorial fixity and exclusivity. Identity or loyalty of the people was not dependent on territory; instead, one's place in the matrix of personal ties was determining one's rights and obligations.[224] Feudalism – public power in private hands – was therefore rule over people rather than land.[225] The church saw itself as a community of believers with no geographic limits to its authority. The Holy

Roman Empire claimed superiority over all other rulers.[226] These systems of complex, crosscutting jurisdictions coexisting next to each other made it possible for individuals to be subject to multiple authorities because government was not defined by mutually exclusive criteria.[227] Even though they were all unified as part of Christendom, power was fragmented and shared by many different parties and there was no clearly defined hierarchy or authority.[228]

The Peace of Westphalia had transformed the international system into a territoriality-based system, simplifying matters by imposing on most persons in Europe an exclusive identity determined by political ties to a sovereign.[229]

> Westphalia symbolized a transformation from a system of political rule based in hierarchical structures of medieval Christianity to one ordered in terms of independent sovereign territorial states: a transition from hierarchy to anarchy.[230]

Back then, the remaining non-territorial unions came into a precarious position.[231] The development towards the sovereign State had started with many unequal units, gradually transforming – through mutual empowerment as well as individuals' choices – into a network of similar actors. Those actors imposed structural limits on the type of units that were possible and would be recognized by them as legitimate forms of organization in international politics.[232]

The City Leagues formed the antithesis of the sovereign, territorial State. They were non-territorial in character.[233] While sovereign States were easily able to coexist with similar types of units in segregated territorial spaces by having the complete authority over their territories and accepting the complete authority of others over their respective territories,[234] City Leagues, like the Hansa did not fit well in this system.[235] The Hansa did not limit its political authority to formal borders. In non-Hansa towns, where the league had important trading interests, it would seek special privileges and rights of jurisdiction over its members within the given areas of the town.[236] Thus, it could not participate in the new order of international politics which was hammered out during the negotiations in Osnabrück and Münster. The organizational principles of territorial States (encompassing a final decision-making structure with a monopoly on violence and justice within certain borders) were incompatible with its own principles.[237] Eventually the league dissolved itself scarcely 20 years later.[238] Spruyt concludes his chapter about the victory of the sovereign State with the following: The emergence of the sovereign State and the territorial State system were mutually reinforcing processes. The competitive system excluded other types of units that were less efficient. Indeed, it "is certainly easier to supervise one's livestock by fencing it in than to follow each head of cattle around, and the most efficient way to control and protect human and natural resources of a given area is probably to patrol its outer margins."[239] Moreover, States preferred to cooperate with other territorial entities, because a clear division of responsibilities (on a territorial basis) was possible.[240]

But there are still non-territorial unions. As such, religious organizations base their rule not on territorial borders but on the community of the faithful – wherever they reside. But the struggle between the territorial mode of authority and the translocal rule claimed by the church was resolved by the treaty of Augsburg in 1555: the principle was set up according to which the secular ruler determines the public character of religion. Through the maxim "*cuius regio eius religio*," political elites established the principle that the territorial unit would publicly adopt the religion of the ruler. This principle was reaffirmed at the end of the Thirty Years War.[241] Nowadays, through human rights, including freedom of religion in particular, there seems to be a change in this regard. But either religion plays an ancillary role in the secular State, or the church works together with the State within its territorial frame.

But although the State system has been spread globally, the tension between transnational religious affinity and territorial rule has not been resolved everywhere to the same extent.[242] By some accounts, the Muslim community of faith differs from the Western concept of sovereign, territorial rule.[243] As such, in the Islamic context, the independence and initiative of the civil society may best be measured not in relation to the State, but in relation to religion, of which, in the Muslim perception, the State itself is a manifestation and an instrument.[244] The dethronement of religion – as Lewis calls it – as the organizing principle of society was attempted much later in the Islamic world, and the attempt was due to European influences. Moreover, it was never really completed, and is perhaps now being reversed. Lewis states in this regard that in Iran, for example, organized religion has returned to something like the status that it enjoyed in the medieval world, both Christian and Islamic.[245]

As long as the church and the State have their own fields of responsibility or agree on how to divide the responsibilities, coexistence can work. If the church has genuine State responsibilities, it only works if and when the State grants the union such responsibilities which most Muslim-majority countries do at some level in their legal framework. Several countries apply the Sharia predominantly or entirely – however, still within their borders. And even within the borders, Jan Michiel Otto argues that the common assumption that the Sharia is binding, i.e., that Muslims are exclusively subject to classical Sharia law, was not the case in practice: Since the early Islamic States of the eighth and ninth centuries the Sharia always existed alongside of other normative systems which could be as binding as or even more binding than particular versions of Sharia.[246]

Opposing our international system of traditional States, there are other examples of non-territorial unions as "al Qaeda's global ummah" "whose constitutional order was not confined to a particular territory or national group," or Hezbollah, a non-State Shiite political-military movement.[247] Also, the so-called Islamic State appeared on the international platform, building a new antagonist in the war on terror,[248] a construct unknown in the Westphalian time characterized by international wars.[249]

More generally, in the course of the emerging right of self-determination, some ethnic movements have destabilized existing sovereign, territorial States.[250] But successful secessionist efforts have subsequently reconstituted themselves as new *territorial* States. (Craven sees this development as maybe turning out to be "one of this century's greatest ironies."[251]) In any case, they are not antithetical to the State system. So, ethnic movements have not essentially been at odds with the principles of territorial demarcation of rule and of a final locus of authority in external affairs. Instead, what they did is, they changed the chronological order of State and nation. While formerly there were States that formed the nation within their territories, nowadays, nations form territorial States.[252]

An exception in this regard, so to say "a break from the given order," are the Roma, a "nation without a state or without a territory"[253] or a "people without any national territory that they can claim as their own."[254] They explicitly do "not want a state:"[255]

> Individuals belonging to the Roma Nation call for a representation of their Nation, which does not want to become a State. We ask for being recognized as a Nation, for the sake of Roma and of non-Roma individuals, who share the need to deal with the nowadays new challenges. We, a Nation of which over half a million persons were exterminated in a forgotten Holocaust, a Nation of individuals too often discriminated, marginalized, victim of intolerance and persecutions, we have a dream, and we are engaged in fulfilling it. We are a Nation, we share the same tradition, the same culture, the same origin, the same language; we are a Nation. We have never looked for creating a Roma State. And we do not want a State today, when the new society and the new economy are concretely and progressively crossing-over the importance and the adequacy of the State as the way how individuals organize themselves.
>
> The will to consubstantiate the concept of a Nation and the one of a State has led and is still leading to tragedies and wars, disasters and massacres. The history of the Roma Nation cuts through such a coincidence, which is evidently not anymore adequate to the needs of individuals. We, the Roma Nation, offer to the individuals belonging to the other Nations our adequacy to the new world.[256]

Engin F. Isin points out that thereby this declaration claims something impossible.

> The order under which we live cannot say yes to this request and its enactment. "We, the people" without a state, without sovereignty, without territory cannot come into being; it can only be a minority. "We, the Roma Nation" is possible only if it demands, claims and requests to become a nation with a state, with sovereignty, with territory.[257]

Thereby, he argues, "the arbitrariness of our order" is pointed out because such a demand is always "trapped in territory and sovereignty."[258]

However, the Roma are becoming increasingly vocal on the international stage. They are represented in the World Bank, the UN, and the EU.[259] Nevertheless, being put on an equal status with States seems impossible because of the equality of States. Making the Roma a sovereign nation without a territory would lead to crosscutting jurisdictions. Crosscutting jurisdictions appear to be only possible when and as long as the actors agree on a prioritization.[260] Generally, if non-territorial systems do not confine their authority with regard to their competences, such a situation will be antithetical to the external equality of States which sovereign territoriality presupposes.[261] As such, Chouinard points out that stateless nations "pose one of the greatest challenges to contemporary political science, as they refute the ideal-type that is the nation-state upon which our entire international system relies."[262] A hierarchical status of domination and subordination between the different territorial and non-territorial subjects is necessary which would abolish the formal equality between States, if other entities were allowed on the same level as States. Ironically, Chouinard points out, stateless nations outnumber States by far. She speaks of between 3,000 and 6,000 nations versus 193 States. Thus, "[s]tateless nations appear, in this light, to be more the norm than the exception in a world that insists on using the nation-state model as an ideal type to be achieved,"[263] a situation that bears some risk for territorial States,[264] by either demanding self-determination (territorially) and thereby questioning the very integrity of existing States, or demanding self-determination (non-territorially), as in the exceptional case of the Roma and thereby eventually questioning the supremacy of territorial States in general.

SOVEREIGN SUBJECTS OF INTERNATIONAL LAW WITHOUT TERRITORY

Jain, who argues that an entity "may retain statehood notwithstanding the loss of territory,"[265] mentions the Sovereign Military Order of Malta and the Holy See as promising examples of exceptions from the necessity of territory with "precedential value."[266]

The Holy See had lost its territory from 1870 onwards until the ratification of the Lateran treaty.[267] While it has acquired territory again since then, it is acknowledged that the Lateran treaty did not change the international personality of the Holy See.[268] Thus, even during the time when it did not have any territory, it was a sovereign subject of international law.

The Order of Malta used to have territorial sovereignty over different territories but remained sovereign after having lost its territory in 1798.[269]

Yet, the comparability of these subjects of international law without a territory with sinking States is questionable. It is true that the Order of Malta used to have territory and was at that time (in contrast to the Templars or the Iberian Orders probably because of its territory)[270] recognized as sovereign subject of international law. It is also true that it still maintains diplomatic relations with 112 states.[271] While it might have kept the sovereign status at first (because of the distinct possibility that the Order might regain territory,[272] as it had done in 1530 when it moved to Malta after having lost Rhodes)[273], the main reason – and the reason why it is still regarded as sovereign is its unique history and humanitarian function, the pursuit of religious objectives, charity, and welfare work (Costituzioni, Titolo I, articolo 10):[274] It is a religious order dedicated to the provision of medical care since its formation in around 1050.[275] As such, the Order of Malta has always (even at times when it had territorial sovereignty) been a non-territorial entity.[276] It enjoyed and still enjoys sovereign immunity (only) to the extent necessary for the execution of its founding purpose – the provision of medical care.[277] The territorial jurisdiction that the Order used to have over Malta was not the international duty of the Order.[278] Its sovereignty was (in contrast to the sovereignty of States or even of governments in exile), independent of territory.[279] When it was recognized by the Bull Pie Postulatio Voluntatis of Pope Paschal II as an autonomous religious Order in 1113 it was dedicated to serve the poor and sick. After the confirmation of this Bull by Pope Calixtus II in 1120, the Order spread outwards from Jerusalem, until there were hospitals, or houses of the Order, throughout Europe.[280] This was its duty. It was thereby always of a supranational character even during the period when it had a territorial ruling.[281] It viewed itself as an essential component of international discussions and action taken concerning peace in the world.[282]

Today, it still only has functional sovereignty in that its sovereignty is based on its international activities and not on the possession of territory, as has been made clear by the cardinalitial tribunal in its decision released 19 February 1953:[283]

> La qualità di Ordine sovrano della Istituzione è funzionale, ossia diretta ad assicurare il raggiungimento dei fini dell'Ordine stesso e il suo sviluppo nel mondo.[284]

Similarly, the Holy See's aims and activities are spiritual. In consideration of that fact, it has maintained its status as person of international law even during the period (1870–1929) during which it was deprived of territory and population, enjoying international personality by "a very special, spiritual, title."[285] Nowadays, it effectively controls the Vatican City (a mere territorial administration) and the Catholic Church (the worldwide network of persons and institutions)[286] holds as such the status of a subject of international law. But – as Kunz makes clear – this should not be confused with its qualification of a State.[287] It is "a subject of international law equal to states," regardless of its territory. As such, it cannot be seen as an example of a State without territory but as an entity having "an international legal personality of its own which permits it to take international actions such as the conclusion of treaties and the maintenance of diplomatic relations."[288]

The "statehood" of these sovereign subjects is thus merely a function of special historical circumstances and the prominent role of Christianity in the development of the Westphalian system of international law[289] and cannot be seen as precedent for sinking island States. These entities were recognized as States or State-like for special reasons and granted *functional* sovereignty as far as necessary for the maintenance of these special reasons. They might therefore well give hope to the thought that island States without territory will not lose (at least not immediately) their status as (partly) sovereign subjects of international law; however, they do not allow a judgment with regard to the status of these entities as *States* under international law.

STATES THAT TEMPORARILY LOST THEIR TERRITORY

No State has, up to now, ever just lost its territory. States that have been recognized as disappearing were regarded as such in situations of State successions.[290]

Claims to the entire territory of a State were made in the context of the admission of Israel, Kuwait, Mauritania, and Belize to the UN. The proposition that a State exists despite claims to the whole of its territory was not generally challenged in these cases.[291]

Some States have temporarily lost their territory. For example,[292] the Baltic States Estonia, Latvia, and Lithuania were formally incorporated by the Soviet Union from 1944–1991.[293] It is generally held that they were resurrected as the same States that had existed prior to their annexation.[294] Even more, they are regarded as having been independent States under illegal occupation during the whole time of the annexation.[295] That might provide insight in the fate of island States, in showing what happens when a State (temporarily) loses its territory. The fact that they were regarded as the same States after having regained their territory might provide an example for small island States at least in the case of them regaining (other) territory. This would lead to the question of how long the identity of a State remains preserved despite its lack of effective control over territory.[296] Several years do not seem to be an obstacle. In the case of Ethiopia, it has been four years, in the case of Austria even seven years.[297] Certainly, once an entity has established itself as a State, it does not (at least not immediately) lose its statehood by losing its territory or effective control over that territory.[298]

However, as island States might not regain their territory at all, it is even more important to explore whether these island States could remain independent States *while* having lost their territory. The analogy of the Baltic States does not seem to go very far, because their continuity was just a legal continuity due to the policy of non-recognition which led to the position that *de jure* there was still an independent State.[299] In the case of sinking island States, the rising seas are "occupying" the territory, against which a non-recognition-policy does not seem suitable.

VIRTUAL STATES

The relevance of territory seems to decline in the concept of the sovereign State in the context of the modern commercial environment, and especially the internet.[300] As such, Rosecrance stated in 1996: "Territory becomes passé."[301] He predicts that "[t]he virtual state – a state that has downsized its territorially based production capability – is the logical consequence of this emancipation from the land."[302] According to Rosecrance, a

> virtual state is a country whose economy is reliant on mobile factors of production. Of course it houses virtual corporations and presides over foreign direct investment by its enterprises. But more than this, it encourages, stimulates, and to a degree even coordinates such activities. […] The virtual state specializes in modern technical and research services and derives its income

> not just from high-value manufacturing, but from product design, marketing, and financing. The rationale for its economy is efficiency attained through productive downsizing. Size no longer determines economic potential. Virtual nations hold the competitive key to greater wealth in the 21st century. They will likely supersede the continent-sized and self-sufficient units that prevailed in the past. Productive specialization will dominate internationally just as the reduced instruction set, or "RISC," computer chip has outmoded its more versatile but slower predecessors.[303]

Nowadays, there are indeed various options to organize the economy (a focus of Rosecrance in his work), even individuals, particularly via the internet. The "growth in both the (horizontal) extent and (vertical) reach of international agreements," etc. leads to a decreasing relevance of national independence.[304]

A certain dispassionateness about territory could even be helpful in avoiding various conflicts concerning borders and territory in general that we currently have to deal with. It would indeed be in line with the trends of humanization and globalization (see in further detail Chapter 4). So maybe a "virtual State" is not a bad idea?

In 2008, the self-proclaimed "world's first internet-based sovereign country"[305] *Wirtland* (term comes from "virtual land")[306] was founded. According to its own statements, it is willing to integrate in the international system and sees the fact that it lacks a territory as advantage, because it thereby avoids the main source of dispute of traditional self-proclaimed States: the dispute about territory.[307] It points out in its Statute:

> While the boundaries of sovereign states are becoming symbolic in Europe, in other world's regions sovereignty is increasingly challenged, and separatism leads to bloodshed and terrorism. Both trends suggest for a serious rethinking of the notion of self-identification in a changing world.[308]

Wirtland states that it wants to be "a country that transcends national borders without breaching or lessening the sovereignty of any involved."[309] However, can there be additional sovereignty without lessening existing sovereignty? Burkett suggests, that as long as its nationals would keep the nationality of the State ex-situ (plan of dual citizenship),[310] the sunken island State could keep its right to exercise jurisdiction over its citizen.[311] She argues that "a deterritorialized statehood is an appropriate means for continued existence [of island States after having lost their territories]."[312] Moore argues that the right of self-determination "lends weight to the idea of a deterritorialised State."[313] Ex-situ nationhood would be a status that protects the peoples forced from their original places.[314] Similarly, Wirtland seems to put some hope into some sort of dual citizenship. As such, it granted *citizenship* to Edward Snowden in 2013 and to Julian Assange in 2010.[315] Interesting in this regard is also Estonia's approach to offer a so-called e-residency: "e-Residency offers to every world citizen a government-issued digital identity and the opportunity to run a trusted company online, unleashing the world's entrepreneurial potential."[316] Granting someone an additional citizenship or letting someone keep its former citizenship would only make sense for the person concerned, if additional rights are connected to this. In the case of Wirtland, no real advantage is visible (yet). In the case of Estonia, the e-residency (which is not *citizenship*)[317] does not allow an e-resident "to vote, or permit someone from outside the EU to travel [to Estonia] without a visa," however "it does confer a number of advantages. It makes it a lot easier to set up a business and open a bank account, and you can use the card to digitally sign documents and contracts."[318] As such, Kaspar Korjus, manager of the project, "is convinced that this is an idea whose time has come, and countries will compete to offer this kind of virtual citizenship: 'We are the first mover – there will be lots of e-Residency programmes'."[319] The number of advantages for an e-resident still remains to be seen. There are some, as can be seen from the example of

> Stanislaw, a painter from Ukraine, who was unable to sell his pictures because his country does not have the infrastructure to allow him to accept foreign payments. [...] Now the artist has established a company in Estonia and is selling his paintings [payments via PayPal] around the world while remaining in Kiev.[320]

Moreover, tax transparency which comes with the program "is now a badge of honour and there are countries like India, Indonesia and Thailand where the most important thing as an entrepreneur is to be trusted."[321] Thus, there are advantages, which might increase with the increasing digitalization of the world, but which are still far from being comparable to actual citizenship.

Actual *citizenship* can be connected with the right of the original State/virtual State for the purpose either of jurisdiction or of diplomatic protection.[322] Territorial jurisdiction seems to be the dominant one as can be seen from several cases, where States were in disagreement about jurisdictions. As there is no real place on Earth where no State is having territorial jurisdiction, it becomes difficult to imagine how such a construct could add to the rights of the people granted such additional citizenship. If there is always sovereign territorial power, sovereign personal jurisdiction seems impossible, because sovereignty is "the highest, final, and supreme political and legal authority and power within the territorially defined domain of a system of direct rule."[323]

Additionally, Art. 9 of the Montevideo Convention[324] (coming right after the prohibition to intervene in the internal or external affairs of another State) tackles the issue of jurisdiction:

> The jurisdiction of states *within the limits of national territory* applies to *all the inhabitants*. Nationals and foreigners are under the same protection of the law and the national authorities and the *foreigners may not claim rights other or more extensive than those of the nationals*.[325]

Thereby it becomes clear that it is impossible for a State to grant special rights to its nationals that inhabit another State.

Diplomatic protection is imaginable. Borchard said in this regard in 1919 that the "right of diplomatic protection constitutes [...] a limitation upon the territorial jurisdiction of the country in which the alien is settled or is conducting business."[326] He added that "[d]iplomatic protection [...] is a complementary or reserved right invoked only when the state of residence fails to conform with this international standard."[327] Thus,

> [i]n the mutual relation of states in international intercourse, the home state of a citizen abroad yields the exercise of its personal control or sovereignty over its citizen in favor of the territorial sovereignty of the state of residence, on the condition that the latter's system of law and administration is in its application to aliens within the standards prescribed by international law and recognized custom. [...].

If not, "the personal sovereignty of the home state reasserts itself and emerges in the form of diplomatic protection."[328] Hence, if the "guest State" remains within the limits of the "international standard," there will not be much room for the State of nationality to exercise its personal jurisdiction; "diplomatic protection is triggered by the breach of primary rules."[329] Moreover, even though there are certainly other examples, diplomatic protection against the will of the territorial State does not seem to be a very strong tool, as famously seen from the LaGrand Case as well as the Avena Case,[330] where diplomatic protection could not prevent the territorial State (in these cases the United States) from executing the death penalty. And last, but not least, diplomatic protection works on the basis of reciprocity.[331] As a State ex-situ is very unlikely to have jurisdiction over the national of any other State (personal jurisdiction is based on nationality and territorial jurisdiction is based on territory), a lasting reciprocal relationship would not be existent.

In addition to jurisdiction and diplomatic protection, one can think of other additional rights that might be useful for the people concerned and could be granted to them via their virtual citizenships. For instance, the citizens of a virtual State (State in-situ) could at least be granted special access to international (human rights) courts. This would be a desirable evolution in the international protection of human rights. However, besides the fact, that it is difficult to imagine that a State of residence would allow better access options for foreigners (citizens of a virtual state) than for its own citizens, the very fact that it would be discriminating against the fellow citizens of the country of residence would most likely not allow a positive discrimination of islanders' nationalities. If a positive discrimination is not practicable, it should better be focused on trying to think about feasible ways of granting stateless people the nationality of their new State of residence, while broadening the field of the international protection of human rights.

Even Rosecrance mentions that the recent developments do not lead to an abolition of States "as territorial entities [...] or that politics can take place without territorial space. ... States [still] require a certain minimum of territory to conduct political business and establish representative institutions differentiated from those of other countries."[332] In this spirit, Wirtland itself proposes, via its institute, "to formally acquire [...] territory [sold by small third world countries], because this web-based micro nation aspires to become a real sovereign country, and therefore needs own legitimate land."[333] Thus, even the self-proclaimed "world's first internet-based sovereign country"[334] accepts that it needs some territory in order to become a "real sovereign country."

On the other hand, crossing different national jurisdictions has become a daily routine even for private persons. Bethlehem reminds us:

> How many of us give a thought to the multiple jurisdictions that we traverse whenever we send an email internationally, and the legal edifice of international law and possibly multiple national laws that makes this possible. Internet Service Providers located in one country routing packets of data through ISPs in another country, on the basis of international telecommunications agreements and other legal arrangements that increasingly address conduct in virtual space, rather than geographic space.[335]

This shows that borders have at least to some extent become less significant than they used to be. As such, the environment is improving for the emergence of a virtual State. In certain regards, the "virtual State" as such could be a desirable alternative to traditional "Westphalian States." Currently, there does not (yet) seem to be "room" for such States in the system of territorial entities.[336]

CONCLUSION

It thus appears that only States seem to be "international juristic persons of general competence," whereas "each type of 'non-State' would have a different sphere of more or less circumscribed international legal competence."[337] Regarding new virtual entities as *unnatural* in comparison to *natural* territorially bundled communities might be a bit shortsighted, because territorial States are also not "natural" in any strict historic or sociological sense.[338] Thus, the possibility of new forms of "States" should not *per se* be excluded while being difficult because full *State sovereignty* is imaginable only with territory.

States' considerations with regard to potential loss of territory

From these analyses it seems that losing the entire territory poses an *existential* threat for States.[339] In particular, for the Marshall Islands, Tuvalu, and Kiribati in the Pacific and the Maldives in the Indian Ocean, this is not simply a theoretical issue. The rising seas are indeed seen as a threat to their continued existence.[340] This section collects some statements in this context, in order to find out what States themselves say about this issue:

As early as 1987, then President of the Republic of the Maldives, Maumoon Abdul Gayoom, raised the issue of the rising sea levels as a possibly existential threat for the

Maldives in front of the UN General Assembly. He explained the scientific findings concerning the greenhouse effects[341] and concluded for his own country:

> […], a mean sea-level rise of 2 metres would suffice virtually to submerge the entire country of 1,190 small islands, most of which barely rise over 2 metres above mean sea level. That would be the death of a nation. With a mere 1 metre rise, also, a storm surge would be catastrophic and possibly fatal to the nation.[342]

Whereas back then, an explanation regarding the greenhouse effect was still necessary, ten years later he was standing in front of the same rostrum again, stating:

> Much has happened since then, [as such no further explanation was needed regarding the greenhouse effect] but the threat to my country has remained as alarming and as urgent as ever.[343]

Also, bigger States started to acknowledge the impacts on small island States by then. For instance, Franck Loy, Under-Secretary for Global Affairs of the United States of America said in 1999:

> Island States are not just vulnerable to the effects of climate change; for many of them it is the transcendent – the life-or-death – issue. Some have already begun to see some impacts; we have had reports that rising sea levels have begun to cause saltwater encroachment into drinking water supplies.[344]

In 2001 the Ambassador and Permanent Representative of Tuvalu to the UN and Chair of the Tuvalu Delegation expressed concern with regard to his country's future:

> As has already been said in this debate, the biggest, long-term threat to the people of Tuvalu is the effects of climate change, in particular the rising sea levels. Recent reports released by the Intergovernmental Panel on Climate Change (IPCC) have confirmed beyond doubt the correlation between accelerated atmospheric warming and sea level rise. In Tuvalu also, it is our strong belief that the weather is growing more severe, hotter, drier, and there is unusually high seas eroding foreshores and intruding into fresh water lenses. We believe the cumulative effect of CO^2 emissions in industrial and other countries into the atmosphere have in sum created a future that is very uncertain in Tuvalu. It may not be known in this Hall but unique within the UN membership are the Maldives, Marshall Islands, Kiribati, and Tuvalu: the four countries are the only Member States that consist entirely of low-lying coral atolls and reef islands. In the event of further rising sea levels, where are we to hide. Asking countries to take us in, eventually, as environmental refugees, is not what Tuvalu is after in the long run. What we prefer is that our great grandchildren grow up the way I did, and the way my wife and our

> brothers and sisters did, in our island communities, learning the traditions, customs, and culture of Tuvalu, and living out our way of life. Tuvalu is not alone in sharing this view. Tens of millions of people who live on islands or in coastal communities face the gloomy onslaught of rising sea levels. The vulnerable geography is everywhere. How ironic it would be if decades from now the last Member to enter the UN, Tuvalu, was the first Member State to withdraw because it has disappeared without a trace.[345]

Whereas back then the fact that "the Maldives, Marshall Islands, Kiribati, and Tuvalu" were particularly vulnerable may according to this statement "not be known in this Hall," from then on statements in this regard were made by pretty much any State: [346]

As such, in 2007, Ms Wieczorek-Zeul from Germany delivered a speech on behalf of the EU saying:

> several small island States are seeing their very existence threatened by rising sea levels.[347]

Puka Temu, Deputy Prime Minister of Papua New Guinea, affirmed in 2008, that

> the adverse impacts of climate change and global warming continue to threaten the existence of many small island States, especially due to rising sea levels. For many small island States, sea level rise and the adverse impacts of climate change are security issues threatening their very survival. We therefore call upon the international community to act urgently in order to ensure the security and welfare of small island developing States.[348]

The representative of Nauru, Ms Moses, introducing a draft resolution on climate change and its possible security implications,[349] stated one year later:

> on behalf of the Pacific small island developing States represented at the UN, namely the Federated States of Micronesia, Fiji, Kiribati, Palau, Papua New Guinea, the Republic of the Marshall Islands, Samoa, Solomon Islands, Tuvalu, Tonga, Vanuatu, and my own country, Nauru: Some of our Pacific countries are in danger of losing their populations and their land as a whole. They will cease to be States.[350]

Similar statements have been made on various occasions by the other affected States, in particular by the Marshall Islands ("climate change [...] poses some very clear and obvious questions with respect to our very existence"),[351] and Kiribati ("For us, any incremental rise in sea level threatens our very existence and our very livelihoods").[352] According to the representative of Palau, back then, the world was

> past the point of debating whether climate change is real, man-made and fundamentally altering the future of human civilization. In Palau, freshwater

resources are dwindling and becoming salinated by salt water. Fields of taro – the food supplies on which my country relies– are being inundated by rising tides. And our culture, which has thrived, developed and endured since the times of Homer and the ancient Greeks, faces the real possibility of being wiped out.[353]

Mr McNee from Canada acknowledged in the same year that

[t]he existential threat facing the Pacific small islands, in particular, gives this important issue a very real, urgent and human dimension.[354]

It is notable and very visible from those statements that loss of statehood is perceived to be a likely consequence of inundation.[355] This view is reaffirmed by a resolution adopted by the General Assembly in the same year saying

that the adverse effects of climate change and sea-level rise present significant risks to the sustainable development of small island developing States, that the effects of climate change may threaten the very existence of some of them and that adaptation to the adverse effects of climate change and sea-level rise therefore remains a major priority for small island developing States.[356]

In 2011, Ms Rice stated for the United States of America:

We have dozens of countries represented in this body and in this very Chamber whose very existence is threatened.[357]

Similarly, Hardeep Singh Puri expressed his view as representative of India that climate change

is a challenge that lies at the forefront of the global development agenda and that is close to the hearts of small island States, for which it poses an existential threat.[358]

Mr Araud [differentiating between existence and territory though] stated for France:

The climate threat concerns us all. It is, in particular, a threat for our small island Pacific State partners, whose very existence is in peril, as is the survival of their territory, culture and identity.[359]

The Group of 77 and China added:

We reiterate that sea-level rise continues to pose a significant risk to small island developing States and to their efforts to achieve sustainable development and that, for some, it represents the gravest of threats to their survival and viability.[360]

Despite all these acknowledgements, the concerns of those affected continue. As such, the Alliance of Small Island States Leaders' Declaration from 2012 starts with the words:

> We are gravely concerned that climate change poses the most serious threat to our territorial integrity, viability and survival, and that it undermines our efforts to achieve sustainable development goals and threatens our very existence. We reaffirm the sovereign rights of all SIDS in light of the adverse impacts of climate change.[361]

Before the climate summit in Paris in 2015, Freundel Stuart, Prime Minister, Minister for National Security, the Public Service and Urban Development of Barbados, expressed his view that it is necessary to

> agree on collective action that will make possible the continued survival of our planet. That is an existential issue for all countries, but in particular for those like mine that are small island developing States. Our countries stand on the edge of the yawning abyss opened up by climate change. For those who framed the Charter of the UN, the cessation of global wars was the single existential threat. While that threat undeniably remains today, it would be to our peril not to accord climate change the same deadly capacity to threaten our planet.[362]

The Prime Minister, Minister for Finance, National Security, and Legal Affairs of Saint Vincent and the Grenadines, Ralph Gonsalves, spoke of the

> "maddening acceleration of global warming" as "an existential issue of" his country's survival.[363]

And Francine Baron, Minister for Foreign Affairs and Caribbean Community Affairs of the Commonwealth of Dominica, stated that

> the impact of climate change represents a real and present danger to the existence of small island States like Dominica.[364]

Mr Malielegaoi, the Prime Minister of Samoa, expressed his view that climate change and its adverse impacts are

> a threat to territorial integrity, security and sovereignty, and in some cases to the very existence, of our islands because of the submersion of existing land and the regression of our maritime heritage.[365]

Similarly, Charles Fernandez, the Minister for Foreign Affairs and International Trade of Antigua and Barbuda stated that

> Small island developing States (SIDS) face a multifaceted set of security challenges that require a pre-emptive response. Ours are not the type of challenges that easily grab headlines, yet they must be tackled to safeguard our very existence.[366]

And Mr Mitchell, Minister for Foreign Affairs and Immigration of the Bahamas, underscored

> that if urgent and ambitious actions are taken to comprehensively address climate change in this context, the security implications associated with climate change will be reduced, thereby diminishing the existential threat faced by some SIDS, including those of us in the Caribbean Community.[367]

The Security Council, where climate change was first considered as a security challenge in 2007,[368] held a special meeting in the year of the Paris climate summit where peace and security challenges facing small island developing States were discussed.[369] Japan, Uruguay, Ukraine, Poland, Belgium, Egypt, South Africa, Angola, Chad, Malaysia, Lithuania, Denmark, Finland, Iceland, Norway, Sweden, Netherlands, Singapore, Luxembourg, and the Observer of the Holy See all agreed that "climate-related threats are [...] an existential threat."[370]

Wong counters, that "the use of the word 'extinction' is inconclusive and is political, rather than a legal term of art (and certainly not *opinio juris*)."[371] Yet, it has to be noted that no State, neither from the region, nor worldwide,[372] has so far expressed the contrary opinion being that a State would not cease to exist when losing its territory. Loss of statehood is thus perceived to be a likely consequence of inundation. There is

> precedent to suggest that, at least for an interim period, [States] would continue to recognize a State as such, even when the full criteria of statehood are lacking. Whether, and for how long, countries like Kiribati and Tuvalu could continue to remain members of the UN in such circumstances would therefore depend on the views of other States.[373]

The views expressed above are indeed political in the way that they are meant to express sympathy for the concerned States and maybe to express the willingness to support, not to de-recognize such States. Therefore, Wong is perhaps right in not taking those common views as an expression of *opinio juris*. Many States now believe that this issue needs further study, as evidenced by feedback on the inclusion of "Sea-level rise in relation to international law" in the ILC's program of work.[374] As for now, no State would probably de-recognize another (former) State, as long as this State's continued existence does not affect other States.

However, at the latest, via jurisdictional conflicts, the existence of States without territory will affect other States. As those States that are allegedly affected first will be rather small with regard to their populations, de-recognition might possibly not be brought forward straight away though. Nevertheless, the currently widely held belief seems to be that States cease to exist when losing their territory.

Conclusion

While Willoughby (and others) originally inclined to the view that a State may conceivably exist without a territory, he later became convinced that the existence of a State is dependent on the claim upon the part of the State to a territory of its own.[375] This is mainly because of the concept of sovereignty. "Sovereignty itself," Shaw argues, "is founded upon the fact of territory." Hence, he continues

> Without territory a legal person cannot be a state. It is undoubtedly the basic characteristic of a state and the one most widely accepted and understood.[376]

Also, Negroponte sees the State as being tied to "space and place, geometry and geography."[377] The contemporary concept of the State is premised on control over territory. A State's purpose is to "ensure that activities within its borders are not regulated by any other State."[378] The ability to control what occurs in a given territory is moreover the basis for the equality of states in international law. Wong explains:

> States are not, as a matter of fact, equal, but sovereignty artificially imposes the equality that the system requires to function. The inviolability of borders, immunity of heads of state and, crucially, the ability of factually weaker states to maintain their significance in the international system all rest on the same fiction: the idea that states are equal.[379]

If all States were not the ultimate authority over the territory in which they existed, the fiction imposed under the rubric of sovereign equality would generate instability. Hence, equality between States would become impossible. Under the current (Westphalian) system of territorial consolidation[380] the continuing existence of non-territorial entities side by side with territorial States is not possible. Seydel sees the difference between a State and a tribe precisely in the territoriality of the former.[381] Indeed, one cannot really contemplate a sovereign State as a kind of disembodied spirit.[382] Wong summarizes: "In short, territory is a leg upon which the state must be created; the leg may be bent, but it must exist."[383] Yet, territoriality of States does not seem to be a logical necessity, but a historically contingent dogma.[384] Brown stated in 1915:

> A state without territory is not perhaps absolutely unthinkable, just as it is conceivable that Switzerland might possess a navy. It is possible that the Gypsies might become so thoroughly organized and obtain such generous

> recognition from existing states as to enable them to assume the responsibilities of an international personality. But taking conditions as they are, territory would seem to be an absolute necessity to the modern state.[385]

This might in its general term still be true today. At least, it is (still) difficult to imagine a State without territory.[386] The territory is the basis upon which peace and security rest. Within the national borders, people can associate and organize themselves. For the State, it is the basis for the exercise of its sovereign power and jurisdiction. The protection of the territory thus represents a fundamental task for the States. The prohibition of interfering in this territorial identity is a fundamental prohibition in international law (cf. as a recent example: A/RES/ES-11/1, para. 5 – Aggression against Ukraine).

El Ouali links the right of a State to existence directly to the principle of territorial integrity,[387] which is to be understood as a sign that a State without territory ceases to exist. Thus, there is a necessity for a State to "own" some territory, but there is no imperative for this territory being the same as the previous one. In the absence of "empty" territory where a State could move to, new territory must either be built or given to the sinking State. Building could be problematic, because wholly man-made structures are currently not allowed to constitute territory: "only structures which make use of a specific piece of the earth's surface can be recognized as State territory within the meaning of international law."[388]

Atapattu sees a chance for the continuing existence of a State that has lost its territory, if the international community "is altruistic and does [...] provide (even for purchase)[389] territory to allow relocation *en masse*."[390] There might even be an obligation to give up territory or a right, to reestablish territorial sovereignty as argued by Angell.[391]

The case of the Boers might be an example of how an entire cultural group migrated while preserving its identity and government.[392] It clearly shows that "the total change of territory by a people which, under the same government and law, settles in a different territory, leaves the identity of the state intact."[393] What would need to be regulated is how to transfer sovereignty or even how to share sovereignty. Coexistence of two sovereigns is theoretically possible, yet it can easily give rise to friction, conflict, and instability. Examples for such not-so-peaceful coexistence can be found in the world today.[394]

On the other hand, if States were only "prepared to take in citizens of small island states on an ad hoc basis, but do not allow them to regain their identity for fear of conflicts with their own citizens," which would be according to Atapattu the "most likely (and realistic) scenario," the State would disappear.[395] The point of the matter might in that case rather lie with the statehood criterion "population" than with the statehood criterion "territory" though.

To come to a conclusion with regard to "territory," a permanent loss of territory does not coercively have to result in the loss of statehood. Territory is merely "one of the ways of ordering the world."[396] Other ways are not *per se* impossible. But without massive changes in the international system deterritorialized statehood appears impossible.[397]

Loss of population

Statehood does not only depend on territory. Judge Cançado Trindade has criticized in his separate opinion to the Advisory Opinion on the independence of Kosovo that "international legal doctrine, obsessed, throughout the twentieth century, with the ideas of State sovereignty and territorial integrity [...] to the exclusion of others, was oblivious of the most precious constitutive element of statehood: human beings, the 'population' or the 'people'."[398] Actually, for many writers since Grotius and Bynkershoek, *population* is the essential element.[399] Verdross identified the State with the State's population.[400] Also, Kelsen, who identified the State with the State's law,[401] explicitly states that "the behavior of a State is reducible to the behavior of individuals representing the State."[402] Akin, the Latin word "populous" and the English and French term "nation" means the "State" rather than the "nation."[403] Hence, indeed, the importance of people in international law should not be forgotten: Even if the climate threatens the existence of their territory, at least the people should be protected from such threat.[404]

The criterion "population" is affected by the rising sea, too. Particularly due to the fact that coasts are most densely populated, the destiny of many people will be affected.[405] Myers warned in 2005 that there could be approximately 200 million climate change migrants by 2050, "when global warming takes hold."[406] The majority of them will "only" be forced to resettle somewhere else within their State. However, for small island States, there might be no territory left to resettle to. The rising seas will lead to a degradation of already scarce groundwater resources, declining productivity of agriculture and fisheries, and increased flooding.[407] Territory will thereby become uninhabitable long before its full disappearance.[408] While this has already occurred within States (the residents of Lohachara Island moved to a nearby island in 2006 and one year later some residents of the Carteret Islands relocated to Bougainville),[409] up to now no entire population of a State has been forced to relocate.[410] Presumably the process of a territory becoming uninhabitable and eventually completely submerged will be a gradual process with different steps that might eventually question the quality of the remaining population to fulfill the population criterion.

In 2018 Fiji offered the following thoughts on the matter:

> It was not clear whether the State would be considered extinct in international law or would not be so considered unless its entire territory was submerged. In the latter case, it was not apparent how international law covered questions of statehood and the rights and freedoms of the population of a State that became uninhabitable long before its territory physically disappeared.[411]

The State's criterion "population" can be defined as comprising all the inhabitants of the respective State's territory plus the State's nationals who stay abroad with regard to their continuing linkage to their home State.

Significant shifts of populations, as have also been experienced by the Democratic Republic of Congo, Sudan, and Iraq, to name a few, through massive refugee crises, do not endanger the State's criterion "population" on the international scene.[412] Nor is there a minimum number of people required. Yet, as soon as there are only a few people left, a problem concerning the quality of these remaining might arise: if they are only caretakers of functions on the remaining territory of an island, one could argue along with the ruling of the German Administrative Court's ruling in the case of the "Principality of Sealand"[413] that this does not suffice for being qualified as "population." Other States would presumably accept them as "population" and would preserve the statehood as a legal fiction,[414] simply because they would thereby avoid being undiplomatic and at the same time, they would avoid having to deal directly with the uncertainties arising from any different reaction. As such, plans to establish a small government outpost on the State's only high ground seem promising (cf. Kiribati).[415] At some point, however, there might be no habitable land left. Such total abandonment of a State's territory by its people would probably be "one of the most striking and well-known examples of the potential human impacts of climate change"[416] and difficult to qualify under our current international law system.

Whereas Judge Dillard noted in his separate opinion to the Western Sahara Advisory opinion that "[i]t is for the people to determine the destiny of the territory and not the territory the destiny of the people,"[417] it looks like the destiny of the territory is – at least in the case of these small island States – determined by climate change-induced rising seas. Thus, if the people in question cannot determine the destiny of their territory, what happens to them once their territory disappears?

One could argue that, as soon as no inhabitant is left on the territory, the criterion "population" is no longer fulfilled.[418] But what about those parts of the population that live somewhere else? The remaining nationals of the State would need to have some continuing linkage to the State. Hestetune suggests that identification with a specific territory is not necessarily defeated by the loss of that territory, it is simply complicated.[419] People might very well remain culturally connected to each other in another country, as for example the Marshallese people in Arkansas.[420]

Wong suggests a distinction between the situations where the people relocate to one place and where they are scattered across various States.[421] This makes sense only when and for how long we see the people as the prime element of the State. If that is the case, the people could indeed continue their State on some other territory without their State being extinct. This suggestion is interesting particularly with regard to the development of the rising importance of the individual in the international system. As soon as the people get scattered around the globe, upholding the quality of a population will become even more difficult. However, the nationals of any ex-situ nation can continue to enjoy a shared purpose. Indeed, this appears to be the most powerful binding force for the Sovereign Order of Malta, whose members remain bounded by history, spirituality, and service, without having their own territory.[422] Also the Jewish diaspora might provide an example of a sufficiently strong community that lacked its own territory until 1948. This example shows also the importance of an actual territory for a population:[423] As such, the Israeli and Palestinian Declarations of Independence "place great importance in grounding their national identity and claim in a specific location, which embodies their histories, memories, cultures, religions and desired futures."[424]

An example of a uniquely strong "population" that stayed together outside its own State's territory is the Tibetan population. It is "far more institutionally organised than any socially networked diasporic community"[425] built abroad "through societal pressure and cultivation of moral authority."[426] The material attributes of the Tibetan citizenship, being the *Rangzen Lag-Teb* or "Green Book" (which Tibetans regard as a "passport"), and the annual payment of *chatrel* (in effect "voluntary" taxes) are key mechanisms through which the Tibetan government in exile and Tibetans in exile reaffirm each other's status as a "legitimate government" and "bona fide Tibetan citizens," respectively, despite not having any legal standing.[427] But there is a very strong link to their homeland: An example for this strong symbolic linkage is the parliamentary election system: it operates through "a unique symbolic quota system whereby members of parliament are elected by voters living in exile to represent the region of Tibet where they or their parents are from."[428] Thereby, a sense of the "inevitable" return to Tibet and "rehearsing" democratic territorial governance is reinforced.[429] Thus, it is a "population-in-waiting ready to return to Tibet; a population-in-training to govern in the homeland; and a population-as-cultural-repository, preserving Tibetan identity outside the home territory."[430] But the population is entirely dependent on the status the host State is willing to grant.[431] Individuals will have to subject themselves to the jurisdiction and sovereignty of the host State,[432] simply because not only are its nationals subject to the sovereignty of a State but, moreover, all foreigners who are for the time being on the territory of the respective State.[433]

While the Tibetans can count as a model for populations of former island States by providing a very strong basis for upholding cultural traditions, etc.; their situation differs from the one of small island States in its possibly temporal character. Unless territory could be protected or territory was ceded by another State, the "exile" of the island State's population (and its government) would presumably be permanent.[434] And permanent residents typically become nationals of the territorial State at some point.[435]

The previously mentioned example of the Boers could be another comparable example to the situation of the population of a sunken island State. The "Great Trek" of the Boers in the first half of the nineteenth century is an example of a population that moved from one territory to another maintaining an identity recognized by the United Kingdom and other States.[436] The government – with its legal system and constitutive rules – and the population changed location, but both kept their identity, intentionally in order to reestablish their colony on an independent basis, with the privileges and liberties the new British sovereign denied them (including that of owning slaves).[437]

The difference between those and the "emigrated" Tibetans is that the Boers went to a territory being *terra nullius*, so they could resettle their sovereignty. Thus, this example does not entirely fit the situation of sinking island States either, because the Boers were able to reestablish themselves somewhere else without having to subordinate under a foreign sovereignty. Nowadays, pretty much any territory on the Earth is under the territorial jurisdiction of a State, or as Knop puts it "a jigsaw puzzle of solid colour pieces fitting neatly together."[438] Thus, a population that lost its territory would necessarily need to subordinate to a foreign State's jurisdiction, except for cases when they would get new territory.

In 2008, then-president of the Maldives, Mohamed Nasheed, made global headlines when he announced plans to examine the possibility of buying land in Australia, India, or Sri Lanka to which he planned to relocate the population of the Maldives once the island nation became uninhabitable due to rising sea levels.[439] Similarly, in 2014 Kiribati concluded the purchase of 2,000 hectares of land in Fiji for the purpose of developing coastal agriculture and thereby enhancing food security for Kiribati's people. Eventually relocating its population had been an openly discussed option.[440] Those options would certainly be possible scenarios in which the criterion of the population would be able to be upheld after having lost its original territory.

However, apart from the practical problems of finding a State to give up parts of its territory, additionally there comes the question of the characteristics of the territory, which could also be seen from the view of the Tibetans, who would probably not want to take over just *any* territory (in contrast to the Boers): Territory shapes a population.[441] It constitutes one of the key imperatives of human behavior.[442] A population also forms a community through cohabiting a certain part of the Earth permanently and somehow separately from other nations. That way it will receive its national independence and idiosyncrasy.[443] The term "nation State" reflects these intimate bonds of people and space.[444] Thus, the new territory would have to be of similar type.

Nonetheless, a population could survive the loss of its former territory. Yet, a population without any territory of its own will – at least under the current territory-focused system – sooner or later cease to qualify as a State's population.[445] Thus this criterion is (also) placed at risk by the rising sea.

To come to a conclusion, with regard to the fate of the statehood criterion population, a distinction has to be made. As long as there are people left on the territory, neither the population criterion nor the statehood should be contested. As soon as there are no people left on the territory, the fate of the remaining nationals abroad becomes decisive.

If they were to be scattered in other States, they would presumably gradually become part of those other States.[446] If they were staying together on some new territory, two scenarios are possible: One possibility is that the population would (have to) subordinate under the sovereignty of the host State. In this case, statehood would probably cease after some time. Another possibility is that the population could stay together in another territory that is being put under their [the sunken State's] sovereignty. In such a case, the State could be regarded as continuing in this transferred territory without altering its quality.

It seems that these two options are not open to a free choice of the affected people: The right to existence of a State is not protected for the sake of the State itself, but for its political independence and connected thereto the right of the population to self-determination.[447] With regard to the right to self-determination, the Declaration on Principles of International Law Concerning Friendly Relations and Cooperation among States in accordance with the Charter of the UN expressively stated that this right cannot be construed as

> authorizing or encouraging any action which would dismember or impair, totally or in part, the territorial integrity or political unity of sovereign and independent States conducting themselves in compliance with the principle of equal rights and self-determination of peoples as described above and thus possessed of a government representing the whole people belonging to the territory without distinction as to race, creed or colour.[448]

Hence, as long as integration into the new host State is not rejected, there might not be a good chance for the population to establish its own new State or uphold its old State against the will of the host State. It will thus depend on the "host State" and its treatment of the dislocated population whether the State ceases to exist or not (comparable to the right to secession).[449]

The special rapporteur of the Sub-commission on the Prevention of Discrimination and Protection of Minorities explained in this regard:

> The principle of equal rights and self-determination, as laid down in the *Charter of the UN*, does not grant an unlimited right of secession to populations living in the territory of an independent sovereign state, and such a right cannot be regarded as a provision of *lex lata*. The right of secession unquestionably exists, however, in a special, but very important case: that of peoples, territories, and entities subjugated in violation of international law. In such cases, the peoples concerned have the right to regain their freedom and constitute themselves independent Sovereign States.[450]

This could be transferable to the case of small island States' populations. But such a transfer could cause hesitations of possible host States to allow entire populations to settle on their territory because thereby they would be forced to either grant them special rights or grant them sovereignty. Such hesitance should be prevented by international law regulations that provide protection for both: The populations in question and the affected host States.

Concluding thoughts on what it takes not to be a State anymore

To come to a conclusion, as soon as no beneficiaries (no people) are left, the continuing existence of a State would be senseless. At the latest, at this point, territorial water (if baselines were to be fixed) would dissolve and become part of the high seas, not owned by any State.

Thus, out of the different criteria, the "population" criterion will be the decisive criterion for the possible continued existence of a State. Without population, a State loses its *raison d'être*. Hence at the very latest, when there is neither anybody left on the territory nor someone bearing the nationality of the State in question, the State will cease to exist. Grote-Stoutenburg makes the continued existence of a State mainly dependent on a remaining "population nucleus" on the remaining territory.[451] Indeed, if only nationals abroad were left, they would probably sooner or later gain an additional (and in this case dominant by way of territorial) nationality which will lead to losing the required link for upholding the former nationality and thereby upholding statehood.

In the end, the loss of territory "presents the major obstacle" because, while "the world has no shortage of groups seeking independence (who would gladly form governments and relations with other states), it does have a shortage of real estate."[452]

At what point, exactly, a State is going to be seen to be extinct internationally will be up to the international community. Yet, the existence of a "fundamental right to survival" has been confirmed by the ICJ in an advisory opinion relating to the legality of the threat or use of nuclear weapons, which recognized the fundamental right of every State to survival as a basis for admitting its right to resort to self-defense in accordance with Art. 51 UN Charter.[453] Hence, the right of States to exist appears to be closely associated with the principle of territorial integrity. It is, as such, not absolute in nature. Thus, "states *can* be territorially diminished and even extinguished." It is merely "illegal to achieve this by an outside use of force, however."[454] Hence, even though States are the primary subjects of international law, there is no actual *right to exist* for States under international law:

> All that international law concerns itself with in this respect is the simple ascertainable fact that states exist as separate, autonomous entities susceptible of rights and obligations. It does not grant, nor is it able to grant, any legal or moral right to a state to exist.[455]

Nevertheless, maybe "it simply cannot be the case that the island state will become extinct as soon as the first wave washes over the last rock."[456] Wong explains how such uncertainty would actually contradict the notion of continuity in international law and calls it "intolerably uncertain if the existence of rights and obligations were to depend on such an unpredictable event."[457] If that were to happen and if international law viewing such is remaining "wedded tightly to Westphalian concepts and principles of states and sovereignty which are increasingly of diminishing relevance to the system it purportedly regulates," it will have difficulties remaining relevant and effective.[458]

Consequently, Wong argues,

> there must be some sort of method, at least in the short-term, for the continued existence of the island state despite the complete loss of sovereign territory. Brownlie speaks of "necessary legal constructions," whereby the state as a legal construct "may be projected on the plane of time for certain purposes although its physical and political existence has ceased."[459]

Yamamoto and Esteban explain in this regard that it is "unlikely that States which have been recognized as such can lose their status even after losing one of the elements required by the Montevideo Convention." They can rely on the recognition of other States. This would have a "reparative effect to compensate for the lack of territory and/or population, giving birth to a State sui generis."[460]

However, the international system as we know it does not offer major chances for a deterritorialized entity to remain a State. This system "is made up of coordinate, juxtaposed, sovereign units."[461] Currently, there are almost 200 separate territorial units. They each have "a different territorial sovereignty and jurisdiction."[462] Thereby, international law, which is based on the concept of the State,[463] "has made the whole world politically a single oikoumene [...] and fragmented it into many often fissiparous states, each claiming ultimate sovereign rule over a segment of the globe."[464] In this system – which is not only a fairly modern one,[465] but also imaginable differently,[466] "the State lies upon the foundation of sovereignty, which expresses internally the supremacy of the governmental institutions and externally the supremacy of the state as a legal person."[467]

Thereby, in this system, States *in situ* are not possible. Changes towards an increasing importance of the people and a decreasing importance of territory are visible though:

> From an element in the definition of statehood, people connected in a community will have to become a de-territorialized subject of international law, with a recognized legal subjectivity under it. The purpose should not be to maintain an illusion, or even a "strong presumption," of the continuity of a state, but to serve the legitimate needs of such a group of people due to their unprecedentedly changed situation.[468]

Hence, *currently*, States are *territorial* entities. The strong presumption against the extinction of States once firmly established[469] comes to an end when the territory of a State disappears entirely.[470] In today's system, the other elements of a State depend on the existence of a territory:

> a permanent population requires a territory for the purposes of its existence and a government must have a territory in its possession to be able to exercise authority at the national level and to participate effectively at the international level.[471]

If deterritorialized States were to be enabled, "the State as organizing idea in the international system is messier, overlapping, with gaps here and there" "[a]s opposed to the clear-cut puzzle pieces" of today's system.[472] International law would have to provide legal rules for when whose jurisdiction would be dominant. Currently, there are no such rules. Thus, it is currently safe to assume that a State exercising any kind of jurisdiction on the territory of another State might be in danger of causing an action for violation of territorial sovereignty.[473]

Nevertheless, again, it is not territory that is the decisive element. Changes towards a deterritorialized personal union/State would be theoretically possible. However,

> [s]ince existing states make international law, it is no surprise that the law is designed to make it very difficult for a new state to form out of an existing state's territory. Territorial integrity, along with sovereignty and political independence, form the "triumvirate of rights" that states enjoy under international law.[474]

It is therefore very doubtful, whether such changes would be made for the States in question. As concerned States are very small, it is unlikely that they would lead to such great changes. On the other hand, proposed changes favoring those small States would probably face less opposition than for bigger States with more numerous populations.

In any case, small changes are already happening: As such, sub-statal governments are increasingly willing and able to project their interests at the international level. The global community could, moreover, organize itself in a way to give voice to affinity groups other than States.[475] Yet, it is probably still true what Hedley Bull said (already in 1977):

> [I]t would be going beyond the evidence to conclude that "groups other than the state" have made such inroads on the sovereignty of states that the states system is now giving way to this alternative.[476]

Without major changes, however, prolonging the fictitious life of a non-territorial entity as a State does not make sense – it is "a denial of reality"[477] – without being of major help for the concerned populations. In the current system, a deterritorialized subject does (at least) face such considerable obstacles that one could doubt whether such a solution is indeed the preferable one for the population.

With a view to small island States, if no changes are made, it seems possible that in the long run some of them will no longer be reasonably considered to exist, and the factual disappearance of the State would likely be followed closely by the legal disappearance of the State.[478]

However, a distinction should be made between loss of statehood and loss of legal personality:[479] Crawford and Rayfuse argue in this regard

> that given the dynamism and flexibility demonstrated by the international community and international law [see Chapter 4], it is reasonable to hypothesize a system whereby states that "lose" key indicia of statehood, through no fault of their own, continue to retain the benefits and privileges of statehood.[480]

Grote-Stoutenburg points out that even if (or when) sea level rise eventually causes "low-lying island States to lose their effective statehood, this does not necessarily mean that they would cease to exist as international legal subjects."[481] This sounds reasonable. Nevertheless, it seems necessary to explore what it actually *means* to be a *State* in international law (not merely a legal subject) and thereafter what it *means* not to be a *State* anymore.

Notes

1 "UN Convention on the Law of the Sea (UNCLOS)" (1982).
2 E. Crawford and R. G. Rayfuse, "Climate change and statehood" in R. Rayfuse, S. V. Scott (eds), *International Law in the Era of Climate Change* (2012), p. 243; cf. N. Myers, "Environmental Refugees in a Globally Warmed World," *43 BioScience* (1993), p. 756.
3 IPCC 2014: L. A. Nurse et al., *IPCC 2014 – Chapter 29 – Small Islands*, p. 1618 ("Indeed, it has been suggested that the very existence of some atoll nations is threatened by rising sea levels associated with global warming."); cf. World Bank, *Turn Down the Heat: Why a 4°c Warmer World Must be Avoided* (2012), p. VIII, XVI, 34.
4 D. K. C. Jones, "Global Warming and Geomorphology," *159 The Geographical Journal* (1993), p. 127.
5 J. R. Crawford, The Creation of States in International Law (2006), p. 705–14; cf. R. Y. Jennings and A. Watts, Oppenheim's International Law (1992), p. 206–8; J. D. Hestetune, *The Invading Waters: Climate Change Dispossession, State Extinction, and International Law* (2013), p. 46, fn. 196–8, D. Wong, "Sovereignty Sunk? The Position of 'Sinking States' at International Law," *14 Melbourne Journal of International Law* (2013), p. 361–2.
6 J. McAdam, *Climate Change, Forced Migration, and International Law* (2012), p. 127; cf. Art. 2(1)(b) "Vienna Convention on the Succession of States in Respect of Treaties: VCSST" (1978).
7 S. Park, *Climate Change and the Risk of Statelessness: The Situation of Low-lying Island States* (2011), p. 6; M. A. Burkett, "Climate Refugees" in S. Alam (ed.), *Routledge Handbook of International Environmental Law* (2013), p. 728.
8 J. R. Crawford, "The Criteria for Statehood in International Law," *48 British Yearbook of International Law* (1976/1977), p. 140; cf. J. R. Crawford, The Creation of States in International Law (2006), p. 90.
9 T. D. Grant, "Defining Statehood: The Montevideo Convention and its Discontents," *37 Columbia Journal of Transnational Law* (1999), p. 435; J. McAdam, *Climate Change, Forced Migration, and International Law* (2012), p. 128; J. McAdam, "'Disappearing States,' Statelessness and the Boundaries of International Law" in J. McAdam (ed.), *Climate change and displacement: Multidisciplinary perspectives* (2010).
10 For example C. Richter, *Collapsed States: Perspektiven nach dem Wegfall von Staatlichkeit* (2011), p. 82.
11 M. Craven, "The Problem of State Succession and the Identity of States under International Law," *9 EJIL* (1998), p. 158; cf. K. Marek, *Identity and Continuity of States in Public International Law* (1968), p. 7.
12 J. R. Crawford, The Creation of States in International Law (2006), p. 715; J. L. Noto, "Creating a Modern Atlantis: Recognizing Submerging States and Their People," *62 Buffalo Law Review* (2014), p. 752, 753; J. D. Hestetune, *The Invading Waters: Climate Change Dispossession, State Extinction, and International Law* (2013), p. 46–7.
13 UNHCR, *Summary of Deliberations on Climate Change and Displacement* (2011), Main messages, p. 2; see also para. 30, p. 7. (Summary of Deliberations on Climate Change and Displacement, UNHCR Expert Roundtable on climate change and displacement, Bellagio, 22–25 February 2011).

14 J. R. Crawford, The Creation of States in International Law (2006), p. 4.
15 K. Marek, *Identity and Continuity of States in Public International Law* (1968), p. 6.
16 I. Ziemele, "State, Extinction of," (last updated March 2009) in R. Wolfrum (ed.), *The Max Planck Encyclopedia of Public International Law: opil.ouplaw.com.home/EPIL* (2012), para. 1; M. Craven, "The Problem of State Succession and the Identity of States under International Law," *9 EJIL* (1998), p. 159.
17 Ibid., p. 159; similarly, L. Yamamoto and M. Esteban, *Atoll Island States and International Law: Climate Change Displacement and Sovereignty* (2014), p. 3.
18 Cf. I. Ziemele, "State, Extinction of," (last updated March 2009) in R. Wolfrum (ed.), *The Max Planck Encyclopedia of Public International Law: opil.ouplaw.com.home/EPIL* (2012), para. 7.
19 Cf. S. Park, *Climate Change and the Risk of Statelessness: The Situation of Low-lying Island States* (2011), p. 7.
20 M. Craven, "The Problem of State Succession and the Identity of States under International Law," *9 EJIL* (1998), p. 159; cf. A. E. Buchanan, "The Right to Self-Determination: Analytical and Moral Foundations," *8 Arizona Journal of International & Comparative Law* (1991), p. 109; F. von Liszt, *Das Völkerrecht: Systematisch dargestellt* (1913), p. 50.
21 J. McAdam, *Climate Change, Forced Migration, and International Law* (2012), p. 127, 128.
22 I. Ziemele, "State, Extinction of," (last updated March 2009) in R. Wolfrum (ed.), *The Max Planck Encyclopedia of Public International Law: opil.ouplaw.com.home/EPIL* (2012), para. 3; cf. G. Kreijen, *State Failure, Sovereignty and Effectiveness: Legal Lessons from the Decolonization of Sub-Saharan Africa* (2004), p. 34; D. Wong, "Sovereignty Sunk? The Position of 'Sinking States' at International Law," *14 Melbourne Journal of International Law* (2013), p. 363.
23 UNHCR, *Climate Change and Statelessness: An Overview* (2009), p. 1.
24 Ibid., p. 1.
25 I. Ziemele, "State, Extinction of," (last updated March 2009) in R. Wolfrum (ed.), *The Max Planck Encyclopedia of Public International Law: opil.ouplaw.com.home/EPIL* (2012), para. 3; G. Jellinek and W. Jellinek, *Allgemeine Staatslehre* (1914), p. 283: "Wenn Naturereignisse das Gebiet eines Staates oder sein Volk zerstören, so hat es auch mit dem Staate ein Ende. Auch Aufhören des Daseins einer Staatsgewalt durch Wegfall der höchsten Organe oder deren Weigerung, ferner zu funktionieren, kann das faktische Ende des Staates durch Lösung der Verbandseinheit herbeiführen."
26 Cf. J. L. Kunz, "Identity of States under International Law," *49 AJIL* (1955), p. 74.
27 D.-E. Khan, *Die deutschen Staatsgrenzen: rechtshistorische Grundlagen und offene Rechtsfragen* (2004), p. 9–10; cf. J. C. Bluntschli and K. Brater, *Deutsches Staats-Wörterbuch* (1861), p. 209 [Land]; U. Di Fabio, *Das Recht offener Staaten: Grundlinien einer Staats- und Rechtstheorie* (1998), p. 2.
28 K. Marek, *Identity and Continuity of States in Public International Law* (1968), p. 15; D. Anzilotti, 'La formazione del Regno d'Italia nei riguardi del diritto internazionale', *1 Rivista di Diritto Internazionale* (1912), p. 9.
29 J. L. Kunz, "Identity of States under International Law," *49 AJIL* (1955), p. 74, fn. 30.
30 Cf. E. Suy, "Reflexions sur la distinction entre la souveraineté et la compétance territoriale" in R. Marcic (ed.), *Internationale Festschrift für Alfred Verdross* (1971), p. 494.
31 A. Torres Camprubí, *Statehood under Water: Challenges of Sea-Level Rise to the Continuity of Pacific Island States* (2016), p. 64–71 (table on vulnerability of islands to the rising sea).
32 Cf. ICJ – The Hague, *North Sea Continental Shelf Judgment* (20 February 1969), para. 46.

33 C. Schaller, T.-S. Schrader, "Der Anstieg des Meeresspiegels als Thema für den VN-Sicherheitsrat," *SWP-Aktuell, Nr. 41, Juni 2020* (2020), p. 3–4.
34 Cf. ILC, *Sea-level rise in relation to international law, First issues paper by Bogdan Aurescu and Nilüfer Oral, Co-Chairs of the Study Group on sea-level rise in relation to international law, Seventy-second session, 28 February 2020* (2020), p. 4 et seq.
35 M. Gerrard and G. E. Wannier, "Dissapearing States: Harnessing International Law to Preserve Cultures and Society" in O. C. Ruppel (ed.), *Climate Change: International Law and Global Governance* (2013), p. 620; cf. ICJ – The Hague, *Case Concerning Maritime Delimitation and Territorial Question between Qatar and Bahrain (Qatar v. Bahrain)* – Judgment (16 March 2001), p. 100 et seq. (particularly p. 101–2, para. 205).
36 C. Schaller, "Der Meeresspiegelanstieg als Herausforderung für die maritime Ordnung – Kann das Seevölkerrecht Stabilität gewährleisten?," *SWP-Studie 1* (2021), p. 19, 20.
37 Ibid., p. 22.
38 J. L. Jesus, "Rocks, New-born Islands, Sea Level Rise and Maritime Space" in J. A. Frowein (ed.), *Verhandeln für den Frieden* (2003), p. 588.
39 Ibid., p. 589.
40 South China Sea Arbitration, *Philippines v. China* (12 July 2016), p. 204.
41 Cf. C. Schaller, "Der Meeresspiegelanstieg als Herausforderung für die maritime Ordnung – Kann das Seevölkerrecht Stabilität gewährleisten?," *SWP-Studie 1* (2021), p. 19.
42 Cf. J. L. Jesus, "Rocks, New-born Islands, Sea Level Rise and Maritime Space" in J. A. Frowein (ed.), *Verhandeln für den Frieden* (2003), p. 593.
43 Permanent Court of Arbitration, *The Grisbadarna Case, Norway v. Sweden* – Award (23 October 1909), p. 6.
44 J. L. Jesus, "Rocks, New-born Islands, Sea Level Rise and Maritime Space" in J. A. Frowein (ed.), *Verhandeln für den Frieden* (2003), p. 594.
45 C. Schaller, T.-S. Schrader, "Der Anstieg des Meeresspiegels als Thema für den VN-Sicherheitsrat," *SWP-Aktuell, Nr. 41, Juni 2020* (2020), p. 4.
46 UNGA, *Sixth Committee – Summary record of the 23rd meeting*, 14 November 2018, para. 76 (Australia).
47 Submission of the Republic of the Maldives, *Information and examples of State practice on "Sea-level rise in relation to international law,"* 31 December 2019, p. 9.
48 Ibid.
49 Cf. Submission of the Pacific Islands Forum, *Submission of the Members of the Pacific Islands Forum to the ILC on the Topic of Sea-Level Rise in Relation to International Law*, 30 December 2019.
50 UNGA, *Sixth Committee – Summary record of the 26th meeting*, 18 November 2019, para. 89 (New Zealand).
51 Submission of the United States, *Comments of the United States Regarding Sea-Level Rise in Relation to the Law of the Sea*, 14 February 2020.
52 Submission of the Netherlands, *Sea-level rise in relation with international law*, 27 December 2019.
53 Submission of Romania, *Romania's Submission in response to the call of the ILC*, 9 January 2020 (however only, if objective modifications are due to natural phenomena which are not related to human activities).
54 Cf. ILC, *Sea-level rise in relation to international law, First issues paper by Bogdan Aurescu and Nilüfer Oral, Co-Chairs of the Study Group on sea-level rise in relation to international law, Seventy-second session, 28 February 2020* (2020), p. 33, para. 88.
55 UNGA, *Sixth Committee – Summary record of the 23rd meeting*, 14 November 2018, para. 50 (Cyprus).

56 Cf. in much detail on the question of freezing the existing baselines or freezing the outer limits of maritime zones: International Law Association, Committee on International Law and Sea Level Rise, "Sea Level Rise and Maritime Zones and Boundaries" in D. Vidas, D. Freestone, J. McAdam (eds), *Report of the International Law Association* (2019), p. 15 et seq.

57 W. Vitzthum, "Aquitoriale Souveränität" in P.-M. Dupuy, B. Fassbender, M. N. Shaw, K.-P. Sommermann (eds), *Völkerrecht als Wertordnung: Festschrift für Christian Tomuschat* (2006), p. 1080–1; cf. J. Grote-Stoutenburg, *Disappearing Island States in International Law* (2015), p. 187 et seq., 253; cf. Art. 2.1. UNCLOS.

58 A. G. Jain, "The 21st Century Atlantis: The International Law of Statehood and Climate Change-Induced Loss of Territory," *50 Stanford Journal of International Law* (2014), p. 8, 9; J. Grote-Stoutenburg, "When do States disappear? Thresholds of Effective Statehood and the Continued Recognition of 'Deterritorialized' Island States" in M. Gerrard, G. E. Wannier (eds), *Threatened Island Nations: Legal Implications of Rising Seas and a Changing Climate* (2013), p. 61.

59 D. Wong, "Sovereignty Sunk? The Position of 'Sinking States' at International Law," *14 Melbourne Journal of International Law* (2013), p. 358. In much more detail: J. Grote-Stoutenburg, *Disappearing Island States in International Law* (2015), p. 30 et seq., 180 et seq.; cf. R. Rayfuse, "Sea Level Rise and Maritime Zones: Preserving the Maritime Entitlements of 'Disappearing' States" in M. Gerrard, G. E. Wannier (eds), *Threatened Island Nations: Legal Implications of Rising Seas and a Changing Climate* (2013), p. 177; cf. UNHCR, *Summary of Deliberations on Climate Change and Displacement* (2011), p. 7, para. 28; J. McAdam, B. Burson, W. Kälin, and S. Weerasinghe, "International Law and Sea-Level Rise: Forced Migration and Human Rights," *FNI Report 1/2016* (2016), p.8.

60 J. Grote-Stoutenburg, "When do States disappear? Thresholds of Effective Statehood and the Continued Recognition of 'Deterritorialized' Island States" in M. Gerrard, G. E. Wannier (eds), *Threatened Island Nations: Legal Implications of Rising Seas and a Changing Climate* (2013), p. 60; D. H. Spennemann, "Water futures and their influence on sovereignty in the Marshall Islands" in D. Ghosh, H. Goodall, S. H. Donald (eds), *Water, Sovereignty and Borders in Asia and Oceania* (2009), p. 52–3; cf. C. Schofield and D. Freestone, "Options to Protect Coastlines and Secure Maritime Jurisdictional Claims in the Face of Global Sea Level Rise" in M. Gerrard, G. E. Wannier (eds), *Threatened Island Nations: Legal Implications of Rising Seas and a Changing Climate* (2013), p. 143.

61 J. Barnett, "Adapting to Climate Change in Pacific Island Countries: The Problem of Uncertainty," *29 World Development* (2001), p. 978; cf. J. McAdam, *Climate Change, Forced Migration, and International Law* (2012), p. 131; L. Elliott, "Sovereignty and the Global Politics of the Environment: Beyond Westpahlia?" in T. Jacobsen, C. J. G. Sampford, R. C. Thakur (eds), *Re-envisioning sovereignty: The end of Westphalia?* (2008), p. 11–12; cf. UNHCR, *Climate Change and Statelessness: An Overview* (2009), p. 2; cf. D. H. Spennemann, "Water futures and their influence on sovereignty in the Marshall Islands" in D. Ghosh, H. Goodall, S. H. Donald (eds), *Water, Sovereignty and Borders in Asia and Oceania* (2009), p. 52 et seq., 62 et seq. for the Marshall Islands.

62 UNGA, *One humanity: shared responsibility*, 2 February 2016, p. 22, para. 79.

63 N. L. Hill, *Claims to Territory in International Law and Relations* (1945), p. 4; M. Gagain, "Climate Change, Sea Level Rise, and Artificial Islands: Saving the Maldives" Statehood and Maritime Claims Through the 'Constitution of the Oceans'," *23 Colorado Journal of International Environmental Law and Policy* (2012), p. 98; J. Grote-Stoutenburg, "When do States disappear? Thresholds of Effective Statehood and the Continued Recognition of 'Deterritorialized' Island States" in M. Gerrard, G. E. Wannier (eds), *Threatened Island Nations: Legal Implications of Rising Seas and a Changing Climate* (2013), p. 60–1.

64 C. Focarelli, *International Law as Social Construct: The Struggle for Global Justice* (2012), p. 158.
65 D. Wong, "Sovereignty Sunk? The Position of 'Sinking States' at International Law," *14 Melbourne Journal of International Law* (2013), p. 361–2.
66 L. Oppenheim and R. Roxburgh, *International Law: A Treatise* (1920), p. 143.
67 Cf. N. Schrijver, "The Impact of Climate Change: Challenges for International Law" in U. Fastenrath, R. Geiger, D.-E. Khan, A. Paulus, S. von Schorlemer, C. Vedder (eds), *From Bilateralism to Community Interest: Essays in Honour of Judge Bruno Simma* (2011), p. 1284; L. Oppenheim and R. Roxburgh, *International Law: A Treatise* (1920), p. 143, mentioning additionally (though only theoretically) emigration of the whole population and permanent anarchy.
68 K. Marek, *Identity and Continuity of States in Public International Law* (1968), p. 7.
69 M. N. Shaw, *International Law* (2008), p. 208, fn. 52; A. Proelß, "Raum und Umwelt im Völkerrecht: Fünfter Abschnitt" in W. Vitzthum, M. Bothe (eds), *Völkerrecht* (2010), p. 407, para. 15.
70 M. N. Shaw, "Territory in International Law," *13 Netherlands Yearbook of International Law* (1982), p. 61.
71 Cf. J. W. Garner, *Introduction to Political Science: A Treatise on the Origin, Nature, Functions, and Organization of the State* (1910), p. 68.
72 R. Y. Jennings and A. Watts, Oppenheim's International Law (1992), § 168, p. 563, similar: A. Proelß, "Raum und Umwelt im Völkerrecht: Fünfter Abschnitt" in W. Vitzthum, M. Bothe (eds), *Völkerrecht* (2010), p. 401, para. 7.
73 J. R. Crawford, The Creation of States in International Law (2006), p. 61.
74 D. Wong, "Sovereignty Sunk? The Position of 'Sinking States' at International Law," *14 Melbourne Journal of International Law* (2013), p. 365, 366; cf. S. P. Sharma, *Territorial Acquisition, Disputes, and International Law* (1997), p. 4; J. D. Hestetune, *The Invading Waters: Climate Change Dispossession, State Extinction, and International Law* (2013), p. 31; D. Raič, *Statehood and the Law of Self-Determination* (2002), p. 62; I. Brownlie, "Rebirth of Statehood" in M. D. Evans (ed.), *International Law* (2006), p. 5, 6; R. Y. Jennings, *The Acquisition of Territory in International Law* (1963), p. 2; R. H. Jackson and A. James, "The Character of Independent Statehood" in R. H. Jackson, A. James (eds), *States in a Changing World: A Contemporary Analysis* (1993), p. 9; M. Lachs, "The Development and general trends of international law in our time," *169 Recueil Des Cours* (1984), p. 36; A. V. Lowe, *International Law* (2007), p. 138.
75 L. Gross, *Essays on International Law and Organization* (1984), p. 3.
76 M. N. Shaw, "Territory in International Law," *13 Netherlands Yearbook of International Law* (1982), p. 62; cf. D.-E. Khan, "Territory and Boundaries" in B. Fassbender, A. Peters (eds), *The Oxford Handbook of the History of International Law* (2012), p. 233 et seq.
77 J. Gottmann, *The Significance of Territory* (1973), pp. 17–26.; cf. M. N. Shaw, 'Territory in International Law', *13 Netherlands Yearbook of International Law* (1982), p. 61; M. N. Shaw, *Title to Territory in Africa: International Legal Issues* (1986), p. 1.
78 D. Wong, "Sovereignty Sunk? The Position of 'Sinking States' at International Law," *14 Melbourne Journal of International Law* (2013), p. 352; cf. P. H. Winfield, *The Foundation & the Future of International Law* (1942), p. 18, 33 et seq.; J. L. Brierly, *The Law of Nations: An Introduction to the International Law of Peace* (1963), p. 162.
79 D. P. O'Connell, *International Law* (1970), p. 403; cf. M. N. Shaw, "Territory in International Law," *13 Netherlands Yearbook of International Law* (1982), p. 62.
80 J. Vidmar, "The Concept of the State and its Right of Existence," *4 Cambridge Journal of International and Comparative Law* (2015), p. 552.

81 D.-E. Khan, "Territory and Boundaries" in B. Fassbender, A. Peters (eds), *The Oxford Handbook of the History of International Law* (2012), p. 234.
82 M. N. Shaw, "Territory in International Law," *13 Netherlands Yearbook of International Law* (1982), p. 62; cf. J. Gottmann, *The Significance of Territory* (1973), p. 27.
83 Cf. M. L. van Creveld, *The Rise and Decline of the State* (1999), p. 57; M. T. Cicero, *De re publica: Cicero. With an English translation by Clinton Walker Keyes* (1928, written 54–51 B.C.E.), book I, XXV, 39: "But a people is not any collection of human beings brought together in any sort of way, but an assemblage of people in large numbers associated in an agreement with respect to justice and a partnership for the common good."
84 Aristotle, *Politics* (translation of 2008, written 350 B.C.E), 1276a40–b4; cf. C. Ebert, *Die Beurteilung der Staatlichkeit politisch-sozialer Verbände* (1988), p. 20; S. Elden, *The Birth of Territory* (2013), p. 45, cf. p. 52.
85 Thucydides, *History of the Peloponnesian war: Thucydides. With an English translation by C. Forster Smith* (1928, written 431 B.C.E.), book VII, LXXVII, 7 (p. 159); cf. M. L. van Creveld, *The Rise and Decline of the State* (1999), p. 57; S. Elden, *The Birth of Territory* (2013), p. 50.
86 M. N. Shaw, *Title to Territory in Africa: International Legal Issues* (1986), p. 1, 2.
87 T. J. Lawrence, *The Principles of International Law* (1895), p. 56.
88 H. Wheaton, *Elements of International Law: With a Sketch of the History of the Science: in Two Volumes* (1880), p. 62.
89 E. de Vattel, *The Law of Nations: Or, Principles of the Law of Nature Applied to the Conduct and Affairs of Nations and Sovereigns* (1797), p. 1.
90 D.-E. Khan, "Territory and Boundaries" in B. Fassbender, A. Peters (eds), *The Oxford Handbook of the History of International Law* (2012), p. 234.
91 Cf. T. D. Grant, "Defining Statehood: The Montevideo Convention and its Discontents," *37 Columbia Journal of Transnational Law* (1999), p. 435; M. A. Burkett, "The Nation Ex-Situ" in M. Gerrard, G. E. Wannier (eds), *Threatened Island Nations: Legal Implications of Rising Seas and a Changing Climate* (2013), p. 89 et seq.
92 J. Bodin, *Über den Staat: Buch I–III* (1986 [1576]), Chapter 1; cited after R. Zippelius, *Geschichte der Staatsideen* (1976), p. 90.
93 S. Sassen, *Territory, Authority, Rights: From Medieval to Global Assemblages* (2006), p. 415; C. W. Morris, *An Essay on the Modern State* (2002), p. 45; B. A. Boczek, *International Law: A Dictionary* (2005), para. 125, p. 117.
94 A. van Staden and H. Vollaard, "The Erosion of State Sovereignty: Towards a Post-territorial World?" in G. Kreijen (ed.), *State, Sovereignty, and International Governance* (2002), p. 166.
95 T. Marauhn, "Changing Role of the State" in D. Bodansky, J. Brunnée, E. Hey (eds), *The Oxford Handbook of International Environmental Law* (2007), p. 730.
96 M. N. Shaw, "The International Court of Justice and the Law of Territory" in C. J. Tams (ed.), *The Development of International Law by the International Court of Justice* (2013), p. 151.
97 A. Hudson, "Beyond the Borders: Globalisation, Sovereignty and Extra-Territoriality" in D. Newman (ed.), *Boundaries, Territory and Postmodernity* (1999), p. 89.
98 Ibid., p. 89.
99 R. Y. Jennings, *The Acquisition of Territory in International Law* (1963), p. 2; cf. J. Gottmann, *The Significance of Territory* (1973), p. 3.
100 G. J. Evans and M. Sahnoun, *The Responsibility to Protect. Report of the International Commission on Intervention and State Sovereignty* (2001), p. 12; cf. W. W. Willoughby, *The Fundamental Concepts of Public Law* (1931), p. 400, 429; A. James, *Sovereign Statehood: The Basis of International Society* (1986), p. 232.

101 ICJ – The Hague, *The Corfu Channel Case* - Individual opinion by Judge Alvarez (9 April 1949), p. 43.
102 House of Lords, Lord Macmillan, *Compania Naviera Vascongado v. Steamship "Cristina"* (13 January 1938), p. 496–7; cf. I. A. Shearer, *Starke's International Law* (2003), p. 184; C. Dupuis, "Règles générales du droit de la paix," *32 Recueil Des Cours* (1930), p. 187; S. D. Krasner, *Sovereignty: Organized Hypocrisy* (1999), p. 4.
103 H. Spruyt, *The Sovereign State and Its Competitors: An Analysis of Systems Change* (1996), p. 17.
104 J. Kokott, "Die Staatsrechtslehre und die Veränderung ihres Gegenstandes: Konsequenzen von Europäisierung und Internationalisierung" in J. Kokott, W. Brugger, C. Gusy, T. Vesting (eds), *Die Staatsrechtslehre und die Veränderung ihres Gegenstandes: Konsequenzen von Europäisierung und Internationalisierung. Gewährleistung von Freiheit und Sicherheit im Lichte unterschiedlicher Staats – und Verfassungsverständnisse/Berichte und Diskussionen auf der Tagung der Vereinigung der Deutschen Strafrechtslehrer in Hamburg vom 1. bis 4. Oktober 2003* (2004), p. 14.
105 ICJ – The Hague, *Sovereignty over Pedra Branca/Pulau Batu Puteh, Middle Rocks and South Ledge (Malaysia/Singapore)* – Judgment (23 May 2008), p. 40, para. 79.
106 N. Schrijver, "The Impact of Climate Change: Challenges for International Law" in U. Fastenrath, R. Geiger, D.-E. Khan, A. Paulus, S. von Schorlemer, C. Vedder (eds), *From Bilateralism to Community Interest: Essays in Honour of Judge Bruno Simma* (2011), p. 1285.
107 Cf. I. A. Shearer, *Starke's International Law* (2003), p. 91; cf. B. Fassbender, "Article 2(1)" in B. Simma, H. Mosler, A. Paulus, E. Chaitidou (eds), *The Charter of the UN: A Commentary* (2012), para. 57 et seq.
108 J. R. Crawford, *Brownlie's Principles of Public International Law* (2012), p. 447; I. A. Shearer, *Starke's International Law* (2003), p. 91; C. d. Visscher, *Theory and Reality in Public International Law* (1968), p. 205.
109 Cf. H. Ruiz-Fabri, "Genèse et disparition de l'État à l'époque contemporaine," *38 Annuaire Français de Droit International* (1992), p. 156.
110 I. A. Shearer, *Starke's International Law* (2003), p. 91; J. R. Crawford, *Brownlie's Principles of Public International Law* (2012), p. 447; B. H. Oxman, "Jurisdiction of States," (last updated March 2009) in R. Wolfrum (ed.), *The Max Planck Encyclopedia of Public International Law: opil.ouplaw.com.home/EPIL* (2012), para. 47.
111 K. Ipsen, *Völkerrecht* (2014), §5 Rn.60, p. 82; s. for example Bundesverfassungericht, *Rechtshilfevertrag zwischen Deutschland und Österreich* (22 March 1983), para. 58.
112 I. A. Shearer, *Starke's International Law* (2003), p. 91; cf. UNSC Res. 138 (1960) of 23 June 1960; cf. B. H. Oxman, "Jurisdiction of States," (last updated March 2009) in R. Wolfrum (ed.), *The Max Planck Encyclopedia of Public International Law: opil .ouplaw.com.home/EPIL* (2012), para. 47; cf. A. Abass, *Complete International Law: Text, Cases, and Materials* (2014), p. 260 et seq.
113 E. Biglieri and G. Prati, *Enclyclopedia of Public International Law* (2014), p. 257 (genocide), p. 357 (kidnapping).
114 Ibid., p. 357 (kidnapping); cf. S. Wilske, "Abduction, Transboundary," (last updated October 2012) in R. Wolfrum (ed.), *The Max Planck Encyclopedia of Public International Law: opil.ouplaw.com.home/EPIL* (2012), para. 2.
115 UNSC Res. 138 (1960) of 23 June 1960.
116 Cf. District Court of Jerusalem, *Attorney-General of the Government of Israel v Adolf Eichmann* – Criminal Case No. 40/61 (11 December 1961), para 40; cf. S. M. Villalpando, "Eichmann Case," (last updated March 2009) in R. Wolfrum (ed.), *The Max Planck Encyclopedia of Public International Law: opil.ouplaw.com.home/EPIL* (2012), para. 4.

117 S. Wilske, "Abduction, Transboundary," (last updated October 2012) in R. Wolfrum (ed.), *The Max Planck Encyclopedia of Public International Law: opil.ouplaw.com.home/EPIL* (2012), para. 3; cf. K. Ipsen, *Völkerrecht* (2014), §5, Rn. 61, p. 82 (cf. BT-Drs. 4/1152, 1).
118 Cf. also A. Orakhelashvili, "Governmental Activities on Foreign Territory," (last updated May 2011) in R. Wolfrum (ed.), *The Max Planck Encyclopedia of Public International Law: opil.ouplaw.com.home/EPIL* (2012), para. 11, 14
119 B. H. Oxman, "Jurisdiction of States," (last updated March 2009) in R. Wolfrum (ed.), *The Max Planck Encyclopedia of Public International Law: opil.ouplaw.com.home/EPIL* (2012), para. 51.
120 G. Acquaviva, "Subjects of International Law: A Power-Based Analysis," *38 Vanderbilt Journal of Transnational Law* (2005), p. 379, 380; cf. B. H. Oxman, "Jurisdiction of States," (last updated March 2009) in R. Wolfrum (ed.), *The Max Planck Encyclopedia of Public International Law: opil.ouplaw.com.home/EPIL* (2012), para. 4, para. 47; W. W. Willoughby, *The Fundamental Concepts of Public Law* (1931), p. 338.
121 ICJ – The Hague, *Case concerning armed activities on the territory of the Congo* – Judgement (19 December 2005), para. 47.
122 A. Orakhelashvili, "Governmental Activities on Foreign Territory," (last updated May 2011) in R. Wolfrum (ed.), *The Max Planck Encyclopedia of Public International Law: opil.ouplaw.com.home/EPIL* (2012), para. 7; cf. ICJ – The Hague, *Case concerning armed activities on the territory of the Congo* – Judgement (19 December 2005), para. 43–7.
123 D. Wong, "Sovereignty Sunk? The Position of 'Sinking States' at International Law," *14 Melbourne Journal of International Law* (2013), p. 372; A. Verdross, B. Simma and R. Geiger, *Territoriale Souveränität und Gebietshoheit: Zur völkerrechtlichen Lage der Oder-Neisse-Gebiete* (1980), p. 24–7.
124 "Hay-Bunau-Varilla Treaty" (1903).
125 Ibid., Art. III; cf. K. Ipsen, *Völkerrecht* (2014), §5, Rn. 63, p. 83; cf. I. Delupis, *International law and the independent state* (1974), p. 166.
126 United States Supreme Court argued in Supreme Court of the United States, *Wilson v. Shaw* – No. 43 (7 January 1907), p. 33 that "it is hypercritical to contend that the title of the United States [to the Canal Zone] was imperfect, and that the territory described does not belong to this Nation, because of the omission of some of the technical terms used in ordinary conveyances of real estate;" cf. M. Arcari, "Panama Canal," (last updated October 2009) in R. Wolfrum (ed.), *The Max Planck Encyclopedia of Public International Law: opil.ouplaw.com.home/EPIL* (2012), para. 13.
127 Ibid., para. 15.
128 Ibid., para. 14; I. Delupis, *International law and the independent state* (1974), p. 200.
129 Supreme Court of the United States, *Canal Zone v. Coulson* – No. 28 (8 May 1907) cited after I. Delupis, *International law and the independent state* (1974), p. 214 et seq.; cf. Supreme Court of the United States, *Luckenbach Steamship Co. v. United States* – No. 32 (23 November 1926).
130 Supreme Court of Panama, *Re Cia. de Transportes de Gelabert* (22 February 1939).
131 Supreme Court of Panama, *Re Burriel* – No. 53 (20 June 1931).
132 Supreme Court of Panama, *Re Kenneth Robert Bartlett* (17 February 1930).
133 Cf. I. Delupis, *International law and the independent state* (1974), p. 215; M. R. Fowler and J. M. Bunck, *Law, Power and the Sovereign State: The Evolution and Application of the Concept of Sovereignty* (1995), p. 89–90.
134 "Agreement Between the United States and Cuba for the Lease of Lands for Coaling and Naval stations" (1903); cf. M. J. Strauss, *Territorial Leasing in Diplomacy and International Law* (2015), p. 165; Y. Ronen, "Territory, Lease," (last updated March

2009) in R. Wolfrum (ed.), *The Max Planck Encyclopedia of Public International Law: opil.ouplaw.com.home/EPIL* (2012), para. 11 et seq.

135 M. R. Fowler and J. M. Bunck, *Law, Power and the Sovereign State: The Evolution and Application of the Concept of Sovereignty* (1995), p. 91 et seq.; I. Delupis, *International law and the independent state* (1974), p. 217; A. Verdross, B. Simma and R. Geiger, *Territoriale Souveränität und Gebietshoheit: Zur völkerrechtlichen Lage der Oder-Neisse-Gebiete* (1980), p. 24–5; cf. M. J. Strauss, *Territorial Leasing in Diplomacy and International Law* (2015), p. 165 ("for the time required for the purposes of coaling and naval stations").

136 D. Wong, "Sovereignty Sunk? The Position of 'Sinking States' at International Law," *14 Melbourne Journal of International Law* (2013), p. 372; cf. I. Delupis, *International law and the independent state* (1974), p. 201–4.

137 Ibid., p. 376; p. 197.

138 A. de Zayas, "Guantánamo Naval Base," (last updated March 2015) in R. Wolfrum (ed.), *The Max Planck Encyclopedia of Public International Law: opil.ouplaw.com .home/EPIL* (2012), para. 4 et seq.; cf. I. Delupis, *International law and the independent state* (1974), p. 217.

139 D. Wong, "Sovereignty Sunk? The Position of 'Sinking States' at International Law," *14 Melbourne Journal of International Law* (2013), p. 372; I. Delupis, *International law and the independent state* (1974), p. 197, 215; cf. N. Bergmann, *Versinkende Inselstaaten: Auswirkungen des Klimawandels auf die Staatlichkeit kleiner Inselstaaten* (2016), p. 93.

140 T. Wang, "International Law in China: Historical and Contemporary Perspectives," *221 Recueil Des Cours* (1990), p. 307–9, 314; cf. O. Schachter, "Sovereignty – Then and Now" in R. S. MacDonald, T. Wang (eds), *Essays in honour of Wang Tieya* (1994), p. 681; cf. A. Verdross, B. Simma, and R. Geiger, *Territoriale Souveränität und Gebietshoheit: Zur völkerrechtlichen Lage der Oder-Neisse-Gebiete* (1980), p. 17; Y. Ronen, "Territory, Lease," (last updated March 2009) in R. Wolfrum (ed.), *The Max Planck Encyclopedia of Public International Law: opil.ouplaw.com.home/EPIL* (2012), para. 4.

141 D. Wong, "Sovereignty Sunk? The Position of 'Sinking States' at International Law," *14 Melbourne Journal of International Law* (2013), p. 372; I. Delupis, *International law and the independent state* (1974), p. 197, 215; cf. N. Bergmann, *Versinkende Inselstaaten: Auswirkungen des Klimawandels auf die Staatlichkeit kleiner Inselstaaten* (2016), p. 93.

142 ILC, *Sea-level rise in relation to international law, Second issues paper by Patrícia Galvão Teles and Juan José Ruda Santolaria* (73rd session of the ILC (2022)), # 138 et seq.

143 S. Magiera, "Governments," (last updated March 2009) in R. Wolfrum (ed.), *The Max Planck Encyclopedia of Public International Law: opil.ouplaw.com.home/EPIL* (2012), para. 30; cf. B. A. Boczek, *International Law: A Dictionary* (2005), para. 79, p. 65.

144 J.-G. A. Hannemann and J. H. Lampe, "The exhaustion of a State: Can a State in reflection to international demographic, political and economical destabilisation cease to exist?," *2013/2 Freilaw* (2013), p. 3; J. McAdam, *Climate Change, Forced Migration, and International Law* (2012), p. 134; cf. S. Talmon, *Recognition of Governments in International Law: With Particular Reference to Governments in Exile* (1998), p. 217, 218.

145 G. Acquaviva, "Subjects of International Law: A Power-Based Analysis," *38 Vanderbilt Journal of Transnational Law* (2005), p. 383.

146 D. Wong, "Sovereignty Sunk? The Position of 'Sinking States' at International Law," *14 Melbourne Journal of International Law* (2013), p. 373, 376; cf. K. Marek, *Identity and Continuity of States in Public International Law* (1968), p. 168; S. Talmon, *Recognition of Governments in International Law: With Particular Reference to*

Governments in Exile (1998), p. 215–18; J. McAdam, *Climate Change, Forced Migration, and International Law* (2012), p. 135–6.

147 D. Wong, "Sovereignty Sunk? The Position of 'Sinking States' at International Law," *14 Melbourne Journal of International Law* (2013), p. 373; cf. A. James, *Sovereign Statehood: The Basis of International Society* (1986), p. 226–7.

148 D. Wong, "Sovereignty Sunk? The Position of 'Sinking States' at International Law," *14 Melbourne Journal of International Law* (2013), p. 373.

149 A. G. Jain, "The 21st Century Atlantis: The International Law of Statehood and Climate Change-Induced Loss of Territory," *50 Stanford Journal of International Law* (2014), p. 80.

150 D. Wong, "Sovereignty Sunk? The Position of 'Sinking States' at International Law," *14 Melbourne Journal of International Law* (2013), p. 370; cf. K. Marek, *Identity and Continuity of States in Public International Law* (1968), p. 168; cf. J. R. Crawford, *Brownlie's Principles of Public International Law* (2012), p. 208.

151 Arbitrator Max Huber (Switzerland), *Island of Palmas case (Netherlands, USA)* (4 April 1928), p. 838.

152 B. Fassbender, "Article 2(1)" in B. Simma, H. Mosler, A. Paulus, E. Chaitidou (eds), *The Charter of the UN: A Commentary* (2012), p. 136, para. 3.

153 K. Ipsen, *Völkerrecht* (2014), §5, para. 27, p. 65; C. W. Morris, *An Essay on the Modern State* (2002), p. 1, 46; D.-E. Khan, "Territory and Boundaries" in B. Fassbender, A. Peters (eds), *The Oxford Handbook of the History of International Law* (2012), p. 247; J. R. Crawford, *Brownlie's Principles of Public International Law* (2012), p. 215; A. R. Harrington, "Is there a Right to Territory in International Law?" in J. C. Smith (ed.), *Property and Sovereignty: Legal and Cultural Perspectives* (2013), p. 66; S. Atapattu, *Human Rights Approaches to Climate Change: Challenges and Opportunities* (2015), p. 235; A. James, *Sovereign Statehood: The Basis of International Society* (1986), p. 31; C. d. Visscher, *Theory and Reality in Public International Law* (1968), p. 205.

154 G. Acquaviva, "Subjects of International Law: A Power-Based Analysis," *38 Vanderbilt Journal of Transnational Law* (2005), p. 380.

155 Ibid., p. 380; cf. E. Crawford and R. G. Rayfuse, "Climate Change, Sovereignty and Statehood," *11/59 Legal Studies Research Paper* (2011), p. 2.

156 D.-E. Khan, "Territory and Boundaries" in B. Fassbender, A. Peters (eds), *The Oxford Handbook of the History of International Law* (2012), p. 234; cf. K. Ipsen, *Völkerrecht* (2014), §23 para. 6 et seq., p. 245; cf. A. G. Jain, "The 21st Century Atlantis: The International Law of Statehood and Climate Change-Induced Loss of Territory," *50 Stanford Journal of International Law* (2014), p. 79.

157 R. Y. Jennings, *The Acquisition of Territory in International Law* (1963), p. 2.

158 G. W. Leibniz, *Entretien De Philarete Et D'Eugene, Sur la question du temps agitée a Nimwegue: Touchant Le Droit D'Ambassade Des Electeurs Et Princes De L'Empire* (1678), p. 20, cited after J. H. Herz, *The Nation-state and the Crisis of World Politics* (1976), p. 105–6.

159 Ibid., p. 107.

160 Czechoslovak Military Court of Appeal in London, *Case 31 – Allied Forces (Czechoslovakia) Case* – Jurisdiction – territorial– exceptional Jurisdiction of foreign Courts within national territory – jurisdiction of zechoslovak Military Courts on British Territory – English Allied Forces Act, 1940 (15 July 1942), p. 124; cf. J. McAdam, "'Disappearing States,' Statelessness and the Boundaries of International Law" in J. McAdam (ed.), *Climate change and displacement: Multidisciplinary perspectives* (2010), p. 115; cf. A. R. Harrington, "Is there a Right to Territory in International Law?" in J. C. Smith (ed.), *Property and Sovereignty: Legal and Cultural Perspectives* (2013), p. 67; S. Talmon, *Recognition of Governments in International Law: With Particular Reference to Governments in Exile* (1998), p. 217.

161 E. Crawford and R. G. Rayfuse, "Climate Change, Sovereignty and Statehood," *11/59 Legal Studies Research Paper* (2011), p. 2.

162 Cf. S. Park, *Climate Change and the Risk of Statelessness: The Situation of Low-lying Island States* (2011), p. 18.

163 M. Arcari, "Panama Canal," (last updated October 2009) in R. Wolfrum (ed.), *The Max Planck Encyclopedia of Public International Law: opil.ouplaw.com.home/EPIL* (2012), para. 14 ("Treaty concerning the Cession of Louisiana (United States of America–France)" (1803); "Treaty concerning the Cession of Alaska (United States of America–Russia)" (1867); cf. L. Yamamoto and M. Esteban, *Atoll Island States and International Law: Climate Change Displacement and Sovereignty* (2014), p. 188; A. Verdross, B. Simma and R. Geiger, *Territoriale Souveränität und Gebietshoheit: Zur völkerrechtlichen Lage der Oder-Neisse-Gebiete* (1980), p. 31–2 with other examples.

164 O. Schachter, "Sovereignty – Then and Now" in R. S. MacDonald, T. Wang (eds), *Essays in honour of Wang Tieya* (1994), p. 680; cf. D.-E. Khan, "Territory and Boundaries" in B. Fassbender, A. Peters (eds), *The Oxford Handbook of the History of International Law* (2012), p. 237.

165 I. A. Shearer, *Starke's International Law* (2003), p. 145.

166 A. James, *Sovereign Statehood: The Basis of International Society* (1986), p. 31–2 with further references.

167 J. Duursma, *Fragmentation and the International Relations of Micro-States: Self-determination and Statehood* (1996), p. 411.

168 R. G. Rayfuse, "International Law and Disappearing States: Utilising Maritime Entitlements to Overcome the Statehood Dilemma: paper 52," *2010 University of New South Wales Faculty of Law Research Series* (2010), p. 10–11, giving the examples of Palestinians, Maori, Nunavut, Inuit, and Tibetans. M. A. Burkett, "The Nation Ex-Situ" in M. Gerrard, G. E. Wannier (eds), *Threatened Island Nations: Legal Implications of Rising Seas and a Changing Climate* (2013), p. 98 adds the example of Taiwan whose exercise of functional sovereignty is recognized internationally.

169 N. van Hear, "Refugees, Diasporas, and Transnationalism" in E. Fiddian-Qasmiyeh, G. Loescher, K. Long, N. Sigona (eds), *The Oxford Handbook of Refugee and Forced Migration Studies* (2014), p. 176; cf. M. A. Burkett, "The Nation Ex-Situ" in M. Gerrard, G. E. Wannier (eds), *Threatened Island Nations: Legal Implications of Rising Seas and a Changing Climate* (2013), p. 96, 101.

170 N. van Hear, "Refugees, Diasporas, and Transnationalism" in E. Fiddian-Qasmiyeh, G. Loescher, K. Long, N. Sigona (eds), *The Oxford Handbook of Refugee and Forced Migration Studies* (2014), p. 178.

171 R. G. Rayfuse, "International Law and Disappearing States: Utilising Maritime Entitlements to Overcome the Statehood Dilemma: paper 52," *2010 University of New South Wales Faculty of Law Research Series* (2010), p. 11.

172 See on practical problems of a deterritorialized State: A. G. Jain, "The 21st Century Atlantis: The International Law of Statehood and Climate Change-Induced Loss of Territory," *50 Stanford Journal of International Law* (2014), p. 78 et seq.

173 M. Greengrass, "Conquest and Coalescence: The Shaping of the State in Early Modern Europe" in M. Greengrass (ed.), *Conquest and Coalescence* (1991), p. 3; cf. D. H. Nexon, *The Struggle for Power in Early Modern Europe: Religious Conflict, Dynastic Empires, and International Change* (2009), p. 92; M. W. Janis, "Sovereignty and International Law: Hobbes and Grotius" in R. S. MacDonald, T. Wang (eds), *Essays in honour of Wang Tieya* (1994), p. 394; O. Schachter, "Sovereignty – Then and Now" in R. S. MacDonald, T. Wang (eds), *Essays in honour of Wang Tieya* (1994), p. 672; L. Glanville, *Sovereignty and the Responsibility to Protect: A New History* (2014), p. 31–3; A. Orford, *International Authority and the Responsibility to Protect* (2011),

p. 143-150; L. Zucca, "A Genealogy of State Sovereignty," *16 Theoretical Inquiries in Law 2* (2015), p. 400.

174 D. Wong, "Sovereignty Sunk? The Position of 'Sinking States' at International Law," *14 Melbourne Journal of International Law* (2013), p. 385; cf. ILC, *Sea-level rise in relation to international law, Second issues paper by Patrícia Galvão Teles and Juan José Ruda Santolaria* (73rd session of the ILC (2022)), # 126 et seq.

175 W. Riphagen, "Some Reflections on 'Functional Sovereignty'," *6 Netherlands Yearbook of International Law* (1975), p. 164.

176 Cf. A. G. Jain, "The 21st Century Atlantis: The International Law of Statehood and Climate Change-Induced Loss of Territory," *50 Stanford Journal of International Law* (2014), p. 79.

177 A. El Ouali, *Territorial Integrity in a Globalizing World: International Law and States' Quest for Survival* (2012), p. 89; cf. M. N. Shaw, "The International Court of Justice and the Law of Territory" in C. J. Tams (ed.), *The Development of International Law by the International Court of Justice* (2013), p. 153–4.

178 ICJ – The Hague, *Western Sahara Advisory Opinion* – Advisory Opinion (16 October 1975), p. 44, para. 95.

179 IC– The Hague, *Sovereignty over Pedra Branca/Pulau Batu Puteh, Middle Rocks and South Ledge (Malaysia/Singapore)* – Judgment (23 May 2008), p. 39, para. 76.

180 Ibid., p. 40, para. 79; cf. M. N. Shaw, "The International Court of Justice and the Law of Territory" in C. J. Tams (ed.), *The Development of International Law by the International Court of Justice* (2013), p. 154.

181 A. El Ouali, *Territorial Integrity in a Globalizing World: International Law and States' Quest for Survival* (2012), p. 34.

182 Cf. D.-E. Khan, "Territory and Boundaries" in B. Fassbender, A. Peters (eds), *The Oxford Handbook of the History of International Law* (2012), p. 228 ("[A] carefully bonded territory has always been viewed as a guarantee of peaceful relations between neighbouring individuals, social or political entities, [...]").

183 H. Spruyt, *The Sovereign State and Its Competitors: An Analysis of Systems Change* (1996), p. 56; cf. W. W. Willoughby, *The Fundamental Concepts of Public Law* (1931), p. 330.

184 A. Giddens, *The Nation-state and Violence* (1985), p. 281.

185 J. R. Crawford, *Brownlie's Principles of Public International Law* (2012), p. 447.

186 Cf. J. Gordley, "Extraterritorial Legal Problems in a World without Nations: What the Medieval Jurists could Teach us" in G. Handl, J. Zekoll, P. Zumbanse (eds), *Beyond Territoriality: Transnational Legal Authority in an Age of Globalization* (2012), p. 36.

187 J. Story, *Commentaries on the Conflict of Laws, Foreign and Domestic: In Regard to Contracts, Rights, and Remedies, and Especially in Regard to Marriages, Divorces, Wills, Successions, and Judgments* (1883), §7: "It is plain that the law of one country can have no intrinsic force, proprio vigore, except within the territorial limits and jurisdiction of that country;" F. C. v. Savigny, *System des heutigen römischen Rechts* (1840–1849), whose starting point was that

1. Every state can require that only its own law is valid within its boundaries.
2. No state can require that its own law be accepted as valid beyond its boundaries.

Cited after J. Gordley, "Exra-territorial Legal Problems in a World without Nations: What the Medieval Jurists could Teach us" in G. Handl, J. Zekoll, P. Zumbanse (eds), *Beyond Territoriality: Transnational Legal Authority in an Age of Globalization* (2012), p. 37.

188 D. Wong, "Sovereignty Sunk? The Position of 'Sinking States' at International Law," *14 Melbourne Journal of International Law* (2013), p. 386; S. D. Krasner, *Sovereignty: Organized Hypocrisy* (1999), p. 4; cf. A. Orford, *International Authority and the Responsibility to Protect* (2011), p. 155 with an historical overview over divided obligations and related conflict potential.

189 H. Spruyt, *The Sovereign State and Its Competitors: An Analysis of Systems Change* (1996), p. 13; C. Richter, *Collapsed States: Perspektiven nach dem Wegfall von Staatlichkeit* (2011), p. 52; cf. in more detail Chapter 4.
190 H. Bull, *The Anarchical Society: A Study of Order in World Politics* (2012), p. 246; cf. C. W. Morris, *An Essay on the Modern State* (2002), p. 53; D. Held and A. G. McGrew, *Globalization/Anti-Globalization: Beyond the Great Divide* (2007), p. 61–2; J. Gordley, "Extraterritorial Legal Problems in a World without Nations: What the Medieval Jurists could Teach us" in G. Handl, J. Zekoll, P. Zumbanse (eds), *Beyond Territoriality: Transnational Legal Authority in an Age of Globalization* (2012), p. 42 et seq. on the comparison with the medieval times; cf. W. Reinhard, "Aufstieg und Niedergang des modernen Staates," *5 Zeitschrift für Staats- und Europawissenschaften* (2007), p. 8, 24.
191 C. Schmitt, *Political Theology II: The Myth of the Closure of any Political Theology* [1970] (2008), p. 114; cf. A. Orford, *International Authority and the Responsibility to Protect* (2011), p. 186.
192 D. H. Nexon, *The Struggle for Power in Early Modern Europe: Religious Conflict, Dynastic Empires, and International Change* (2009), p. 282; B. Marquardt, *Universalgeschichte des Staates: Von der vorstaatlichen Gesellschaft zum Staat der Industriegesellschaft* (2009), p. 247; A. James, *Sovereign Statehood: The Basis of International Society* (1986), p. 4; cf. Chapter D.
193 D. H. Nexon, *The Struggle for Power in Early Modern Europe: Religious Conflict, Dynastic Empires, and International Change* (2009), p. 278.
194 Ibid., p. 293.
195 Cf. ibid., p. 295.
196 J. Branch, *The Cartographic State: Maps, Territory, and the Origins of Sovereignty* (2014), p. 84.
197 A. El Ouali, *Territorial Integrity in a Globalizing World: International Law and States' Quest for Survival* (2012), p. 41.
198 A. El Ouali, *Territorial Integrity in a Globalizing World: International Law and States' Quest for Survival* (2012), p. 41.
199 Art. 2(1)(b) of both Conventions.
200 N. Schrijver, "The Impact of Climate Change: Challenges for International Law" in U. Fastenrath, R. Geiger, D.-E. Khan, A. Paulus, S. von Schorlemer, C. Vedder (eds), *From Bilateralism to Community Interest: Essays in Honour of Judge Bruno Simma* (2011), p. 1286 who argues that "novel solutions may have to be found to accommodate such scenarios."
201 Cf. C. Grabenwarter and M. Holoubek, *Verfassungsrecht – Allgemeines Verwaltungsrecht* (2009), p. 28 para. 3.
202 M. A. Burkett, "The Nation Ex-Situ" in M. Gerrard, G. E. Wannier (eds), *Threatened Island Nations: Legal Implications of Rising Seas and a Changing Climate* (2013), p. 95.
203 Ibid., p. 105–6.
204 J. Gottmann, *The Significance of Territory* (1973), p. 3; cf. D. Wong, "Sovereignty Sunk? The Position of 'Sinking States' at International Law," *14 Melbourne Journal of International Law* (2013), p. 366; J. Klabbers, *International Law* (2013), p. 76.
205 Non-territorial entities that enjoy sovereignty only enjoy functional sovereignty.
206 H.-E. Folz, "Die unmittelbaren Rechte der Staaten" in H. Miehsler, E. Mock, B. Simma, I. Tammelo (eds), *Jus Humanitatis: Festschrift zum 90. Geburtstag von Alfred Verdross* (1980), p. 420.
207 A. G. Jain, "The 21st Century Atlantis: The International Law of Statehood and Climate Change-Induced Loss of Territory," *50 Stanford Journal of International Law* (2014), p. 23; cf. J. Gottmann, *The Significance of Territory* (1973), p. 64–8.
208 H. Spruyt, *The Sovereign State and Its Competitors: An Analysis of Systems Change* (1996), p. 153.

209 A. G. Jain, "The 21st Century Atlantis: The International Law of Statehood and Climate Change-Induced Loss of Territory," *50 Stanford Journal of International Law* (2014), p. 23; cf. J. Gottmann, *The Significance of Territory* (1973), p. 64–8.
210 M. N. Shaw, "The International Court of Justice and the Law of Territory" in C. J. Tams (ed.), *The Development of International Law by the International Court of Justice* (2013), p. 151 (footnote omitted).
211 W. W. Willoughby, *The Fundamental Concepts of Public Law* (1931), p. 63–4.
212 B. H. Oxman, "Jurisdiction of States," (last updated March 2009) in R. Wolfrum (ed.), *The Max Planck Encyclopedia of Public International Law: opil.ouplaw.com.home/EPIL* (2012), para. 9; cf. M. N. Shaw, "Territory in International Law," *13 Netherlands Yearbook of International Law* (1982), p. 62.
213 R. Y. Jennings, *The Acquisition of Territory in International Law* (1963), p. 1.
214 A. Orakhelashvili, "Governmental Activities on Foreign Territory," (last updated May 2011) in R. Wolfrum (ed.), *The Max Planck Encyclopedia of Public International Law: opil.ouplaw.com.home/EPIL* (2012), para. 36; cf. R. Lawson, "The Concept of Jurisdiction and Extraterritorial Acts of State" in G. Kreijen (ed.), *State, Sovereignty, and International Governance* (2002), p. 281 et seq.
215 Cf. J. C. Bluntschli and K. Brater, *Deutsches Staats-Wörterbuch* (1861), p. 209: "Ohne Land kein Staat."
216 W. W. Willoughby, *The Fundamental Concepts of Public Law* (1931), p. 65.
217 W. Vitzthum, "Aquitoriale Souveränität" in P.-M. Dupuy, B. Fassbender, M. N. Shaw, K.-P. Sommermann (eds), *Völkerrecht als Wertordnung: Festschrift für Christian Tomuschat* (2006), p. 1067; "State without sovereignty is a contradiction in terms." (N. Schrijver, "The Impact of Climate Change: Challenges for International Law" in U. Fastenrath, R. Geiger, D.-E. Khan, A. Paulus, S. von Schorlemer, C. Vedder (eds), *From Bilateralism to Community Interest: Essays in Honour of Judge Bruno Simma* (2011), p. 1285.)
218 A. Hudson, "Beyond the Borders: Globalisation, Sovereignty and Extra-Territoriality" in D. Newman (ed.), *Boundaries, Territory and Postmodernity* (1999), p. 102.
219 Cf. D. Wong, "Sovereignty Sunk? The Position of 'Sinking States' at International Law," *14 Melbourne Journal of International Law* (2013), p. 352; cf. G. Abi-Saab, "International Law and the International Community: The long road to Universality" in R. S. MacDonald, T. Wang (eds), *Essays in honour of Wang Tieya* (1994), p. 36–7.
220 T. J. Lawrence, *The Principles of International Law* (1895), p. 59.
221 C. W. Morris, *An Essay on the Modern State* (2002), p. 38.
222 D. H. Nexon, *The Struggle for Power in Early Modern Europe: Religious Conflict, Dynastic Empires, and International Change* (2009), p. 18; C. W. Morris, *An Essay on the Modern State* (2002), p. 3; see Chapter D.
223 Ibid., p. 3, 51; cf. C. Tilly, "Reflections on the History of European State-making" in C. Tilly, G. Ardant (eds), *The Formation of national States in Western Europe* (1975), p. 26–7.
224 H. Spruyt, *The Sovereign State and Its Competitors: An Analysis of Systems Change* (1996), p. 35; C. W. Morris, *An Essay on the Modern State* (2002), p. 33.
225 J. R. Strayer, *Feudalism* (1965), p. 13; H. Spruyt, *The Sovereign State and Its Competitors: An Analysis of Systems Change* (1996), p. 40, with further references; cf. C. W. Morris, *An Essay on the Modern State* (2002), p. 33.
226 H. Spruyt, *The Sovereign State and Its Competitors: An Analysis of Systems Change* (1996), p. 35; B. Marquardt, *Universalgeschichte des Staates: Von der vorstaatlichen Gesellschaft zum Staat der Industriegesellschaft* (2009), p. 111.
227 H. Spruyt, *The Sovereign State and Its Competitors: An Analysis of Systems Change* (1996), p. 55; C. W. Morris, *An Essay on the Modern State* (2002), p. 33; B. Marquardt,

Universalgeschichte des Staates: Von der vorstaatlichen Gesellschaft zum Staat der Industriegesellschaft (2009), p. 120.

228 C. W. Morris, *An Essay on the Modern State* (2002), p. 33; cf. T. M. Franck, *The Empowered Self: Law and Society in an Age of Individualism* (1999), p. 99; B. Marquardt, *Universalgeschichte des Staates: Von der vorstaatlichen Gesellschaft zum Staat der Industriegesellschaft* (2009), p. 125.

229 H. Spruyt, *The Sovereign State and Its Competitors: An Analysis of Systems Change* (1996), p. 170; T. M. Franck, *The Empowered Self: Law and Society in an Age of Individualism* (1999), p. 99; A. Eyffinger, "Europe in the Balance: An Appraisal of the Westphalian System," *45 Netherlands international law review* (1998), p. 174.

230 J. Larkins, *From Hierarchy to Anarchy: Territory and Politics before Westphalia* (2009), p. 3.

231 H. Spruyt, *The Sovereign State and Its Competitors: An Analysis of Systems Change* (1996), p. 170.

232 Ibid., p. 180.

233 Ibid., p. 153; cf. D. H. Nexon, *The Struggle for Power in Early Modern Europe: Religious Conflict, Dynastic Empires, and International Change* (2009), p. 75.

234 H. Spruyt, *The Sovereign State and Its Competitors: An Analysis of Systems Change* (1996), p. 169.

235 Ibid., p. 170; cf. M. L. van Creveld, *The Rise and Decline of the State* (1999), p. 109.

236 H. Spruyt, *The Sovereign State and Its Competitors: An Analysis of Systems Change* (1996), p. 170 with further references; cf. M. L. van Creveld, *The Rise and Decline of the State* (1999), p. 109 et seq.

237 D. B. Goldman, *Globalisation and the Western Legal Tradition: Recurring Patterns of Law and Authority* (2008), p. 119, 120; H. Spruyt, *The Sovereign State and Its Competitors: An Analysis of Systems Change* (1996), p. 28.

238 Ibid., p. 171.

239 D.-E. Khan, "Territory and Boundaries" in B. Fassbender, A. Peters (eds), *The Oxford Handbook of the History of International Law* (2012), p. 226.

240 H. Spruyt, *The Sovereign State and Its Competitors: An Analysis of Systems Change* (1996), p. 179–80.

241 Ibid., p. 191.

242 Ibid., p. 191.

243 Ibid., p. 191.

244 B. Lewis, *What Went Wrong?: Western Impact and Middle Eastern Response* (2002), p. 112.

245 Ibid., p. 112.

246 J. M. Otto, *Sharia Incorporated: A Comparative Overview of the Legal Systems of Twelve Muslim Countries in Past and Present* (2010), p. 615–16.

247 D. H. Nexon, *The Struggle for Power in Early Modern Europe: Religious Conflict, Dynastic Empires, and International Change* (2009), p. 20.

248 P. Bobbitt, "Waging War against Terror: An Essay for Sandy Levinson," *40 Georgia Law Review* (2006), p. 754.

249 R. N. Rosecrance, *The Rise of the Virtual State: Wealth and Power in the Coming Century* (1999), p. xiii.

250 In this context, Ödalen argues, that sovereignty is "but an endpoint of a continuum consisting of several different ways of institutionalizing self-determination." J. Ödalen, "Underwater self-determination: Sea-level rise and deterritorialized Small Island States," *17 (2) Ethics, Policy & Environment* (2014), p. 225 et seq.

251 M. Craven, R. Parfitt, "Statehood, Self-determination, and Recognition" in M. D. Evans (ed.), *International Law* (2018), p. 221.

252 H. Spruyt, *The Sovereign State and Its Competitors: An Analysis of Systems Change* (1996), p. 191–2.

253 R. Kastoryano, "Transnational nationalism: redefining nation and territory" in S. Benhabib, I. Shapiro, D. Petranovich (eds), *Identities, Affiliations, and Allegiances* (2007), p. 167; cf. S. Chouinard, 'Stateless Nations' in K. Cordell, S. Wolff (eds), *The Routledge Handbook of Ethnic Conflict* (2016), p. 55–6.
254 I. Pogany, "Accommodating an Emergent National Identity: The Roma of Central and Eastern Europe" in S. Tierney (ed.), *Accommodating National Identity: New Approaches in International and Domestic Law* (2000), p. 179.
255 E. F. Isin, *Citizens Without Frontiers* (2012), p. 161.
256 "Declaration of a Roma Nation (IRU)" (2001).
257 E. F. Isin, *Citizens Without Frontiers* (2012), p. 161.
258 Ibid., p. 161.
259 R. Kastoryano, "Transnational nationalism: redefining nation and territory" in S. Benhabib, I. Shapiro, D. Petranovich (eds), *Identities, Affiliations, and Allegiances* (2007), p. 167.
260 H. Spruyt, *The Sovereign State and Its Competitors: An Analysis of Systems Change* (1996), p. 6.
261 Ibid., p. 17, with further references.
262 S. Chouinard, "Stateless Nations" in K. Cordell, S. Wolff (eds), *The Routledge Handbook of Ethnic Conflict* (2016), p. 54.
263 Ibid., p. 55.
264 Cf. ibid., p. 56.
265 A. G. Jain, "The 21st Century Atlantis: The International Law of Statehood and Climate Change-Induced Loss of Territory," *50 Stanford Journal of International Law* (2014), p. 46.
266 Ibid., p. 45; cf. also R. G. Rayfuse, "International Law and Disappearing States: Utilising Maritime Entitlements to Overcome the Statehood Dilemma: paper 52," *2010 University of New South Wales Faculty of Law Research Series* (2010), p. 10; J. Grote-Stoutenburg, *Disappearing Island States in International Law* (2015), p. 234; L. Yamamoto and M. Esteban, *Atoll Island States and International Law: Climate Change Displacement and Sovereignty* (2014), p. 203 et seq.; M. A. Burkett, "The Nation Ex-Situ" in M. Gerrard, G. E. Wannier (eds), *Threatened Island Nations: Legal Implications of Rising Seas and a Changing Climate* (2013), p. 97; cf. E. Suy, "New Players in International Relations" in G. Kreijen (ed.), *State, Sovereignty, and International Governance* (2002), p. 373; ILC, *Sea-level rise in relation to international law, Second issues paper by Patrícia Galvão Teles and Juan José Ruda Santolaria* (73rd session of the ILC (2022)), # 113 et seq.
267 D. Wong, "Sovereignty Sunk? The Position of 'Sinking States' at International Law," *14 Melbourne Journal of International Law* (2013), p. 357; Y. Abdullah, "The Holy See at the UN Conferences: State of Church?", *96 Columbia Law Review* (1996), p. 1856; cf. G. Westdickenberg, "Holy See," (last updated March 2009) in R. Wolfrum (ed.), *The Max Planck Encyclopedia of Public International Law: opil.ouplaw.com .home/EPIL* (2012), para. 18 et seq.
268 J. L. Kunz, "The Status of the Holy See in International Law," *46 AJIL* (1952), p. 312; cf. S. R. J. Araujo, "The International personality and sovereignty of the Holy See," *50 Catholic University Law Review* (2001), p. 299 et seq.; G. Acquaviva, "Subjects of International Law: A Power-Based Analysis," *38 Vanderbilt Journal of Transnational Law* (2005), p. 357: "It is the same subject as the Holy See before 1808, the same subject as that which existed between the fall of Napoleon and 1870, and the same subject as that which existed between 1870 and 1929."
269 F. Gazzoni, "Malta, Order of," (last updated November 2009) in R. Wolfrum (ed.), *The Max Planck Encyclopedia of Public International Law: opil.ouplaw.com.home/EPIL* (2012), para. 4, para. 12; N. Cox, "The Acquisition of Sovereignty by Quasi-States: The Case of the Order of Malta," *6 Mountbatten Journal of Legal Studies* (2002), p. 34,

37; E. Crawford and R. G. Rayfuse, "Climate Change, Sovereignty and Statehood," *11/59 Legal Studies Research Paper* (2011), p. 10–11; J. R. Crawford, The Creation of States in International Law (2006), p. 221 et seq.; O. Dörr, K. Schmalenbach (eds), *Vienna Convention on the Law of Treaties: A Commentary* (2012), p. 66.

270 See N. Cox, "The Acquisition of Sovereignty by Quasi-States: The Case of the Order of Malta," *6 Mountbatten Journal of Legal Studies* (2002), p. 37 in greater detail; see also ibid., p. 45–6: "Neither the Templars, nor less well-known orders, such as the St Lazarus, ever achieved sovereign status, as they never obtained control of territory. The Teutonic Order lost its sovereign status when it ceased to rule territory in Germany after 1525."

271 Order of Malta, Bilateral Relations with Countries: https://www.orderofmalta.org.uk/press-and-media/bilateral-relations-with-countries/ (last visited 21 May 2022). Cf. D. Wong, "Sovereignty Sunk? The Position of 'Sinking States' at International Law," *14 Melbourne Journal of International Law* (2013), p. 357.

272 N. Cox, "The Acquisition of Sovereignty by Quasi-States: The Case of the Order of Malta," *6 Mountbatten Journal of Legal Studies* (2002), p. 37.

273 Cf. F. Gazzoni, "Malta, Order of," (last updated November 2009) in R. Wolfrum (ed.), *The Max Planck Encyclopedia of Public International Law: opil.ouplaw.com.home/EPIL* (2012), para. 3.

274 N. Cox, "The Acquisition of Sovereignty by Quasi-States: The Case of the Order of Malta," *6 Mountbatten Journal of Legal Studies* (2002), p. 37, 40; cf. Tribunale Cardinalizio, *Acta Apostolicae Sedis XLV (15): 30 November 1953* (19 February 1953), p. 766.

275 F. Gazzoni, "Malta, Order of," (last updated November 2009) in R. Wolfrum (ed.), *The Max Planck Encyclopedia of Public International Law: opil.ouplaw.com.home/EPIL* (2012), para. 4, para. 12; N. Cox, "The Acquisition of Sovereignty by Quasi-States: The Case of the Order of Malta," *6 Mountbatten Journal of Legal Studies* (2002), p. 34, 37; E. Crawford and R. G. Rayfuse, "Climate Change, Sovereignty and Statehood," *11/59 Legal Studies Research Paper* (2011), p. 10–11; J. R. Crawford, The Creation of States in International Law (2006), p. 221 et seq.; O. Dörr, K. Schmalenbach (eds), *Vienna Convention on the Law of Treaties: A Commentary* (2012), p. 66.

276 F. Gazzoni, "Malta, Order of," (last updated November 2009) in R. Wolfrum (ed.), *The Max Planck Encyclopedia of Public International Law: opil.ouplaw.com.home/EPIL* (2012), para. 12.

277 E. Crawford and R. G. Rayfuse, "Climate Change, Sovereignty and Statehood," *11/59 Legal Studies Research Paper* (2011), p. 10–11; cf. D. Wong, "Sovereignty Sunk? The Position of 'Sinking States' at International Law," *14 Melbourne Journal of International Law* (2013), p. 357.

278 R. Prantner, *Malteserorden und Völkergemeinschaft* (1974), p. 71.

279 Ibid., p. 71, 76, 113 (in greater detail); cf. A. C. Breycha-Vauthier, "L'Ordre S. M. Jérosolymitain de Malte. Evolutions récentes autour d'une ancienne organisation internationale," *16 Zeitschrift für ausländisches Öffentliches Recht und Völkerrecht* (1955/56), p. 507–8, 512.

280 N. Cox, "The Acquisition of Sovereignty by Quasi-States: The Case of the Order of Malta," *6 Mountbatten Journal of Legal Studies* (2002), p. 33.

281 F. Gazzoni, "Malta, Order of," (last updated November 2009) in R. Wolfrum (ed.), *The Max Planck Encyclopedia of Public International Law: opil.ouplaw.com.home/EPIL* (2012), para. 5.

282 S. R. J. Araujo, "The International personality and sovereignty of the Holy See," *50 Catholic University Law Review* (2001), p. 306.

283 N. Cox, 'The Acquisition of Sovereignty by Quasi-States: The Case of the Order of Malta', *6 Mountbatten Journal of Legal Studies* (2002), p. 40; cf. N. Bergmann,

Versinkende Inselstaaten: Auswirkungen des Klimawandels auf die Staatlichkeit kleiner Inselstaaten (2016), p. 140 et seq.

284 Tribunale Cardinalizio, *Acta Apostolicae Sedis XLV (15): 30 November 1953* (19 February 1953), p. 767.

285 G. Arangio-Ruiz, "On the Nature of the International Personality of the Holy See," *1996/2 Revue Belge de Droit International* (1996), p. 361, 362.

286 G. Acquaviva, "Subjects of International Law: A Power-Based Analysis," *38 Vanderbilt Journal of Transnational Law* (2005), p. 356.

287 J. L. Kunz, "The Status of the Holy See in International Law," *46 AJIL* (1952), p. 309, 311.

288 J. Duursma, *Fragmentation and the International Relations of Micro-States: Self-determination and Statehood* (1996), p. 386; cf. D. Wong, "Sovereignty Sunk? The Position of 'Sinking States' at International Law," *14 Melbourne Journal of International Law* (2013), p. 358.

289 A. G. Jain, "The 21st Century Atlantis: The International Law of Statehood and Climate Change-Induced Loss of Territory," *50 Stanford Journal of International Law* (2014), p. 70.

290 J. R. Crawford, The Creation of States in International Law (2006), p. 715.

291 M. S. Fusillo, "The legal regime of uninhabited "rocks" lacking an economic life of their own," *4 The Italian Yearbook of International Law* (1978–1979), p. 478, para. 17.

292 Other examples: Albania, Austria, Czechoslovakia, and Ethiopia, which were annexed by Germany or Italy or the Soviet Union respectively. (R. Hofmann, "Annexation," (last updated February 2013) in R. Wolfrum (ed.), *The Max Planck Encyclopedia of Public International Law: opil.ouplaw.com.home/EPIL* (2012) para. 15); cf. J. L. Kunz, "Identity of States under International Law," *49 AJIL* (1955), p. 75.

293 P. van Elsuwege, "Baltic States," (last updated April 2012) in R. Wolfrum (ed.), *The Max Planck Encyclopedia of Public International Law: opil.ouplaw.com.home/EPIL* (2012), para. 1; cf. A. Cassese, "Self-Determination of Peoples and the Recent Break-up of USSR and Yugoslavia" in R. S. MacDonald, T. Wang (eds), *Essays in honour of Wang Tieya* (1994), p. 133 et seq.; cf. D. Wong, "Sovereignty Sunk? The Position of 'Sinking States' at International Law," *14 Melbourne Journal of International Law* (2013), p. 377 with further references.

294 R. Hofmann, "Annexation," (last updated February 2013) in R. Wolfrum (ed.), *The Max Planck Encyclopedia of Public International Law: opil.ouplaw.com.home/EPIL* (2012) para. 15.

295 S. for Estonia D. J. Smith, *Estonia: Independence and European Integration, Postcommunist States and Nations* (2001), p. xx.

296 P. van Elsuwege, "Baltic States," (last updated April 2012) in R. Wolfrum (ed.), *The Max Planck Encyclopedia of Public International Law: opil.ouplaw.com.home/EPIL* (2012), para. 18.

297 J. L. Kunz, "Identity of States under International Law," *49 AJIL* (1955), p. 75

298 J. Grote-Stoutenburg, *Disappearing Island States in International Law* (2015), p. 265

299 D. J. Smith, *Estonia: Independence and European Integration, Postcommunist States and Nations* (2001), p. xix, xx.

300 N. Cox, "The Acquisition of Sovereignty by Quasi-States: The Case of the Order of Malta," *6 Mountbatten Journal of Legal Studies* (2002), p. 47.

301 R. N. Rosecrance, "The Rise of the Virtual State," *75 Foreign Affairs* (1996), p. 45.

302 Ibid., p. 46.

303 http://institute.wirtland.com/ (last visited 21 May 2022).

304 N. Cox, "The Acquisition of Sovereignty by Quasi-States: The Case of the Order of Malta," *6 Mountbatten Journal of Legal Studies* (2002), p. 31, cf. p. 46–7.

305 http://www.wirtland.com/ (last visited 21 May 2022).

306 http://wirtland.agilityhoster.com/FAQ.html (last visited 21 May 2022).

307 http://wirtland.agilityhoster.com/legal.html (last visited 21 May 2022).
308 http://www.wirtland.com/ (last visited 21 May 2022).
309 Ibid.
310 M. A. Burkett, "The Nation Ex-Situ" in M. Gerrard, G. E. Wannier (eds), *Threatened Island Nations: Legal Implications of Rising Seas and a Changing Climate* (2013), p. 115.
311 Ibid., p. 116; cf. J. L. Blackman, "State Successions and Statelessness: The Emerging Right to an Effective Nationality Under International Law," *19 Michigan Journal of International Law* (1998), p. 1149.
312 M. A. Burkett, "The Nation Ex-Situ" in M. Gerrard, G. E. Wannier (eds), *Threatened Island Nations: Legal Implications of Rising Seas and a Changing Climate* (2013), p. 95.
313 C. Moore, "Waterworld: Climate change, Statehood and the right to self-determination," in O. Quirico, M. Boumghar (eds), *Climate Change and Human Rights: An international and comparative law perspective* (2016), p. 111.
314 M. A. Burkett, "The Nation Ex-Situ" in M. Gerrard, G. E. Wannier (eds), *Threatened Island Nations: Legal Implications of Rising Seas and a Changing Climate* (2013), p. 90.
315 The Times of Wirtland, *Wirtland citizenship for Edward Snowden* (2013); cf. A. Martín, *El país que une a Snowden, Assange y Obama* (2015).
316 https://e-estonia.com/e-residents/about (last visited 30 June 2019).
317 M. Shearlaw, "A Brexit bolthole? For €100 you can become an e-resident of an EU country you've never visited," The Guardian, 15 September 2016: "e-residents are not citizens."
318 R. Cellan-Jones, *Becoming a virtual Estonian* (2016).
319 Ibid.: "He has been set a target of attracting 10 million e-Estonians by 2025. That sounds ridiculously ambitious, but this tiny country has already shown that, when it comes to being digital, it can punch far above its weight."
320 Ibid.
321 M. Shearlaw, "A Brexit bolthole? For €100 you can become an e-resident of an EU country you've never visited," *The Guardian*, 15 September 2016.
322 J. L. Blackman, "State Successions and Statelessness: The Emerging Right to an Effective Nationality Under International Law," *19 Michigan Journal of International Law* (1998), p. 1149; cf. D. P. O'Connell, *State Succession in Municipal Law and International Law* (1967), p. 498.
323 C. W. Morris, *An Essay on the Modern State* (2002), p. 205; cf. S. Besson, "Sovereignty," (last updated March 2012) in R. Wolfrum (ed.), *The Max Planck Encyclopedia of Public International Law: opil.ouplaw.com.home/EPIL* (2012), para. 1; seen differently by M. A. Burkett, "The Nation Ex-Situ" in M. Gerrard, G. E. Wannier (eds), *Threatened Island Nations: Legal Implications of Rising Seas and a Changing Climate* (2013), p. 116.
324 "Convention on Rights and Duties of States: Montevideo Convention" (1933).
325 Emphasis added.
326 E. M. Borchard, *The Diplomatic Protection of Citizens Abroad: Or, The Law of International Claims* (1919), Preface.
327 Ibid., p. 28.
328 Ibid., p. 346.
329 C. F. Amerasinghe, *Diplomatic Protection* (2008), p. 2.
330 B. Sepúlveda Amor, "Diplomatic and Consular Protection: The Rights of the State and the Rights of the Individual in the 'Lagrand' and 'Avena' Cases" in U. Fastenrath, R. Geiger, D.-E. Khan, A. Paulus, S. von Schorlemer, C. Vedder (eds), *From Bilateralism to Community Interest: Essays in Honour of Judge Bruno Simma* (2011), p. 1098 et seq. with further details on the cases: ICJ – The Hague, *LaGrand Case – Germany v. USA* – Judgment (27 June 2001) and ICJ – The Hague, *Case concerning Avena and other Mexican Nationals – Mexico v. USA* – Judgment (31 March 2004); cf. A. A. C.

Trindade, "International Law for Humankind: Towards a New Jus Gentium," part 2, *317 Recueil Des Cours* (2005), p. 139.

331 Cf. C. F. Amerasinghe, *Diplomatic Protection* (2008), p. 24

332 R. N. Rosecrance, *The Rise of the Virtual State: Wealth and Power in the Coming Century* (1999), p. 4.

333 Wirtland Institute, *How to sell a square mile of wasteland for 2.6 billion dollars? A micronation proposes new way to raise money to help developing countries* (2010).

334 http://www.wirtland.com/ (last visited 21 May 2022).

335 D. Bethlehem, "The End of Geography: The Changing Nature of the International System and the Challenge to International Law," *25 EJIL* (2014), p. 19; cf. also S. D. Brunn, "A Treaty of Silicon for the Treaty of Westphalia? New Territorial Dimensions of Modern Statehood" in D. Newman (ed.), *Boundaries, Territory and Postmodernity* (1999), p. 122.

336 Additionally, it would have to be "satisfactory to its members" as Burkett points out. M. A. Burkett, "The Nation Ex-Situ" in M. Gerrard, G. E. Wannier (eds), *Threatened Island Nations: Legal Implications of Rising Seas and a Changing Climate* (2013), p. 102.

337 G. Arangio-Ruiz, "On the Nature of the International Personality of the Holy See," *1996/2 Revue Belge de Droit International* (1996), p. 363.

338 T. M. Franck, *The Empowered Self: Law and Society in an Age of Individualism* (1999), p. 92.

339 Cf. Final Draft IPCC 2022: IPCC WGII Sixth Assessment Report, *Chapter 3*, Projected risks to coastal communities, infrastructure and ecosystems.

340 "Barbados Declaration" (1994), p. 79 (Opening Statement by HE Mr L. E. Sandiford, Prime Minister of Barbados and President of the Global Conference (Annex II); M. A. Burkett, "Climate Refugees" in S. Alam (ed.), *Routledge Handbook of International Environmental Law* (2013), p. 728.

341 UNGA, *Provisional verbatim record of the forty-first meeting*, 19 October 1987, p. 15–16.

342 Ibid., p. 17.

343 UNGA, *19th Special Session, 3rd plenary meeting*, 24 June 1997, p. 4; cf. Submission of the Republic of the Maldives, *Submission of the Maldives to the Office of the UN High Commissioner for Human Rights under Resolution HRC 7/23*, 25 September 2008, p. 47 (nation "faces extinction"), cf. H. H. Shihab, *General Debate of the Second Committee: Permanent Mission of the Republic of the Maldives to the UN New York* (2012), p. 1.

344 UNGA, *Review and appraisal of the implementation of the Programme of Action for the Sustainable Development of Small Island Developing States*, 28 September 1999, p. 17.

345 E. S. Sopoaga, *Statement by His Excellency Mr Enele S Sopoaga Ambassador and Permanent Representative of Tuvalu to the UN Chair of the Tuvalu Delegation at the General Debate of the Fifty-Sixth Session of the UNGA* (2001) (Statement by His Excellency Mr Enele S Sopoaga, Ambassador and Permanent Representative of Tuvalu to the UN Chair of the Tuvalu Delegation at the General Debate of the Fifty-Sixth Session of the UNGA Friday 16th November 2001).

346 To cite just a few: UNSC, *Maintenance of international peace and security: Impact of climate change: Letter dated 1 July 2011 from the Permanent Representative of Germany to the UN addressed to the Secretary-General (S/2011/408)*, 20 July 2011, p. 17 (South Africa); UNGA, *63rd Session, 85th Plenary meeting*, 3 June 2009, p. 7 (Samoa); UNSC, *Maintenance of international peace and security: Impact of climate change: Letter dated 1 July 2011 from the Permanent Representative of Germany to the UN addressed to the Secretary-General (S/2011/408)*, 20 July 2011, p. 16 (Lebanon); ibid., p. 20 (Portugal); UNGA, *63rd Session, 85th Plenary meeting*, 3 June 2009, p. 15 (Fiji); UNGA, *70th Session, 19th Plenary meeting*, 30 September

2015, p. 10–11 (Croatia); UNGA, *Integrated and coordinated implementation of and follow-up to the outcomes of the major UN conferences and summits in the economic, social and related fields*, 25 September 2015, p. 3 (Uganda); UNGA, *Agenda item 8*, 2 October 2015, p. 17 (Colombia).

347 UNSC, *Sixty-second year, 5,663rd meeting*, 17 April 2007, p. 20.
348 UNGA, *Agenda item 8*, 27 September 2008, p. 3.
349 UNGA, *Climate change and its possible security implications*, 18 May 2009.
350 UNGA, *63rd Session, 85th Plenary meeting*, 3 June 2009, p. 2.
351 Ibid., p. 8 (Mr Muller).
352 Anote Tong, President of Kiribati in UNSC, *Peace and security challenges facing small island developing States*, 30 July 2015, p. 29.
353 UNGA, *63rd Session, 85th Plenary meeting*, 3 June 2009, p. 10.
354 Ibid., p. 16.
355 D. Wong, "Sovereignty Sunk? The Position of 'Sinking States' at International Law," *14 Melbourne Journal of International Law* (2013), p. 367, 368.
356 UNGA Res. 63/213 of 10 February 2009, p. 2.
357 UNSC, *Maintenance of international peace and security: Impact of climate change: Letter dated 1 July 2011 from the Permanent Representative of Germany to the UN addressed to the Secretary-General (S/2011/408)*, 20 July 2011, p. 7.
358 Ibid., p. 18; same phrase used by Mr Marles (Australia), p. 24.
359 Ibid., p. 14.
360 Ibid., p. 28.
361 "Alliance of Small Island States Leaders' Declaration" (2012), p. 1.
362 UNGA, *Agenda item 8*, 2 October 2015, p. 8.
363 UNGA, *Integrated and coordinated implementation of and follow-up to the outcomes of the major UN conferences and summits in the economic, social and related fields*, 25 September 2015, p. 12.
364 UNGA, *Agenda item 8*, 3 October 2015, p. 11.
365 UNSC, *Peace and security challenges facing small island developing States*, 30 July 2015, p. 5.
366 Ibid., p. 31.
367 Ibid., p. 32.
368 UNSC, *Sixty-second year, 5,663rd meeting*, 17 April 2007, albeit the five veto powers are still divided among themselves as to whether the Security Council should deal with climate issues (cf. C. Schaller, T.-S. Schrader, "Der Anstieg des Meeresspiegels als Thema für den VN-Sicherheitsrat," SWP-Aktuell, Nr. 41, Juni 2020 (2020), p. 3).
369 UNSC, *Peace and security challenges facing small island developing States*, 30 July 2015.
370 Ibid., p. 59.
371 D. Wong, "Sovereignty Sunk? The Position of 'Sinking States' at International Law," *14 Melbourne Journal of International Law* (2013), p. 367, 368.
372 J. Barnett, "The dilemmas of normalising losses from climate change: Towards hope for Pacific atoll countries," *58 Asia Pacific Viewpoint* (2017), p. 5.
373 J. McAdam, *Climate Change, Forced Migration, and International Law* (2012), p. 138.
374 ILC, *Sea-level rise in relation to international law, First issues paper by Bogdan Aurescu and Nilüfer Oral, Co-Chairs of the Study Group on sea-level rise in relation to international law, Seventy-second session, 28 February 2020* (2020), p. 4 et seq.
375 W. W. Willoughby, *The Fundamental Concepts of Public Law* (1931), p. 63–4.
376 M. N. Shaw, *International Law* (2014), p. 352.
377 N. Negroponte, *Being digital* (1996); cf. J. Everard, *Virtual States: The Internet and the Boundaries of the Nation-state* (2000), p. 7.

378 A. V. Lowe, *International Law* (2007), p. 138; cf. D. Wong, "Sovereignty Sunk? The Position of 'Sinking States' at International Law," *14 Melbourne Journal of International Law* (2013), p. 367.
379 Ibid., p. 370.
380 D. B. Goldman, *Globalisation and the Western Legal Tradition: Recurring Patterns of Law and Authority* (2008), p. 141; S. Beaulac, *The Power of Language in the Making of International Law: The Word Sovereignty in Bodin and Vattel and the Myth of Westphalia* (2004), p. 77.
381 M. v. Seydel, *Grundzüge einer allgemeinen Staatslehre* (1873), p. 5.
382 UNSC, *Third Year, 383rd Meeting*, 2 December 1948, p. 11.
383 D. Wong, "Sovereignty Sunk? The Position of 'Sinking States' at International Law," *14 Melbourne Journal of International Law* (2013), p. 355.
384 J. Grote-Stoutenburg, *Disappearing Island States in International Law* (2015), p. 259; cf. T. Darsow, *Zum Wandel des Staatsbegriffs: Unter besonderer Berücksichtigung der Lehre und Praxis internationaler Organisationen, der Mikrostaaten und der PLO* (1984), p. 1.
385 P. M. Brown, "The Theory of the Independence and Equality of States," *9 AJIL* (1915), p. 317.
386 Cf. N. Schrijver, "The Impact of Climate Change: Challenges for International Law" in U. Fastenrath, R. Geiger, D.-E. Khan, A. Paulus, S. von Schorlemer, C. Vedder (eds), *From Bilateralism to Community Interest: Essays in Honour of Judge Bruno Simma* (2011), p. 1248–85.
387 Cf. A. El Ouali, *Territorial Integrity in a Globalizing World: International Law and States' Quest for Survival* (2012), p. 9-10, citing A. S. Hershey, *The Essentials of International Public Law* (1927), p. 230–1 and M. Sibert, *Traité de droit international public* (1951), p. 230.
388 D. Wong, "Sovereignty Sunk? The Position of 'Sinking States' at International Law," *14 Melbourne Journal of International Law* (2013), p. 384, citing Administrative Court of Cologne, *In re duchy of Sealand* (3 May 1978), p. 685.
389 J. L. Noto, "Creating a Modern Atlantis: Recognizing Submerging States and Their People," *62 Buffalo Law Review* (2014), p. 757, 784.
390 S. Atapattu, *Human Rights Approaches to Climate Change: Challenges and Opportunities* (2015), p. 235.
391 K. Angell, "New territorial rights for sinking island states," *20 (1) European Journal of Political Theory* (2021), p. 104 et seq.
392 L. Yamamoto and M. Esteban, *Atoll Island States and International Law: Climate Change Displacement and Sovereignty* (2014), p. 189 with further details; cf. D. Wong, "Sovereignty Sunk? The Position of 'Sinking States' at International Law," *14 Melbourne Journal of International Law* (2013), p. 360.
393 J. L. Kunz, "Identity of States under International Law," *49 AJIL* (1955), p. 72; G. Acquaviva, "Subjects of International Law: A Power-Based Analysis," *38 Vanderbilt Journal of Transnational Law* (2005), p. 359; cf. K. Marek, *Identity and Continuity of States in Public International Law* (1968), p. 48.
394 Cf. S. Atapattu, *Human Rights Approaches to Climate Change: Challenges and Opportunities* (2015), p. 241.
395 Ibid., p. 235.
396 S. Elden, *The Birth of Territory* (2013), p. 330.
397 Arguing for the loss of statehood: D. Wong, "Sovereignty Sunk? The Position of 'Sinking States' at International Law," *14 Melbourne Journal of International Law* (2013), p. 367; cf. S. Park, *Climate Change and the Risk of Statelessness: The Situation of Low-lying Island States* (2011), p. 6–8; cf. N. Bergmann, *Versinkende Inselstaaten: Auswirkungen des Klimawandels auf die Staatlichkeit kleiner Inselstaaten* (2016), p. 63 et seq., 138.
398 ICJ – The Hague, *Accordance with international law of the unilateral declaration of independence in respect of Kosovo* – Advisory Opinion – Separate opinion of Judge

Cançado Trindade (22 July 2010), p. 553 para. 77; cf. D.-E. Khan, "Territory and Boundaries" in B. Fassbender, A. Peters (eds), *The Oxford Handbook of the History of International Law* (2012), p. 248; cf. D. Wong, "Sovereignty Sunk? The Position of 'Sinking States' at International Law," *14 Melbourne Journal of International Law* (2013), p. 391.

399 J. L. Kunz, "Identity of States under International Law," *49 AJIL* (1955), p. 74.

400 A. Verdross, *Völkerrecht* (1950), p. 68; cf. K. Marek, *Identity and Continuity of States in Public International Law* (1968), p. 48.

401 H. Kelsen, *Hans Kelsen oder die Reinheit der Rechtslehre* (1988; ed. F. Koja), p. 76; H. Kelsen, *Allgemeine Staatslehre* (1925), p. 16.

402 H. Kelsen, General Theory of Law and State (1945/2007, translation by A. Wedberg), p. 364.

403 J. L. Kunz, "Identity of States under International Law," *49 AJIL* (1955), p. 74.

404 Cf. D. Wong, "Sovereignty Sunk? The Position of 'Sinking States' at International Law," *14 Melbourne Journal of International Law* (2013), p. 391.

405 R. Rayfuse, "Sea Level Rise and Maritime Zones: Preserving the Maritime Entitlements of 'Disappearing' States" in M. Gerrard, G. E. Wannier (eds), *Threatened Island Nations: Legal Implications of Rising Seas and a Changing Climate* (2013), p. 167; O. H. Pilkey and R. Young, *The rising sea* (2009), p. xi.

406 N. Myers, *Environmental Refugees: An Emergent Security Issue* (2005), p. 1; cf. N. Myers, "Environmental Refugees in a Globally Warmed World," *43 BioScience* (1993); cf. M. Gerrard and G. E. Wannier, "Overview" in M. Gerrard, G. E. Wannier (eds), *Threatened Island Nations: Legal Implications of Rising Seas and a Changing Climate* (2013), p. 5.

407 S. A. G. Jain, "The 21st Century Atlantis: The International Law of Statehood and Climate Change-Induced Loss of Territory," *50 Stanford Journal of International Law* (2014), p. 8 with further references; cf. J. McAdam, *Climate Change, Forced Migration, and International Law* (2012), p. 124; UNHCR, *Climate Change and Statelessness: An Overview* (2009), p. 2; D. H. Spennemann, "Water futures and their influence on sovereignty in the Marshall Islands" in D. Ghosh, H. Goodall, S. H. Donald (eds), *Water, Sovereignty and Borders in Asia and Oceania* (2009), p. 62 et seq. (for the Marshall Islands).

408 D. Wong, "Sovereignty Sunk? The Position of 'Sinking States' at International Law," *14 Melbourne Journal of International Law* (2013), p. 359 with further references; cf. J. Campbell, "Climate-Induced Community Relocation in the Pacific: The Meaning and Importance of Land" in J. McAdam (ed.), *Climate change and displacement: Multidisciplinary perspectives* (2010), p. 58 et seq.; J. McAdam, "'Disappearing States', Statelessness and the Boundaries of International Law" in J. McAdam (ed.), *Climate change and displacement: Multidisciplinary perspectives* (2010), p. 105; UNHCR, *Climate Change and Statelessness: An Overview* (2009), p. 2.

409 Cf. D. Wong, "Sovereignty Sunk? The Position of 'Sinking States' at International Law," *14 Melbourne Journal of International Law* (2013), p. 359; cf. C. Schofield, "Rising Waters, Shrinking States: The Potential Impacts of Sea Level Rise on Claims to Maritime Jurisdiction," *53 German Yearbook of International Law* (2010), p. 215.

410 E. Crawford and R. G. Rayfuse, "Climate Change, Sovereignty and Statehood," *11/59 Legal Studies Research Paper* (2011), p. 10 with further thoughts about total displacement.

411 UNGA, *Sixth Committee – Summary record of the 23rd meeting*, 14 November 2018, para. 63 (Fiji).

412 Cf. M. Sterio, "On the Right to External Self-Determination: 'Selfistans,' Secession and the Great Powers' Rule," *19 Minnesota Journal of International Law* (2010), p. 148 with further references.

413 Verwaltungsgericht Köln, *"Fürstentum Sealand"* (3 May 1978).
414 J. Grote-Stoutenburg, "When do States disappear? Thresholds of Effective Statehood and the Continued Recognition of 'Deterritorialized' Island States" in M. Gerrard, G. E. Wannier (eds), *Threatened Island Nations: Legal Implications of Rising Seas and a Changing Climate* (2013), p. 66.
415 Cf. J. McAdam, "'Disappearing States,' Statelessness and the Boundaries of International Law" in J. McAdam (ed.), *Climate change and displacement: Multidisciplinary perspectives* (2010), p. 126; M. A. Burkett, "The Nation Ex-Situ" in M. Gerrard, G. E. Wannier (eds), *Threatened Island Nations: Legal Implications of Rising Seas and a Changing Climate* (2013), p. 117, cf. J. Grote-Stoutenburg, *Disappearing Island States in International Law* (2015), p. 274.
416 S. Park, *Climate Change and the Risk of Statelessness: The Situation of Low-lying Island States* (2011), p. 1.
417 ICJ – The Hague, *Western Sahara Advisory Opinion* – Separate Opinion of Judge Dillard (16 October 1975), p. 122; cf. D. Wong, "Sovereignty Sunk? The Position of 'Sinking States' at International Law," *14 Melbourne Journal of International Law* (2013), p. 391.
418 I. Seidl-Hohenveldern, *Lexikon des Rechts* (2001), p. 380; T. Schweisfurth, *Völkerrecht* (2006), p. 10, § 25; F. von Liszt, *Das Völkerrecht: Systematisch dargestellt* (1913), p. 50.
419 J. D. Hestetune, *The Invading Waters: Climate Change Dispossession, State Extinction, and International Law* (2013), p. 32.
420 J. H. Hinzel, C. Jose and K. Wall, "Wo die Welt gerade untergeht," Süddeutsche Zeitung, 27 November 2015; J. H. Hinzel, C. Jose and K. Wall, "Der große Exodus," *Süddeutsche Zeitung*, 1 December 2015.
421 D. Wong, "Sovereignty Sunk? The Position of 'Sinking States' at International Law," *14 Melbourne Journal of International Law* (2013), p. 360.
422 M. A. Burkett, "The Nation Ex-Situ" in M. Gerrard, G. E. Wannier (eds), *Threatened Island Nations: Legal Implications of Rising Seas and a Changing Climate* (2013), p. 117.
423 Cf. D.-E. Khan, "Territory and Boundaries" in B. Fassbender, A. Peters (eds), *The Oxford Handbook of the History of International Law* (2012), p. 228.
424 O. Yiftachel, "Territory as the Kernel of the Nation: Space, Time and Nationalism in Israel/Palestine," *7 Geopolitics* (2002), p. 216 (with further references).
425 F. McConnell, "De facto, displaced, tacit: The sovereign articulations of the Tibetan Government-in-Exile," *28 Political Geography* (2009), p. 343.
426 Ibid., p. 346.
427 Ibid., p. 347; cf. F. McConnell, *Rehearsing the State: The Political Practices of the Tibetan Government-in-Exile* (2016), p. 140, 180.
428 F. McConnell, "De facto, displaced, tacit: The sovereign articulations of the Tibetan Government-in-Exile," *28 Political Geography* (2009), p. 348.
429 Ibid., p. 348.
430 Ibid., p. 346.
431 UNHCR, *Climate Change and Statelessness: An Overview* (2009), p. 2.
432 A. G. Jain, "The 21st Century Atlantis: The International Law of Statehood and Climate Change-Induced Loss of Territory," *50 Stanford Journal of International Law* (2014), p. 10; cf. A. James, *Sovereign Statehood: The Basis of International Society* (1986), p. 226–7.
433 Czechoslovak Military Court of Appeal in London, *Case 31 – Allied Forces (Czechoslovakia) Case* – Jurisdiction – territorial – exceptional Jurisdiction of foreign Courts within national territory – jurisdiction of Czechoslovak Military Courts on British Territory – English Allied Forces Act, 1940 (15 July 1942), p. 124.
434 UNHCR, *Climate Change and Statelessness: An Overview* (2009), p. 2.

435 Cf. N. Bergmann, *Versinkende Inselstaaten: Auswirkungen des Klimawandels auf die Staatlichkeit kleiner Inselstaaten* (2016), p. 100.

436 G. Acquaviva, "Subjects of International Law: A Power-Based Analysis," *38 Vanderbilt Journal of Transnational Law* (2005), p. 357, 358: "The British government recognized that the Transvaal was constituted by the 'emigrant farmers beyond the Vaal river'."

437 Ibid., p. 357, 359.

438 K. Knop, "Statehood: territory, people, government" in J. R. Crawford, M. Koskenniemi (eds), *The Cambridge Companion to International Law* (2012), p. 95.

439 L. Yamamoto and M. Esteban, *Atoll Island States and International Law: Climate Change Displacement and Sovereignty* (2014), p. 190; A. R. Harrington, "Is there a Right to Territory in International Law?" in J. C. Smith (ed.), *Property and Sovereignty: Legal and Cultural Perspectives* (2013), p. 72–3, citing: BBC NEWS, *Plan for new Maldives homeland* (2008).

440 Cf. A. Torres Camprubí, *Statehood under Water: Challenges of Sea-Level Rise to the Continuity of Pacific Island States* (2016), p. 107, citing L. Caramel, *Besieged by the rising tides of climate change, Kiribati buys land in Fiji* (2014); cf. A. R. Harrington, "Is there a Right to Territory in International Law?" in J. C. Smith (ed.), *Property and Sovereignty: Legal and Cultural Perspectives* (2013), p. 73, citing: N. Perry, *Entire Pacific nation could one day move to Fiji* (2012).

441 O. Yiftachel, "Territory as the Kernel of the Nation: Space, Time and Nationalism in Israel/Palestine," *7 Geopolitics* (2002), p. 216.

442 D.-E. Khan, "Territory and Boundaries" in B. Fassbender, A. Peters (eds), *The Oxford Handbook of the History of International Law* (2012), p. 226.

443 P. Heilborn, "Staaten und Staatenverbindungen" in K. Strupp (ed.), *Wörterbuch des Völkerrechts und der Diplomatie* (1925), p. 571; cf. M. Viroli, *Die Idee der republikanischen Freiheit: Von Machiavelli bis heute* (2002); p. 107, who argues that the idiosyncrasy comes first, seeing not such a big role in the territory.

444 G. W. White and E. A. White, *Nation, State, and Territory: Origins, Evolutions, and Relationships* (2007), p. 3.

445 J. R. Crawford, *Brownlie's Principles of Public International Law* (2012), p. 128; J. McAdam, *Climate Change, Forced Migration, and International Law* (2012), p. 124; D. Wong, "Sovereignty Sunk? The Position of 'Sinking States' at International Law," *14 Melbourne Journal of International Law* (2013), p. 359.

446 D. Wong, "Sovereignty Sunk? The Position of 'Sinking States' at International Law," *14 Melbourne Journal of International Law* (2013), p. 385.

447 S. Kadelbach, *Zwingendes Völkerrecht* (1992), p. 215; cf. P. M. Brown, "The Theory of the Independence and Equality of States," *9 AJIL* (1915), p. 321, stating that a continued existence might be ethically desirable, but not legally necessary.

448 UNGA Res. 25/2625 of 24 October 1970, p. 7.

449 Cf. D. Murswiek, "The Issue of a Right of Secession – Reconsidered" in C. Tomuschat (ed.), *Modern Law of Self-Determination* (1993), p. 25 et seq.

450 A. Cristescu, *The Right to Self-Determination: Historical and Current Development on the Basis of UN Instruments*, 1981, para. 173.

451 J. Grote-Stoutenburg, *Disappearing Island States in International Law* (2015), p. 297.

452 P. R. Williams, "What Makes a State? Territory," *106 Proceedings of the Annual Meeting (American Society of International Law)* (2012), p. 449.

453 O. T. Magoon, H. Converse, and L. T. Tobin, *Coastal Zone: Post-conference volume: third symposium on coastal and ocean management, Coastal Zone* (1984), p. 568, para. 28; ICJ – The Hague, *Legality of the threat or use of nuclear weapons* - Advisory Opinion (8 July 1996), p. 263; cf. J. Vidmar, "The Concept of the State and its Right of Existence," *4 Cambridge Journal of International and Comparative Law* (2015), p. 553.

454 Ibid., p. 562.
455 P. M. Brown, "The Theory of the Independence and Equality of States," *9 AJIL* (1915), p. 322.
456 D. Wong, "Sovereignty Sunk? The Position of 'Sinking States' at International Law," *14 Melbourne Journal of International Law* (2013), p. 376.
457 Ibid., p. 376.
458 D. S. Koller, "The End of Geography: The Changing Nature of the International System and the Challenge to International Law: A Reply to Daniel Bethlehem," *25 EJIL* (2014), p. 26; cf. T. M. Franck, *The Empowered Self: Law and Society in an Age of Individualism* (1999), speaking about "A World of 2000 States," p. 21 et seq.
459 D. Wong, "Sovereignty Sunk? The Position of 'Sinking States' at International Law," *14 Melbourne Journal of International Law* (2013), p. 376–7; citing I. Brownlie, *Principles of Public International Law* (2008), p. 78.
460 L. Yamamoto and M. Esteban, *Atoll Island States and International Law: Climate Change Displacement and Sovereignty* (2014), p. 212.
461 G. Poggi, *The Development of the Modern State: A Sociological Introduction* (1978), p. 88.
462 M. N. Shaw, *International Law* (2014), p. 352.
463 Ibid., p. 352; B. Finucane, "Fictitious States, Effective Control, and the Use of Force Against Non-State Actors," *30 Berkeley Journal of International Law* (2012), p. 40.
464 G. Poggi, *The Development of the Modern State: A Sociological Introduction* (1978), p. 89.
465 J. A. Andrews, "The Concept of Statehood and the Acquisition of Territory in the Nineteenth Century," *94 The Law Quarterly Review* (1978), p. 412.
466 T. M. Franck, *The Empowered Self: Law and Society in an Age of Individualism* (1999), p. 30–1, 76, 79, 92.
467 M. N. Shaw, *International Law* (2014), p. 352.
468 D. Vidas, "Sea-Level Rise and International Law," *4 Climate Law* (2014), p. 84.
469 J. R. Crawford, The Creation of States in International Law (2006), p. 715.
470 I. Ziemele, "State, Extinction of," (last updated March 2009) in R. Wolfrum (ed.), *The Max Planck Encyclopedia of Public International Law: opil.ouplaw.com.home/EPIL* (2012), para. 3; cf. K. Marek, *Identity and Continuity of States in Public International Law* (1968), p. 7–9.
471 N. Schrijver, "The Impact of Climate Change: Challenges for International Law" in U. Fastenrath, R. Geiger, D.-E. Khan, A. Paulus, S. von Schorlemer, C. Vedder (eds), *From Bilateralism to Community Interest: Essays in Honour of Judge Bruno Simma* (2011), p. 1285.
472 K. Knop, "Statehood: territory, people, government" in J. R. Crawford, M. Koskenniemi (eds), *The Cambridge Companion to International Law* (2012), p. 100, 101.
473 Cf. A. Abass, *Complete International Law: Text, Cases, and Materials* (2014), p. 263.
474 P. R. Williams, "What Makes a State? Territory," *106 Proceedings of the Annual Meeting (American Society of International Law)* (2012), p. 449.
475 T. M. Franck, *The Empowered Self: Law and Society in an Age of Individualism* (1999), p. 30–1; for the global city, s. H. P. Aust, *Das Recht der globalen Stadt: Grenzüberschreitende Dimensionen kommunaler Selbstverwaltung* (2017), p. 52 et seq.
476 H. Bull, *The Anarchical Society: A Study of Order in World Politics* (2012), p. 265.
477 J. R. Crawford, *The Creation of States in International Law* (2006), p. 4.
478 J. D. Hestetune, *The Invading Waters: Climate Change Dispossession, State Extinction, and International Law* (2013), p. 49.
479 Cf. International Law Association, Committee on International Law and Sea Level Rise, "Issues of Statehood and International Legal Personality in the Case of Total

Loss of State Territory or Its Becoming Permanently Uninhabitable" in D. Vidas, D. Freestone, J. McAdam (eds), *Report of the International Law Association* (2019), p. 41 et seq.

480 E. Crawford and R. G. Rayfuse, "Climate Change, Sovereignty and Statehood," *11/59 Legal Studies Research Paper* (2011), p. 12.

481 J. Grote-Stoutenburg, "When do States disappear? Thresholds of Effective Statehood and the Continued Recognition of 'Deterritorialized' Island States" in M. Gerrard, G. E. Wannier (eds), *Threatened Island Nations: Legal Implications of Rising Seas and a Changing Climate* (2013), p. 58.

4 What it means to be a State – the emergence of the modern State and its significance today

States were the original, and remain, the primary actors in the international legal system.[1] They are the only "born" or "natural" persons of international law and the only entities enjoying sovereign equality.[2] However, the "State," as such a relatively recent phenomenon, is a feature of modern times, initially European.[3]

While there are also other subjects of international law that appeared on the international stage,[4] it is fair to say that "[w]e live in a world of states."[5] The State is the "fundamental concept and building block"[6] of our current system of international law. One can ask, with Craven, "why has statehood come to assume such a central and powerful role in the world today, in which there appears 'no alternative' to either being part of a State or the object of its coercive power?"[7] The term "State" came into political and legal vocabulary in parallel with the "gradual growth of the idea of an entity, which would simultaneously be the source of its own legitimacy and the cradle of every public power that it would exercise under that name."[8] It "became, especially as it derived from the same cultural context as Machiavelli, the name par excellence of the territorial political organization."[9] However, the State as such is changing in accordance with the developments of the world around it. Higgins points out in this regard:

> In a rapidly changing world, the definition of "a state" has remained virtually unchanged and continues to be well described by the traditional provisions of the Montevideo Convention on the Rights and Duties of States. [...] But it should not be thought that, because the formal definition of statehood has remained unchanged, the concept of statehood is rigid and immutable. Its component elements have always been interpreted flexibly, depending on the circumstances and the context in which the claim of statehood is made.[10]

There is an increasingly diametrically opposed relationship between the territorial nature of the States which still form the basic feature of the international system and trans-territorial or non-territorial problems of today's world order. Hence, Mathews argued:

> [T]he clash between the fixed geography of states and the nonterritorial nature of today's problems and solutions, which is only likely to escalate, strongly suggests that the relative power of states will continue to decline.[11]

DOI: 10.4324/9781003263593-4

This chapter shall therefore investigate what it means to be a State in the twenty-first century by taking a look at the challenges the modern State faces in the current world order. This examination is important because, after having found out that States are actually threatened in their existence due to the rising sea, one should explore what it actually means when a *State* is threatened. Therefore, it will be interesting to investigate the importance of territory in the course of time (which is the element most threatened by the rising sea) and the importance of the individual (which is factually but not imperatively dependent on territory).

Rights of a modern State

The modern State has developed and has become the dominant form of territorial subject all over the world and "the fundamental unit of legal personality in the international legal system."[12] Yet, despite "statehood" being without a question "an attractive status,"[13] Crawford argues that "statehood does not involve any inherent substantive rights."[14] However, he lists five "exclusive and general legal characteristics of States:"[15]

(1) States have plenary competence to perform acts, make treaties and so on, in the international sphere.
(2) States are exclusively competent with respect to their internal affairs, a principle reflected by Article 2(7) of the UN Charter – "exclusive" means plenary and not subject to control by other States.
(3) States are not subject to international process without their consent.
(4) States are regarded in international law as "equal," a principle reflected by Article 2(1) of the UN Charter. it is a formal, not a moral or political, principle.
(5) States are entitled to benefit from the Lotus presumption, especially that any derogation from the previous principles must be clearly established.[16]

According to Crawford, "[t]hese five principles [...] constitute in legal terms the core of the concept of statehood, the essence of the special position of States in general international law."[17] And under these principles, States certainly do have rights. Often States' rights are associated with their territorial sovereignty.[18] As such, it is important that States have the power to enact, amend, or terminate rules of international law in accordance with the processes of international law, a right as such not explicitly stated by the aforementioned Draft Declaration. The State as an independent entity is also entitled to pursue its own projects and the international system as a pluralistic union recognizes this independence. The legal independence of each State is also strengthened by the fact that a State is protected from binding "legislative" or judicial proceedings by the requirement of the State's consent in each case, which is, as State immunity, a customary law principle of international law. The principles also establish formal equality between States. This right is enshrined in Art. 2(1) of the Charter. It means, among other things, that all States gain the same from these principles. In the end, these principles are a strong self-preservation mechanism for the State as such, and the importance of the "statehood" status since any change or deviation from these principles requires – again— the consent of the State.[19]

Together the rights and duties established through these principles find themselves in one way or another also in the Draft Declaration on Rights and Duties of States prepared by the International Law Commission (ILC)[20] and the Declaration on Principles of International Law concerning Friendly Relations and Cooperation among States in accordance with the Charter of the UN.[21]

The ILC covered four rights:

> The rights are those of independence, comprehending the right of the State to exercise freely all its legal powers, including the choice of its form of government; of jurisdiction over State territory in accordance with international law; of equality in law; and of self-defence, individual or collective, against armed attack.[22]

In addition, the ILC speaks of ten duties:

> The duties [...] include the duty of the State to conduct its international relations in accordance with international law and to observe its legal obligations. They also include the duty to settle disputes by peaceful means and in accordance with law and justice, and to refrain from intervention and from resorting to war or other illegal use of force. The duties of refraining from assisting any State resorting to war or other illegal use of force, or any State against which the UN is taking preventive or enforcement action, and of refraining from recognizing any territorial acquisition resulting from war or other illegal use of force, are likewise stated as corollaries of the foregoing. And, finally, there are set out the duties of the State to refrain from fomenting civil strife in the territory of other State and to prevent the organized incitement thereof from within its own territory; to ensure in general that conditions in its territory do not menace international peace and order; and to treat all persons within its jurisdiction with due respect for human rights and fundamental freedoms for all, without distinction as to race, sex, language, or religion.[23]

Kelsen criticized that

> [c]ertain rights and duties formulated in the draft Declaration are evidently not established by existing general international law, but by the Charter of the UN; as, for instance, the duty to settle disputes by peaceful means, formulated in Article 8 of the draft Declaration. Some rights and duties, formulated in conformity with the Charter, have a narrower scope than the corresponding right or duty established by general international law; as, for instance, the right of self-defense, stipulated in Article 12 of the draft Declaration. The duty to treat persons with respect for human rights and fundamental

> freedoms, laid down in Article 6 of the draft Declaration, even goes beyond the duties established by the Charter.[24]

Even more "problematical in view of the number and variety of principles and rules it embodies,"[25] however unanimously adopted by the UN General Assembly among the events celebrating the 25th anniversary of the UN is the *Declaration on Principles of International Law concerning Friendly Relations and Cooperation among States in accordance with the Charter of the UN*.[26]

Speaking of the UN General Assembly, also membership in international organizations is largely reserved for States – and thus a factual right of a State. For example, even though the founding members of the UN were aware of the fact that several of the participants at the San Francisco Conference were not "States" in an international legal sense, they made clear that for members admitted later, being a State was a constitutive feature.[27] This was different at the time of the Covenant of the League of Nations,[28] where also non-State "members" were enabled to become members (back then, particularly the British Dominions).[29] Today, "[n]ot being a State is to be denied independent access to those forums that States – themselves or through international organizations – still control."[30] The same applies to the ICJ, where, according to Art. 34(1) of the Statute of the ICJ, only States have standing. In addition, States have the power (but not the right) to establish diplomatic relations with other States.[31] And, last but not least, the State is the only association whose existence does not depend on other powers. Moreover, according to Möllers, the State's universal task of order is necessary, not only possible, as are the tasks of order limited to individual questions of fact.[32]

Also, Nicholson argues that "merely by virtue of being defined as a state, a state has more rights than" those in the Friendly Relations Declaration, etc.: "It has legal relations in every area of customary international law," which cannot be "exhaustively listed; they are in flux."[33]

However, Warbrick restricts that "[t]he development of rules which create other categories of international person means that [the enjoyment of plentitude of rights and duties in international law] is no longer the case."[34] Developments in this context indeed challenge the contemporary concept of the State:

Challenges for the contemporary concept of a State

Various commentators have already suggested that the very concept of the nation State is outdated.[35] As such, Carl Schmitt famously said in 1963:

> The era of the State is coming to an end. No need to waste a word on that. … The State as the model of political unity, the State as the bearer … of the monopoly of political decision … is becoming dethroned.[36]

Others assume, that "[i]t is possible that the attention being given today to the State portends that its dusk is not far ahead."[37] Thus, indeed, the State is not taken for granted anymore.[38]

Many others argue contrarily:

> States continue, and will long if not always continue, to be the basic units of organization of the international community […].[39]

And indeed, the claim that the territorial State is on its last legs may be exaggerated.[40] Alvarez says:

> The Westphalian system may be a blink of an eye in the scope of human history but we are living in its time. No one unfortunate enough to be outside Koskenniemi's "wonderful artificiality" of statehood believes that it is a myth [or withering away[41]]. Ask a Palestinian.[42]

Undeniably, a view into world politics shows how "being (or having) a State still matters." As such, Schrijver mentions the

> wave of self-determination movements evident in the former socialist countries (former Yugoslavia, former Czechoslovakia, Chechnya), industrialized countries (Scotland, Quebec, Catalonia) and developing countries (Eritrea, Palestine, Indonesian provinces) [which] is grounded in a desire for greater autonomy or ultimately even the establishment of a sovereign State.[43]

Disaffected ethnic and religious groups rarely claim to create a form of organization that is universalistic or based on translocal affinity, but mainly wish to form a territorial and sovereign *State* of their own.[44] Thus, as Nijman puts it: the "end-of-the-State theories turn a blind eye to reality."[45] Hence, it is rather unlikely that the State as such will disappear in the foreseeable future.[46]

Nevertheless, it is probably not exaggerated to argue, that today the description by Hall from 1880

> States [...] are independent beings, subject to no control, and owning no superior; no person or body of persons exists to whom authority has been delegated to declare law for the common good; a State is only bound by rules which it feels itself obliged in conscience after reasonable examination to submit.[47]

is not entirely valid anymore. The concept of *sovereignty* was understood as describing a status of being, by definition, above the law, and therefore legally unbindable.[48] The monarch had to have authoritative control over feudal princes in order to prevent instability and disorder, seen as obstacles to a stable society. The conflicts of the time were seen as only to be overcome by strong governments that would establish "firm and effective 'sovereignty' over territory and populations."[49]

Lillich suggests that such a "concept of sovereignty in international law is an idea whose time has come and gone."[50] He advances three major premises: first he argues that humanity must be "the *raison d'être* of any legal system." Second, he criticizes how the international system for over 300 years, since the Peace of Westphalia, has not been fulfilling what should be "its primary function, namely, the protection and development of the human dignity of the individual." And last, but not least, he demands

> that any proposed "new world order" should be structured so as to maximize benefits not for States but for individuals living within States, all the way from freedom of speech and elections, on the one hand, to freedom from hunger and the right to education on the other hand.[51]

Sovereignty (still) is "the one and only organising principle in respect of the dry surface of the globe"[52] and "the basic constitutional doctrine of the law of nations, which governs a community consisting primarily of states having, in principle, a uniform legal personality."[53] But the unlimitedly sovereign State developed to a primarily territorially defined entity which nowadays is bound by various obligations from international law.[54] Phlogaitēs states as such that the "glorious times" of the unlimitedly sovereign State "were mainly the eighteenth and the nineteenth centuries, because in that period they became rationalized, well organized, and powerful and were respected by both citizens and the international world."[55] Sovereignty "was conceived to be 'all or nothing,' i.e., either unlimited or non-existent." It could not be questioned, neither from inside nor from outside.[56] Today, such a "state does not exist anymore [...], because the states have created an international community, composed of states and international organizations, but also of all sorts of other international players, including individuals."[57]

Moreover, there has been a profound change in the international legal order which leads some authors to proclaim the so-called post-Westphalian order whose main characteristics are "interdependence" and "co-operation" in comparison to the Westphalian order that was characterized by "independence" and "co-existence."[58] Indeed, both the individual human being and the international organization have increasingly found recognition in rules of international law as (acting) "entities" which are more than mere "creatures" of the sovereign States.[59] In particular, the experience of two world wars played a major role in enabling this gradual shift away from the pure doctrine of self-binding and self-interest.[60]

Thus, while the State might well remain a significant, perhaps even the most significant, actor on the international stage, a certain shift is undeniable. There is "a parallel impact of the global (macro) and local (micro) at the expense of the meso (state) level of political and territorial ordering."[61] Two major developments have thereby shaped the international system and with it the national State– on the one hand, *humanization* and, on the other, *globalization*. Schrijver describes those developments as the challenge from "bottom-up" (particularly the growing international recognition of the rights and claims of individuals and peoples) and the challenge "top-down" (States deciding to transfer certain aspects of their national sovereignty to supranational organizations seeking to retain control over the exercise of the powers so transferred and generally being tied together in an ever tighter global net).[62] Thus, while "[i]t can hardly be denied that the state remains a political institution of utmost importance,"[63] "both external [globalization] and internal [humanization] pressures have put state structures under strain."[64] The developments

> have called into question the ability of the Western state – as a distinctive regime form – to adequately provide the normative goods that have traditionally been used to justify its existence: peace and physical security, liberty and legal certainty, democracy and self-determination, economic growth and social welfare.[65]

They are gradually and inexorably eroding the authority of States.[66]

Bethlehem speaks of

> a pretty formidable array of challenges, which in many respects, and certainly in scale, go beyond Westphalian conceptions of society and Westphalian conceptions of international law. While states will continue to be key instruments of international interaction, organization, and law-making for a considerable time to come, and notions of sovereignty, jurisdiction, and territoriality will continue to inform our approach to new challenges, we will have to move beyond our traditional notions of Westphalia if we are to engage effectively with these challenges.[67]

This shall be looked at in the following sections:

Humanization – the increasing importance of the individual

At least since 1648 there had been an explicit assumption that the international system is an association of sovereign States where the State is the "sole actor in the international order." The individual has meaning solely through association with a State via its citizenship or nationality.[68] Thus, traditional inter*national* law was – despite its name which refers to the nation – essentially a law between sovereign territorial *States*.[69] The treatment of citizens was seen as an internal matter of the respective State.[70] It was one of the "firm bulwarks of national sovereignty" over which other States had no say. This had a stabilizing influence over international relations in comparison to the time before the Peace of Westphalia.[71] The only violations that "mattered" extraterritorially (in terms of the injury done not to the individual but to the State of his nationality) were violations of rights of aliens. Those, however, were regulated on the inter-State level through diplomatic protection.[72]

This changed considerably after WWII, which had featured a massive betrayal of the lives and liberties of persons. A "tectonic shift"[73] occurred – away from the "state-centric focus of international law" towards a new system characterized by the emergence of new actors and the internationalization of the protection of human rights, as well as an increasing interdependence between States.[74] Trindade speaks of "an extraordinary development, which gradually took the shape of an historical process of its [International Law] humanization."[75] There was a "transition from a culture of violence to a more enlightened culture of peace" and a "transition from a culture of sovereign impunity to a culture of national and international accountability"[76] – in particular with respect to the treatment of individuals. As Lillich points out, topics like "The Individual in international law" have become almost commonplace since WWII in academic literature.[77] Whereas beforehand, international law was essentially silent on the question of human rights, the Charter of the UN proclaimed as one of its principle purposes "[t]o achieve international co-operation in solving international problems of an economic, social, cultural, or humanitarian character, and in promoting and encouraging respect for human rights and for fundamental freedoms for all without distinction as to race, sex, language, or religion."[78] Human rights became internationalized.[79] The world "witnessed a gradual shift in that balance, making respect for human rights more and more mandatory and respect for sovereignty less and less stringent."[80] Out of the desire to prevent the recurrence of such crimes against humanity through development of an international system for the protection of human rights, individuals got international rights. And the punishment of war criminals at Nuremberg and Tokyo, on the other hand, showed that individuals also bear international duties.[81] This "international criminal liability of even a high State official is not matched by equivalent criminal liability of his State,"[82] as Warbrick points out. Thus, "[r]esponsibility for violations of international law is not limited to responsibility by States but includes responsibility by individuals."[83]

> Just as the French Revolution ended the divine rights of kings, the human rights revolution that began at the 1945 San Francisco Conference of the UN has deprived the sovereign states of the lordly privilege of being the sole possessors of rights under international law. States have had to concede to ordinary human beings the status of subjects of international law, to concede that individuals are no longer mere objects, mere pawns in the hands of states.[84]

Hence, human beings became at least partly subjectivized.[85] The shift becomes visible already in the preamble of the Charter of the UN.[86] It is written in the name of "we the peoples," reaffirming "faith in fundamental human rights, in the dignity and worth of the human person."[87] Then US President Carter pointed out:

> All the signatories of the U.N. Charter have pledged themselves to observe and to respect basic human rights. Thus, no member of the UN can claim that mistreatment of its citizens is solely its own business.[88]

Hence, even though the UN is an organization of States, "masses of individuals rather than states constitute the basic element of the organization."[89] The UN General Assembly is charged with the supervision of international cooperation and with assisting in "the realization of human rights and fundamental freedoms for all."[90]

Today, "every single State in the world has ratified at least one human rights treaty that imposes legal obligations on them."[91] The starting point of the story of the humanization of international law was therefore 1945–1948.[92] The Universal Declaration of Human Rights that was established shortly afterwards in 1948 by the UN General Assembly is "one of the greatest political statements in world history."[93] A qualitatively unique system emerged. For the first time ever, governments internationally agreed among themselves to abide by these proclamations.[94] Human rights became an international concern and thereby – so to say – stepped out of the internal affairs of a sovereign State. A big step in this transition was certainly the emergence of the human rights treaties of the 1960s and 1970s. "[T]here was an evolving human rights narrative, which formed the foundation for the notion of an international or collective responsibility to protect people [...]."[95] "No longer is an individual's international protection limited to the state of his nationality and subject to its whims."[96]

Something interesting in this regard is the resolution on "The Protection of Human Rights and the Principle of Non-intervention in Internal Affairs of States"[97] of the Institut de Droit International from 1989 which states in its Art. 1:

> Human rights are a direct expression of the dignity of the human person. The obligation of States to ensure their observance derives from the recognition of this dignity as proclaimed in the Charter of the UN and in the Universal Declaration of Human Rights.
>
> This international obligation, as expressed by the International Court of Justice, is *erga omnes*; it is incumbent upon every State in relation to the international community as a whole, and every State has a legal interest in the protection of human rights. The obligation further implies a duty of solidarity among all States to ensure as rapidly as possible the effective protection of human rights throughout the world.

Some argue, though, that the subjectivity of an individual under international law can only be seen as such if there is an international treaty providing a procedure under which the individual can make his own claims. Emerging new jurisdictions do allow citizens to take their grievances outside of the State territory.[98] An example for such a procedure is Art. 34 of the European Convention on Human Rights[99] which provides for an individual complaints mechanism. Individuals can complain about violations through their respective State at the European Court for Human Rights which is furnished in this regard with decisive power, meaning its decisions are considered binding on the concerned States. Internationally, there is no such possibility (yet).[100] However, international organizations, such as the International Labour Organization and the World Bank, develop procedures that allow complaints by individuals.[101] Human beings have started "having recourse to the international tribunal, to protect [themselves] by norms of International Law from the arbitrariness of the State."[102] Some human rights have gained the status of obligations *erga omnes*, meaning that the State does not only have to subject itself under the provisions with respect to the individual, but also internationally. At least with regard to such rights, a (partial) subjectivity is to be presumed.[103]

Generally, acknowledging that human rights are a legitimate concern of the international community has a direct effect on State sovereignty: one aspect of each State's control and authority over its activities on its territory and within its jurisdiction is now subject to international legal review.[104] Thus, up until the end of WWII, sovereignty was used as a kind of curtain behind which it was not allowed to do anything, but behind which it was basically possible to do anything, because it was not being looked behind by other States.[105]

While the global community is still dominated by States,[106] tensions began to emerge between the idea of the international promotion of human rights and the prevailing understanding of sovereignty.[107] In 1933, Goebbels is reported to having responded to critics concerning the treatment of Jews in Germany that "[a] man is master in his own home."[108] Such concept of unlimited sovereignty was being questioned with a view to the experience of the two world wars.[109]

According to Henkin, the hated "S" word [sovereignty] needed to be banned from polite lawyerly discourse.[110] Sovereignty as such became seen as either redundant or as a dangerous fiction, and "Statism" a derogatory label attached to any approach to international law that prioritizes what States do or say "at the expense of individuals and communities over whom they hold authority."[111] In retrospect, it was seen "as having paved the way for the two World Wars."[112]

> Examples of the illegitimacy of premising international legal norms on the Westphalian primacy of the sovereign state have reached a point at which the question is not whether the focus should shift from national sovereignty to human security, but rather how this normative shift should be formulated.[113]

The emergence of international human rights law after WWII thoroughly transformed this old concept.[114] Hence, Art. 14 of the 1949 ILC Draft Declaration on Rights and Duties of States reads quite differently from what was accepted as law beforehand:

> Every State has the duty to conduct its relations with other States in accordance with international law and with the principle that the sovereignty of each State is subject to the *supremacy* of international law.[115]

It is now a matter of legitimate international concern how a State treats its citizens within its borders.[116] The core content of the principle of sovereignty is no longer the right to control territory, but the responsibility towards its inhabitants.[117] Thereby, "the traditional relationship between the state and the citizen [...] has been reversed."[118] States became expected to be "the servants of their peoples, and not vice versa."[119] Today, neither State sovereignty nor the principle of non-interference should provide a shield behind which human rights could be massively violated.[120] Tomuschat stated in this regard:

> Must national sovereignty be understood as the paramount rule of international law that overrides any other value? Giving an affirmative response to

these two questions would totally deprive international law of its essential value content.[121]

Similarly, the ICTY stated in its Tadić decision of 1995:

> It would be a travesty of law and a betrayal of the universal need for justice, should the concept of State sovereignty be allowed to be raised successfully against human rights. Borders should not be considered as a shield against the reach of the law and as a protection for those who trample underfoot the most elementary rights of humanity.[122]

Hence, States are no longer "sovereign" in the sense of being entitled to act at liberty on their own territory and with respect to their own nations.[123] Juridically, "little remains of the traditional sovereignty of states."[124] There has been some sort of a return of the ideas of natural law which had disappeared in the positivist international legal order of the nineteenth and early twentieth centuries. Paragraphs 4 and 7 of Art. 2 of the Charter (and probably also Art. 2(1)) that demand for adherence with the sovereignty of other States, the prohibition of the use of force and the prohibition to intervene[125] are counterbalanced by an elaborate body of international human rights. Thus, "if the Charter were to be written today, there would be an Article 2.8 saying that nothing contained in the present Charter shall authorize Member States to terrorize their own people."[126] Therefore, the international protection of human rights imposes the idea of an emerging constitutional system on the traditional notion of sovereignty.[127] State sovereignty is thereby limited by human rights and should even "be seen to exist only in function of humanity." Therefore, Peters suggests, that "conflicts between state sovereignty and human rights should not be approached in a balancing process in which the former is played off against the latter on an equal footing, but should be tackled on the basis of a presumption in favour of humanity."[128]

This leads Peters to announce that "[t]oday, human rights have come to outrank sovereignty."[129] Schachter points out that some international lawyers maintain that the principle of sovereignty is no longer relevant at all in regard to the human rights which have been internationalized and refers to Henkin, who says:[130]

> Mankind, and States that represent it in the international system, recognised and commited to additional values and to institutions of governance to realise them. To invoke the myth of "sovereignty" to frustrate those human values and those institutions, is reactionary and archaic. There is no place for such mythology in the world order of the twenty-first Century.[131]

Secretaries-General Javier Pérez de Cuéllar and Boutros Boutros-Ghali were at the forefront of calls for a redefinition of sovereignty in the early 1990s, building on developments in the international promotion of human rights in the 1970s and 1980s.[132] The human rights policy of the Carter administration "strongly contributed to eroding the domestic jurisdiction argument, to redefining sovereignty as a form of responsibility to one's citizens, promoting international pressure on behalf of human rights and to demonstrating willingness to subject violating states to a range of penalties."[133] The humanization of sovereignty thus appears to open the way for humanitarian interventions,[134] which probably shows the most radical shift of powers of the State towards needs and rights of the individual.[135] In this regard, the adoption of the doctrine of "responsibility to protect" (*R2P*) as an inevitable step in this progression, shall be mentioned.[136] In 2005, the UN World Summit Agreement "was something of a watershed moment for humanitarian intervention"[137] and a big further step towards responsible sovereignty. "[T]he concept of R2P takes human needs as a starting point and shifts the focus from states' rights to states' obligations (or responsibilities)."[138]

> While continuing to recognize sovereignty as the basis for the international system, new thinking began to emphasize the responsibility of states to provide for the security and well-being of their populations and the obligation of the international community to become involved when governments fail in these responsibilities, putting large numbers at risk.[139]

As such, in 2011, the Security Council authorized, for the first time, the use of force against a functioning sovereign State, Libya, without its consent, for the purpose of protecting civilians from mass atrocities, which was indeed a drastic departure from the Cold War understanding of sovereignty.[140] Other internationally authorized actions against sovereign States for the protection of people had taken place in Somalia, Liberia, Cote d'Ivoire, Congo, Bosnia and Herzegovina, and Rwanda. Additionally, there was forcible pro-democratic action in Haiti and last, but not least, the establishment of international criminal tribunals in relation to Yugoslavia and Rwanda.[141] Thus, the concept of solidarity between the members of the international community has qualified the criticized concept of unlimited sovereignty significantly.[142] So if sovereignty in the traditional Westphalian sense is interpreted as the supreme authority within a territory, there was a big change towards a concept based on human security and social justice, consequently carrying with it responsibilities to protect people.[143]

However, the idea, that sovereignty entails responsibility is not new but "has deep historical roots."[144] Sovereign authority has always been understood to involve varied and evolving responsibilities since it was first articulated in the sixteenth and seventeenth century.[145] Peters cites Hobbes saying

> The obligation of Subjects to the Soveraign, is understood to last as long, and no longer, than the power lasteth, by which he is able to protect them.[146]

The State was conceived as artificially created "for our ends, our protection and defense."[147] Thus, the "absolute and exclusive sovereignty [...] was in fact never so absolute as it was conceived to be in theory."[148] Even Bodin's doctrine of absolute sovereignty was no defense of tyranny; it was absolute in the sense that it was supreme and irresistible, but absolute authority did not equate to arbitrary authority. It rather entailed both rights and responsibilities.[149] Hence, according to Glanville, the sovereign right of non-interference was held from its earliest articulation in tension with responsibilities to eschew tyranny and oppression, as can be seen from Vattel and Pufendorf.[150] Thus, whether the change towards the emerging "responsible sovereignty" is as dramatic as some authors describe it,[151] is debatable.[152] It appears that the shift from sovereignty as control to sovereignty as responsibility was "less radical than suggested by its history."[153]

Certainly, though, the focus in the law of State responsibility has shifted. It did so from bilateralism to community interest:[154] Today, in order to evoke State responsibility, bilaterally felt damage is not necessary anymore. Violating the rights of individuals is "sufficient."[155] Whereas "[o]ne hundred years ago, there could be no doubt that the specific relationship between a State and its citizens came under its exclusive domestic jurisdiction,"[156] the protection of human rights gradually became an international duty. Thereby, what happens inside a State could become of concern for other States when human rights were concerned.[157]

Human rights "are intended to shield individuals even against their own governments: A concept hitherto virtually unknown in international law and state practice."[158] They are "the yardstick by which the lawfulness of the conduct of States vis-à-vis their citizens is measured."[159] Yet, it is still an "unfinished revolution." Pulling away the curtain does not *per se* lead to a change in the practice. Violations of human rights have not stopped occurring. But since 1948, they cannot hide easily in the darkness anymore, which is "not a bad beginning."[160]

While in 1947 the UN Commission on Human Rights noted that it had "no power to take any action in regard to any complaints concerning human rights,"[161] by 2006, the Human Rights Council as the successor body to the Commission was able to adopt the undertaking of a universal periodic review[162] of the human rights of all UN member States. This is an extraordinary evolution in thinking from a strict State-centered system in which sovereignty was absolute to one in which the behavior of States towards their own citizens became a matter of international concern and scrutiny.[163] In the end, "States are no more than instruments whose inherent function it is to serve the interests of their citizens as legally expressed in human rights."[164]

Traditional concepts of peace and security have also changed in the course of humanization: Recent Security Council practice shows a tendency to "humanize" the "threat to international peace and security" as conceived under Chapter VII of the UN Charter: It assimilates the distress of civil populations and the flagrant and systematic violation of human rights (in other words, any overwhelming humanitarian crisis) to a threat to international peace and security.[165] The international community sees itself bound to the pursuit of common goals, such as peace and security, whereby it is understood that international protection of human rights and the maintenance of world peace were inextricably connected.[166] This is interesting: While, traditionally, the concept of international security was perceived as primarily a problem of State security, an additional concept has emerged – that of human security, acknowledging that threats cannot only come from States and non-State actors, but can also exist to the security of both, States and the people.[167]

The jurisdiction of the ICJ shows signs of the "humanization of the World Court," too.[168] While the case law of its predecessor, the Permanent Court of International Justice, "can only be described as pronouncedly deferential to national sovereignty,"[169] the ICJ "has become a major player in a process in which human rights and general international law mutually impact upon one another: human rights 'modernize' international law, while international law 'mainstreams,' or 'domesticates,' human rights."[170]

The transformation of the individual within international law is ongoing: Some argue the individual is transforming "from subject of international law to international citizen" which is a "part of the transformation of the international legal system from a Vattelian inter-state system into a universal constitutional democracy in which the individual is not only imputed with international rights and duties but in which he is (directly) represented."[171]

At a regional level, there are developments in such a direction: The Maastricht Treaty created a "citizenship of the Union" which gives legal expression to broader political identifications going beyond the State of the individual's nationality. European citizens enjoy freedom of movement and residence in the entire Community. Moreover, they are – irrespective of the place of residence within the Community – allowed to participate in local elections and in elections for the European Parliament.[172] As such, "EU law recognises that *individuals*, to be 'free and equal,' must be capable ('sovereign') of exercising human rights and developing personal autonomy in economic, social and political affairs across frontiers."[173]

For the international level, Anne Peters suggests a General Assembly representing natural persons.[174] Andreas Paulus points out that a liberal concept of international community focuses on individual rights and duties. Thus, "[l]iberals and neoliberals demand a reconstruction of international law on an inter-individual basis."[175] While Kant described the "world citizen" as early as 1903 as "no high-flown or exaggerated notion,"[176] he was still careful in distinguishing between *jus gentium* (providing something like a constitutional order among States) and *jus cosmopoliticum* (providing rules for the relationships between individuals and foreign States).[177] Crawford is less optimistic with regard to developments towards a more individual-focused "constitution;" yet he accepts that "the possibility that international law might develop in these directions cannot be ruled out, major changes to the system would be required."[178] Indeed, as Simma points out, "international law is developing, [… but …] one must not forget that traditionally patterned, bilaterist international law still constitutes the basis on which the new developments are taking shape – and a rather pertinacious basis at that."[179]

Franck aims for "an individualism that empowers each person to define his or her own unique identity protected by a new regime of national and international laws."[180]

Thereby, the individual becomes increasingly independent.

> [...] individual sovereignty – and by this I mean the human rights and fundamental freedoms enshrined in our charter – has been enhanced by a renewed consciousness of the right of every individual to control his or her own destiny.[181]

Thus, today, there are various loyalties which compete with the loyalty to the State. Facilitated by the communications revolution, there is a "growing awareness of new affinity options" based neither on shared genes nor on territoriality:[182] Franck lists environmentalists, human rights activists, women, children, animal rights advocates, consumers, disabled, gays, indigenous people, Mafiosi, drug smugglers, terrorists who have "all gone international." Indeed, individuals identify themselves increasingly according to social and political solidarity with others on an autonomous basis instead of exogenous or preordained affiliations such as their race or nationality.[183] They are seeking new forms of organization, asserting their identities in different ways – on the local, regional, and international level.[184] With it comes an "emerging right to individuality."[185] The "new individualists" "see themselves as the alien other, in opposition to the old territorially determined communal identity."[186] This does not mean that the individual's relationship with his State, nation, or tribe, is not completely broken off. It becomes merely one of many relationships through which the self is defined.[187]

Fixed personalized loyalty (made visible by citizenship since the French Revolution) that came into being after the Peace of Westphalia and was replacing the formerly overlapping loyalties for a clear-cut-puzzle of States is now challenged by the claim of a growing number of individuals to invent their own identity.[188] Thereby, the clear-cut-puzzle becomes less clear-cut. Overlapping affiliations as they were known before the Peace of Westphalia, re-emerge (however in a different pattern). "What is emerging [...] is a global system increasingly characterized by overlapping communities and multivariegated personal loyalties yielding more complex personal identities," precedented by the overlapping authority patterns of medieval Europe.[189]

Moreover, not only have individuals become subjectivized in the course of humanization and play an increasingly "distinct and important role in the clarification and interpretation of international law."[190] Also other actors have arrived on the international stage: Actors in their capacity as potential protectors and as potential violators of human rights.[191] As such, the ICJ pronounced in 1949 in the Reparation for injuries case[192]

> the end of the old orthodoxy that States are the only subjects of international law, by advising that the UN, though not a State, had the capacity to bring certain kinds of claims directly against a State on the plane of international law.[193]

The increasing importance of the right to self-determination can be seen in this context. Because, as Warbrick points out, "the right to self-determination of a colonial people is not a right of States."[194] Indeed, the focus of the right to self-determination is on human beings,[195] instead of on States: It can, on the one hand, have the effect of modifying the traditional criteria of statehood, lowering for instance the degree of effectiveness expected from governments in decolonization situations. On the other hand, it can also act as an additional, "modern" criterion whose application can lead to the denial of statehood to effective international legal entities that have been created in contravention to its premises, as happened for example when international recognition was denied to the self-proclaimed State of Rhodesia.[196]

With regard to the right of self-determination of peoples, States were rather cautious not to allow them "to replace States or even to have a say on the international scene."[197] Except for colonial peoples, peoples subjected to belligerent occupation or foreign domination and represented by an organization, and peoples subjected to extreme racial discrimination and denied access to government, peoples have been denied proper access to the international community.[198]

In conclusion, the "humanization" of international law generally seeks to enhance the status of human beings as legal subjects in international society.[199] As Anne Peters puts it: The ratio of the emancipation of the human being from State guardianship speaks for the transferability of the concept of the inherent legal capacity of the human being and thus also for the existence of a general principle of law, which states that human beings are original or *a priori* subjects of international law.[200] The transformation from international law as a State-centered system to an individual-centered system has not yet found a definitive new equilibrium though.[201] The State's importance became merely qualified and (importantly) the State's sovereignty stopped being a shield behind which States could do whatever they wanted.

Eventually, the identity of Franck's "world citizen" would not depend at all anymore on "accident of birth or some liege-lords' fiat."[202] Thus, humanization would not only lead to an increasing importance of the individual, but also to a decreasing importance of territory. However, this is true up to now only to a certain extent and mainly on the regional level. The importance of territory – in the sense of the importance of where someone is born – still depends very much on the progress of globalization which will be looked at in more detail in the following pages.

Globalization – the decreasing importance of territory?

Territory is still important as a basis for jurisdiction,[203] as source of economic resources,[204] as source of historical and cultural resources,[205] and also as a source of security.[206] However, this importance might decrease. Through globalization, new tasks and opportunities for action are emerging for the State (participation in decision-making processes at the international level),[207] globalization also "diminishes the role of the state and opens up society for new actors."[208] Hence, "[w]ith the exponential growth and impact of *globalization* in the twentieth century, the Westphalian order, as well as the realist theory of international relations, came increasingly under attack."[209] While Kant was already pronouncing in 1795 that the international community was so interconnected that a violation in one place of the world is felt all over the world,[210] this is even more so today.

Globalization thereby encompasses three domains: "the staggering growth in worldwide telecommunication; [...] the increased mobility; and [...] the burgeoning number of environmental problems like acid rain, deforestation, and global warming that cross national borders."[211]

Indeed, the importance, volume, speed, and scope of cross-border flows of ideas, money, commodities, and people is constantly increasing and obliterating borders.[212] Also, the tools of new media make "a rigid Westphalian distinction among nations, communities and societies" no longer legitimate nor executable.[213] Hence, globalization is compressing the global space. Today, it is both easy and less time-consuming to travel to a country on the other side of the globe. Through satellite and internet and the TV it is also easily possible to get information about anywhere in the world in real time ("communication revolution").[214] This, in combination with the humanization described above has certainly led to a situation where States cannot hide behind closed curtains anymore, which is certainly a positive development. With regard to the ever-growing global challenges, it is also a necessary development. Moreover, it led to a decreasing importance of territory. As such, in cyberspace, territoriality is no longer an issue.[215]

In the economic field, the growing economic interdependence challenges State sovereignty: James Carville's catchphrase "It's the economy, stupid," which characterized Bill Clinton's successful bid for the US Presidency, dates back to 1992 and captures well the story of international law in the post-Cold War period.[216] Financial institutions that move vast amounts of capital worldwide "in the blink of an eye" make the territorial State less relevant.[217]

Another example is the environmental field. Clearly, the notion of State sovereignty as outlined in the conventional story is strongly challenged: On the one hand when a State becomes the victim of the environmental policy of another State, on the other hand when a State is required to curtail or abandon activities within its own territory because those activities will have an impact on other States.[218]

As such, according to Art. 2 of the Rio Declaration on Environment and Development, States have the

> responsibility to ensure that activities within their jurisdiction or control do not cause damage to the environment of other States or of areas beyond the limits of national jurisdiction.[219]

Moreover, today it is clear that due to the interconnectivity of States

> no State has the right to use or permit the use of its territory in such a manner as to cause injury by fumes in or to the territory of another or the properties or persons therein, when the case is of serious consequence and the injury is established by clear and convincing evidence.[220]

The UN Convention to Combat Desertification[221] states in Art. 3(b):

> the Parties should, in a spirit of international solidarity and partnership, improve cooperation and coordination at subregional, regional and international levels, and better focus financial, human, organizational and technical resources where they are needed."

In the field of climate change, the need for cooperation is particularly obvious. This apparent necessity, together with the disappointing results of some of the past Climate summits – Copenhagen, Durban, Doha – even led to an evasion of other forms of action, strengthening new (in this case communal) actors, as pointed out by Helmut Aust.[222] In this context, it is also interesting to note the initial reactions to then US President Trump's announcement that he would withdraw from the Paris Agreement: On the same day that Trump declared his decision, the *New York Times* published the following:

> Representatives of American cities, states and companies are preparing to submit a plan to the UN pledging to meet the United States' greenhouse gas emissions targets under the Paris climate accord, despite President Trump's decision to withdraw from the agreement.
>
> The unnamed group – which, so far, includes 30 mayors, three governors, more than 80 university presidents and more than 100 businesses – is negotiating with the UN to have its submission accepted alongside contributions to the Paris climate deal by other nations.[223]

Disappointment about the non-action of States with regard to climate change[224] also propelled several recent cases in the field of climate litigation before different courts around the world, either against States themselves or against private companies that violate environmental laws without the State interfering. Most of the procedures up to 2017 concern administrative issues in concrete projects. Within the last years, the importance of more general strategic procedures seem to have increased:[225]

> Climate change litigation is increasingly viewed as a tool to influence policy outcomes and corporate behaviour. Strategic cases are designed to press national governments to be more ambitious on climate or to enforce existing legislation, while cases against major emitters seek compensation for loss and damage. Routine planning and regulatory cases are increasingly including climate change arguments, exposing courts to climate science and climate-related arguments even where incidental to the main claim.[226]

The first case in which a State government was successfully sued to adopt stricter emission reduction targets was *Urgenda Foundation v. State of the Netherlands*: The Urgenda Foundation (a Dutch environmental group) together with 900 Dutch citizens alleged that the Dutch government's revision of greenhouse gas (GHG) emissions reduction goals amounted to a violation of the State's constitutionally imposed duty of care.[227]

> In view of [...] the State's "procrastination," meaning its failure to commit to a greater emission reduction by end-2020, Urgenda is of the opinion that the State has acted unlawfully towards it, because such conduct violates proper social conduct and is contrary to the positive and negative duty of care expressed in Articles 2 (the right to life) and 8 ECHR (the right to family life, which also covers the right to be protected from harmful environmental influences of a nature and scope this serious).[228]

The court in the Hague agreed with the plaintiffs and ordered the Dutch State to reduce its GHG emissions by at least 25 percent by 2020 (compared to 1990). Its existing pledge to reduce emissions by 17 percent was found insufficient to meet the State's fair contribution towards the goal of keeping global temperature increases within 2°C of pre-industrial conditions, which was codified in the Paris Agreement.[229] It thereby not only rejects the 17 percent target of the Netherlands, but also the reduction targets for GHG emissions formulated by the EU (minus 20 percent).[230] Several projections for GHG reduction paths in the climate policy discussion are illustrated in the reasoning for the judgment illustrates with the help of graphic representations.[231] The government appealed, *inter alia*, on the grounds that the decision of the Regional Court in 2015 infringed the principle of the balance of powers. The Court of Appeal of the Hague[232] rejected, in October 2018, all the Dutch Government's objections. It held that the decision was not an inadmissible interference in the political decision-making process and that the positive obligations of the government of the Netherlands to protect human rights implied a general mitigation obligation. It interpreted this general mitigation obligation as an obligation to reduce national GHG emissions by at least 25 percent of 1990 levels by 2020. On 24 May 2019 the case was heard before the Supreme Court.[233] On 13 September 2019 the Deputy Procurator General of the Supreme Court published the advisory opinion that "the appeal seeking cassation must be rejected."[234] In any case, the judgement was then already seen as a "spectacular judicial success."[235] And indeed, on 20 December 2019, the Dutch Supreme Court upheld the previous decisions in its *landmark decision* and thereby contributed to a "historic victory for climate justice."[236]

Together with the US constitutional youth climate lawsuit (*Juliana v. US*)[237] that was dismissed on 17 January 2020 in a split decision, the Urgenda case has influenced the filing of similar cases in other jurisdictions.[238] By determining their State's obligations under domestic law, these domestic courts significantly draw on States' international obligations relating to the mitigation of climate change.[239]

In addition, the Urgenda decision is considered groundbreaking on the supranational level because it considered the European Convention on Human Rights to have been violated. Not surprisingly, on 7 September 2020, six Portuguese children and young adults (aged eight to 21) issued an application to the European Court of Human Rights[240] against 33 Council of Europe member States for failing to do their part to avert the ongoing and worsening impact of climate change, which contribute to global warming and result, *inter alia*, in heatwaves which are affecting the applicants' living conditions and health of the applicants. In November 2020 the court gave notice of the application to the defending governments and required each one of them to respond to the complaint.[241]

Another remarkable case (and the first case in this context at supranational level) was the *People's Climate Case*:[242] Ten families from Portugal, Germany, France, Italy, Romania, Kenya, Fiji, and Sáminuorra, the Swedish Saami Youth Association, all of whom operate in the agricultural or tourism sectors, filed the case against the European Parliament and European Council in an effort to force lawmakers to increase their ambition. In May 2019, it was dismissed on procedural grounds. The European General Court stated that the plaintiffs are not sufficiently or directly affected by EU policies to challenge these in court:[243]

> The applicants have not established that the contested provisions of the legislative package infringed their fundamental rights and distinguished them individually from all other natural or legal persons concerned by those provisions just as in the case of the addressee."[244] "[T]he fact that the effects of climate change may be different for one person than they are for another does not mean that, for that reason, there exists standing to bring an action against a measure of general application.[245]

Nevertheless, the court acknowledged that "It is true that every individual is likely to be affected one way or another by climate change, that issue being recognised by the European Union and the Member States who have, as a result, committed to reducing emissions."[246] The applicants lodged an appeal with the Court of Justice of the European Union on 23 July 2019, which was however dismissed in its entirety by judgment of 25 March 2021 due to a "lack of individual concern."[247]

A case before the district court Essen in Germany[248] took a different approach to tackling climate change: A farmer from the Peruvian Andes filed a civil claim against the German energy company RWE because of an alleged violation of property rights. His village in the Andes is existentially threatened from flooding by a glacier lake situated above the village. The flooding results from the continuous melting of the glaciers due to steadily rising temperatures. These steadily rising temperatures are attributed to CO^2 emissions. The defendant contributed 0.47 percent to this situation as this percentage corresponds to its share of global greenhouse gas emissions. Thus, the farmer demanded 0.47 percent of the costs needed for a protective dam for his village. The lawsuit was dismissed in December 2016 before the District Court in Essen. The lawyer promised to continue fighting for the rights of the farmer in the further instances.[249]

Accordingly, the Higher Regional Court of Hamm in North Rhine Westphalia accepted the case *Lliuya v. RWE* on 13 November 2017,[250] which actually marked the first time that a court acknowledged that a private company can be responsible for its share in causing climate damages, if concrete damages or risks to private persons or their property can partly be assigned to the activities of the relevant company. Thus, the appeals court recognized the complaint as well-pled and admissible. The case thereby moved forward into the evidentiary phase on 30 November 2017. Now, it is the task for the plaintiff to provide evidence for his claim before the court.[251]

Rodríguez-Garavito sees a "second wave of lawsuits" in the field of climate litigation filed in countries of the Global South with a particular focus on human rights and indigenous rights.[252] As such, taking a similar approach as *Lliuya v. RWE*, the Philippine Human Rights Commission was mandated by Greenpeace Southeast Asia and other local environmental groups in 2016 to determine whether 47 of the world's largest fossil fuel companies – including Shell, BP, ExxonMobil, and Total – are violating the rights of Filipino citizens. On 9 December 2019, Commission Leader Roberto Cadiz announced the commission's conclusions during the international climate negotiations at COP25 in Madrid (which generally seem to have an increasing focus on human rights issues): Large fossil fuel companies can be held legally responsible for the impact of their carbon emissions. The final report states that these companies have clear legal and moral obligations to act, "including shifting away from fossil fuels and investing in cleaner energy sources."[253]

All these cases, whether citizens and non-governmental organizations, hold their governments accountable for their climate-related commitments, or large corporations for the impact of their actions abroad, strengthen the understanding to deal responsibly with climate change. At the same time, they show new actors in a field of activity which until recently had been reserved for States.

More generally, particularly in the second half of the twentieth century, a growing number of new actors emerged on the international scene: International organizations and other bodies that are (partly) now recognized as subjects of international law. These include (in addition to individuals that have been examined in more detail in the previous section) public institutions (intergovernmental international organizations), private institutions (e.g., non-governmental organizations or multinational corporations), and mixed institutions (such as, for instance, international sports associations).[254] The standard-setting activity of such non-territorial actors growing both in (horizontal) extent and (vertical) reach led to one of the most noticeable transformations in contemporary international society and currently challenges the traditional State-centered structure of the Westphalian order.[255] International organizations, in particular the UN, "have much fostered the duty of international cooperation," whereby the search for consensus is sometimes even "evolved from the individual consent of States."[256]

Nexon concludes that non-State transnational actors may determine the fate of great-power struggles.[257] Indeed, it may appear tempting to recount this development as another chapter "in the saga about the decline of the State." This however is not compelling. It can also be a step towards a new element, a complement to classical forms of the State.[258]

Moreover, the early modern European experience cautions against declaring the premature death of the "State" as a significant corporate actor in world politics.[259] So if the State continues to carry out its tasks and other actors are taking over global/sub-Statal tasks, this should be the best way to handle the current world order. Addis, after strengthening the ambiguity of territory and boundaries in the current globalized world, argues therefore for a "thin" State "in this era of thick globalism."[260] This "thin State" would necessarily have to be accompanied by new actors, taking over tasks that the State cannot handle (on its own): Indeed, there seems to be "an unstoppable march of globalization" towards the construction of global institutions.[261] "States have not ceased to be active in providing security, liberty, self-determination, and wealth, 'but have increasingly lost their autonomy in guaranteeing for these goods' provision'."[262] Peters argues that "on the promise that need and want the delivery of the basic goods [...] given the fact that states have less autonomy and capacity for their delivery, international institutions must become more effective in furnishing these goods."[263] Otherwise, if this (self-)transformation of the State does not come hand in hand with a compensating transformation of the international system, the legitimacy of the international system is seriously challenged.[264] Thus,

> States, which had defined themselves from Thukydides to Bismarck by their claims to sovereign independence, gradually came together to create international organizations to promote peace, curb aggression, regulate diplomatic affairs, devise an international code of law, encourage social development, and foster prosperity.[265]

Luhmann has described this development as a move from territoriality to functionality, from a world of sovereign territorial States to a world of functional institutions.[266] The territorially bound State can no longer be the sole vehicle of public policy[267] and "[t]he current paradigm whose theoretical foundation is thick statism will not be able to support international legal institutions in the twenty-first century."[268] Hence, parallel to the trend of humanization, there is a trend towards an internationalization of State functions.[269]

Sovereignty, the crucial term of the architecture of the Westphalian regime,[270] is being altered due to globalization and the ensuing practical necessities.[271] "[G]lobalization has ended the nation state's monopoly over internal sovereignty, which was formerly guaranteed by territory."[272] The vital question is whether the current development diminishes the sovereignty and territorial supremacy of the States.[273]

Judge Alvarez of the ICJ stated in his individual opinion to the advisory opinion on the Conditions of Admission of a State to Membership in the UN (using community and society differently than here):

> the old *community* of nations has been transformed into a veritable international *society,* though it has neither an executive power, nor a legislative power, nor yet a judicial power, which are the characteristics of a national society, but not of international society. This society comprises all States throughout the world, without there being any need for consent on their part or on that of other States; it has aims and interests of its own; States

> no longer have an absolute sovereignty but are interdependent; they have not only rights, but also *duties* towards each other and towards this society; finally, the latter is organized and governed, to an ever increasing extent, by a law of a character quite different from that of customary law.[274]

Indeed, sovereignty has been subject to persistent pressures "of global integration and sub-state fragmentation."[275] Crawford, when thinking about the future of sovereignty sees it as being challenged by "the mass movement of persons, capital, ideas and information – summed up as 'globalization'."[276] And Schrijver concludes that "national sovereignty in 2000 does indeed differ greatly from the concept held in the mid-seventeenth century, and [...] has been qualified in various ways:"[277]

> [T]he idea of sovereignty as the supreme governing principle of the State system is no longer implicitly accepted. Increasingly, questions are raised as to its significance in a world where national frontiers are of decreasing importance. Economics, technology, ecology, communications, human contracts have radically changed the perception of self-contained independent States. The metaphors of the "global village" and the "space-ship earth" reflect new conditions that seem incompatible with the primacy of State sovereignty.[278]

Allott predicts that "[s]overeignty over territory will disappear as a category from the theory of international society and from its international law."[279]

The UN Charter itself does not even speak of sovereignty of States but uses the expression "sovereign equality of States" instead. Sovereign equality means that no State is superior to another State, but it does not mean that any State is superior to the international community. It rather implies that every State is subordinated under the international community.[280] As such, Kelsen also defined sovereignty under public international law as a State's "legal independence from other States."[281]

Thus, a contemporary definition of national sovereignty needs to take into account the increased community-relatedness of the State: The sovereignty of the State is its autonomy which is granted and guaranteed by the constitution of the international community, notably the UN Charter.[282] The Charter thereby is itself an example of an international obligation voluntarily accepted by member States.[283] They

> not only benefit from the privileges of sovereignty but also accept its responsibilities. Whatever perceptions may have prevailed when the Westphalian system first gave rise to the notion of State sovereignty, today it clearly carries with it the obligation of a State to protect the welfare of its own peoples and meet its obligations to the wider international community.
>
> But history teaches us all too clearly that it cannot be assumed that every State will always be able, or willing, to meet its responsibilities to protect its own people and avoid harming its neighbors. And in those circumstances, the

> principles of collective security mean that some portion of those responsibilities should be taken up by the international community, acting in accordance with the Charter of the UN and the Universal Declaration of Human Rights, to help build the necessary capacity or supply the necessary protection, as the case may be.
>
> What we seek to protect reflects what we value. The Charter of the UN seeks to protect all States, not because they are intrinsically good but because they are necessary to achieve the dignity, justice, worth and safety of their citizens. These are the values that should be at the heart of any collective security system for the twenty-first century, but too often States have failed to respect and promote them. The collective security we seek to build today asserts a shared responsibility on the part of all States and international institutions, and those who lead them, to do just that.[284]

Within the European Union a certain deviation from the sovereign rule in this regard is visible.[285] On the international level such signs are not visible to that extent (yet). Paulus summarizes the signs of such a true community (as a separate actor in addition to the State) in the *ius cogens* norms, obligations *erga omnes*, the concept of the common heritage of mankind, the alleged "constitutionalization" of the UN security system and of the World Trade Organization (WTO) trading system as well as in the preamble of the 1998 Rome Statute of the International Criminal Court (ICC), referring to Tomuschat and Thouvenin, Dupuy, Fassbender, and Petersmann.[286]

As such, the era of globalization is, so to say, "post-imperial."[287] Territorial States on their own "have a difficult task." They remain territorial entities in the extreme, linked to frontiers and sustained by defined relationships with their populations, while the importance of territory and borders is reduced by radical socioeconomic change and the functions of territory are losing their relevance.[288] Even with regard to jurisdiction, one of the main functions of territory, States are increasingly forced to exercise extraterritorial jurisdiction and tolerate similar exercises by other States.[289] There has been a noticeable trend towards the exercise of jurisdiction on the basis of criteria other than that of territorial location due to the increasing speed of communications, the more sophisticated structure of commercial organizations or enterprises with transnational ramifications, and the growing international character of criminal activities (narcotic drugs and currency transactions).[290]

The post-Westphalian system is characterized by the concept of solidarity and a "willingness to privilege the interests of threatened populations over traditional conceptions of state sovereignty and non-intervention."[291] In Western Europe, the new guiding idea of supranationality countered with and restricted sovereignty.[292] As such, the preamble of the Treaty establishing the European Coal and Steel Community (which subsequently became part of the European Union) reads:

> CONSIDERING that world peace may be safeguarded only by creative efforts equal to the dangers which menace it; CONVINCED that the contribution

> which an organized and vital Europe can bring to civilization is indispensable to the maintenance of peaceful relations; CONSCIOUS of the fact that Europe can be built only by concrete actions which *create a real solidarity* and by the establishment of common bases for economic development; DESIROUS of assisting through the expansion of their basic production in raising the standard of living and in furthering the works of peace; RESOLVED to substitute for historic rivalries a fusion of their essential interests; to establish, by creating an economic community, the foundation of a broad and independent community among peoples long divided by bloody conflicts; and to lay the bases of institutions capable of giving direction to their future common destiny; HAVE DECIDED to create a European Coal and Steel Community.[293]

Likewise, the Inter-American States affirmed their commitment to international solidarity: For instance, in the Act of Chapultepec, the Inter-American Conference approved, on 6 March 1945, a resolution on reciprocal assistance and solidarity.[294] Goldman sees in the twentieth century in general the "return of universalist law" after it had been divided into separate sovereign States after the Peace of Westphalia.[295] It developed into a shift towards solidarity between the States (due to globalization) and with the population (due to humanization) even of foreign States.[296]

The UN with its purpose "[t]o achieve international cooperation in solving international problems of an economic, social, cultural, or humanitarian character …"[297] has certainly marked the beginning of the concept of international solidarity which gradually emerged and led to "the new era of Cooperation" starting at the end of the Cold War.[298]

This challenges the exclusive territorial authority of sovereign States or even leads to a crisis of State territoriality.[299] While

> [f]or roughly the last 500 years, a bordered territory has been considered a suitable framework to organize government over people […] in recent years there are increasing signs that the traditional and rather categorical symbiosis between territory and power may no longer lay a legitimate claim for exclusivity.[300]

A lesser focus on territory is probably not a bad idea, as territory and boundaries despite being "designed to avoid strife among individuals and peoples" have "in the long course of history […] evolved into the prime cause for belligerent unrest in the world."[301]

A lesser focus on territory seems also appropriate: Today's global economy requires open economies that make effective territorial security very difficult. Nuclear weapons can make borders totally irrelevant. Terrorists can infiltrate elaborate border controls and unleash devastation with lethal devices that can be contained in briefcases. Thus, the security function of territory has also been compromised.[302] In relations with and among the WTO, NAFTA, and the EU extraterritorial disputes and competing claims to jurisdiction proliferate and assume increasing prominence.[303] A common currency like the one in the EU is, according to Tomuschat, "the prototype of a matter which lacks any territorial links."[304]

Additionally, due to the expansion of international trade, the physical resources inherent in territory are no longer critical to the survival of a State. Human capital far outweighs physical territorial resources, and it is possible for a State to exist as a service economy powered by tertiary sector services.[305]

But "globalisation and deterritorialisation impact different places unevenly:"[306] While boundaries are becoming more permeable to the movement of goods and people, and diffusion of ideas and transactions, the fences of national and ethnic separation continue to be erected – Newman adds "in other parts of the world."[307] This is very true in many parts of the world. While, for example, the European Union seemed to be a symbol for permeable boundaries, the "refugee crisis" showed, that this permeability has not at all yet reached a point of real permeability: States quickly reinstalled impermeable borders. Also, "[m]ore and more people see their respective nation state, and not the European Union or another international institution, as the only reliable 'area of freedom, security and justice' which must be shielded against foreign or international interference or disturbance."[308] Accordingly, the outcome of the Brexit referendum is seen as (at least partly) being influenced by the people's fears about the permeability of their borders.[309]

> Ethnic and national groups are still prepared to fight and die for their territorial homelands, as well as to practice policies of ethno-territorial exclusion, cleansing and purification as they seek to erect new territorial boundaries and fences of separation.[310]

Schachter points out an irony where an outburst of nationalism occurs hand in hand with the diminishing significance of boundaries in the lives of most people.[311] What we are witnessing is "an ambivalent move consisting in an increasing economic opening of borders concomitant with a political closure of national spaces where sometimes even new walls and fences of separation are being erected."[312]

> The very fact that the national State appears to be diminished by globalization and new structures of authority can appear to its citizens as a loss of their control.[313]

As such Boutros-Ghali said in 1992:

> We have entered a time of global transition marked by uniquely contradictory trends. Regional and continental associations of States are evolving ways to deepen cooperation and ease some of the contentious characteristics of sovereign and nationalistic rivalries. National boundaries are blurred by advanced communications and global commerce, and by the decisions of States to yield some sovereign prerogatives to larger, common political associations. At the same time, fierce new assertions of nationalism and sovereignty spring up,

> and the cohesion of States is threatened by brutal ethnic, religious, social, cultural or linguistic strife. Social peace is challenged on the one hand by new assertions of discrimination and exclusion and, on the other, by acts of terrorism seeking to undermine evolution and change through democratic means.[314]

Moreover, statistics show that even within the EU where borders are permeable, natural persons are extremely reluctant to move to another country. Exceptions are people from the very bottom and the very top of the income scale. Thus, the assumption of a stable and definite territorial basis for the respective population has obviously been loosened through globalization and migration, but it has not been dissolved.[315] On the whole, State borders "in a world where states appear to be overwhelmed by transnational flows of capital, information, and commodities"[316] did not lose their relevance. Khan argues in this regard that despite the abolition of border controls and intensified cooperation at all levels of cross-border interaction, the territory remains relevant. The exclusional function of borders remains intact, creating the domestic/foreign dichotomy. Hence, the territoriality of sovereign States remains important.[317]

Shaw adds in this regard:

> The rise of globalization and supranational organizations and enterprises notwithstanding, the concepts of territorial sovereignty and territorial integrity constitute the beating heart of international law.[318]

Moreover, while it is true that "new multilayered loyalty references are emerging" "a balanced view of tendencies at the end of the twentieth century reveals that powerful centripetal and centrifugal loyalties coexist with resilient statist patriotism."[319]

The State becomes so to say "reterritorialized" due to territorial ideologies at both the concrete and symbolic levels.[320] Whether this is indeed a necessity – at least the age of territoriality appears as one of relative order and safety when compared with the age of anarchy and insecurity before[321] – or whether it is due to the fact that the minds of people are not yet at the point of accepting the deterritorializing effects of globalization, remains to be seen.

It has to be acknowledged, that the system based on territorial demarcation and mutual recognition creates a systematized pattern of interaction in international affairs.[322] Today, there is some kind of imbalance: It might develop into tensions between conflicting modes of organization based on the deterritorialized global capitalist system, on the one hand, and on a territorial nation State system, on the other.[323] The increasingly closer relations between States led to their ever greater interdependence.[324] At the same time, though, the structure is losing its clarity of the Westphalian time. By moving towards a crosscutting set of jurisdictions at the national and supranational levels, there is a change in the locus of authority.[325]

This change comes along with the change from a world of coexisting States towards a world of cooperating States. Today, no State can be regarded as isolated in itself. All are linked and connected to other actors of international relations.[326] Multilateral treaties put obligations onto contracting States. There emerges a legal interest of the other contracting States who may, if in their view a contractual obligation is violated, denounce these injuries, and impose remedial measures without infringing the non-intervention requirement. As a result, today there is hardly any area of public life that would be closed to criticism and influence by other States and international organizations.[327] Due to the international system for the protection of human rights, but also in the fields of the protection of the environment, many issues that originally belonged to the internal affairs of a State have become the responsibility of the international community.[328] It has been claimed that "[i]f the world survives [...] it cannot go on as a congeries of wholly independent watertight political communities."[329] From an anarchic society, the States are moving towards a new legal system with mutual responsibilities, "which may be labelled 'international community'."[330] Thus, while Larkins was examining territory and politics before Westphalia and identifying a development from hierarchy to anarchy,[331] today, examining territory and politics after Westphalia, a development from anarchy to hierarchy becomes visible.

The international law system was originally based on the coexistence of States,[332] later on cooperating States,[333] and today on a legal system based upon common values.[334] The post-Westphalian system has thus replaced the Westphalian system of exclusive bilateral relations.[335] Originally, international law was mainly concerned with bilateral issues. Nowadays it often "cannot be adequately analyzed through the prism of bilateral relationships. Some multilateral conventions represent broad statements of community values in which every State party has a legal interest in the integrity of the treaty and its observance by all the parties."[336] Because of this system change, many scholars question "Westphalia's capacity to make a constructive contribution to world order in the twenty-first century."[337] The juxtaposition of independent States, which corresponds to the sovereignty of the nineteenth century, does neither provide sufficient security against attacks, nor does it permit reasonable progress in attaining social and economic justice, protecting the environment, or conserving scarce resources.[338]

Today, there is a demand for international cooperation:[339] As such, growing economic interdependence, widespread dangers represented by ecological problems, and the international nature of much military conflict can be seen as the main contemporary challenges to States.[340] "[G]lobalization – for better or for worse – brought the world closer together than ever," and "the advent of global warming and global terrorism has increased the necessity of global regulation to a point where national sovereignty itself seems to be at stake."[341] Thus, even though "States have always constituted nomads eager to look after their own interests and unmindful of collective needs, let alone universal values, [...] collective arrangement[s] for protecting joint of common interests" are increasingly made.[342] Hence, today's system is "far more complex than a system of sovereign states."[343]

Nevertheless, while authorities might be shifting, the State remains the prevalent organizational source of authority and to variable extents the dominant one.[344] "[T]he starting point is always that limitations of the sovereignty of a state over its territory are not to be presumed." States "are free to consent to modifications of the exercise of jurisdiction over their territory."[345] Moreover, one should not entirely ignore the sovereign rights of the States. For example, the European Court of Human Rights has acknowledged a margin of appreciation in determining the implementation of human rights.[346] Sovereignty is still "used to justify and define the 'privacy' of States, their political independence and territorial integrity; their rights and the rights of their peoples to be let alone and to go their own way."[347] Hence, sovereignty cannot be seen as obsolete: It should merely no longer be seen as

> an absolute and individual right of every State, as used to be done under the old law founded on the individualist régime, according to which States were only bound by the rules which they had accepted. [...] The sovereignty of States has now become an *institution*, an *international social function* of a psychological character, which has to be exercised in accordance with the new international law.[348]

However, international law is still reliant on States to be implemented and international, as well as supranational organizations are dependent on their States as long as the latter do not agree to transfer sovereignty.[349] As long as sovereignty remains an essential part of international relations, the State will continue to exist.[350] Anything else "is premature, to say the least."[351]

Schermers and Blokker point out, though, that today there is "the remarkable paradox that, to remain sovereign, they [the States] must cooperate, *inter alia*, through international organisations."[352] Herberg states in this regard that

> [i]n the long run, the manifold interconnections might very well sum up to a new model of interlocked governance and statehood, with the state regaining its operational responsibility as well as its regulatory competence inside and, to some extent, also outside of the national territory.[353]

In this development, international organizations rather strengthen than weaken the existing State system.[354]

The cure for jurisdictional conflicts lies in a constitutionalization of the system.[355] This is not new. The Italian lawyer Baldus de Ubaldis (1327–1400) realized back in the fourteenth century that in order to handle conflicts among different actors that would all "not accept any superiors," "a general and legal principle to be accepted as a leading norm" ("*jus gentium*") was needed.[356] Also Kelsen concluded that holding the State as being "sovereign" was not entirely correct because its sovereignty was derived from international law. Therefore, in the end, only international law is sovereign.[357] Hart sees that as "one of the persistent sources of perplexity."[358] Crawford suggests that the term sovereignty can still be used "when we find it convenient" particularly in phrases such as "sovereign equality."[359]

In the case of supra-territorial issues (such as human rights and climate change) a stronger commitment to and subordination under "superior principles" is needed.

Thereby, such a process

> has the potential of determining the establishment of a renewed international legal order, based on the emergence of additional subjects and actors, an expansion of the role of substantive international law and the establishment of innovative accountability mechanisms at the international level. For a number of reasons, globalization and its consequential effects, is bound to further adjust the doctrine of fundamental rights and duties of States as it was originally envisaged.[360]

Concluding thoughts on what it means to be a State

The concept of the State has been challenged significantly within the last century. Globalization and humanization "are deterritorializing much of the political landscape."[361] However, those challenges do not point to the demise of the State as such.[362]

> If we pause to ask ourselves, at the dawn of the twenty-first century, which political institutions constitute the world's major depositories of power, we would have to reply: states. It is the same answer that any seasoned observer would have given in 1815.[363]

Indeed, the present day is not that different from hundreds of years ago in that States are still the primary actors of the international legal system.[364] In particular, States are still the holders of the implementing power.[365] Effective and legitimate states are well suited to ensure that the benefits of the internationalization of trade, investment, technology, and communications are equitably distributed[366] and provide protection to all citizens on the basis of equality and justice. A reduction in autonomy does not mean the demise of States.[367] Also, as Peters reminds us, "[t]here is simply no other political institution in sight which would possess a comparable capacity and legitimacy as the state"[368] and

> in security terms, a cohesive and peaceful international system is far more likely to be achieved through the cooperation of effective states, confident of their place in the world, than in an environment of fragile, collapsed, fragmenting or generally chaotic state entities.[369]

Andreas Paulus says in this context that "all agree that the state is here to stay as the only institution in which political decisions can be legitimized by democratic means and which can provide indispensable social services and other public goods."[370] Also Louis Henkin makes clear that he assumes a world of States. He nevertheless suggests

> that it is time to bring sovereignty down to Earth, cut it down to size, discard its overblown rhetoric; to examine, analyse, reconceive the concept and

> break out its normative content; to repackage it, even rename it, and slowly ease the term out of polite language in international relations, particularly in law.[371]

Indeed, globalization and the expansion of the activities of international institutions and new non-state actors are often cited as examples that point to the decline of State sovereignty.[372]

Kingsbury argues, though, that

> discarding sovereignty in favour of a functional approach will intensify inequality, weakening restraints on coercive intervention, diminishing critical roles of the state as a locus of identity and an autonomous zone of politics, and re-dividing the world into zones. The traditional normative concept of sovereignty is strained and flawed, but in the absence of better means to manage inequality it remains preferable to any of the alternatives on offer.[373]

In any case, the concept of sovereignty has been qualified.[374] This relativity of sovereignty shows that the once-held notions of absolute sovereignty are far from today's legal conception and practice. They do not, however, show that sovereignty has lost its political and legal significance.[375] It "is still at the core of most rules of international law," even though "both the individual human being and the international organisation have increasingly found recognition in rules of international law as (acting) 'entities' which are more than mere 'creatures' of the sovereign State." But the changes are slow and do not yet truly undermine the international system of coexisting sovereign States.[376] Hence, Shinoda suggests to neither attack nor defend sovereignty, "but to contemplate carefully a healthy development of the constitutional rules of international society."[377] In this context, Evans says about the modern understanding of the meaning of sovereignty that it "implies a dual responsibility: externally – to respect the sovereignty of other states, and internally, to respect the dignity and basic rights of all the people within the state."[378]

This, however, does not even go far enough. Sovereignty also implies the respect of the dignity and basic rights of peoples outside the own sovereign territory of a State. International citizenship involves the concept of sovereignty as responsibility.[379] The term international citizenship itself is indicative of humanization in international law. Although states remain the primary international legal subjects, individuals have been recognized as international legal subjects in their own right as citizens of the world.[380] Humanization has thus begun to reshape the international system, but it has so far been felt more at the regional (European) level than at the truly international level.[381]

Thus, it is clear that it is not the UN Charter as such that is unable to handle these difficulties. Rather, it is a failure to apply its principles to a new era, where the traditional notion of sovereignty can no longer meet the aspirations of peoples to realize their human rights.[382] The Charter must always be seen as "a living document." Nothing in there "precludes a recognition that there are rights beyond borders" but "its very letter and spirit are an affirmation of those fundamental human rights."[383]

If the State and (subsidiarily) the international community act in order to protect the individual, no individual must be denied the benefits of globalization. Global risks must be managed so that the costs and burdens are shared equitably and those who suffer have a right to help from those who benefit most.[384]

Borders are (and should be) losing their importance.[385] "The transformation of the 'old' inter-state international law into a genuine global order with the individual at its centre is at first sight geared towards making the state redundant and obsolete."[386] However, with the economy, it appears that "[t]ime zone borders are more important than state borders,"[387] and generally "issues of boundaries, sovereignty, identity, representation, power, and alliances [...] assume some additional significance in a world where speed, instant communication, new and multiple state and non-state actors are characteristic,"[388] in the field of human rights the actors that would have to become increasingly active are often still too hesitant to actually overcome borders globally. Thus, as Shaw points out "the territorial pattern of international law remains the dominant one even if its predominance has been modified."[389] Indeed, concepts of territorial sovereignty and the multilateralism upon which international law operates even achieve an underappreciated balance between State and individual rights that often serves as a foundational prerequisite for human rights to flourish.[390]

The classical Westphalian system envisaged a coexistence of different States, which aimed to remain internally independent.[391] The "new world order" or post-Westphalian system is more complex, "with power being diffused both upwards and downwards from the State, and with boundaries taking on multi-dimensions of bordering, excluding and including not only territories but also social groups and virtual communities."[392] The era can thereby rightfully be described as an "era of cooperation."[393]

Some argue, though, that the international legal order is by now in its third stage (after coexistence and cooperation).[394] Indeed, no State can stand wholly alone in in the twenty-first century, more than ever before. Collective strategies, collective institutions, and a sense of collective responsibility are indispensable.[395] International law also builds the "blueprint for social life," encompassing "matters previously thought to be shielded from any outside interference" – in particular: Human rights.[396]

Thereby, while international law does increasingly allow for rights for individuals and other non-State entities, this increasing recognition of rights is (up to now) explicitly a result of State consent. International organizations are consensual associations of States, human rights are accepted and enforced through the consent of States, and investor-state arbitration is premised on investment treaties which are negotiated between States.[397] Thus, the new actors,[398] such as international organizations and individuals themselves, often remain "mere third-party beneficiar[ies]."[399]

Indeed, while the developments above are "unsurprising to any observer of international affairs [...] yet [they] cannot fit with the fictions of the dominant legal doctrine. For that doctrine ignores any participation or relationships in the international community other than those by or between States."[400] The international community largely still lacks a sufficient level of institutionalization and cohesion.[401] The Universal Declaration of Human Rights and the two Covenants are "important milestones"[402] that paved the way for a potentially very different new world order. However, the dilemma of the new era is that "[o]n the one hand, the state is often incapable of meeting the demands of sovereignty in the complex circumstances of the contemporary world. On the other hand, no adequate replacement for the state is in place or even in sight."[403]

This is particularly grave for human rights and transnational environmental matters: Human rights have long been subordinate to considerations of State sovereignty. The same can certainly be said about environmental matters.

As such, the UNFCCC explicitly reconfirms the importance of national sovereignty in various places. Its preamble reiterates that "States have, in accordance with the UN Charter and the principles of international law, the *sovereign right* to exploit their resources on the basis of their own environmental and development policies"[404] – a passage taken over from Principle 2 of the Rio Declaration on Environment and Development, repeating the well-known Principle 2 I of the 1972 Stockholm Declaration. Newly added in the Rio Declaration and the Climate Change Convention are the words "and developmental," which is intended to stress the primacy of the freedom of sovereign States to formulate their own policies in the area of environment and economics. Art. 2 of Kyoto[405] reads in this regard: Each industrialized country "shall implement *and/or* further elaborate policies and measures in accordance with its *national circumstances*." The Protocol then mentions various measures as examples, but States are free to decide in these matters. Sovereignty is left intact.[406] Also the Paris Agreement merely requires all parties to put forward their best efforts through "nationally determined contributions."[407]

Individuals and their sufferings and need for protection are not mentioned. Thus, the transition towards a real humanization is far from completed (but is still ongoing).[408]

The Secretary-General acknowledged that

> Any such evolution in our understanding of state sovereignty and individual sovereignty will, in some quarters, be met with distrust, skepticism, even hostility. But it is an evolution that we should welcome.
>
> Why? Because, despite its limitations and imperfections, it is testimony to a humanity that cares more, not less, for the suffering in its midst, and a humanity that will do more, and not less, to end it.[409]

The State will need to show a "supple willingness to shift power down towards the local level and up towards international organizations, which the state has a hand in running."[410] Global issues that cannot be dealt with by one State alone must be dealt with by the international community as a separate actor. The protection of human rights that is the prime function of the State must become the responsibility of the international community if the State cannot provide or is not providing such protection. Up to now, the system is, despite all the changes and transitions described above, still very much State-centered.

There remains much to be done by the States, individuals, and particularly by the international community. Thereby it is important to notice that the international community does not and should not lead to the irrelevance of national States. Even if there are common interests and common values, there will remain a need for differing traditions and values. The international community should find compromises "rather than [postulate] a common philosophy which would miraculously neutralize the divergence of individual interests and values."[411] Generally, the interests of individuals worldwide are interestingly very similar to each other, though. They differ far less from each other than from the interests of their respective States. The interests of States again are similar to each other, too. Thus, humanization could lead to the stronger implementation of people's interest.[412] Then, "[p]erhaps there is indeed an international system of 'interlocking communities'[413] looming on the horizon, made up of individuals, organizations (economic and others) and States with overlapping memberships and allegiances."[414]

Such a "global community" would not only require individuals who define their personal self, but also States that "recognize individualism as a right to personal self-determination and to acknowledge that freedom of conscience is a human right that is protected by international institutions and law."[415] Fassbender suggests that "the concept of equal rights for peoples, already familiar to the international law in connection with the right of self-determination, could take over some of the functions until now performed by the principle of sovereign equality of states."[416] Additionally, a strong international community as specific actor is needed. When this doctrinal move has been completed, international law will, could and should be an "individual-centered system."[417]

Thus, this chapter showed that there are ongoing developments with regard to the State, developments that might – in the end – make it easier for the individual to search for protection internationally, and for the international community to offer protection internationally. These developments are far from being "completed." They might well never become complete. However, the findings of this chapter are important for the analysis in the next chapter when it comes to exploring what it actually means to lose a State. It might come out that through the developments described above, a human rights regime with "forward-looking, trans-boundary mechanisms of monitoring and protection that no longer rely on the state as the central domain of moral concern, or risk"[418] becomes possible. These developments might provide "a normative basis for an inclusive, flexible, cosmopolitan framework with the capacity to address issues of inundation, loss of sovereignty, and denial of basic human rights more effectively than a rigid, compartmentalised system premised on state sovereignty."[419]

Notes

1 C. Warbrick, "States and Recognition in International Law" in M. D. Evans (ed.), *International Law* (2006), p. 218; cf. B. Fassbender, "Die Souveränität des Staates als Autonomie im Rahmen der völkerrechtlichen Verfassung" in H.-P. Mansel (ed.), *Festschrift für Erik Jayme* (2004), p. 38; C. Tomuschat, "Self-Determination in a Post-Colonial World" in C. Tomuschat (ed.), *Modern Law of Self-Determination* (1993), p. 10; A. L. Paulus, *Die internationale Gemeinschaft im Völkerrecht: Eine Untersuchung zur Entwicklung des Völkerrechts im Zeitalter der Globalisierung* (2001), p. 228; E. Suy, "New Players in International Relations" in G. Kreijen (ed.), *State, Sovereignty, and International Governance* (2002), p. 373.

2 Cf. B. Fassbender, "Sovereignty and Constitutionalism in International Law" in N. Walker (ed.), *Sovereignty in Transition* (2003), p. 133, 138.

3 A. Cassese, "States: Rise and Decline of the Primary Subjects of the International Community" in B. Fassbender, A. Peters (eds), *The Oxford Handbook of the History of International Law* (2012), p. 49; M. Craven, R. Parfitt, "Statehood, Self-determination, and Recognition" in M. D. Evans (ed.), *International Law* (2018), p. 177; R. McCorquodale, "International Community and State Sovereignty: An Uneasy Symbiotic Relationship" in C. Warbrick, S. Tierney (eds), *Towards an "International Legal Community"?: The Sovereignty of States and the Sovereignty of International Law* (2006), p. 246–7.

4 Cf. A. A. C. Trindade, "International Law for Humankind: Towards a New Jus Gentium," part 1, *316 Recueil Des Cours* (2005), p. 203 ("The domain of the subjects of International Law, which in the past was largely devoted [...] to States, has lately been much enriched with the acknowledgment of international organizations and individuals as also subjects of the law of nations."); cf. H. Mosler, "The International Society as a Legal Community," *140 Recueil Des Cours* (1974), p. 22; M. A. Burkett, "The Nation Ex-Situ" in M. Gerrard, G. E. Wannier (eds), *Threatened Island Nations: Legal Implications of Rising Seas and a Changing Climate* (2013), p. 98, mentioning the EU and Taiwan that enjoy recognition of their sovereignty at the international level.

5 C. W. Morris, *An Essay on the Modern State* (2002), p. 1.

6 I. Österdahl, "Relatively Failed. Troubled Statehood and International Law," *14 Finnish Yearbook of International Law* (2003), p. 49.

7 M. Craven, R. Parfitt, "Statehood, Self-determination, and Recognition" in M. D. Evans (ed.), *International Law* (2018), p. 177, 220.

8 S. I. Phlogaitēs, *The Evolution of Law and the State in Europe: Seven Lessons* (2014), p. 52.

9 Ibid., p. 52.

10 R. Higgins, *Problems and Process: International Law and How We Use It* (1995), p. 39.

11 J. T. Mathews, "Power Shift," *76 Foreign Affairs* (1997), p. 65.

12 C. Warbrick, "States and Recognition in International Law" in M. D. Evans (ed.), *International Law*, 2nd edn (2006), p. 247.

13 Ibid., p. 224.

14 J. R. Crawford, *The Creation of States in International Law* (2006), p. 45.

15 Ibid, pp. 40–1.

16 Cf. C. Warbrick, "States and Recognition in International Law" in M. D. Evans (ed.), *International Law*, 2nd edn. (2006), p. 242, citing J. R. Crawford, *The Creation of States in International Law* (2006), pp. 40–1.

17 J. R. Crawford, *The Creation of States in International Law* (2006), p. 42.

18 Cf. I. A. Shearer, *Starke's International Law* (2003), p. 91; cf. B. Fassbender, "Article 2(1)" in B. Simma, H. Mosler, A. Paulus, E. Chaitidou (eds), *The Charter of the UN: A Commentary* (2012), para. 57 et seq.

19 Cf. C. Warbrick, "States and Recognition in International Law" in M. D. Evans (ed.), *International Law*, 2nd edn. (2006), p. 242–3
20 "Draft Declaration on Rights and Duties of States" (1949).
21 UNGA, Resolution 25/2625: *Declaration on Principles of International Law concerning Friendly Relations and Cooperation among States in accordance with the Charter of the UN*, 24 October 1970.
22 Ibid., p. 289, para. 48 (summary of contents).
23 Ibid.
24 H. Kelsen, "The Draft Declaration on Rights and Duties of States," *44 AJIL* (1950), pp. 261.
25 G. Arangio-Ruiz, *The UN Declaration on Friendly Relations and the System of the Sources of International Law* (1979), p. 3.
26 UNGA, Resolution 25/2625: *Declaration on Principles of International Law concerning Friendly Relations and Cooperation among States in accordance with the Charter of the UN*, 24 October 1970. Cf. C. Warbrick, "States and Recognition in International Law" in M. D. Evans (ed.), *International Law*, 2nd edn (2006), p. 243; G. Arangio-Ruiz, *The UN Declaration on Friendly Relations and the System of the Sources of International Law* (1979), p. 3.
27 U. Fastenrath, "Article 3," in B. Simma, H. Mosler, A. Randelzhofer, C. Tomushat, R. Wolfrum (eds), *The Charter of the UN: A Commentary* (1994), p. 155 et seq. (para. 6).
28 "Covenant of the League of Nations" (1919).
29 Cf. R. Nicholson, *Statehood and the State-Like in International Law* (2019), p. 2.
30 J. R. Crawford, *The Creation of States in International Law* (2006), p. 44.
31 C. Warbrick, "States and Recognition in International Law" in M. D. Evans (ed.), *International Law*, 2nd edn (2006), p. 243
32 C. Möllers, *Staat als Argument* (2000), p. 101, citing Smend (R. Smend, *Verfassung und Verfassungsrecht* (1928), p. 84).
33 R. Nicholson, *Statehood and the State-Like in International Law* (2019), p. 101.
34 C. Warbrick, "States and Recognition in International Law" in M. D. Evans (ed.), *International Law*, 2nd edn. (2006), p. 242.
35 Cf. A. Addis, "The Thin State in Thick Globalism: Sovereignty in the Information Age," *37 Vanderbilt Journal of Transnational Law* (2004), p. 4 with further references; cf. H. J. Morgenthau, "The Intellectual and Political Functions of a Theory of International Relations" in H. V. Harrison (ed.), *The Role of Theory in International Relations* (1964), p. 116.
36 C. Schmitt, *Der Begriff des Politischen* [1932] (1963), p. 10 (translation by the author). "Die Epoche der Staatlichkeit geht jetzt zu Ende. Darüber ist kein Wort mehr zu verlieren. … Der Staat als das Modell der politischen Einheit, der Staat als Träger … des Monopols der politischen Entscheidung … wird entthront." Cf. J. Kokott, "Die Staatsrechtslehre und die Veränderung ihres Gegenstandes: Konsequenzen von Europäisierung und Internationalisierung" in J. Kokott, W. Brugger, C. Gusy, T. Vesting (eds), *Die Staatsrechtslehre und die Veränderung ihres Gegenstandes: Konsequenzen von Europäisierung und Internationalisierung. Gewährleistung von Freiheit und Sicherheit im Lichte unterschiedlicher Staats- und Verfassungsverständnisse/Berichte und Diskussionen auf der Tagung der Vereinigung der Deutschen Strafrechtslehrer in Hamburg vom 1. bis 4. Oktober 2003* (2004), p. 9; cf. H. Bull, *The Anarchical Society: A Study of Order in World Politics* (2012), p. 248.
37 C. W. Morris, *An Essay on the Modern State* (2002), p. 55.
38 A. L. Paulus, *Die internationale Gemeinschaft im Völkerrecht: Eine Untersuchung zur Entwicklung des Völkerrechts im Zeitalter der Globalisierung* (2001), p. 103; W. Reinhard, "Aufstieg und Niedergang des modernen Staates," *5 Zeitschrift für Staats- und Europawissenschaften* (2007), p. 19, 23.

39 C. W. Jenks, *The Common Law of Mankind* (1958), p. 37; cf. J. E. Alvarez, "The return of the State," *20 Minnesota Journal of International Law* (2011), p. 262–3; R. A. Falk, "Revisiting Westphalia, Discovering Post-Westphalia," *6 The Journal of Ethics* (2002), p. 338.

40 A. Addis, "The Thin State in Thick Globalism: Sovereignty in the Information Age," *37 Vanderbilt Journal of Transnational Law* (2004), p. 107.

41 M. Koskenniemi, "The Wonderful Artificiality of States," *88 Proceedings of the Annual Meeting (American Society of International Law)* (1994), p. 22, citing Friedrich Engels.

42 J. E. Alvarez, "The return of the State," *20 Minnesota Journal of International Law* (2011), p. 263; M. Koskenniemi, "The Wonderful Artificiality of States," *88 Proceedings of the Annual Meeting (American Society of International Law)* (1994), p. 22.

43 N. Schrijver, "The Changing Nature of State Sovereignty," *70 British Yearbook of International Law* (1999), p. 66; cf. O. Yiftachel, "Territory as the Kernel of the Nation: Space, Time and Nationalism in Israel/Palestine," *7 Geopolitics* (2002), p. 217; D. Newman, "Geopolitics Renaissant: Territory, Sovereignty, and the World Political Map" in D. Newman (ed.), *Boundaries, Territory and Postmodernity* (1999), p. 6–7; S. Chouinard, "Stateless Nations" in K. Cordell, S. Wolff (eds), *The Routledge Handbook of Ethnic Conflict* (2016), p. 55.

44 H. Spruyt, *The Sovereign State and Its Competitors: An Analysis of Systems Change* (1996), p. 192; cf. S. Chouinard, "Stateless Nations" in K. Cordell, S. Wolff (eds), *The Routledge Handbook of Ethnic Conflict* (2016), p. 54 et seq.

45 J. E. Nijman, *The Concept of International Legal Personality: An Inquiry Into the History and Theory of International Law* (2004), p. 423. But one has to admit that "[t]oday, for us to recognize the existence of a society without territory or political administration merely on the grounds that it maintains itself by an active exchange of goods and messages, as well as highly developed sense of common purpose, requires a very special effort" (E. W. Fox, *History in Geographic Perspective: The other France* (1972), p. 38–9).

46 O. Schachter, "The Decline of the Nation-State and its Implications for International Law," *36 Columbia Journal of Transnational Law* (1997), p. 22; cf. M. Craven, "Statehood, Self-determination, and Recognition" in M. D. Evans (ed.), *International Law* (2014), p. 205.

47 W. E. Hall, *A treatise on international law* (1895), p. 4; cited by B. Fassbender, "Der Schutz der Menschenrechte als zentraler Inhalt des völkerrechtlichen Gemeinwohls," *30 Europäische Grundrechte-Zeitschrift* (2003), p. 3.

48 C. Schmitt, *Politische Theologie: Vier Kapitel zur Lehre von der Souveränität* (1922), p. 9; cf. A. Peters, "Membership in the Global Constitutional Community" in J. Klabbers, A. Peters, G. Ulfstein (eds), *The Constitutionalization of International Law* (2009), p. 184.

49 F. M. Deng, "Frontiers of Sovereignty: A Framework of Protection, Assistance, and Development for the Internally Displaced," *8 Leiden Journal of International Law* (1995), p. 261; cf. C. Tomuschat, "How the Classical Concept of Sovereignty has Evolved" in M. Delević Dilas, V. Derić, V. Dimitrijević (eds), *The International and the National: Essays in honour of Vojin Dimitrijević* (2003), p. 27; R. Cohen, "From Sovereign Responsibility to R2P" in W. A. Knight, F. Egerton (eds), *The Routledge Handbook of the Responsibility to Protect* (2012), p. 17.

50 R. B. Lillich, "Sovereignty and Humanity: Can they converge?" in A. Grahl-Madsen, J. Toman (eds), The Spirit of Uppsala (1984), p. 406.

51 Ibid., p. 406–7; cf. F. M. Deng, "Frontiers of Sovereignty: A Framework of Protection, Assistance, and Development for the Internally Displaced," *8 Leiden Journal of International Law* (1995), p. 267.

52 A. James, *Sovereign Statehood: The Basis of International Society* (1986), p. 34: "being divided among single entities of a sovereign, or constitutionally independent, kind."
53 J. R. Crawford, *Brownlie's Principles of Public International Law* (2012), p. 447.
54 B. Fassbender, "Die Souveränität des Staates als Autonomie im Rahmen der völkerrechtlichen Verfassung" in H.-P. Mansel (ed.), *Festschrift für Erik Jayme* (2004), p. 1093.
55 S. I. Phlogaitēs, *The Evolution of Law and the State in Europe: Seven Lessons* (2014), p. 99.
56 A. Jakab, "Neutralizing the Sovereignty Question Compromise Strategies in Constitutional Argumentations before European Integration and since," *2 European Constitutional Law Review* (2006), 376.
57 S. I. Phlogaitēs, *The Evolution of Law and the State in Europe: Seven Lessons* (2014), p. 99; cf. R. McCorquodale, "International Community and State Sovereignty: An Uneasy Symbiotic Relationship" in C. Warbrick, S. Tierney (eds), *Towards an "International Legal Community"?: The Sovereignty of States and the Sovereignty of International Law* (2006), p. 260.
58 G. Kreijen, *State Failure, Sovereignty and Effectiveness: Legal Lessons from the Decolonization of Sub-Saharan Africa* (2004), p. 8; cf. W. G. Friedmann, *The Changing Structure of International Law* (1964), p. 60 et seq.; A. van Staden and H. Vollaard, "The Erosion of State Sovereignty: Towards a Post-territorial World?" in G. Kreijen (ed.), *State, Sovereignty, and International Governance* (2002), p. 165.
59 W. Riphagen, "Some Reflections on 'Functional Sovereignty'," *6 Netherlands Yearbook of International Law* (1975), p. 121.
60 B. Fassbender, "Der Schutz der Menschenrechte als zentraler Inhalt des völkerrechtlichen Gemeinwohls," *30 Europäische Grundrechte-Zeitschrift* (2003), p. 3, 12.
61 D. Newman, "Geopolitics Renaissant: Territory, Sovereignty, and the World Political Map" in D. Newman (ed.), *Boundaries, Territory and Postmodernity* (1999), p. 8.
62 N. Schrijver, "The Changing Nature of State Sovereignty," *70 British Yearbook of International Law* (1999), p. 76–7; C. Möllers, *Staat als Argument* (2000), p. 146.
63 A. Hurrelmann, S. Leibfried, K. Martens and P. Mayer, "The Transformation of the Golden-Age Nation State: Findings and Perspectives" in A. Hurrelmann, S. Leibfried, K. Martens, P. Mayer (eds), *Transforming the Golden-Age Nation State* (2007), p. 193.
64 Ibid., p. 193; cf. J. E. Nijman, *The Concept of International Legal Personality: An Inquiry Into the History and Theory of International Law* (2004), p. 350.
65 A. Hurrelmann, S. Leibfried, K. Martens, and P. Mayer, "The Transformation of the Golden-Age Nation State: Findings and Perspectives" in A. Hurrelmann, S. Leibfried, K. Martens, P. Mayer (eds), *Transforming the Golden-Age Nation State* (2007), p. 193.
66 A. Cassese, "States: Rise and Decline of the Primary Subjects of the International Community" in B. Fassbender, A. Peters (eds), *The Oxford Handbook of the History of International Law* (2012), p. 65.
67 D. Bethlehem, "The End of Geography: The Changing Nature of the International System and the Challenge to International Law," *25 EJIL* (2014), p. 18.
68 T. M. Franck, *The Empowered Self: Law and Society in an Age of Individualism* (1999), p. 5.
69 Cf. E. d. Vattel, *Le droit des gens ou Principes de la loi naturelle appliqués à la conduite et aux affaires des nations et des souverains* (1758).
70 C. Schreuer, "The Waning of the Sovereign State: Towards a New Paradigm for International-Law?," *4 EJIL* (1993), p. 465; A. G. Jain, "The 21st Century Atlantis: The International Law of Statehood and Climate Change-Induced Loss of Territory," *50 Stanford Journal of International Law* (2014), p. 7; A. Cassese, "States: Rise and

Decline of the Primary Subjects of the International Community" in B. Fassbender, A. Peters (eds), *The Oxford Handbook of the History of International Law* (2012), p. 54.

71 C. Tomuschat, "How the Classical Concept of Sovereignty has Evolved" in M. Delević Dilas, V. Derić, V. Dimitrijević (eds), *The International and the National: Essays in honour of Vojin Dimitrijević* (2003), p. 27; R. Cohen, "From Sovereign Responsibility to R2P" in W. A. Knight, F. Egerton (eds), *The Routledge Handbook of the Responsibility to Protect* (2012), p. 17; F. M. Deng, "Frontiers of Sovereignty: A Framework of Protection, Assistance, and Development for the Internally Displaced," *8 Leiden Journal of International Law* (1995), p. 261.

72 C. Schreuer, "The Waning of the Sovereign State: Towards a New Paradigm for International-Law?," *4 EJIL* (1993), p. 465; A. G. Jain, "The 21st Century Atlantis: The International Law of Statehood and Climate Change-Induced Loss of Territory," *50 Stanford Journal of International Law* (2014), p. 7; R. Y. Jennings, "An International Lawyer Takes Stock," *39 International & Comparative Law Quarterly* (1990), p. 522; G. Hafner, "The Emancipation of the Individual from the State under International Law," *358 Recueil Des Cours* (2011), p. 373.

73 T. M. Franck, *The Empowered Self: Law and Society in an Age of Individualism* (1999), p. 196–8.

74 C. Schreuer, "The Waning of the Sovereign State: Towards a New Paradigm for International-Law?," *4 EJIL* (1993), p. 465; A. L. Parrish, "Rehabilitating Territoriality in Human Rights," *32 Cardozo Law Review* (2011), p. 1099; F. M. Deng, "Frontiers of Sovereignty: A Framework of Protection, Assistance, and Development for the Internally Displaced," *8 Leiden Journal of International Law* (1995), p. 265; K. Knop, "Statehood: territory, people, government" in J. R. Crawford, M. Koskenniemi (eds), *The Cambridge Companion to International Law* (2012), p. 96; A. de Hoogh, "The Sovereigns are Dead, Long Live the Sovereigns – Reflections on State Sovereignty and International Law" in K. Wellens, E. R. Rieter, H. C. F. J. A. d. Waele (eds), *Evolving principles of international law: Studies in honour of Karel C. Wellens* (2012), p. 194.

75 A. A. C. Trindade, "International Law for Humankind: Towards a New Jus Gentium," part 2, *317 Recueil Des Cours* (2005), p. 269.

76 G. J. Evans and M. Sahnoun, *The Responsibility to Protect. Report of the International Commission on Intervention and State Sovereignty* (2001), p. 14.

77 R. B. Lillich, "Sovereignty and Humanity: Can they converge?" in A. Grahl-Madsen, J. Toman (eds), The Spirit of Uppsala (1984), p. 408.

78 Art. 1(3) "Charter of the UN" (1945); cf. R. B. McKay, "The 'Common Core' of Human Rights" in A. H. Henkin (ed.), *Human Dignity: The Internationalization of Human Rights: with Selected International Human Rights Documents: Essays Based on an Aspen Institute Workshop* (1978), p. 66.

79 S. Kadelbach, "The Territoriality and Migration of Fundamental Rights" in G. Handl, J. Zekoll, P. Zumbanse (eds), *Beyond Territoriality: Transnational Legal Authority in an Age of Globalization* (2012), p. 303.

80 UNGA, *54th Session, 13th Plenary meeting*, 24 September 1999, p. 23; seen differently for example by China in UNGA, *54th Session, 8th Plenary meeting*, 22 September 1999, p. 8.

81 L. B. Sohn, "The New International Law: Protection of the Rights of Individuals Rather than States," *32 The American University Law Review* (1982), p. 9–10; since Nuremberg and Tokyo, it is clear that individuals can even be held accountable for gross violations of international law (cf. A. G. Jain, "The 21st Century Atlantis: The International Law of Statehood and Climate Change-Induced Loss of Territory," *50 Stanford Journal of International Law* (2014), p. 8, fn50.); cf. A. Cassese, "States: Rise and Decline of the Primary Subjects of the International Community" in

B. Fassbender, A. Peters (eds), *The Oxford Handbook of the History of International Law* (2012), p. 67.

82 C. Warbrick, "States and Recognition in International Law" in M. D. Evans (ed.), *International Law*, 2nd edn. (2006), p. 242.

83 R. McCorquodale, "International Community and State Sovereignty: An Uneasy Symbiotic Relationship" in C. Warbrick, S. Tierney (eds), *Towards an "International Legal Community"?: The Sovereignty of States and the Sovereignty of International Law* (2006), p. 260.

84 L. B. Sohn, "The New International Law: Protection of the Rights of Individuals Rather than States," *32 The American University Law Review* (1982), p. 1.

85 K. Parlett, *The Individual in the International Legal System: Continuity and Change in International Law* (2011), p. 353, 362; cf. A. A. C. Trindade, "International Law for Humankind: Towards a New Jus Gentium," part 1, *316 Recueil Des Cours* (2005), p. 252 et seq.; A. Peters, *Jenseits der Menschenrechte: Die Rechtsstellung des Individuums im Völkerrecht* (2014), p. 363, 364; cf. R. McCorquodale, "The Individual in the International Legal System" in M. D. Evans (ed.), *International Law* (2014), p. 283 with further references.

86 Cf. B. Fassbender, "Der Schutz der Menschenrechte als zentraler Inhalt des völkerrechtlichen Gemeinwohls," *30 Europäische Grundrechte-Zeitschrift* (2003), p. 3; cf. ICJ – The Hague, *Conditions of Admission of a State to Membership in the UN (Article 4 of the Charter)* – Advisory Opinion – Individual Opinion by M. Alvarez (28 May 1948), p. 68.

87 "Charter of the UN" (1945), preamble.

88 J. Carter, *Address Before the General Assembly* (1977).

89 W. Schiffer, *The Legal Community of Mankind: A Critical Analysis of the Modern Concept of World Organization* (1972), p. 285; cf. K. A. Annan, *We the Peoples: The Role of the UN in the Twenty-first Century* (2000), p. 6.

90 P. M. Kennedy, *The Parliament of Man: The Past, Present, and Future of the UN* (2007), p. 33.

91 R. McCorquodale, "International Community and State Sovereignty: An Uneasy Symbiotic Relationship" in C. Warbrick, S. Tierney (eds), *Towards an "International Legal Community"?: The Sovereignty of States and the Sovereignty of International Law* (2006), p. 260.

92 Ibid., p. 178.

93 Ibid., p. 180.

94 Ibid., p. 178.

95 W. A. Knight, "Concluding Thoughts" in W. A. Knight, F. Egerton (eds), *The Routledge Handbook of the Responsibility to Protect* (2012), p. 277.

96 L. B. Sohn, "The New International Law: Protection of the Rights of Individuals Rather than States," *32 The American University Law Review* (1982), p. 1, 23.

97 Institut de droit international, "The Protection of Human Rights and the Principle of Non-intervention in Internal Affairs of States," *63 Institut de Droit International Annuaire 338* (1989); cf. T. Meron, *The Humanization of International Law* (2006), p. 265.

98 D. B. Goldman, *Globalisation and the Western Legal Tradition: Recurring Patterns of Law and Authority* (2008), p. 247-248; cf. J. Kokott, "Die Staatsrechtslehre und die Veränderung ihres Gegenstandes: Konsequenzen von Europäisierung und Internationalisierung" in J. Kokott, W. Brugger, C. Gusy, T. Vesting (eds), *Die Staatsrechtslehre und die Veränderung ihres Gegenstandes: Konsequenzen von Europäisierung und Internationalisierung. Gewährleistung von Freiheit und Sicherheit im Lichte unterschiedlicher Staats- und Verfassungsverständnisse / Berichte und Diskussionen auf der Tagung der Vereinigung der Deutschen Strafrechtslehrer in Hamburg vom 1. bis 4. Oktober 2003* (2004), p. 13, 36.

99 "Convention for the Protection of Human Rights and Fundamental Freedoms" (1950).
100 Cf. G. Hafner, "The Emancipation of the Individual from the State under International Law," *358 Recueil Des Cours* (2011), p. 395, 399.
101 R. McCorquodale, "International Community and State Sovereignty: An Uneasy Symbiotic Relationship" in C. Warbrick, S. Tierney (eds), *Towards an "International Legal Community"?: The Sovereignty of States and the Sovereignty of International Law* (2006), p. 260.
102 A. A. C. Trindade, "International Law for Humankind: Towards a New Jus Gentium," part 1, *316 Recueil Des Cours* (2005), p. 286; s. for an early examination: J. Spiropoulos, "L'individu et le droit international," *30 Recueil Des Cours* (1929), p. 245 et seq.
103 Cf. N. Bergmann, *Versinkende Inselstaaten: Auswirkungen des Klimawandels auf die Staatlichkeit kleiner Inselstaaten* (2016), p. 147; s. B. H. Oxman, "Jurisdiction of States," (last updated March 2009) in R. Wolfrum (ed.), *The Max Planck Encyclopedia of Public International Law: opil.ouplaw.com.home/EPIL* (2012), para. 38–9 for human rights violations leading to universal jurisdictions.
104 R. McCorquodale, "The Individual in the International Legal System" in M. D. Evans (ed.), *International Law* (2014), p. 285.
105 B. Fassbender, "Die Souveränität des Staates als Autonomie im Rahmen der völkerrechtlichen Verfassung" in H.-P. Mansel (ed.), *Festschrift für Erik Jayme* (2004), p. 1092–3.
106 A. Peters, "Membership in the Global Constitutional Community" in J. Klabbers, A. Peters, G. Ulfstein (eds), *The Constitutionalization of International Law* (2009), p. 179; C. W. Jenks, *The Common Law of Mankind* (1958); p. 17.
107 L. Glanville, *Sovereignty and the Responsibility to Protect: A New History* (2014), p. 135 with further references.
108 Van der Vyver, Johan D., "Sovereignty" in D. L. Shelton (ed.), *The Oxford Handbook of International Human Rights Law* (2013), p. 379.
109 B. Fassbender, "Die Souveränität des Staates als Autonomie im Rahmen der völkerrechtlichen Verfassung" in H.-P. Mansel (ed.), *Festschrift für Erik Jayme* (2004), p. 1092–3.
110 J. E. Alvarez, "The return of the State," *20 Minnesota Journal of International Law* (2011), p. 225 ("'S' word as a troublesome hindrance," p. 228); citing L. Henkin, "The Mythology of Sovereignty" in R. S. MacDonald, T. Wang (eds), *Essays in honour of Wang Tieya* (1994); cf. J. R. Crawford, "Chance, Order, Change: The Course of International Law, General Course on Public International Law," *365 Recueil Des Cours* (2013), p. 84.
111 M. Craven, "Statehood, Self-determination, and Recognition" in M. D. Evans (ed.), *International Law* (2014), p. 204; cf. ICJ – The Hague, *The Corfu Channel Case –* Individual opinion by Judge Alvarez (9 April 1949), p. 43.
112 B. Fassbender, "Article 2(1)" in B. Simma, H. Mosler, A. Paulus, E. Chaitidou (eds), *The Charter of the UN: A Commentary* (2012), p. 140, para. 14; cf. A. A. C. Trindade, "International Law for Humankind: Towards a New Jus Gentium," part 1, *316 Recueil Des Cours* (2005), p. 217 ("purely inter-state law has led to abuse of power by those who held it").
113 L. A. Malone, "Green Helmets: Eco-Intervention in the TwentyFirst Century," *103 Proceedings of the Annual Meeting (American Society of International Law)* (2009), p. 26.
114 L. Glanville, *Sovereignty and the Responsibility to Protect: A New History* (2014), p. 11–12 with further references, pointing out that also sovereignty has a "rich history" (p. 14) and has not always been as absolute as it is suggested today, even at the time of the peace of Westphalia (p. 49); A. Peters, "Humanity as the A and Ω of Sovereignty," *20 EJIL* (2009), p. 543.

115 "Draft Declaration on Rights and Duties of States" (1949), emphasis added.

116 Van der Vyver, Johan D., "Sovereignty" in D. L. Shelton (ed.), *The Oxford Handbook of International Human Rights Law* (2013), p. 379, citing House of Lords, *Regina v Bow Street Metropolitan Stipendiary Magistrate, ex parte Pinochet Ugarte (No. 1)* (25 November 1998); cf. R. McCorquodale and R. Pangalangan, "Pushing Back the Limitations of Territorial Boundaries," *21 EJIL* (2001), p. 881.

117 C. Stahn, "Responsibility to Protect: Political Rhetoric or Emerging Legal Norm?" *101 AJIL* (2007), p. 102; cf. G. J. Evans and M. Sahnoun, *The Responsibility to Protect. Report of the International Commission on Intervention and State Sovereignty* (2001), p. 13; cf. A. Peters, *Jenseits der Menschenrechte: Die Rechtsstellung des Individuums im Völkerrecht* (2014), p. 218

118 A. Peters, "Humanity as the A and Ω of Sovereignty," *20 EJIL* (2009), p. 543.

119 K. A. Annan, "The Legitimacy to Intervene," Financial Times, 10 January 2000, p. 19; cf. A. Addis, "The Thin State in Thick Globalism: Sovereignty in the Information Age," *37 Vanderbilt Journal of Transnational Law* (2004), p. 70; A. A. C. Trindade, "International Law for Humankind: Towards a New Jus Gentium," part 1, *316 Recueil Des Cours* (2005), p. 219; W. Mannens, "Shared Sovereignty? Minority Claims and the Effectiveness of State Authority" in G. Kreijen (ed.), *State, Sovereignty, and International Governance* (2002), p. 155.

120 S. S. Kim, "Sovereignty in the Chinese Image of World Order" in R. S. MacDonald, T. Wang (eds), *Essays in honour of Wang Tieya* (1994), p. 433; cf. J. Pérez de Cuéllar, "Report of the Secretary-General on the work of the Organization," *45 Yearbook of the UN* (1991), p. 7.

121 C. Tomuschat, "International Law: Ensuring the Survival of Mankind on the Eve of a New Century," *281 Recueil Des Cours* (1999), p. 224.

122 International Tribunal for the Prosecution of Persons Responsible for Serious Violations of International Humanitarian Law Committed in the Territory of the Former Yugoslavia since 1991, *Decision on the Defence Motion for Interlocutory Appeal on Jurisdiction – Prosecutor v. Duško Tadić* (2 October 1995), para. 58.

123 M. S. Fusillo, "The legal regime of uninhabited 'rocks' lacking an economic life of their own," *4 The Italian Yearbook of International Law* (1978–79), p. 483, para. 50.

124 B. Fassbender, "Sovereignty and Constitutionalism in International Law" in N. Walker (ed.), *Sovereignty in Transition* (2003), p. 139; s. C. Tomuschat, "International Law: Ensuring the Survival of Mankind on the Eve of a New Century," *281 Recueil Des Cours* (1999), p. 70.

125 E. Schmeer, *Responsibility to Protect und Wandel von Souveränität: Untersucht am Fallbeispiel des Krieges in Darfur* (2010), p. 10–11.

126 UNGA, *54th Session, 13th Plenary meeting*, 24 September 1999, p. 23 (Mr van Aartsen (Netherlands)); seen differently for example by China in UNGA, *54th Session, 8th Plenary meeting*, 22 September 1999, p. 8.

127 S. C. Breau, *The Responsibility to Protect in International Law: An Emerging Paradigm Shift* (2016), p. 92.

128 A. Peters, "Humanity as the A and Ω of Sovereignty," *20 EJIL* (2009), p. 513, 514.

129 UNGA, *54th Session, 13th Plenary meeting*, 24 September 1999, p. 23 (Mr van Aartsen (Netherlands)).

130 O. Schachter, "Sovereignty – Then and Now" in R. S. MacDonald, T. Wang (eds), *Essays in honour of Wang Tieya* (1994), p. 677 referring to L. Henkin, "Human Rights and Domestic Jurisdiction" in T. Buergenthal (ed.), Human Rights, International Law, and the Helsinki Accord (1977), p. 29–40.

131 L. Henkin, "The Mythology of Sovereignty" in R. S. MacDonald, T. Wang (eds), *Essays in honour of Wang Tieya* (1994), p. 358.

132 L. Glanville, *Sovereignty and the Responsibility to Protect: A New History* (2014), p. 173.

133 R. Cohen, "From Sovereign Responsibility to R2P" in W. A. Knight, F. Egerton (eds), *The Routledge Handbook of the Responsibility to Protect* (2012), p. 11; cf. p. 10: While the Carter administration "regularly emphasized that it was the responsibility of governments first and foremost to protect the human rights of their citizens in accordance with national and international human rights standards" they already affirmed that "if they failed to do so, the United States had a right and a responsibility to act on the basis of its laws and international commitments." Taking action could go from diplomatic intercessions to military and economic aid cutoffs. (cf. H. Cleveland, "The Internationalization of internal affairs" in A. H. Henkin (ed.), *Human Dignity: The Internationalization of Human Rights: with Selected International Human Rights Documents: Essays Based on an Aspen Institute Workshop* (1978), p. 43 et seq.).

134 A. Peters, "Humanity as the A and Ω of Sovereignty," *20 EJIL* (2009), p. 533.

135 A. Peters, *Jenseits der Menschenrechte: Die Rechtsstellung des Individuums im Völkerrecht* (2014), p. 218; cf. A. Addis, "The Thin State in Thick Globalism: Sovereignty in the Information Age," *37 Vanderbilt Journal of Transnational Law* (2004), p. 21; C. W. Morris, *An Essay on the Modern State* (2002), p. 53. Various military interventions (Cambodia, Bangladesh, Kosovo, Iraq, Afghanistan, Georgia, and Libya) "indicate a softening, if not an actual erosion, of the Westphalian notion of sovereignty." (W. A. Knight, "Concluding Thoughts" in W. A. Knight, F. Egerton (eds), *The Routledge Handbook of the Responsibility to Protect* (2012), p. 276).

136 M. Weller, *Contested Statehood: Kosovo's Struggle for Independence* (2009), p. 261; L. A. Malone, "Green Helmets: Eco-Intervention in the TwentyFirst Century," *103 Proceedings of the Annual Meeting (American Society of International Law)* (2009), p. 26.

137 J. Pattison, *Humanitarian Intervention and the Responsibility to Protect: Who Should Intervene?* (2010), p. 3.

138 A. Peters, "Membership in the Global Constitutional Community" in J. Klabbers, A. Peters, G. Ulfstein (eds), *The Constitutionalization of International Law* (2009), p. 185; s. M. Byers, "International law and the responsibility to protect" in C. M. Chinkin, F. Baetens (eds), *Sovereignty, Statehood and State Responsibility: Essays in Honour of James Crawford* (2015), p. 24 et seq. on the development of R2P.

139 R. Cohen, "From Sovereign Responsibility to R2P" in W. A. Knight, F. Egerton (eds), *The Routledge Handbook of the Responsibility to Protect* (2012), p. 17.

140 L. Glanville, *Sovereignty and the Responsibility to Protect: A New History* (2014), p. 171; cf. A. Addis, "The Thin State in Thick Globalism: Sovereignty in the Information Age," *37 Vanderbilt Journal of Transnational Law* (2004), p. 20–1; M. Byers, "International law and the responsibility to protect" in C. M. Chinkin, F. Baetens (eds), *Sovereignty, Statehood and State Responsibility: Essays in Honour of James Crawford* (2015), p. 34 et seq.

141 M. Weller, *Contested Statehood: Kosovo's Struggle for Independence* (2009), p. 260.

142 B. Fassbender, "Die Souveränität des Staates als Autonomie im Rahmen der völkerrechtlichen Verfassung" in H.-P. Mansel (ed.), *Festschrift für Erik Jayme* (2004), p. 1092–3; K. A. Annan, "The Legitimacy to Intervene," Financial Times, 10 January 2000, p. 19.

143 A. Peters, *Jenseits der Menschenrechte: Die Rechtsstellung des Individuums im Völkerrecht* (2014), p. 222; cf. ILC, *Protection of persons in the event of disasters: Texts and titles of draft articles 6, 7, 8, and 9, provisionally adopted by the Drafting Committee on 6,7, and 8 July 2010*, 14 July 2010, Art. 9; L. Glanville, *Sovereignty and the Responsibility to Protect: A New History* (2014), p. 192; F. M. Deng, S. Kimaro, T. Lyons and D. Rothchild, *Sovereignty as Responsibility: Conflict Management in Africa* (1996), p. xviii; cf. A. Orford, *International Authority and the Responsibility to Protect* (2011), p. 13–14; J. Pattison, *Humanitarian Intervention and the Responsibility to Protect: Who Should Intervene?* (2010), p. 3; UN Secretary

General K. A. Annan, *Secretary-General reflects on 'intervention' in thirty-fifth annual Ditchley Foundation Lecture*, 26 June 1998; W. A. Knight, "Concluding Thoughts" in W. A. Knight, F. Egerton (eds), *The Routledge Handbook of the Responsibility to Protect* (2012), p. 276; R. Cohen, "From Sovereign Responsibility to R2P" in W. A. Knight, F. Egerton (eds), *The Routledge Handbook of the Responsibility to Protect* (2012), p. 13; P. Hilpold, "From Humanitarian Intervention to Responsibility to Protect: Making Utopia True?" in U. Fastenrath, R. Geiger, D.-E. Khan, A. Paulus, S. von Schorlemer, C. Vedder (eds), *From Bilateralism to Community Interest: Essays in Honour of Judge Bruno Simma* (2011), p. 468; A. Peters, "Humanity as the A and Ω of Sovereignty," *20 EJIL* (2009), p. 513; M. Horsman and A. Marshall, *After the Nation-state: Citizens, Tribalism and the New World Disorder* (1994). P. 263; D. Wallace, "Introduction: security and global climate change" in D. Wallace, D. Silander (eds), *Climate Change, Policy and Security: State and Human Impacts* (2018), p. 5 et seq.

144 L. Glanville, "The Responsibility to Protect Beyond Borders," *12 Human Rights Law Review* (2012), p. 4.

145 L. Glanville, *Sovereignty and the Responsibility to Protect: A New History* (2014), p. 1, 5, 43.

146 A. Peters, "Humanity as the A and Ω of Sovereignty," *20 EJIL* (2009), p. 525; citing T. Hobbes/A. P. Martinich, *Leviathan* (2005 [1651]), ch. 21, para. 114, (p. 166).

147 C. W. Morris, *An Essay on the Modern State* (2002), p. 5, cf. T. Hobbes/A. P. Martinich, *Leviathan* (2005 [1651]), introduction, para. 1 (p. 9): "[the state] is but an artificial man; though of greater stature and strength than the natural, for whose protection and defense it was intended; …"

148 B. Boutros-Ghali, "Empowering the UN," *71 Foreign Affairs* (1992), p. 98, 99.

149 L. Glanville, *Sovereignty and the Responsibility to Protect: A New History* (2014), p. 36.

150 Ibid., p. 58 with further references; cf. W. Schiffer, *The Legal Community of Mankind: A Critical Analysis of the Modern Concept of World Organization* (1972), p. 57; D. J. B. Trim, "'If a prince use tyrannie towards his people': interventions on behalf of foreign populations in early modern Europe" in B. Simms, D. J. B. Trim (eds), *Humanitarian Intervention: A History* (2011), p. 29 et seq.

151 C. Tomuschat, "How the Classical Concept of Sovereignty has Evolved" in M. Delević Dilas, V. Derić, V. Dimitrijević (eds), *The International and the National: Essays in honour of Vojin Dimitrijević* (2003), p. 21.

152 Stahn argues, that "[t]he understanding that a state exercises the functions of an agent and trustee for the human beings […] is not a twentieth-century principle but can be traced much further back. […] as early as the time of Hugo Grotius whose conception of law was based on the assumption that the rules governing the organization and behavior of states exist ultimately for the benefit of the actual subjects of the rights and duties concerned, individual human beings." (C. Stahn, "Responsibility to Protect: Political Rhetoric or Emerging Legal Norm?," *101 AJIL* (2007), p. 111).

153 Ibid., p. 111; cf. G. J. Evans and M. Sahnoun, *The Responsibility to Protect. Report of the International Commission on Intervention and State Sovereignty* (2001), p. 13, para. 2.14, 2.15; A. Peters, *Jenseits der Menschenrechte: Die Rechtsstellung des Individuums im Völkerrecht* (2014), p. 218.

154 Cf. B. Simma, "From bilateralism to community interest in international law," *250 Recueil Des Cours* (1994), p. 229 et seq.

155 T. Meron, *The Humanization of International Law* (2006), p. 249.

156 C. Tomuschat, "How the Classical Concept of Sovereignty has Evolved" in M. Delević Dilas, V. Derić, V. Dimitrijević (eds), *The International and the National: Essays in honour of Vojin Dimitrijević* (2003), p. 27.

157 T. Schweisfurth, *Völkerrecht* (2006), p. 13 §36.

158 T. M. Franck, *The Empowered Self: Law and Society in an Age of Individualism* (1999), p. 280; cf. J. E. Nijman, *The Concept of International Legal Personality: An Inquiry Into the History and Theory of International Law* (2004), p. 422.
159 C. Tomuschat, "How the Classical Concept of Sovereignty has Evolved" in M. Delević Dilas, V. Derić, V. Dimitrijević (eds), *The International and the National: Essays in honour of Vojin Dimitrijević* (2003), p. 27.
160 P. M. Kennedy, *The Parliament of Man: The Past, Present, and Future of the UN* (2007), p. 205.
161 UN Commission on Human Rights, *Report of the Sub-Committee on the handling of communications*, 6 February 1947.
162 UNGA Res. 60/251 of 4 April 2006, p. 3, para. 5(e).
163 R. Cohen, "From Sovereign Responsibility to R2P" in W. A. Knight, F. Egerton (eds), *The Routledge Handbook of the Responsibility to Protect* (2012), p. 8–9.
164 A. Peters, "Humanity as the A and Ω of Sovereignty," *20 EJIL* (2009), p. 514.
165 N. Aloupi, "The Right to Non-intervention and Non-interference," *4 Cambridge Journal of International and Comparative Law* (2015), p. 582.
166 T. M. Franck, *The Empowered Self: Law and Society in an Age of Individualism* (1999), p. 196–8; cf. L. Glanville, *Sovereignty and the Responsibility to Protect: A New History* (2014), p. 135; R. Grote, "Westphalian System," (last updated March 2009) in R. Wolfrum (ed.), *The Max Planck Encyclopedia of Public International Law: opil.ouplaw.com.home/EPIL* (2012), p. 873, para. 15; C. W. Jenks, *The Common Law of Mankind* (1958); p. 17; W. G. Friedmann, *The Changing Structure of International Law* (1964), p. 65; B. Fassbender, "Der Schutz der Menschenrechte als zentraler Inhalt des völkerrechtlichen Gemeinwohls," *30 Europäische Grundrechte-Zeitschrift* (2003), p. 3; M. Koskenniemi, *From Apology to Utopia: The Structure of International Legal Argument* (2015), p. 211.
167 R. Wolfrum, "Article 1" in B. Simma, H. Mosler, A. Paulus, E. Chaitidou (eds), *The Charter of the UN: A Commentary* (2012), para. 12.
168 Cf. R. Wilde, "Human Rights beyond Borders at the World Court" in C. M. Chinkin, F. Baetens (eds), *Sovereignty, Statehood and State Responsibility: Essays in Honour of James Crawford* (2015), p. 56 et seq.
169 Cf. B. Simma, "Human Rights Before the International Court of Justice: Community Interests Coming to Life?" in C. J. Tams (ed.), *The Development of International Law by the International Court of Justice* (2013), p. 303.
170 Ibid., p. 325.
171 J. E. Nijman, *The Concept of International Legal Personality: An Inquiry Into the History and Theory of International Law* (2004), p. 424.
172 C. Schreuer, "The Waning of the Sovereign State: Towards a New Paradigm for International-Law?," *4 EJIL* (1993), p. 469.
173 E.-U. Petersmann, "From State Sovereignty to the 'Sovereign of Citizens' in the International Relations Law of the EU?" in N. Walker (ed.), *Sovereignty in Transition* (2003), p. 152 (emphasis added).
174 A. Peters, "Membership in the Global Constitutional Community" in J. Klabbers, A. Peters, G. Ulfstein (eds), *The Constitutionalization of International Law* (2009), p. 196; cf. A. Peters, "Dual Democracy" in J. Klabbers, A. Peters, G. Ulfstein (eds), *The Constitutionalization of International Law* (2009), p. 319–26; cf. T. M. Franck, *The Empowered Self: Law and Society in an Age of Individualism* (1999), p. 37: "There, factions, minorities, and other affinity groups could make themselves heard without secession and the pursuit of sovereignty, choosing instead to aggregate their interests through transnational political parties and coalitions."
175 A. L. Paulus, "The Emergence of the International Community and the Divide between International and Domestic Law" in A. Nollkaemper, J. E. Nijman (eds), *New Perspectives on the Divide Between National and International Law* (2007),

p. 223; A. L. Paulus, "International law and international community" in J. D. Armstrong, J. Brunée (eds), *Routledge Handbook of International Law* (2009), p. 48.

176 I. Kant/M. C. Smith, R. Latta, and J. Donaldson, *Perpetual Peace: A Philosophical Essay by Immanuel Kant 1795 translated with introduction and notes by M. Campbell Smith, M.A. With a preface by Professor Latta* (1903), Third definitive Article; I. Kant, *Zum ewigen Frieden* (1795), p. 46 ("so ist die Idee des Weltbürgerrechts keine phantastische und überspannte Vorstellungsart des Rechts, sondern eine nothwendige Ergänzung des ungeschriebenen Kodex…").

177 I. Kant/H. B. Nisbet (transl.), and H. Reiss (ed.), *Kant: Political Writings* (1996), p. 98–9 (I. Kant, *Zum ewigen Frieden* (1795)).

178 J. R. Crawford, "Chance, Order, Change: The Course of International Law, General Course on Public International Law," *365 Recueil Des Cours* (2013), p. 332.

179 B. Simma, "From bilateralism to community interest in international law," *250 Recueil Des Cours* (1994), p. 230.

180 T. M. Franck, *The Empowered Self: Law and Society in an Age of Individualism* (1999), p. 44; cf. J. E. Nijman, *The Concept of International Legal Personality: An Inquiry Into the History and Theory of International Law* (2004), p. 418.

181 K. A. Annan, "The Legitimacy to Intervene," Financial Times, 10 January 2000, p. 19; cf. A. Addis, "The Thin State in Thick Globalism: Sovereignty in the Information Age," *37 Vanderbilt Journal of Transnational Law* (2004), p. 70.

182 T. M. Franck, *The Empowered Self: Law and Society in an Age of Individualism* (1999), p. 3.

183 Ibid., p. 79, partly citing P. J. Spiro, "New Global Communities: Nongovernmental Organizations in International Decision-Making Institutions," *18 The Washington Quarterly* (1995), p. 45.

184 M. Horsman and A. Marshall, *After the Nation-state: Citizens, Tribalism and the New World Disorder* (1994), p. 263–4.

185 T. M. Franck, *The Empowered Self: Law and Society in an Age of Individualism* (1999), p. 1.

186 Ibid., p. 1. Franck argues later with regard to such "alternative" associations: "The prefatory words 'virtual' or 'emerging' make some people think, they are not as 'natural' as territorially 'bundled' communities. Yet, territorial states themselves are not 'natural' in any strict historic or sociological sense, but invented constructs of shifting boundaries and populations. Even older communities like nations were 'unnatural' conveniences invented by ancient ethnie, tribes, and clans" (p. 92).

187 Cf. J. E. Nijman, *The Concept of International Legal Personality: An Inquiry Into the History and Theory of International Law* (2004), p. 418.

188 T. M. Franck, *The Empowered Self: Law and Society in an Age of Individualism* (1999), p. 99–100.

189 Ibid., p. 99; A. van Staden and H. Vollaard, "The Erosion of State Sovereignty: Towards a Post-territorial World?" in G. Kreijen (ed.), *State, Sovereignty, and International Governance* (2002), p. 177 et seq.; but cf. H. Bull, *The Anarchical Society: A Study of Order in World Politics* (2012), p. 254–5; 246: The mere existence of actors other than the State, does not provide any indication of a trend towards a new medievalism though.

190 R. McCorquodale, "International Community and State Sovereignty: An Uneasy Symbiotic Relationship" in C. Warbrick, S. Tierney (eds), *Towards an "International Legal Community"?: The Sovereignty of States and the Sovereignty of International Law* (2006), p. 261.

191 C. Schreuer, "The Waning of the Sovereign State: Towards a New Paradigm for International-Law?," *4 EJIL* (1993), p. 465; A. L. Parrish, "Rehabilitating Territoriality in Human Rights," *32 Cardozo Law Review* (2011), p. 1099; A. G.

Jain, "The 21st Century Atlantis: The International Law of Statehood and Climate Change-Induced Loss of Territory," *50 Stanford Journal of International Law* (2014), p. 8.

192 ICJ – The Hague, *Reparation for Injuries Suffered in the Service of the UN* – Advisory Opinion (11 April 1949)

193 R. Y. Jennings, "An International Lawyer Takes Stock," *39 International & Comparative Law Quarterly* (1990), p. 522; citing ICJ – The Hague, *Reparation for Injuries Suffered in the Service of the UN* – Advisory Opinion (11 April 1949), p. 174 et seq.

194 C. Warbrick, "States and Recognition in International Law" in M. D. Evans (ed.), *International Law*, 2nd edn (2006), p. 242.

195 Cf. for many: A. A. C. Trindade, "International Law for Humankind: Towards a New Jus Gentium," part 2, *317 Recueil Des Cours* (2005), p. 118.

196 J. Grote-Stoutenburg, *Disappearing Island States in International Law* (2015), p. 245; cf. M. N. Shaw, *International Law* (2008), p. 206; D. J. Devine, "The Requirements of Statehood Re-Examined," *34 The Modern Law Review* (1971), p. 410 et seq.

197 A. Cassese, "States: Rise and Decline of the Primary Subjects of the International Community" in B. Fassbender, A. Peters (eds), *The Oxford Handbook of the History of International Law* (2012), p. 67.

198 Ibid., p. 67.

199 R. Kwiecień, "On Some Contemporary Challenges to Statehood in the International Legal Order: International Law Between Lotus and Global Administrative Law," *51 Archiv des Völkerrechts* (2013), p. 279.

200 A. Peters, *Jenseits der Menschenrechte: Die Rechtsstellung des Individuums im Völkerrecht* (2014), p. 379 (translation by the author).

201 A. Peters, "Humanity as the A and Ω of Sovereignty," *20 EJIL* (2009), p. 514; citing C. Tomuschat, "International Law: Ensuring the Survival of Mankind on the Eve of a New Century," *281 Recueil Des Cours* (1999), p. 161–2.

202 T. M. Franck, *The Empowered Self: Law and Society in an Age of Individualism* (1999), p. 60; cf. J. E. Nijman, *The Concept of International Legal Personality: An Inquiry Into the History and Theory of International Law* (2004), p. 422.

203 Cf. A. G. Jain, "The 21st Century Atlantis: The International Law of Statehood and Climate Change-Induced Loss of Territory," *50 Stanford Journal of International Law* (2014), p. 23; cf. I. A. Shearer, *Starke's International Law* (2003), p. 144; C. Dupuis, "Règles générales du droit de la paix," *32 Recueil Des Cours* (1930), p. 187 et seq.

204 A. G. Jain, "The 21st Century Atlantis: The International Law of Statehood and Climate Change-Induced Loss of Territory," *50 Stanford Journal of International Law* (2014), p. 23; cf. G. W. White and E. A. White, *Nation, State, and Territory: Origins, Evolutions, and Relationships* (2007), p. 37; R. McCorquodale and R. Pangalangan, "Pushing Back the Limitations of Territorial Boundaries," *21 European Journal of International Law* (2001), p. 883.

205 A. G. Jain, "The 21st Century Atlantis: The International Law of Statehood and Climate Change-Induced Loss of Territory," *50 Stanford Journal of International Law* (2014), p. 23; cf. G. W. White and E. A. White, *Nation, State, and Territory: Origins, Evolutions, and Relationships* (2007), p. 37; D.-E. Khan, "Territory and Boundaries" in B. Fassbender, A. Peters (eds), *The Oxford Handbook of the History of International Law* (2012), p. 227.

206 A. G. Jain, "The 21st Century Atlantis: The International Law of Statehood and Climate Change-Induced Loss of Territory," *50 Stanford Journal of International Law* (2014), p. 23; D. B. Goldman, *Globalisation and the Western Legal Tradition: Recurring Patterns of Law and Authority* (2008), p. 142; cf. D.-E. Khan, "Territory and Boundaries" in B. Fassbender, A. Peters (eds), *The Oxford Handbook of the History of International Law* (2012), p. 227.

207 R. Mayntz, "Die Handlungsfähigkeit des Nationalstaats in Zeiten der Globalisierung" in L. Heidbrink, A. Hirsch (eds), *Staat ohne Verantwortung, Zum Wandel der Aufgaben von Staat und Politik* (2007), p. 269, 270.

208 A. L. Paulus, "The International Lawyer between Globalization and Postmodernity" in J. I. Drolshammer, M. Pfeifer (eds), *The Internationalization of the Practice of Law* (2001), p. 387.

209 W. A. Knight, "Concluding Thoughts" in W. A. Knight, F. Egerton (eds), *The Routledge Handbook of the Responsibility to Protect* (2012), p. 276.

210 I. Kant/M. C. Smith, R. Latta and J. Donaldson, *Perpetual Peace: A Philosophical Essay by Immanuel Kant 1795 translated with introduction and notes by M. Campbell Smith, M.A. With a preface by Professor Latta* (1903), Third definitive Article; I. Kant, *Zum ewigen Frieden* (1795), p. 46 ("Da es nun mit der unter den Völkern der Erde einmal durchgängig überhandgenommenen (engeren oder weiteren) Gemeinschaft so weit gekommen ist, dass die *Rechtsverletzung an einem Platz der Erde an allen gefühlt* wird: …").

211 C. W. Kegley, G. A. Raymond, *Exorcising the Ghost of Westphalia: Building World Order in the New Millennium* (2002), p. 157; referring to R. T. Kudrle, "Three Types of Globalization: Communication, Market, and Direct" in R. Väyrynen (ed.), *Globalization and Global Governance* (1999), p. 3 et seq.

212 A. Hudson, 'Beyond the Borders: Globalisation, Sovereignty and Extra-Territoriality' in D. Newman (ed.), *Boundaries, Territory and Postmodernity* (1999), p. 89; A. El Ouali, *Territorial Integrity in a Globalizing World: International Law and States' Quest for Survival* (2012), p. 92; O. Schachter, "The Decline of the Nation-State and its Implications for International Law," *36 Columbia Journal of Transnational Law* (1997), p. 8; cf. W. Mannens, "Shared Sovereignty? Minority Claims and the Effectiveness of State Authority" in G. Kreijen (ed.), *State, Sovereignty, and International Governance* (2002), p. 147 et seq., 162.

213 R. Balleste and J. Kulesza, "Signs and Portents in Cyberspace: The Rise of Jus Internet as New Order in International Law," *23 Fordham Intellectual Property, Media and Entertainment Law Journal* (2013), p. 1319.

214 B. Marquardt, *Universalgeschichte des Staates: Von der vorstaatlichen Gesellschaft zum Staat der Industriegesellschaft* (2009), p. 615; cf. A. Addis, "The Thin State in Thick Globalism: Sovereignty in the Information Age," *37 Vanderbilt Journal of Transnational Law* (2004), p. 25 et seq. in much greater detail; M. Albert, *A Theory of World Politics* (2016), p. 29.

215 R. Balleste and J. Kulesza, "Signs and Portents in Cyberspace: The Rise of Jus Internet as New Order in International Law," *23 Fordham Intellectual Property, Media and Entertainment Law Journal* (2013), p. 1330.

216 E. Milano, "The Deterritorialization of International Law," *2 ESIL Reflections* (2013), p. 2; C. W. Morris, *An Essay on the Modern State* (2002), p. 52.

217 H. Spruyt, *The Sovereign State and Its Competitors: An Analysis of Systems Change* (1996), p. 183.

218 A. Addis, "The Thin State in Thick Globalism: Sovereignty in the Information Age," *37 Vanderbilt Journal of Transnational Law* (2004), p. 20.

219 "Rio Declaration on Environment and Development: Rio Declaration" (1992).

220 Warren, Charles; Greenshields, Robert A. E; Hostie, Jan Frans, *Trail smelter case (USA, Canada)* – Arbitration Award (16 April 1938 and 11 March 1941), p. 1965.

221 "Convention to Combat Desertification" (1994).

222 H. P. Aust, "Auf dem Weg zu einem Recht der globalen Stadt?: 'C40' und der 'Konvent der Bürgermeister' im globalen Klimaschutzregime," *73 Zeitschrift für ausländisches Öffentliches Recht und Völkerrecht* (2013), p. 676; H. P. Aust, *Das Recht der globalen Stadt: Grenzüberschreitende Dimensionen kommunaler Selbstverwaltung* (2017), p. 169.

223 H. Tabuchi and H. Fountain, "Bucking Trump, These Cities, States and Companies Commit to Paris Accord," *The New York Times*, 1 June 2017; cf. M. Rosso Grossman, "Climate Change and the Individual," *66 The American Journal of Comparative Law* (2018), p. 347, who suggests "Despite this withdrawal, however, the United States could meet its Paris goals through the efforts of cities, states, and businesses."
224 A. Coen, "RWE: Hält dieser Mann den Klimawandel auf?" *Die Zeit*, 8 June 2017.
225 Cf. J. Setzer; R. Byrnes, *Global trends in climate change litigation: 2019 snapshot* (2019).
226 Ibid., p. 1.
227 Setzer; R. Byrnes, *Global trends in climate change litigation: 2019 snapshot* (2019), p. 6; cf. B. Mayer, *The International Law on Climate Change* (2018), p. 245.
228 Gerechtshof Den Haag, *The State of the Netherlands (Ministry of Infrastructure and the Environment) v. Urgenda Foundation* (2018), para. 29.
229 Cf. UN Environment Programme, *The Status of Climate Change Litigation – A Global Review*, May 2017 (2017), p. 15.
230 J. Saurer; K. Purnhagen, "Klimawandel vor Gericht – Der Rechtsstreit der Nichtregierungsorganisation 'Urgenda' gegen die Niederlande und seine Bedeutung für Deutschland," *Zeitschrift für Umweltrecht (ZUR)* (2016), p. 19–20.
231 Ibid., p. 19.
232 Gerechtshof Den Haag, *The State of the Netherlands (Ministry of Infrastructure and the Environment) v. Urgenda Foundation* (9 October 2018).
233 J. Setzer; R. Byrnes, *Global trends in climate change litigation: 2019 snapshot* (2019), p. 6; B. Mayer, "Interpreting States' general obligations on climate change mitigation: A methodological review," *Review of European Community & International Environmental Law* (2019), p. 2; cf. I. Kaminski, *Final Appeal in Historic Urgenda Case May Hinge on Human Rights* (28 May 2019).
234 Procurator General of the Supreme Court of the Netherlands, *The State of the Netherlands (Ministry of Infrastructure and the Environment) v. Urgenda Foundation*, 13 September 2019.
235 J. Saurer; K. Purnhagen, "Klimawandel vor Gericht – Der Rechtsstreit der Nichtregierungsorganisation 'Urgenda' gegen die Niederlande und seine Bedeutung für Deutschland," *Zeitschrift für Umweltrecht (ZUR)* (2016), p. 16.
236 https://www.urgenda.nl/en/themas/climate-case/, *Landmark decision by Dutch Supreme Court* (last visited 21 May 2022); cf. Hoge Raad der Nederlanden, *De Staat der Nederlanden tegen Stichting Urgenda*, 20 December 2019.
237 Ninth Circuit Court of Appeals in Portland, Oregon, *Juliana v. United States*, Case: 18-36082, 17 January 2020: youth plaintiffs asserted that the Government's actions that cause climate change violate their constitutional rights to life, liberty, and property.
238 J. Setzer, R. Byrnes, *Global trends in climate change litigation: 2019 snapshot* (2019), p. 6; B. Mayer, "Interpreting States' general obligations on climate change mitigation: A methodological review," *Review of European Community & International Environmental Law* (2019), p. 6.
239 G. Liston, "Enhancing the efficacy of climate change litigation: how to resolve the 'fair share question' in the context of international human rights law," *Cambridge International Law Journal, Vol. 9 No. 2* (2020), p. 242.
240 https://youth4climatejustice.org/wp-content/uploads/2020/12/Application-form-annex.pdf (last visited 29 December 2020).
241 European Court of Human Rights, *Cláudia Duarte Agostinho and others against Portugal and 33 other States*, Request No. 39371/20, Statement of 13 November 2020.
242 General Court of the European Union (EGC), Second Chamber, *People's Climate Case (Carvalho and Others v Parliament and Council)*, Case T-330/18, 8 May 2019.

243 J. Setzer; R. Byrnes, *Global trends in climate change litigation: 2019 snapshot* (2019), p. 6; B. Mayer, "Interpreting States' general obligations on climate change mitigation: A methodological review," *Review of European Community & International Environmental Law* (2019), p. 7.
244 General Court of the European Union (EGC), Second Chamber, *People's Climate Case (Carvalho and Others v Parliament and Council)*, Case T-330/18, 8 May 2019, para. 49.
245 Ibid., para. 50.
246 Ibid.
247 European Court of Justice, *People's Climate Case (Carvalho and Others v Parliament and Council)*, Case C-565/19 P, Judgment of the Court (Sixth Chamber) of 25 March 2021.
248 Landgericht Essen, *Zur Störereigenschaft eines Unternehmens, das klimaschädliche Gase emittiert in Bezug auf durch den Klimawandel drohende Umweltschäden* (15 December 2016).
249 Ibid., para. 11, 24.
250 Oberlandesgericht Hamm, Rechtsstreit Lliuya ./. RWE (Az. 5 U 15/17 OLG Hamm).
251 W. Frank, C. Bals, J. Grimm, "The Case of Huaraz: First Climate Lawsuit on Loss and Damage Against an Energy Company Before German Courts" in R. Mechler, L. M. Bouwer et al. (eds), *Loss and Damage from Climate Change: Concepts, Methods and Policy Options* (2019), p. 479.
252 C. Rodríguez-Garavito, "Human Rights: The Global South's Route to Climate Litigation," *114 AJIL Unbound* (2020), p. 40, 41.
253 Cf. I. Kaminski, *Fossil fuel firms "could be sued" for climate change* (10 December 2019).
254 R. Kwiecień, "On Some Contemporary Challenges to Statehood in the International Legal Order: International Law Between Lotus and Global Administrative Law," *51 Archiv des Völkerrechts* (2013), p. 298; N. Cox, "The Acquisition of Sovereignty by Quasi-States: The Case of the Order of Malta," *6 Mountbatten Journal of Legal Studies* (2002), p. 31; A. van Staden and H. Vollaard, "The Erosion of State Sovereignty: Towards a Post-territorial World?" in G. Kreijen (ed.), *State, Sovereignty, and International Governance* (2002), p. 181; R. McCorquodale, "International Community and State Sovereignty: An Uneasy Symbiotic Relationship" in C. Warbrick, S. Tierney (eds), *Towards an "International Legal Community"?: The Sovereignty of States and the Sovereignty of International Law* (2006), p. 257 et seq.
255 J. E. Nijman, *The Concept of International Legal Personality: An Inquiry Into the History and Theory of International Law* (2004), p. 354 with further references; R. Kwiecień, "On Some Contemporary Challenges to Statehood in the International Legal Order: International Law Between Lotus and Global Administrative Law," *51 Archiv des Völkerrechts* (2013), p. 298; N. Cox, "The Acquisition of Sovereignty by Quasi-States: The Case of the Order of Malta," *6 Mountbatten Journal of Legal Studies* (2002), p. 31, 46.
256 A. A. C. Trindade, "International Law for Humankind: Towards a New Jus Gentium," part 1, *316 Recueil Des Cours* (2005), p. 238, 239.
257 D. H. Nexon, *The Struggle for Power in Early Modern Europe: Religious Conflict, Dynastic Empires, and International Change* (2009), p. 300; de Hoogh adds that it is also "premature to conduct a post-mortem on the concept of sovereignty" (A. de Hoogh, "The Sovereigns are Dead, Long Live the Sovereigns – Reflections on State Sovereignty and International Law" in K. Wellens, E. R. Rieter, H. C. F. J. A. d. Waele (eds), *Evolving principles of international law: Studies in honour of Karel C. Wellens* (2012), p. 195).
258 H. P. Aust, "Auf dem Weg zu einem Recht der globalen Stadt?: 'C40' und der 'Konvent der Bürgermeister' im globalen Klimaschutzregime," *73 Zeitschrift für ausländisches Öffentliches Recht und Völkerrecht* (2013), p. 698.

259 D. H. Nexon, *The Struggle for Power in Early Modern Europe: Religious Conflict, Dynastic Empires, and International Change* (2009), p. 300; de Hoogh adds that it is also "premature to conduct a post-mortem on the concept of sovereignty" (A. de Hoogh, "The Sovereigns are Dead, Long Live the Sovereigns – Reflections on State Sovereignty and International Law" in K. Wellens, E. R. Rieter, H. C. F. J. A. d. Waele (eds), *Evolving principles of international law: Studies in honour of Karel C. Wellens* (2012), p. 195).

260 A. Addis, "The Thin State in Thick Globalism: Sovereignty in the Information Age," *37 Vanderbilt Journal of Transnational Law* (2004), p. 106.

261 A. L. Paulus, "International Community," (last updated March 2013) in R. Wolfrum (ed.), *The Max Planck Encyclopedia of Public International Law: opil.ouplaw.com .home/EPIL* (2012), para. 20.

262 A. Peters, 'Membership in the Global Constitutional Community' in J. Klabbers, A. Peters, G. Ulfstein (eds), *The Constitutionalization of International Law* (2009), p. 198; citing A. Hurrelmann, S. Leibfried, K. Martens and P. Mayer, "The Transformation of the Golden-Age Nation State: Findings and Perspectives" in A. Hurrelmann, S. Leibfried, K. Martens, P. Mayer (ed.), *Transforming the Golden-Age Nation State* (2007), p. 200, 204.

263 A. Peters, "Membership in the Global Constitutional Community" in J. Klabbers, A. Peters, G. Ulfstein (eds), *The Constitutionalization of International Law* (2009), p. 198.

264 Ibid., p. 198.

265 P. M. Kennedy, *The Parliament of Man: The Past, Present, and Future of the UN* (2007), p. xiii.

266 A. L. Paulus, "International Community," (last updated March 2013) in R. Wolfrum (ed.), *The Max Planck Encyclopedia of Public International Law: opil.ouplaw.com.home/EPIL* (2012), para. 20; N. Luhmann, *Das Recht der Gesellschaft* (1993), p. 571.

267 M. Horsman and A. Marshall, *After the Nation-state: Citizens, Tribalism and the New World Disorder* (1994), p. 265.

268 A. Addis, "The Thin State in Thick Globalism: Sovereignty in the Information Age," *37 Vanderbilt Journal of Transnational Law* (2004), p. 107.

269 A. Hurrelmann, S. Leibfried, K. Martens, and P. Mayer, "The Transformation of the Golden-Age Nation State: Findings and Perspectives" in A. Hurrelmann, S. Leibfried, K. Martens, P. Mayer (eds), *Transforming the Golden-Age Nation State* (2007), p. 193.

270 Cf. R. Balleste and J. Kulesza, "Signs and Portents in Cyberspace: The Rise of Jus Internet as New Order in International Law," *23 Fordham Intellectual Property, Media and Entertainment Law Journal* (2013), p. 1319.

271 A. Peters, "Membership in the Global Constitutional Community" in J. Klabbers, A. Peters, G. Ulfstein (eds), *The Constitutionalization of International Law* (2009), p. 182; A. van Staden and H. Vollaard, "The Erosion of State Sovereignty: Towards a Post-territorial World?" in G. Kreijen (ed.), *State, Sovereignty, and International Governance* (2002), p. 165 et seq.

272 W. H. Reinicke, "Global Public Policy," *76 Foreign Affairs* (1997), p. 137; cf. C. W. Kegley, G. A. Raymond, *Exorcising the Ghost of Westphalia: Building World Order in the New Millennium* (2002), p. 158.

273 H. Bull, *The Anarchical Society: A Study of Order in World Politics* (2012), p. 254–5; 246.

274 ICJ – The Hague, *Conditions of Admission of a State to Membership in the UN (Article 4 of the Charter)* – Advisory Opinion – Individual Opinion by M. Alvarez (28 May 1948), p. 68; cf. M. Koskenniemi, *From Apology to Utopia: The Structure of International Legal Argument* (2015), p. 213.

275 S. S. Kim, "Sovereignty in the Chinese Image of World Order" in R. S. MacDonald, T. Wang (eds), *Essays in honour of Wang Tieya* (1994), p. 425.

276 J. R. Crawford, "Chance, Order, Change: The Course of International Law, General Course on Public International Law," *365 Recueil Des Cours* (2013), p. 86.
277 N. Schrijver, "The Changing Nature of State Sovereignty," *70 British Yearbook of International Law* (1999), p. 65.
278 O. Schachter, "Sovereignty – Then and Now" in R. S. MacDonald, T. Wang (eds), *Essays in honour of Wang Tieya* (1994), p. 671.
279 P. Allott, *Eunomia: New Order for a New World* (1990), p. 329.
280 B. Fassbender, "Die Souveränität des Staates als Autonomie im Rahmen der völkerrechtlichen Verfassung" in H.-P. Mansel (ed.), *Festschrift für Erik Jayme* (2004), p. 1093–5; cf. B. Fassbender, "Sovereignty and Constitutionalism in International Law" in N. Walker (ed.), *Sovereignty in Transition* (2003), p. 128, 132.
281 H. Kelsen, "The Principle of Sovereign Equality of States as a Basis for International Organization," *53 The Yale Law Journal* (1944), p. 208; cf. B. Fassbender, "Friede durch Recht: Hans Kelsen und die Vereinten Nationen" in H. Brunkhorst, R. Voigt (eds), *Rechts-Staat: Staat, internationale Gemeinschaft und Völkerrecht bei Hans Kelsen* (2008), p. 142.
282 B. Fassbender, "Der Schutz der Menschenrechte als zentraler Inhalt des völkerrechtlichen Gemeinwohls," *30 Europäische Grundrechte-Zeitschrift* (2003), p. 5.
283 G. J. Evans and M. Sahnoun, *The Responsibility to Protect. Report of the International Commission on Intervention and State Sovereignty* (2001), p. 13, para. 2.14; cf. A. Peters, *Jenseits der Menschenrechte: Die Rechtsstellung des Individuums im Völkerrecht* (2014), p. 218.
284 UNGA, *A more secure world: our shared responsibility,* Report of the High-level Panel on Threats, Challenges and Change, 2 December 2004, p. 21–2, 29–30.
285 H. Spruyt, *The Sovereign State and Its Competitors: An Analysis of Systems Change* (1996), p. 189–91; cf. C. W. Morris, *An Essay on the Modern State* (2002), p. 53; O. Schachter, "The Decline of the Nation-State and its Implications for International Law," *36 Columbia Journal of Transnational Law* (1997), p. 11; M. Craven, "Statehood, Self-determination, and Recognition" in M. D. Evans (ed.), *International Law* (2014), p. 204.
286 A. L. Paulus, "International Community," (last updated March 2013) in R. Wolfrum (ed.), *The Max Planck Encyclopedia of Public International Law: opil.ouplaw.com .home/EPIL* (2012), para. 18, with further references; cf. K. Wellens, "Revisiting Solidarity as a (Re-)Emerging Constitutional Principle: Some Further Reflections" in C. Kojima, R. Wolfrum (eds), *Solidarity: A Structural Principle of International Law* (2010), p. 9 et seq.
287 A. Peters, "Humanity as the A and Ω of Sovereignty," *20 EJIL* (2009), p. 532 with further references.
288 M. Horsman and A. Marshall, *After the Nation-state: Citizens, Tribalism and the New World Disorder* (1994), p. 263.
289 S. A. G. Jain, "The 21st Century Atlantis: The International Law of Statehood and Climate Change-Induced Loss of Territory," *50 Stanford Journal of International Law* (2014), p. 24, who brings the example of American antitrust-law.
290 I. A. Shearer, *Starke's International Law* (2003), p. 183.
291 M. Weller, *Contested Statehood: Kosovo's Struggle for Independence* (2009), p. 260.
292 B. Fassbender, "Article 2(1)" in B. Simma, H. Mosler, A. Paulus, E. Chaitidou (eds), *The Charter of the UN: A Commentary* (2012), p. 140, para. 14.
293 "Treaty establishing the European Coal and Steel Community: Treaty of Paris ECSC" (1951) (emphasis added).
294 The provisions were incorporated in part in the inter-American treaty of reciprocal assistance of Sept. 2, 1947 ("Inter-American reciprocal assistance and solidarity: Act of Chapultepec" (1945)), and in part in the Charter of the Organization of American States ("Charter of the Organization of American States" (1948)); cf. on the solidarity

between Latin-American States J. M. Yepes, "La contribution de l'Amérique latine au développement du droit international public et privé," *32 Recueil Des Cours* (1930), p. 699 et seq.

295 D. B. Goldman, *Globalisation and the Western Legal Tradition: Recurring Patterns of Law and Authority* (2008), p. 213 et seq.

296 R. Wolfrum, "Solidarity amongst States: An Emerging Structural Principle of International Law" in P.-M. Dupuy, B. Fassbender, M. N. Shaw, K.-P. Sommermann (eds), *Völkerrecht als Wertordnung: Festschrift für Christian Tomuschat* (2006), p. 1099.

297 Art. 1(3) "Charter of the UN" (1945).

298 E. McWhinney and D. Ross, "The End of the Cold War: The 'New Thinking' and the New International Cooperation" in E. McWhinney, D. Ross, G. Tunkin, V. Vereshchetin (eds), *From Coexistence to Cooperation. International Law and Organization in the Post-Cold War Era* (1991), p. 5.

299 A. Hudson, "Beyond the Borders: Globalisation, Sovereignty and Extra-Territoriality" in D. Newman (ed.), *Boundaries, Territory and Postmodernity* (1999), p. 89; A. El Ouali, *Territorial Integrity in a Globalizing World: International Law and States' Quest for Survival* (2012), p. 92; J. E. Nijman, *The Concept of International Legal Personality: An Inquiry Into the History and Theory of International Law* (2004), p. 363.

300 D.-E. Khan, "Territory and Boundaries" in B. Fassbender, A. Peters (eds), *The Oxford Handbook of the History of International Law* (2012), p. 248.

301 Ibid., p. 229.

302 A. G. Jain, "The 21st Century Atlantis: The International Law of Statehood and Climate Change-Induced Loss of Territory," *50 Stanford Journal of International Law* (2014), p. 24 with further references; H. Spruyt, *The Sovereign State and Its Competitors: An Analysis of Systems Change* (1996), p. 183; A. van Staden and H. Vollaard, "The Erosion of State Sovereignty: Towards a Post-territorial World?" in G. Kreijen (ed.), *State, Sovereignty, and International Governance* (2002), p. 169.

303 A. Hudson, "Beyond the Borders: Globalisation, Sovereignty and Extra-Territoriality" in D. Newman (ed.), *Boundaries, Territory and Postmodernity* (1999), p. 102.

304 C. Tomuschat, "How the Classical Concept of Sovereignty has Evolved" in M. Delević Dilas, V. Derić, V. Dimitrijević (eds), *The International and the National: Essays in honour of Vojin Dimitrijević* (2003), p. 26–7.

305 A. G. Jain, "The 21st Century Atlantis: The International Law of Statehood and Climate Change-Induced Loss of Territory," *50 Stanford Journal of International Law* (2014), p. 24–5.

306 D. Newman, "Geopolitics Renaissant: Territory, Sovereignty, and the World Political Map" in D. Newman (ed.), *Boundaries, Territory and Postmodernity* (1999), p. 7.

307 Ibid., p. 6.

308 B. Fassbender, "The state's unabandoned claim to be the center of the legal universe," *16 International Journal of Constitutional Law 4* (2018), p. 1214.

309 J. W. Scott, "European Crisis and its Consequences for Borders and Cooperation – Editorial Introduction" *Cross-Border Review* (2016), p. 5.

310 D. Newman, "Geopolitics Renaissant: Territory, Sovereignty, and the World Political Map" in D. Newman (ed.), *Boundaries, Territory and Postmodernity* (1999), p. 5 (mentioning Basques, Catalonians, Scots as well as Palestinians and Kurds; today one could add the rebuilt or reinforced fences within and around the European Union in the course of the refugee crisis).

311 O. Schachter, "Sovereignty – Then and Now" in R. S. MacDonald, T. Wang (eds), *Essays in honour of Wang Tieya* (1994), p. 682.

312 A. El Ouali, *Territorial Integrity in a Globalizing World: International Law and States' Quest for Survival* (2012), p. 98.

313 O. Schachter, "Sovereignty – Then and Now" in R. S. MacDonald, T. Wang (eds), *Essays in honour of Wang Tieya* (1994), p. 682.
314 B. Boutros-Ghali, *An Agenda for Peace: Preventive Diplomacy, Peacemaking and Peace-keeping: Report of the Secretary-General Pursuant to the Statement Adopted by the Summit Meeting of the Security Council on 31 January 1992* (1992), para. 11.
315 A. Peters, "Extraterritorial Naturalizations: Between the Human Right to Nationality, State Sovereignty and Fair Principles of Jurisdiction," *53 German Yearbook of International Law* (2010), p. 724; cf. S. Chouinard, "Stateless Nations" in K. Cordell, S. Wolff (eds), *The Routledge Handbook of Ethnic Conflict* (2016), p. 56.
316 G. Ó Tuathail, "De-Territorialised Threats and Global Dangers: Geopolitics and Risk Society," *3 Geopolitics* (1998), p. 17.
317 D.-E. Khan, *Die deutschen Staatsgrenzen: rechtshistorische Grundlagen und offene Rechtsfragen* (2004), p. 10, cf. U. Di Fabio, *Das Recht offener Staaten: Grundlinien einer Staats- und Rechtstheorie* (1998), p. 135; cf. J. Everard, *Virtual States: The Internet and the Boundaries of the Nation-state* (2000), preface by Michael Talalay, p. xi, who argues "In a sense, the existence of the state hinges on the condition of autarky."
318 M. N. Shaw, "The International Court of Justice and the Law of Territory" in C. J. Tams (ed.), *The Development of International Law by the International Court of Justice* (2013), p. 151.
319 T. M. Franck, *The Empowered Self: Law and Society in an Age of Individualism* (1999), p. 61.
320 D. Newman, "Geopolitics Renaissant: Territory, Sovereignty, and the World Political Map" in D. Newman (ed.), *Boundaries, Territory and Postmodernity* (1999), p. 5.
321 J. H. Herz, *The Nation-state and the Crisis of World Politics* (1976), p. 102 with further explanations about the change towards territoriality.
322 H. Spruyt, *The Sovereign State and Its Competitors: An Analysis of Systems Change* (1996), p. 192.
323 K. Rygiel, *Globalizing Citizenship* (2011), p. 1.
324 ICJ – The Hague, *Conditions of Admission of a State to Membership in the UN (Article 4 of the Charter)* – Advisory Opinion – Individual Opinion by M. Alvarez (28 May 1948), p. 68; cf. M. Koskenniemi, *From Apology to Utopia: The Structure of International Legal Argument* (2015), p. 213.
325 H. Spruyt, *The Sovereign State and Its Competitors: An Analysis of Systems Change* (1996), p. 190.
326 D. Thürer, "Recht der internationelen Gemeinschaft und Wandel der Staatlichkeit" in D. Thürer, J.-F. Aubert, J. P. Müller (eds), *Verfassungsrecht der Schweiz* (2001), p. 39, para. 6.
327 B. Fassbender, "Die souveräne Gleichheit der Staaten – ein angefochtenes Grundprinzip des Völkerrechts," *43 Aus Politik und Zeitgeschichte, Beilage zur Wochenzeitung* (2004), p. 12.
328 Ibid., p. 12; U. Haltern, "Tomuschats Traum: Zur Bedeutung der Souveränität im Völkerrecht" in P.-M. Dupuy, B. Fassbender, M. N. Shaw, K.-P. Sommermann (eds), *Völkerrecht als Wertordnung: Festschrift für Christian Tomuschat* (2006), p. 872, 887.
329 W. Schiffer, *The Legal Community of Mankind: A Critical Analysis of the Modern Concept of World Organization* (1972), p. v.
330 C. Tomuschat, "How the Classical Concept of Sovereignty has Evolved" in M. Delević Dilas, V. Derić, V. Dimitrijević (eds), *The International and the National: Essays in honour of Vojin Dimitrijević* (2003), p. 21.
331 J. Larkins, *From Hierarchy to Anarchy: Territory and Politics before Westphalia* (2009).

332 W. G. Friedmann, *The Changing Structure of International Law* (1964), p. 60.
333 Ibid., p. 61; G. Abi-Saab, "Whither the International Community?," *9 EJIL* (1998), p. 248.
334 R. Wolfrum, "Solidarity amongst States: An Emerging Structural Principle of International Law" in P.-M. Dupuy, B. Fassbender, M. N. Shaw, K.-P. Sommermann (eds), *Völkerrecht als Wertordnung: Festschrift für Christian Tomuschat* (2006), p. 1088; cf. H. Mosler, "The International Society as a Legal Community," *140 Recueil Des Cours* (1974), p. 17 et seq.; R. Wolfrum, "Solidarity" in D. L. Shelton (ed.), *The Oxford Handbook of International Human Rights Law* (2013), p. 403.
335 M. W. Zacher, "The dacaying pillars of the Westphalian temple: implications for international order and governance" in J. N. Rosenau, E. O. Czempiel (eds), *Governance Without Government: Order and Change in World Politics* (1992), p. 100; cf. A. L. Paulus, *Die internationale Gemeinschaft im Völkerrecht: Eine Untersuchung zur Entwicklung des Völkerrechts im Zeitalter der Globalisierung* (2001), p. 111, 116.
336 T. Meron, *The Humanization of International Law* (2006), p. 257.
337 C. W. Kegley, G. A. Raymond, *Exorcising the Ghost of Westphalia: Building World Order in the New Millennium* (2002), p. 155.
338 U. Scheuner, "Solidaritat unter den Nationen als Grundsatz in der gegenwärtigen internationalen Gemeinschaft" in J. Delbrück, K. Ipsen, D. Rauschning (eds), *Recht im Dienst des Friedens: Festschrift für Eberhard Menzel zum 65. Geburtstag am 21. Januar 1976* (1975), p. 270; R. A. Falk, *A study of future worlds* (1975), p. 68; C. W. Kegley, G. A. Raymond, *Exorcising the Ghost of Westphalia: Building World Order in the New Millennium* (2002), p. 155.
339 U. Scheuner, "Solidaritat unter den Nationen als Grundsatz in der gegenwärtigen internationalen Gemeinschaft" in J. Delbrück, K. Ipsen, D. Rauschning (eds), *Recht im Dienst des Friedens: Festschrift für Eberhard Menzel zum 65. Geburtstag am 21. Januar 1976* (1975), p. 270.
340 C. W. Morris, *An Essay on the Modern State* (2002), p. 52
341 A. L. Paulus, "Reciprocity Revisited" in U. Fastenrath, R. Geiger, D.-E. Khan, A. Paulus, S. von Schorlemer, C. Vedder (eds), *From Bilateralism to Community Interest: Essays in Honour of Judge Bruno Simma* (2011), p. 113.
342 A. Cassese, "States: Rise and Decline of the Primary Subjects of the International Community" in B. Fassbender, A. Peters (eds), *The Oxford Handbook of the History of International Law* (2012), p. 62, 69.
343 J. N. Rosenau, "Turbulence in World Politics: A Theory of Change and Continuity" in R. W. Mansbach, E. J. Rhodes (eds), *Global Politics in a Changing World: A Reader* (2008), p. 13.
344 S. Sassen, *Territory, Authority, Rights: From Medieval to Global Assemblages* (2006), p. 419; cf. D. Wong, "Sovereignty Sunk? The Position of 'Sinking States' at International Law," *14 Melbourne Journal of International Law* (2013), p. 347, 348.
345 M. N. Shaw, "The International Court of Justice and the Law of Territory" in C. J. Tams (ed.), *The Development of International Law by the International Court of Justice* (2013), p. 153, with further references (footnotes omitted).
346 Cf. O. Schachter, "Sovereignty – Then and Now" in R. S. MacDonald, T. Wang (eds), *Essays in honour of Wang Tieya* (1994), p. 677.
347 L. Henkin, "The Mythology of Sovereignty" in R. S. MacDonald, T. Wang (eds), *Essays in honour of Wang Tieya* (1994), p. 351; cf. van der Vyver, Johan D., "Sovereignty" in D. L. Shelton (ed.), *The Oxford Handbook of International Human Rights Law* (2013), p. 388 et seq.
348 ICJ– The Hague, *The Corfu Channel Case* – Individual opinion by Judge Alvarez (9 April 1949), p. 43.
349 W. Vitzthum, "Aquitoriale Souveränität" in P.-M. Dupuy, B. Fassbender, M. N. Shaw, K.-P. Sommermann (eds), *Völkerrecht als Wertordnung: Festschrift für Christian*

Tomuschat (2006), p. 1068; K. A. Annan, *We the Peoples: The Role of the UN in the Twenty-first Century* (2000), p. 13; cf. D. Thürer, "Recht der internationelen Gemeinschaft und Wandel der Staatlichkeit" in D. Thürer, J.-F. Aubert, J. P. Müller (eds), *Verfassungsrecht der Schweiz* (2001), p. 55, para. 40.

350 B. Fassbender, "Die Souveränität des Staates als Autonomie im Rahmen der völkerrechtlichen Verfassung" in H.-P. Mansel (ed.), *Festschrift für Erik Jayme* (2004), p. 1089 ("Viel spricht dafür, daß erst sein [Souveränitätsbegriff] Verschwinden in einem noch unbekannten Zeitpunkt der Zukunft das wirkliche Ende des modernen Staates markieren wird."); cf. I. Brownlie, "Rebirth of Statehood" in M. D. Evans (ed.), *International Law* (2006), p. 5.

351 N. Schrijver, "The Changing Nature of State Sovereignty," *70 British Yearbook of International Law* (1999), p. 65.

352 H. G. Schermers and N. Blokker, *International Institutional Law: Unity Within Diversity* (2011), p. 1212, §1888; cf. N. Schrijver, "The Changing Nature of State Sovereignty," *70 British Yearbook of International Law* (1999), p. 71–2; cf. L. Zucca, "A Genealogy of State Sovereignty," *16 Theoretical Inquiries in Law 2* (2015), p. 422.

353 M. Herberg, "From Diffusion to Interplay: Rethinking the Constitutional State in the Age of Global Legal Pluralism" in A. Hurrelmann, S. Leibfried, K. Martens, P. Mayer (eds), *Transforming the Golden-Age Nation State* (2007), p. 79.

354 H. Spruyt, *The Sovereign State and Its Competitors: An Analysis of Systems Change* (1996), p. 192; cf. D. Thürer, "Recht der internationelen Gemeinschaft und Wandel der Staatlichkeit" in D. Thürer, J.-F. Aubert, J. P. Müller (eds), *Verfassungsrecht der Schweiz* (2001), p. 55, para. 40; B. Fassbender, "Article 2(1)" in B. Simma, H. Mosler, A. Paulus, E. Chaitidou (eds), *The Charter of the UN: A Commentary* (2012), para. 63–4.

355 A. L. Paulus, "International Community," (last updated March 2013) in R. Wolfrum (ed.), *The Max Planck Encyclopedia of Public International Law: opil.ouplaw.com .home/EPIL* (2012), para. 20.

356 Cf. M. Kintzinger, "From the late Middle Ages to the Peace of Westphalia" in B. Fassbender, A. Peters (eds), *The Oxford Handbook of the History of International Law* (2012), p. 627, 623.

357 H. Kelsen, *Allgemeine Staatslehre* (1925), p. 103; H. Kelsen, "Les rapports de système entre le droit interne et le droit international public," *14 Recueil Des Cours* (1926), p. 251, 256; H. Kelsen, "Sovereignty and International Law," *48 Georgetown Law Journal* (1959), p. 627; cf. A. Jakab, "Neutralizing the Sovereignty Question Compromise Strategies in Constitutional Argumentations before European Integration and since," *2 European Constitutional Law Review* (2006), p. 381; cf. J. R. Crawford, "Chance, Order, Change: The Course of International Law, General Course on Public International Law," *365 Recueil Des Cours* (2013), p. 75.

358 H. L. A. Hart, *The Concept of Law* (1994), p. 220.

359 J. R. Crawford, "Chance, Order, Change: The Course of International Law, General Course on Public International Law," *365 Recueil Des Cours* (2013), p. 86.

360 S. M. Carbone, L. S. di Pepe, "States, Fundamental Rights and Duties," (last updated January 2009) in R. Wolfrum (ed.), *The Max Planck Encyclopedia of Public International Law: opil.ouplaw.com.home/EPIL* (2012), para. 35.

361 C. W. Kegley, G. A. Raymond, *Exorcising the Ghost of Westphalia: Building World Order in the New Millennium* (2002), p. 156 (speaking of "globalization, democratization, and humanitarianism" that lead to a deterritorialization).

362 A. Hurrelmann, S. Leibfried, K. Martens and P. Mayer, "The Transformation of the Golden-Age Nation State: Findings and Perspectives" in A. Hurrelmann, S. Leibfried, K. Martens, P. Mayer (eds), *Transforming the Golden-Age Nation State* (2007), p. 200; cf. A. van Staden and H. Vollaard, "The Erosion of State Sovereignty: Towards a

Post-territorial World?" in G. Kreijen (ed.), *State, Sovereignty, and International Governance* (2002), p. 184.

363 D. Archibugi, "Cosmopolitical Democracy" in D. Archibugi (ed.), *Debating cosmopolitics* (2003), p. 1; cf. A. Addis, "The Thin State in Thick Globalism: Sovereignty in the Information Age," *37 Vanderbilt Journal of Transnational Law* (2004), p. 107, fn. 373.

364 A. G. Jain, "The 21st Century Atlantis: The International Law of Statehood and Climate Change-Induced Loss of Territory," *50 Stanford Journal of International Law* (2014), p. 9.

365 D. Thürer, "Recht der internationelen Gemeinschaft und Wandel der Staatlichkeit" in D. Thürer, J.-F. Aubert, J. P. Müller (eds), *Verfassungsrecht der Schweiz* (2001), p. 55, para. 40.

366 G. J. Evans and M. Sahnoun, *The Responsibility to Protect. Report of the International Commission on Intervention and State Sovereignty* (2001), p. 7.

367 O. Schachter, "The Decline of the Nation-State and its Implications for International Law," *36 Columbia Journal of Transnational Law* (1997), p. 23.

368 A. Peters, "Membership in the Global Constitutional Community" in J. Klabbers, A. Peters, G. Ulfstein (eds), *The Constitutionalization of International Law* (2009), p. 200.

369 G. J. Evans and M. Sahnoun, *The Responsibility to Protect. Report of the International Commission on Intervention and State Sovereignty* (2001), p. 8.

370 A. L. Paulus, "The International Lawyer between Globalization and Postmodernity" in J. I. Drolshammer, M. Pfeifer (eds), *The Internationalization of the Practice of Law* (2001), p. 388.

371 L. Henkin, "The Mythology of Sovereignty" in R. S. MacDonald, T. Wang (eds), *Essays in honour of Wang Tieya* (1994), p. 352.

372 H. Shinoda, *Re-Examining Sovereignty: From Classical Theory to the Global Age* (2000), p. 1.

373 B. Kingsbury, "Sovereignty and Inequality," *9 EJIL* (1998), p. 599.

374 For many: T. Schilling, "Die neue Weltordnung und die Souveränität der Mitglieder der Vereinten Nationen," *33 Archiv des Völkerrechts* (1995), p. 69.

375 O. Schachter, "Sovereignty – Then and Now" in R. S. MacDonald, T. Wang (eds), *Essays in honour of Wang Tieya* (1994), p. 679.

376 W. Riphagen, "Some Reflections on 'Functional Sovereignty'," *6 Netherlands Yearbook of International Law* (1975), p. 121.

377 H. Shinoda, *Re-Examining Sovereignty: From Classical Theory to the Global Age* (2000), p. 162.

378 G. J. Evans and M. Sahnoun, *The Responsibility to Protect. Report of the International Commission on Intervention and State Sovereignty* (2001), p. 8.

379 Ibid., p. 8.

380 A. Peters, "Extraterritorial Naturalizations: Between the Human Right to Nationality, State Sovereignty and Fair Principles of Jurisdiction," *53 German Yearbook of International Law* (2010), p. 724.

381 T. M. Franck, *The Empowered Self: Law and Society in an Age of Individualism* (1999), p. 100; cf. J. E. Nijman, *The Concept of International Legal Personality: An Inquiry Into the History and Theory of International Law* (2004), p. 425.

382 UN Secretary General K. A. Annan, *The Secretary-General Address to The UNGA*, 20 September 1999.

383 Ibid.

384 K. A. Annan, *We the Peoples: The Role of the UN in the Twenty-first Century* (2000), p. 77.

385 Cf. E. Milano, "The Deterritorialization of International Law," *2 ESIL Reflections* (2013), p. 3 et seq. "For instance, the 61 pages of the Ahtisaari Plan for the

Comprehensive Settlement of Kosovo detail to an unprecedented extent the democratic and pluralist governance of Kosovo but feature one paragraph only dealing with the territory of the new State - with an entire annex devoted to the internal borders among municipalities." (p. 3).

386 H. P. Aust, "Fundamental Rights of States: Constitutional Law in Disguise?," *4 Cambridge Journal of International and Comparative Law* (2015), p. 539; referring to A. A. C. Trindade, "International Law for Humankind: Towards a New Jus Gentium," part 1, *316 Recueil Des Cours* (2005).

387 Cf. S. D. Brunn, "A Treaty of Silicon for the Treaty of Westphalia? New Territorial Dimensions of Modern Statehood" in D. Newman (ed.), *Boundaries, Territory and Postmodernity* (1999), p. 114.

388 Ibid., p. 128.

389 M. N. Shaw, *Title to Territory in Africa: International Legal Issues* (1986), p. 11.

390 A. L. Parrish, "Rehabilitating Territoriality in Human Rights," *32 Cardozo Law Review* (2011), p. 1099.

391 A. L. Paulus, *Die internationale Gemeinschaft im Völkerrecht: Eine Untersuchung zur Entwicklung des Völkerrechts im Zeitalter der Globalisierung* (2001), p. 221.

392 D. Newman, "Geopolitics Renaissant: Territory, Sovereignty, and the World Political Map" in D. Newman (ed.), *Boundaries, Territory and Postmodernity* (1999), p. 13.

393 W. G. Friedmann, *The Changing Structure of International Law* (1964), p. 251; E. McWhinney and D. Ross, "The End of the Cold War: The 'New Thinking' and the New International Cooperation" in E. McWhinney, D. Ross, G. Tunkin, V. Vereshchetin (eds), *From Coexistence to Cooperation. International Law and Organization in the Post-Cold War Era* (1991), p. 5.

394 Cf. B. Fassbender, "Sovereignty and Constitutionalism in International Law" in N. Walker (ed.), *Sovereignty in Transition* (2003), p. 139.

395 UNGA, *A more secure world: our shared responsibility,* Report of the High-level Panel on Threats, Challenges and Change, 2 December 2004, p. 15.

396 C. Tomuschat, "International Law: Ensuring the Survival of Mankind on the Eve of a New Century," *281 Recueil Des Cours* (1999), p. 63–70.

397 A. G. Jain, "The 21st Century Atlantis: The International Law of Statehood and Climate Change-Induced Loss of Territory," *50 Stanford Journal of International Law* (2014), p. 12.

398 D. Thürer, "Recht der internationelen Gemeinschaft und Wandel der Staatlichkeit" in D. Thürer, J.-F. Aubert, J. P. Müller (eds), *Verfassungsrecht der Schweiz* (2001), p. 41, para. 12; cf. S. D. Brunn, "A Treaty of Silicon for the Treaty of Westphalia? New Territorial Dimensions of Modern Statehood" in D. Newman (ed.), *Boundaries, Territory and Postmodernity* (1999), p. 113; A. Cassese, "States: Rise and Decline of the Primary Subjects of the International Community" in B. Fassbender, A. Peters (eds), *The Oxford Handbook of the History of International Law* (2012), p. 65–6.

399 J. Cerone, "The Status of the Individual: A Critical Appraisal," *100 Proceedings of the Annual Meeting (American Society of International Law)* (2006), p. 259–60.

400 R. McCorquodale, "International Community and State Sovereignty: An Uneasy Symbiotic Relationship" in C. Warbrick, S. Tierney (eds), *Towards an "International Legal Community"?: The Sovereignty of States and the Sovereignty of International Law* (2006), p. 263.

401 Cf. A. A. C. Trindade, "International Law for Humankind: Towards a New Jus Gentium," part 2, *317 Recueil Des Cours* (2005), p. 104.

402 G. J. Evans and M. Sahnoun, *The Responsibility to Protect. Report of the International Commission on Intervention and State Sovereignty* (2001), p. 14.

403 F. M. Deng, "Frontiers of Sovereignty: A Framework of Protection, Assistance, and Development for the Internally Displaced," *8 Leiden Journal of International Law* (1995), p. 249 (footnote omitted).

404 "UNFCCC" (1992), preamble – emphasis added.
405 "Kyoto Protocol to the UNFCCC" (1997).
406 N. Schrijver, "The Changing Nature of State Sovereignty," *70 British Yearbook of International Law* (1999), p. 84.
407 "Paris Agreement" (2016), Art. 3.
408 L. Viikari, "Responsibility to Protect and Environmental Considerations: A Fundamental Mismatch or the Way Forward?" in P. Hilpold (ed.), *The Responsibility to Protect (R2P): A New Paradigm of International Law?* (2014), p. 348.
409 UN Secretary General K. A. Annan, *The Secretary-General Address to The UNGA*, 20 September 1999; cf. L. Glanville, *Sovereignty and the Responsibility to Protect: A New History* (2014), p. 176.
410 M. Horsman and A. Marshall, *After the Nation-state: Citizens, Tribalism and the New World Disorder* (1994), p. 265.
411 B. Simma and A. L. Paulus, "The 'International Community': Facing the Challenge of Globalization," *9 EJIL* (1998), p. 272; cf. A. L. Paulus, *Die internationale Gemeinschaft im Völkerrecht: Eine Untersuchung zur Entwicklung des Völkerrechts im Zeitalter der Globalisierung* (2001), p. 160–1.
412 Cf. P. Kunig, "Das Völkerrecht und die Interessen der Bevölkerung" in P.-M. Dupuy, B. Fassbender, M. N. Shaw, K.-P. Sommermann (eds), *Völkerrecht als Wertordnung: Festschrift für Christian Tomuschat* (2006), p. 379.
413 Cf. J. Thompson, *Justice and World Order: A Philosophical Inquiry* (1992).
414 B. Fassbender, "Article 2(1)" in B. Simma, H. Mosler, A. Paulus, E. Chaitidou (eds), *The Charter of the UN: A Commentary* (2012), para. 69 et seq., citing A. L. Paulus, *Die internationale Gemeinschaft im Völkerrecht: Eine Untersuchung zur Entwicklung des Völkerrechts im Zeitalter der Globalisierung* (2001), p. 446.
415 J. E. Nijman, *The Concept of International Legal Personality: An Inquiry Into the History and Theory of International Law* (2004), p. 426.
416 B. Fassbender, "Sovereignty and Constitutionalism in International Law" in N. Walker (ed.), *Sovereignty in Transition* (2003), p. 141.
417 A. Peters, "Humanity as the A and Ω of Sovereignty," *20 EJIL* (2009), p. 544; citing C. Tomuschat, "International Law: Ensuring the Survival of Mankind on the Eve of a New Century," *281 Recueil Des Cours* (1999), p. 162.
418 Willcox, S., "A Rising Tide: The Implications of Climate Change Inundation for Human Rights and State Sovereignty," *9 Essex Human Rights Review 1* (2012), p. 1.
419 Ibid, p. 16.

5 What it means not to be a State anymore – the consequences of the loss of statehood for the State's population and the international community

The rising seas are endangering the statehood of several members of the international community. This necessitates the question of what it means not to be a State anymore. What are the consequences of losing statehood?

All in all, the consequences of extinction are unclear.[1] There are no international law regimes that govern circumstances in which no successor State exists, and the predecessor State has been rendered uninhabitable or has physically disappeared.[2]

But statehood is important for different reasons:[3] For example, membership of the UN and other international organizations is limited to States. UN membership is providing a cost-effective method of maintaining international contacts, and thereby avoiding the need for a worldwide diplomatic apparatus, which is crucial for small States.[4] Yet, there is no procedure for entities losing statehood and thereby losing UN membership. The only foreseen possibility to be expelled from the UN by the General Assembly is according to Art. 6 of the UN Charter when States persistently break the principles of the Charter and only after recommendations of the Security Council.[5] No longer (entirely) fulfilling the entry criteria is not an explicit (or guaranteed) reason to be expelled. Thus, it is not clear whether an entity losing its statehood would automatically lose its UN membership. The same is true for other privileges (normally reserved for States) such as diplomatic immunity, trade relations, eligibility for development loans, or aid from the International Monetary Fund (IMF) and the World Bank.[6]

Moreover, standing before the International Court of Justice (ICJ) is limited to States. Uncontroversial access to this court is critical particularly when a State is vulnerable.[7] Whether or not a former State would be able to have access to the ICJ is not clear. The State is also still the prime protector of the human rights of its populations. By losing statehood, an entity loses the right to negotiate international law as a sovereign equal, and the right to invoke international law on behalf of its people who simultaneously lose their livelihood.[8]

For a State to be reduced to the status of a group is tantamount to losing its international legal personality.[9] International law privileges States in comparison to people.[10] At best, the State will lose its status as a State but remain "a subject of international law … capable of possessing international rights and duties," thus retaining the capacity to bring international claims. At worst, the State will just

DOI: 10.4324/9781003263593-5

be totally extinct.[11] International law would by all means need to provide rules for such an unprecedented event.

Loss of statehood and its effects on the respective populations – individual and collective dimension

Up to now, no State has disappeared through climate change-induced rising sea levels. However, climate change does already systematically undermine the widespread enjoyment of human rights;[12] currently mainly factually, but in the foreseeable future most likely also legally. In this context, the Human Rights Council has held various sessions devoted to climate change and produced six resolutions on the matter to date.[13] Many rights that already appear barely protected in practice, will be even more impaired as climate change hits harder.[14] "Human-induced climate change will disrupt, indeed devastate, the protection of Covenant rights for many millions of persons."[15] The question of sea-level rise and – in the long run – the disappearance of a State is only one aspect of a threat to the enjoyment of human rights through climate change, and it bears in itself many separate aspects.[16] The focus, as Vidas points out, should thereby always be "on *humankind* – from the individual person, to people connected in a community by belonging to a nation, and to other forms of joint identity as well."[17]

All in all, "the 'international conditions' for the fulfilment of human rights are worsening. Many millions are finding their human rights less available for 'enjoyment.' And some are more vulnerable than others to human rights threats or to their loss altogether."[18] The impacts for small island States

> include loss of coastal land and infrastructure due to erosion, inundation, sea-level rise and storm surges; an increase in the frequency and severity of cyclones, creating risks to life, health and homes; loss of coral reefs, with attendant implications for food security and the ecosystems on which many islanders' livelihoods depend; changing rainfall patterns, leading to flooding in some areas, drought in others and threats to fresh water supplies; salt-water intrusion into agricultural land; and extreme temperatures.[19]

That all raises important considerations in terms of the protection of the rights of the affected individuals, being a people with specific social and cultural identity, history, and traditions.[20]

While all human rights are implicated by climate change, given that it affects the totality of the living space where human existence unfolds,[21] this chapter focuses only on a few selected human rights that are particularly affected by the rise of the sea and – ultimately – the resulting loss of statehood.

In the following, the right to nationality is singled out and virtually placed in front of the parentheses. On the one hand because this right is particularly closely connected with the existence of the State, on the other hand because the analysis of this right will make clear how important the State (still) is today for the enjoyment of *internationally* guaranteed human rights.

Nationality and why having a State is (still) important for the protection of human rights

When statehood ceases, the remaining nationals of the respective State would lose their nationality, because nationality being the "'belonging' of an individual to a State, presupposes the co-existence of States"[22] and – certainly – the existence of the respective State. "Obviously, once a State ceases to exist, so does its nationality."[23] This is without precedent,[24] however, not pure fantasy for States such as the Maldives, Tuvalu, Kiribati, and the Marshall Islands anymore.[25] Whether they would then be *de facto* or *de jure* stateless[26] depends on the actual handling of the sunken "State," whether it is seen to be still a State. The international community could agree that the affected States would continue to exist nonetheless as a State or State-like entity.[27] States would probably not immediately be declared as extinct, anyway. If the ability of the deterritorialized State to issue passports is recognized, the issue of preserving the nationality of its citizens becomes more straightforward.[28] Practically however, the people in question would be likely to find themselves largely in a situation that would be similar to, if not the same, as if statehood had ceased. They would be considered at least *de facto* stateless[29] and thereby lose in any case the *content* of the right to a nationality. But what is the content of the right to a nationality? And why is having a nationality today at all important for internationally granted human rights?

The modern concept of nationality emerged following the Peace of Westphalia of 1648 and the rise of separate sovereign States.[30] Under traditional international law the meaning of nationality was that of "excluding others" and to defend the territory if the nation was under attack from external forces. It then gradually changed to the status of membership of a community based upon a common history, culture, ethnicity, and/or common political convictions and values.[31] While in the beginning it was seen as an issue "within [each State's] reserved domain,"[32] over the years it became more and more internationalized. And assumingly less important for the protection of human rights.

Indeed, while the US Supreme Court stated in 1958 as to the conditions of statelessness:

> There is, instead, the total destruction of the individual's status in organized society. It is a form of punishment more primitive than torture, for it destroys for the individual the political existence that was centuries in the development. The punishment strips the citizen of his status in the national and international political community. His very existence is at the sufferance of the country in which he happens to find himself.[33]

Today, the "development of human rights law has resulted in an increasing move away from citizenship as the right to have rights, as described by the US Supreme Court, and towards the 'denationalisation' of protection."[34] which "deeply affected the very significance of nationality."[35] Rather than citizenship being the right to have rights, "[t]he principles of human rights would maintain that being human is the right to have human rights."[36] Individuals were provided with certain rights directly on the basis of international law. Each State was obliged to recognize these rights vis-à-vis its own nationals. "The rights in question were termed 'human rights' – a label conveying the sentiment that they are owed to all people, everywhere, on the basis of their 'humanity' rather than being conditional upon the possession of a particular legal status such as citizenship."[37] This development, also described above as "Humanization" has "led many to point out that modern human rights norms now call into question the very relevance of nationality for the enjoyment of rights as citizens rights made way for human rights."[38] However, "in reality there are numerous ways in which the enjoyment of human rights by non-nationals may differ from that of nationals, both through divergence in the applicability of legal norms and through state practice."[39] So van Waas concludes that the vision of the needlessness of nationality "is a utopia for the stateless who have no nationality to rely on."[40]

Interestingly, the *human right* to a nationality,[41] was included as Art. 15 in the Universal Declaration of Human Rights:

(1) Everyone has the right to a nationality.
(2) No one shall be arbitrarily deprived of his nationality nor denied the right to change his nationality.[42]

This recognition reaffirms "the enduring relevance of nationality: The human rights system can only maintain its aspiration of universality with the guarantee that every human will also hold a nationality."[43] Although stateless people are perhaps less right-less today (Hannah Arendt equated the condition of being without a nationality to being right-less)[44] than they were "prior to the advent of the major human rights instruments,"[45] nationality is still important. The Inter-American Court of Human Rights clarifies with regard to Art. 20 of the Inter-American Convention on Human Rights:[46]

> [T]he right to a nationality established therein provides the individual with a minimal measure of legal protection in international relations through the link his nationality establishes between him and the state in question; and, second, the protection therein accorded the individual against the arbitrary deprivation of his nationality, without which he would be deprived for all practical purposes of all of his political rights as well as of those civil rights that are tied to the nationality of the individual.[47]

Thus, nationality is not only a human right, it also entitles the individual to certain rights:[48] Rights generally associated with holding a nationality are the right to re-enter and reside permanently in the territory of the State of one's nationality (cf. Art. 12(4) ICCPR), the right to consular assistance, the right to vote and participate in public life and the right to economic, social, and cultural advancement.[49]

The right to (re-)enter the State and to remain on its soil, which is an automatic and absolute right of someone holding a State's nationality and which offers this individual both stability and certainty,[50] is of course null and void for people from sunken island States.

Also, several rights are or can be restricted on the basis of nationality.[51] Such differential treatment between nationals and non-nationals with regard to political rights[52] but also with regard to social rights[53] occurs for many reasons, mostly around non-implementation of obligations. Many governments have, for example, not fully complied with their international human rights obligations or they reserve some rights only for nationals. Many national constitutions regulate the relationship between the sovereign and its citizens only.[54] For example, "the right to vote, to be elected and to work in public service"[55] is mainly reserved for nationals. All in all, nationality is critical to full participation in society.[56] It became "to mean empowerment."[57]

> The importance of nationality is that, as the political and legal bond that connects a person to a specific State, it allows the individual to acquire and exercise rights and obligations inherent in membership in a political community. As such, nationality is a requirement for the exercise of specific rights.[58]

In addition, the chance to profit from the State's right to offer diplomatic protection,[59] which certainly is an important component of the substance of nationality[60] is nonexistent without a State. Diplomatic protection is based on the notion that whoever mistreats a citizen indirectly violates the State. On this basis, States have the right to protect their citizens against violations by another State.[61] This right is not to be underestimated. Kesby argues that for example "for some detainees at Guantánamo Bay, diplomatic protection proved more efficacious in securing their release than assertions of their human rights."[62]

Also, in the opinion of the International Law Commission's (ILC) Special Rapporteur on Diplomatic Protection, John R. Dugart, the development of international human rights law has not rendered diplomatic protection "obsolete."[63] "As long as the State remains the dominant actor in international relations, the espousal of claims by States for the violation of the rights of their nationals remains the most effective remedy for the promotion of human rights."[64]

Thus, "[i]n underlining the importance of diplomatic protection as a remedy for human rights violations, we again see the privileging of the legal status of nationality and thus of the significance of the right to a nationality for the protection of human rights."[65] Indeed, in international law, the State is generally still the prime protector for human rights and in the absence of a truly global protection mechanism, probably the sole protector.[66] Nationality thereby safeguards the individual's rights and obligations in international law.[67] It gives rise on the part of the State to personal jurisdiction over the individual, and standing *vis-à-vis* other States under international law.[68]

Accordingly, while individuals "may hold rights under customary international law and international conventions, their capacity to enforce those rights is limited."[69] The "efficacy of human rights law is dependent on a body capable of providing protection."[70] The case of the sinking island States makes it particularly obvious: Only as "long as every individual holds a nationality, the universality of [human rights] documents remains intact: everyone can enjoy these rights in relation to at least one country, so no one is excluded."[71] And despite "tireless and somewhat tiresome efforts to find an alternate basis for citizenship, the status has no logic, power, or moral force outside a nation state."[72] Hence,

> inhabitants of a state whose legal status becomes ambiguous due to loss of territory risk [by becoming stateless, lose] the "only link between individuals and their rights, benefits and duties of international law," and therefore a stateless human being is an "object of international law for whom no subject of international law is responsible.[73]

This has dire consequences on individuals' rights and living conditions.[74] It makes persons "politically, socially and culturally marginalized."[75]

Moreover, statehood forms part of an individual's identity and bears as such certain values and functions for the individual: It gives a "feeling of belonging to a group" which provides security.[76] Branthwaite quotes a Palestinian Arab leader saying:

> A flag, a sense of nationality, a passport are essential. In the modern world, State membership is a fundamental part of identity ... With a passport we would not be pariahs. We could be the beneficiaries of reciprocity ... We would have a place to go back to if in a plight.[77]

Similarly, an Israeli general recalled his experience as a 14-year-old boy arriving in Israel as when he began to feel "like a normal person, with land, a State and an army."[78] Nationality, as part of identity, sets up simple ways of understanding the world in terms of in-groups and out-groups. These divisions help in evaluating the world, deciding where loyalties lie on issues, and what is right and wrong. It acts as a guide to the interpretation of events, even attributing blame and responsibility,[79] and gives a

> sense of security [arising] out of individuals' experiences within families, which gradually widens and is generalized to other social groups that enclose us. [...] This special sequence, radiating outwards from the home, helps in generalizing the ties of affection and loyalty that begin in the family.[80]

International law is theoretically aware of this situation. A "negative duty arising from the right to nationality"[81] is the prevention of statelessness. As such, there are two conventions covering the topic of statelessness: the 1954 Convention relating to the status of stateless persons, defining such a person as someone "who is not considered as a national by any State under the operation of its law"[82] and the 1961 Convention on the Reduction of statelessness.[83] The definition is widely seen as customary international law.[84]

The islanders of the States that will have ceased or are about to cease to exist might well become such persons (probably gradually from *de facto* to *de jure* stateless), due to the fact that their States, even before being extinct, cannot offer their nationals even the minor protection nor the right to return once they are rendered uninhabitable (or the inhabitable parts become too small for all the nationals).

It seems like international law is unprepared for people actually losing their statehood. Tellingly, van Waas mentions the draft text on the *elimination* of statelessness that states in its Art. 1:

> A person who would otherwise be stateless shall acquire *at birth* the nationality of the Party in whose territory he is born.[85]

Putting such a provision in contrast to the actual provision in the text on the *reduction* of statelessness gives the impression of confidence that by such a rule, statelessness could be eliminated. Unfortunately, the islanders who lose their nationality *after* birth would not be covered even by such a comprehensive rule. While practice shows that there is almost universal acceptance of the principle according to which children are entitled to a nationality by reason of their birth,[86] no obligation to grant nationality through naturalization has arisen so far, even when the individual in question is *de jure* or *de facto* stateless.[87] There is little the international community can do to ensure the granting of citizenship or refugee status in any particular receiving State.[88] The UN and the International Law Commission have adopted a number of articles on the topic, but no general multilateral convention exists yet. In 1999, the General Assembly adopted some articles, whose main political impetus was to prevent statelessness from occurring. The guiding presumption laid down by Art. 5 was that individuals will have the nationality of the State on whose territory they habitually reside.[89] However, States are generally[90] recognized as possessing the power to expel and deport aliens.[91] Such unqualified rights (to be able to exclude all aliens at will) is seen as an essential attribute of sovereign government.[92] Thus, under general international law, there is no duty to admit aliens or to grant them a certain period of stay once admitted.[93] Therefore,

> [i]t is strict but fair to conclude that, to date, international law has failed to fully remedy any of the core difficulties that are presented by the situation of statelessness. Yes, there is a specially devised instrument that offers a minimum standard of treatment to be enjoyed by the stateless. And yes, human rights law has progressively denationalised protection with the result that the "rights gap" into which the stateless tumble is narrowing. Yet, the "big issues" remain outstanding. Those rights and entitlements that traditionally belong to the very heart and function of citizenship still generally hover just beyond the reach of the stateless: the right to enter and remain in a state, the right to participate in government ant the opportunity to enjoy diplomatic protection.[94]

In the end, as Arendt concludes:

> The rights of man had been defined as "inalienable" because they were supposed to be independent of all governments, but it turned out that the moment human beings lacked their own government and had to fall back upon their minimum rights, no authority was left to protect them and no institution was willing to guarantee them.[95]

Emerging infringements on the human rights of (indigenous) peoples from small island States due to rising sea levels

Attention must also be paid to the concept of "indigenous peoples." Indigenous peoples can be identified in certain geographical areas by the presence in varying degrees of the following characteristics:

(a) a close attachment to ancestral territories and to the natural resources in these areas;
(b) self-identification and identification by others as members of a distinct cultural group;
(c) an indigenous language, often different from the national language;
(d) presence of customary social and political institutions; and
(e) primarily subsistence-oriented production.[96]

Being indigenous means "that there is a relationship through time between the people and a particular environment."[97] While not all islanders will qualify as indigenous peoples, some of them will. Indigenous peoples in countries like Kiribati, Nuie, Marshall Islands, Tokelau, Papua New Guinea, and Vanuatu "stand to lose everything because of rising sea levels."[98] They "will not only lose their lands, natural resources and their livelihoods but also their countries. The loss of their lands and resources will affect their cultural and social identity."[99] Indeed, the unique relationship of indigenous peoples to their territories is crucial for the cultural identity of these peoples and their physical survival.[100] Therefore, indigenous rights understandably place a special emphasis on the maintenance of the homeland territory. As such, Art. 13 of the Indigenous and Tribal Peoples Convention, 1989 (No. 169)[101] states:

1. In applying the provisions of this Part of the Convention governments shall respect the special importance for the cultures and spiritual values of the peoples concerned of their relationship with the lands or territories, or both as applicable, which they occupy or otherwise use, and in particular the collective aspects of this relationship.
2. The use of the term lands in Articles 15 and 16 shall include the concept of territories, which covers the total environment of the areas which the peoples concerned occupy or otherwise use.

Similarly, the UN Declaration on the Rights of Indigenous Peoples, while explicitly "recognizing the urgent need to respect and promote the inherent rights of indigenous peoples which derive from their political, economic and social structures and from their cultures, spiritual traditions, histories and philosophies, especially their rights to their lands, territories and resources,"[102] states in its Art. 25:

> Indigenous peoples have the right to the lands, territories and resources which they have traditionally owned, occupied or otherwise used or acquired.

Despite these explicit rights, there does not seem to be a plan regarding the mitigation, remediation, and potential relocation of many indigenous cultures around the world that are threatened by the rising seas.[103] Yet, for indigenous peoples in particular, and for many islanders in general, "the central importance of land and territory to group identity and culture"[104] must not be underestimated.

Therefore, the concept of "indigenous peoples" is also interesting for the aspect of collective human rights protection discussed next.

Collective dimension of human rights infringements due to climate change

In addition to recognizing the endangered rights, in the context of climate change it is necessary to transcend "the traditional notion of human rights as an individual entitlement" and capture "the intrinsic, collective and global dimension of climate change and its inter-generational nature."[105] Generally, particularly in indigenous/traditional societies, where persons are not defined principally as individuals, but more as members of a group,[106] these groups must be protected more collectively than individually. For indigenous peoples, the relevant regulations explicitly emphasize the importance of collective protection. For example, Art. 1 of the UN Declaration on the Rights of Indigenous Peoples[107] states:

> Indigenous peoples have the right to the full enjoyment, as a collective or as individuals, of all human rights and fundamental freedoms ...

And the American Declaration on the Rights of Indigenous Peoples[108] contains a separate article on collective rights: Art. VI:

> Indigenous peoples have collective rights that are indispensable for their existence, well-being, and integral development as peoples.

Moreover, some of the rights threatened by climate change are collective rights due to their very nature: As such, self-determination[109] is often seen as "collective right."[110] Also "cultural rights refer to a community's way of life."[111] And the right to nationality, or citizenship, must be interpreted as a universal right to a particular group right,[112] "[u]nless one believes that the only citizenship compatible with a universal human rights regime is cosmopolitan citizenship in a world state – a conception of citizenship that is not countenanced by the UDHR."[113] However, a collectively understood right of nationality would probably provide the basis for a claim for such a population to a territory of its own to replace the territory it has lost.[114] Thus, Statelessness is not only a source of difficulties for the stateless person himself, but also for the receiving State.[115]

The core meaning of human rights "refers to indispensable conditions for an existence worthy of a human being. Such conditions may include interests belonging to collectivities of human beings."[116]

However, at least at the universal level, the development of a collective dimension in the human rights provisions of the two UN Covenants has been rather modest: Most cases dealing with environmental change were brought before the UN Human Rights Committee under the minority protection clause of Art. 27 ICCPR. This provision explicitly refers to the rights of "persons belonging to such minorities" and not to the collective rights of the group as such. Accordingly, the UN Human Rights Committee has addressed the environmental impact on the traditional lives of minorities with regard to the "individual" rights of minority members and not of the community.[117] Hence, environmentally related "rights" (just like human rights in general) have essentially been conceived as "individual rights."[118]

According to Francioni, this

> rigid maintenance of this approach contributes to the 'stagnation' of international law, and more particularly to the confinement of the idea of 'human rights' within an individualistic horizon, which remains blind to the intrinsic linkage between the individual and the collective interests of society.[119]

The *Teitiota Case* is interesting in this regard. In this case, a man from Kiribati, Mr Ioane Teitiota, moved to New Zealand with his wife in 2007. There, they had three children who were, even though they were born in New Zealand, not entitled to New Zealand citizenship under the Citizenship Act 1977. Following the expiration of their visas in October 2010, the family remained in the country illegally. Subsequently, in order to avoid deportation, Mr Teitiota applied for refugee status under Part 5 of the Immigration Act 2009, which incorporates the 1951 Convention Relating to the Status of Refugees into domestic law.[120] The New Zealand Court of Appeal stated that, although it has

> every sympathy with the people of Kiribati, Mr. Teitiota's claim for recognition as a refugee is fundamentally misconceived. It attempts to stand the Convention on its head.[121]

It pointed out that the family would have to be *affected differently* from the other nationals of the respective country.[122] This understanding is fully in accordance with the individualistic direction of the traditional refugee understanding. Also, the panelists of the 2019 Berlin Climate and Security Conference pointed to the gap in international law as the Geneva Refugee Convention does not cover displacement linked to environmental and climate change.[123] Refugee law and human rights law in general was "developed before climate change was understood to be a looming threat to human security."[124]

Remarkably, in 2019, the UN Human Rights Committee recognized that Teitiota could qualify as climate refugee. Hence, States were responsible "to take into account in future deportation cases the situation at the time in Kiribati and new and updated data on the effects of climate change and rising sea levels thereupon."[125] It held that New Zealand could have acted in violation of Teitiota's right to life under Art. 6 of the ICCPR by removing him to Kiribati, however it left the burden of proof entirely on the applicant, setting a very high threshold, which, in the case of Teitiota, it did not consider satisfied.[126]

Thereby, whereas in the end rejecting Teitiota's claim (with two dissenting opinions), the Committee paved the way for human rights bodies as a forum to litigate issues related to climate change and environmental matters. States' non-refoulement obligations, as well as their policies and responses (or lack thereof) vis-à-vis climate change need to be looked at more closely.[127]

Moreover, cases like the Teitiota case necessitate a broader and collective understanding because the populations in question are threatened *collectively*. Generally, a "human rights approach to climate change must be conceived of in such a way as to transcend the traditional notion of fundamental rights as individual entitlements and capture the collective dimension of the impact of climate change on society and humanity as a whole."[128] In this respect, Committee member Duncan Laki Muhumuza concluded his dissenting opinion to the Human Rights Committee's finding in the Teitiota case by saying:

> The action taken by New Zealand is more like forcing a drowning person back into a sinking vessel, with the "justification" that after all, there are other passengers on board. Even as Kiribati does what it takes to address the conditions, for as long as they remain dire, the life and dignity of persons remains at risk.[129]

Wider in its scope and exemplary in this regard is the Banjul Charter and its implementing jurisprudence, where environmentally related "rights" are seen as "collective right[s] of the community affected by the disputed environmental impact."[130] Also the Inter-American system shows a "somewhat more progressive attitude with respect to the conceptualization of environmental rights as 'collective' rather than purely individual."[131] While the African system is still "better positioned to develop a jurisprudence adequate for addressing collective rights,"[132] both systems seek to go beyond the individualistic approach to environmental rights found in the jurisprudence of the European Court of Justice and interpret human rights guarantees collectively as legitimate community claims.[133] Thereby, these systems deal with the problem of collective human rights violations more appropriately, which could set a good (but internationally probably not well received) example.

> The plea is therefore for more advanced jurisprudence in the field of human rights which recognizes the collective dimension of the right to a decent and sustainable environment as an indispensable condition of human security and

human welfare.[134] ... a plea for a more imaginative approach based on the consideration of the collective-social dimension of human rights affected by environmental degradation.[135]

Conclusion

The rising sea level and eventual loss of their home State means great hardship for the affected individuals and peoples. International law seems rather unprepared for such a situation.

People living on atolls are particularly vulnerable, principally because of the characteristics of the ecosystem in which they live. Unlike most vulnerable communities, the vulnerability of atoll populations cannot be reduced merely by the enhancement of human rights at the level of their home State alone.[136]

Above all, the necessity of relocation will pose a challenge on the individuals in question, their States, and States where the people will relocate to. Realistically, it is unlikely that populations will move all at once; instead, their movement will be gradual and most likely, also quite random. There will be legal, economic, financial, educational, cultural, and other types of obstacles. International law will need to be developed and it should be pre-emptive in character, focusing on the real needs and perceptions of the affected populations.[137] The legal status of displaced people should be clarified in advance. Generally, under international law, a State may determine for itself to whom it will grant citizenship. Consequently, at least at present, there is no right for a citizen of a sinking State to obtain citizenship in the host State. However, while in the case of refugees from non-sinking States, (dual) citizenship of the State of origin carries with it some rights (diplomatic protection, right of return, etc.), the rights associated with citizenship of the sinking State will become increasingly weak and eventually irrelevant. Therefore, it seems important and right to grant special status to the citizens of sinking States in this regard and distinguish stateless migrants from non-stateless migrants (in terms of the possibility of acquiring the citizenship of the host State, qualified right of permanent residence, etc.) in order to compensate for the loss of their State. The international community must, moreover, "provide social, cultural, political, and economic support and guidance for a people forced to abandon their lands, without hope of return. Regardless of how such a response develops, the law must adapt to address the reality of the situations it seeks to regulate."[138] The parties to the Paris Agreement were

> [a]*cknowledging* that climate change is a common concern of humankind, [hence] Parties should, when taking action to address climate change, respect, promote and consider their respective obligations on human rights, [...].[139]

If, however, no pre-emptive solutions are provided, there will be a vague "responsibility" of various/all States and a big practical burden for some (other?) neighboring States, who will most likely not be willing to take this responsibility alone. Thereby, those forced to leave their homes will "become victims twice: first of the environmental disasters, but second, by the international community whose failure to take the necessary steps to protect and classify them rendered them stateless and homeless."[140]

The prime protector of human rights is the national State. This has a long pedigree in political theory and has been recognized in both international human rights law and the law of State responsibility:[141] "[T]he first obligation of a government is to respect and to ensure to all individuals within its territory and subject to its jurisdiction" the enjoyment of their human rights by not violating those rights and ensuring, through specific activities, the enjoyment of the recognized rights.[142]

In particular, it is the responsibility of States "to prevent and protect people from displacement, mitigate its consequences, provide protection and humanitarian assistance and find durable solutions."[143] They even must take preventive measures,[144] "[w]here there are indications that an individual is at risk of having his/her rights violated, or where a situation exists which gives rise to such a risk," in order to ensure, to the fullest extent possible, that these risks do not materialize.[145] Here are clear "indications that an individual is at risk of having his/her rights violated." The Report of the Special Rapporteur on the issue of human rights obligations relating to the enjoyment of a safe, clean, healthy, and sustainable environment stated in this context in 2016:

> States have *obligations* to protect the enjoyment of human rights from environmental harm. These obligations encompass climate change. The *foreseeable* adverse effects of *climate change* on the *enjoyment of human rights* give *rise to duties of States* to take actions to protect against those effects.[146]

However, in the context of climate change, particular issues arise with regard to the shared responsibility of States and international cooperation.[147] The jurisprudence of the European Court of Human Rights might give some indication of how a failure to take measures against foreseeable risks could possibly amount to a violation of human rights: it found a violation of the right to life in a case where State authorities had failed to implement land-planning and emergency relief policies while they were aware of an increasing risk of a large-scale mudslide. The Court also noted that the population had not been adequately informed about the risk.[148]

If relocation becomes necessary, the obligation includes the provision of access to housing away from hazardous zones. Moreover, communities that are relocated away from hazardous zones must be protected. This includes protection against forced evictions without appropriate forms of legal or other protection and adequate consultation with affected persons.[149]

With regard to livelihood, the Special Rapporteur on housing notes that attention must be paid to the location of the alternative site when people are being relocated.[150] Any response to the loss of land and the concomitant rootedness and spirituality would moreover do well to be mindful of the interrelationship of land and culture.[151] Early planning would maybe permit cultural and communal artifacts to be preserved.[152] However, as soon as relocation within the affected State's territory is not possible anymore, the duty is ill-placed with the affected State.

The State moreover has the obligation to promote the realization of the right to self-determination.[153] The positive duty of the affected State here is difficult to imagine though, because the infringement of the right comes from the sinking of the State. However, "as a fundamental principle of human rights, the right of self-determination is not an optional concept, but a compulsion under the regime of international law," interference in which "demands response from the international community."[154]

Similarly, with regard to a right to nationality, it is simply impossible to leave the duty to protect it with the State in question whose extinction is causing the loss of nationality. Ideally, multilateral comprehensive agreements would provide for where and on what legal basis such populations would be permitted to move elsewhere and their status. To prevent temporary statelessness, acquisition of an effective nationality should be foreseen prior to the dissolution of the affected State. Dual nationality may therefore need to be permitted at least for a transitional period.[155]

Generally, the possibilities of a sinking State to provide protection are obviously limited (and becoming more limited, the higher the sea rises). Eventually, the sinking island State is missing. It is extinct, submerged by the sea. Therefore, there is a legal vacuum regarding the prime protector of human rights. It seems like there must be someone else to take over the responsibility for the affected individuals. Who is responsible for their fate?

Loss of statehood – triggering a responsibility of the international community?

Is a State's existence protected at all under international law? When the ILC drafted its Declaration on Rights and Duties of States in 1947, the delegation of Panama had submitted the basic draft, which noted that a State does not only have a right to exist (Art. 1), but is also "entitled to have this right respected and protected by all the other States" (Art. 9).[156] This would clearly point towards an obligation of the other States to protect threatened island States from sinking. However, back in 1947, such a formulation already drew criticism from several States: For example, India said: "The words 'and protected' may be omitted, as it would be neither possible nor desirable to throw the responsibility of protecting any other State in the world on the rest of the States."[157] In the final ILC draft, these two articles do not feature.[158] Explicitly stating a right of existence was seen to be "tautological" and "superfluous."[159]

> They also thought it superfluous to declare the right of a State to preserve its existence in view of articles in the draft Declaration concerning self-defence and non-intervention by other States.[160]

Hence, at least back in 1949, one did apparently not think of a danger to the existence of a State by anything but other States. Today, one does, but there is still a lack of any explicit obligation to protect the existence of the State members of the international community.[161]

However, the general rule is that under international law, States are obliged to cooperate.[162] Also, the idea that States have a responsibility to protect populations even beyond their borders is not new.[163] Thus, there might be an obligation towards the people (which could lead indirectly to a protection of the State).

In the current globalized world, the extinction of States will have an (legal but also practical) impact on other States. With regard to failing States, the international order, and especially international law, was said to

> not simply leave [them] to their fate. On the contrary, the collapse of a State anywhere in the world is seen as a matter of concern for the international community, since the international system as a whole is felt to be endangered if one of its State members is no longer functioning.[164]

This feeling seems to be less intimidating if the failing State does not leave behind a territory which could potentially become a safe haven for terrorists. However, the failing, or in this case sinking, State does also leave something behind, namely its population. While Branthwaite points out warning examples of cultural or ethnic identity without statehood that lead to instability and build a potential source of terrorism and revolution,[165] the neighboring States will notice the practical impacts of the refugees even without such projections.[166] But are those neighboring States the ones who should be let alone to deal with the issue? The so-called "refugee crisis" in Europe is striking in that it shows that it is certainly not a good idea to leave neighboring countries alone to deal with the situation.[167] Thus, even presumably less-affected States would maybe want to be protected from enormous refugee flows.

But who should be seen as "responsible" then? Boyle suggests (without reaching a conclusion) the UK, US, and Germany whose historical emissions have unpredictably caused the problem, or China and India whose current emissions are predictably making the situation worse, or the US or Canada that have pulled out of the Kyoto Protocol and have failed to take adequate action to limit further emissions to stabilize global temperatures at 1990 levels? Or the governments of the Association of Small Island States, which may have conceded far too much in ratifying the Kyoto Protocol or in subsequent climate negotiations (and even in the Paris Agreement, although they were much more visible there)?[168] The nature of climate change, which directly affects the majority of States and much of humanity,[169] makes it necessary to consider how human rights norms apply to a global environmental threat. Usual environmental issues that have been examined by human rights bodies have causes and effects that are felt within one country. In those cases, the application of human rights law is possible. They can and should be addressed primarily by that State. Climate change is different regarding responsibility and causation – and, in the end, regarding the addressee.[170]

Human rights approach

The inhabitants of sinking islands may justifiably complain of human rights infringements caused by climate change and eventually the cessation of their State due to climate change-induced rising sea levels.[171]

A possible obligation to protect these populations could be derived from the *erga omnes* nature of some human rights. Generally, "[a] human right can be understood as an interest so fundamentally important to human dignity that it imposes duties on others for its fulfillment."[172] The previously mentioned rights are certainly indispensable in securing human dignity. The issue of whether States are legally bound to take action upon the breach of *erga omnes* obligations is controversial, though. In the Wall Advisory Opinion, the majority of judges of the ICJ held, with respect to the right of self-determination and certain obligations under international law, that due to the *erga omnes* character of these norms, other States were obliged not to recognize the illegal situation resulting from such violations.[173] Judges Higgins and Kooijmans objected in their separate opinions that *erga omnes* violations would not tackle obligations for third States.[174]

However, the human rights approach "identifies rightsholders and their entitlements and corresponding duty-bearers and their obligations, and works towards strengthening the capacities of rights-holders to make their claims and of duty-bearers to meet their obligations."[175] It "places the individual at the centre."[176] Applied, this approach would not only "encourage transparent and participatory processes for decision-making, implementation, monitoring and evaluation."[177] It would also widen the view to other responsible persons if the primary responsible person does not fit.

In the case of sinking island States, it is obvious that the duty to protect the human rights of the affected individuals cannot remain by their very nature with the affected States. As each State is still the prime protector of human rights, losing one's State means losing one's prime protector of human rights for the affected individuals. The populations of climate change-related sinking island States "will neither be able to avail themselves of protection of the country of their nationality nor be able to return to that country."[178]

In this case, there must be a fallback bearer of that responsibility. As there is no obvious fallback option under international law, such a bearer needs to be found. And it needs to be found before the prime protector has ceased to exist.

The best option would be that the individuals had actual rights against the *international community*. Certainly, populations of extinct States deserve, need, and should be entitled to the aide of the international community.[179] However, the international human rights system is, while emerging, not (yet) at a stage where individuals could file claims with it, without the support of their respective State, except for the provisions in the regional European system and gradually in the inter-American system.[180] Internationally, there is no such option (yet).

Following the developments in the field of human rights, particularly with regard to humanization, (enforceable) rights of individuals in the context of human rights infringements would be consequent. Thus, a rights-based approach in the context of climate change (and natural disasters) would do justice to the place of the individual in the contemporary international legal order.[181]

Some authors already speak of a paradigm shift from States' powers towards needs and possibly even rights of individuals. Particularly, such a shift becomes visible in the law of non-intervention.[182] This is (or would be) just. As such, Judge Cançado Trindade reminded us of the purpose of the law, which is "to preserve and promote the values of freedom and human dignity for individuals," particularly in the international arena.[183]

Indeed, the positive dimension of human rights (obligation to fulfill and to protect) requires a State to act. In the case of climate change, no State alone can actually ensure the protection of its populations on its own. From a justice point of view, individuals would not even have to primarily sue their own national State. After all, the cause is global, so the corresponding duty for the right of the individual should be with the culprit, in this case, the international community as a whole. While human rights in general could remain under the primary protection of the national State, there should be subsidiary rights that are the responsibility of the international community.

But, as international law is not about how it should be but about how it is, a view into the current reality is sobering: Positive duties are primarily duties of the territorial State.[184] While extraterritorial obligations, including the duty to actively do something about human suffering, were worked out in particular in the *Maastricht Principles on Extraterritorial Obligations of States in the Area of Economic, Social and Cultural Rights*[185] by a group of international lawyers and human rights experts, even these principles are not formulated in the language of the rights of the individuals, but in the language of objective duties.[186] Rights of the individual to humanitarian assistance exist solely against the State.[187] Thus, there is no subjective right to international assistance in contemporary international law.[188]

There are exceptions, though, when the parties involved agree to make exceptions: In 1989, within the *Operation Lifeline Sudan* framework, "the warring parties conceded the principle that civilians caught in conflict have a right to humanitarian assistance and that the international community has a right to provide it."[189] In the case of sinking island States, the agreement about the necessity to provide assistance is not even as complicated to find as in war-torn Sudan back in 1989. However, action to provide assistance internationally is still rare.

As mentioned by Breau, at least with regard to economic, social, and cultural rights, the international community has obligations to assist States in providing development.[190] Indeed, the ICESCR[191] does not contain restrictions on the territory, as, for example, the ICCPR does,[192] but mentions explicitly "international assistance and cooperation" (Art. 2(1), Art. 11(1); Art. 23 ICESCR).[193] This could be read in a way that economic, social, and cultural obligations do actually exist extraterritorially.[194]

By referring to Arts. 55 and 56 of the UN Charter and to principles of international law, the Committee on Economic, Social, and Cultural Rights stated in its General Comment No. 3 that international cooperation for development, i.e., for the realization of economic, social, and cultural rights, would constitute an obligation of all States – in particular of those States, which would be in a position to assist others in that regard.[195]

Yet, Ammer points out that extraterritorial obligations might be "not doubted by the international community" as long as obligations to respect and to protect are concerned. What is contested is "the scope of the obligation 'to fulfil'."[196] This obligation comprises the obligations to fulfill-facilitate, the obligation to fulfill-promote and the obligation to fulfill-provide. While the obligation to fulfill-provide would be the most helpful obligation for the affected islanders, this duty is highly disputed.[197] Vandenhole states that such a duty can be assumed if the following four conditions are fulfilled:

> Subsidiarity to the obligation of the country of origin, i.e., only if the country of origin is itself not capable – for reasons outside its control – to guarantee this right, the State has already asked for international support, the extraterritorial obligation only has to be fulfilled progressively (the obligation is dependent on the resources available; whether means are available should be dependent on how much of the national budget is dedicated for development assistance), the obligation refers only to core obligations, i.e., obligations regarding a minimum level of a right.[198]

These conditions could all be fulfilled in the case of sinking States. With regard to the (contested) question of which States should be obliged, it could be argued in the context of climate change and the principle of common but differentiated responsibilities of the UNFCCC that particularly developed Parties to the UNFCCC (Annex I) should be targeted by this obligation.[199] The

> obligation on "developed countries" in the UNFCCC to "promote, facilitate and finance access to and transfer of environmentally sound technologies" arguably fleshes out the references to "international assistance and cooperation" in the UNFCCC – being essentially a rare concrete formulation of such assistance in the form of an obligation.[200]

In this context, it is important to notice that the respective populations are small. The total population of the four most threatened island nations is approximately 500,000, which is about one third of the total number of migrants accepted annually by the United States, Australia, and New Zealand.[201] Therefore, maybe it should not be too hard to find rules that regulate their special situations in a manner that respects and dignifies human rights. In any case, currently

> greater clarity and guidance is needed on the ways in which international and regional human rights law obligates States [and the international community] to take action to adapt to and address the impacts of sea-level rise.[202]

Responsibility that comes with solidarity

As the human rights approach did not give a clear answer, maybe another approach offers better help: One basic principle of the international community is the principle of solidarity. Solidarity means responsibility towards all the members of the international community.[203]

Thus, here we have a population suffering and a State being unable to protect its citizens (up to a point that we do not even have a State anymore). Atapattu suggests that "at least with regard to the populations on small island states" human rights should be regarded as creating *erga omnes* obligations based on the *principle of cooperation* to provide a home to these populations.[204] But is there indeed such an obligation on other States or the international community? "Considering that the abandonment of the victims of natural disasters and similar emergency situations without humanitarian assistance constitutes a threat to human life and an offence to human dignity."[205] the answer should be clearly *yes*. Moreover, without a doubt, "[d]eveloping countries and the world's poor cannot avert these setbacks by acting alone – nor should they have to."[206] Due to the global nature of the problem, global action is needed. It is "not an option but an imperative."[207] Unfortunately, in practice, it is not as clear, though. Mr Tong, president of Kiribati said in 2015

> that climate change was the biggest moral challenge facing humankind. It threatened the very survival of peoples and nations. It was a global problem demanding global leadership. To spur action, the human face of climate change must be understood. The previous week, Kiribati had recorded its highest tides, which caused substantial damage to a hospital and a road construction project. In countries on the front line, immediate action to prevent, mitigate and adapt to climate change was essential. Despite this, he said, Kiribati would continue to gradually fall victim to the rising tides. Mr Tong asked what the Human Rights Council and others would do about it.[208]

With the presence of the UN, whose stated purpose is "[t]o achieve international cooperation in solving international problems of an economic, social, cultural, or humanitarian character ...,"[209] one would assume that such a problem would be dealt with by the international community. Moreover, "international cooperation is not only expedient but also a human rights obligation and [...] its central objective is the realization of human rights,"[210] as stated in the Report of the Office of the UN High Commissioner for Human Rights on the relationship between climate change and human rights.

Back in 1949, Prof. Brierly was still a bit skeptical when he said

> [i]t is still a misnomer to speak of the society of states as a genuine community. It is not a community because its parts have not yet any strongly held common purpose of loyalty, and so long as the present ideological rift between the East and the West continues to divide our world into two rival power systems, we cannot look for the development of community on a world scale.[211]

But things have changed. Today, Fassbender, along with Mosler, Tomuschat, and Simma of the "international community school"[212] come to a different conclusion:

"The community is more than the sum of its constituent parts."[213] It is "an entity committed to humankind as a whole, having its own legal personality and purposes which it can set against the opinion and action of a recalcitrant State."[214] Authors such as Schücking, Verdross, or Lauterpacht established the idea of an international legal community, a community bound together by an international or global law that defined the common interests and translated them into legal rights and obligations towards the international community.[215]

Thus, the international community is adding a communal dimension of solidarity to the purely selfish and antagonistic understanding of States' interests,[216] which is the characteristic of the community as an aim in itself, in contrast to the society which solely serves the individual purposes of its members.[217] In such a global community, States are no longer able to solely protect their own self-interest; rather, the moral responsibility to aid States threatened with extinction must be transformed into a legal obligation to act.[218] Ethical and moral concerns are introduced into this international legal system.[219]

From this self-concept of the international community, there would thus clearly follow a responsibility, otherwise such a community is barely worthy of its name. A well-defined understanding of the concept of an "International Community" remains to be found:[220] Paulus suggests a "communal idea of a universal community based on common values such as peace, human rights, and the preservation of the global commons such as the environment or the high seas."[221] Such a community would bear responsibility for its members. Moreover, in a community where human rights are seen as universal, there must be a responsibility for human rights impairments that are globally caused. The international human rights system that enables individuals to complain against their States would lose much credibility if it would not take over responsibility for individuals suffering from *environmental genocide* perpetrated by the community of States. "Save for refugee and asylum law," however, as well as "general statements concerning universality in the international treaties, the vision of human rights [...] mainly [focuses] on the sovereign state and its obligations towards its own citizens or those who seek protection within its borders."[222]

Nevertheless, during the last century "the idea of an international community bound together by shared values, benefits and responsibilities, and common rules and procedures, took hold of people's imaginations."[223] These "imaginations" are present and put some pressure on the international community and some anticipation towards a reaction –particularly in topics, which exceed the individual interests of individual States, not being tangible in the classical intergovernmental paradigm of international relations.[224] Such a topic is by its very nature the fight against climate change or the "duty to protect the natural environment" in general. Fassbender mentions additionally, "[t]he prohibition of the use of force [and] the obligation to respect fundamental human rights and freedoms."[225] The international community is based on an agreement of this limited set of fundamental rules.[226] The common feature of the various content provisions of the common interest of the international community is the protection of the individual.[227] This is "all the 'homogeneity' which is needed"[228] in order to speak of the international community as a "community."

A view into *jus cogens* (defined in Art. 53 Vienna Convention on the Law of Treaties) is interesting in this regard. Those norms which are peremptory and enjoy "higher rank in the international hierarchy than treaty law or even 'ordinary' customary rules"[229] are characteristic of the international community because they exceed the individual State's rules and bind the States even against their will.[230] Violations of such norms entail universal jurisdiction.

> Identified with general principles of law enshrining common and superior values shared by the international community as a whole, jus cogens ascribes an ethical content to the new jus gentium, the International Law for humankind. [...], jus cogens exists indeed to the benefit of human beings, and ultimately of humankind.[231]

Thus, even though the prohibition to emit climate change-causing substances is not a *jus cogens* norm[232] (and will at least in such a radical form probably never become one, because of practical reasons), it clearly has significant commonalities with the accepted *jus cogens* norms: Those are communal values that are there for the protection of individuals (in contrast to pure State values).[233] Moreover, these norms rest upon the right to exist, the equality and the self-determination of States, groups of persons and individuals.[234] Maguire and McGee argue that

> there is an ethical obligation on States to engage in mitigation strategies to protect unique indigenous ways of life and relationships to land, the devastation of which would be catastrophic to indigenous survival. The integration of self-determination principles in climate change governance could extend this ethical obligation into a legal obligation, not only to indigenous peoples, but to all vulnerable populations facing climate-change-induced forced migration.[235]

In any case, the prohibition to add to man-made climate change, which itself is violating rights of individuals and undoubtedly exceeds pure State values, would fit in there rather well and would ideally have to be treated as such. Such a duty is supported by various articles in the UN Charter. As such, Art. 55 requires the UN to promote "universal respect for, and observance of, human rights and fundamental freedoms for all," and according to Art. 56 "all Members pledge themselves to take joint and separate action in co-operation with the Organization for the achievement of the purposes set forth in Article 55." Thereby, the Charter of the UN seeks to protect all States – and what it protects reflects what we value. States are not protected "because they are intrinsically good but because they are necessary to achieve the dignity, justice, worth and safety of their citizens."[236]

Similarly, Art. 2(1) ICESCR requires each of its parties to take steps not only individually, but also "through international assistance and cooperation," towards the progressive realization of the rights recognized in the Covenant.[237] The ICJ has interpreted the obligation to ensure the enjoyment of human rights as "*erga omnes*." The obligation implies a duty of solidarity among all States to ensure as rapidly as possible the effective protection of human rights throughout the world.[238] Solidarity, thereby, is "because of its nature rightly referred to as 'a value-driven principle' with 'a strong ethical underpinning'."[239] Hence, it is not merely a strong moral claim, but "also a value reflected in international law."[240]

But is this responsibility actually borne out in reality to reflect how it sounds in theory? Or is the term "International Community" giving a wrong impression of coziness in the harsh realities of this world?[241] Practice seems to point towards the latter. In the end, "the international community remains dominated by powerful states and the overriding concern for protection of their sovereignty and security."[242] This leads to the following cynical situation:

> A finding of state failure would not necessarily lead to international action as the next step, but at least it would create some kind of expectation that something constructive will follow. The cynicism of the international community will be more evident if said community first finds a case of state failure and then stops short of further measures [...].[243]

Responsibility to protect

We have seen that the world has changed from coexisting to cooperating States. Yet, these developments did not directly lead to a global solidarity providing for a subsidiary responsibility of the international community in case a State is not able to protect its citizens (in the case of sinking island States in the beginning, because it is impossible for the State to tackle climate change on its own, in the end because the State itself disappeared).

In the context of people suffering human rights violations and States not being able to protect them properly, another concept comes to mind, that came up in the course of humanization and could impose a duty to assist for the international community: The concept of the Responsibility to Protect (*R2P*).[244]

First developed in the 2001 Report of the International Commission on Intervention and State Sovereignty (ICISS) in order to "remind States of their basic obligations vis-à-vis the men, women and children under their jurisdiction,"[245] the concept aims at a collective responsibility to protect populations when States fail to do so.[246] Under the premise that tasks should be performed by whoever can perform them most effectively and assuming an international principle of solidarity in the multi-level system of our globalized world, the responsibility to protect proceeds from the territorial State to the international community.[247]

Thereby it led to a fundamental shift from a right to intervene to a duty to intervene, from non-intervention[248] to non-indifference.[249] Thus, it has been explicitly stated in the ICISS report:

> While the state whose people are directly affected has the default responsibility to protect, a residual responsibility also lies with the broader community of states. This fallback responsibility is activated when a particular state is clearly either unwilling or unable to fulfill its responsibility to protect or is

> itself the actual perpetrator of crimes or atrocities; or where people living outside a particular state are directly threatened by actions taking place there. This responsibility also requires that in some circumstances action must be taken by the broader community of states to support populations that are in jeopardy or under serious threat.[250]

Deng thus suggested that when States fail to carry out their responsibilities, the international community has not merely a right but a responsibility to step in.[251] Axworthy and Rock see therein "the most significant adjustment to national sovereignty in 360 years" (since the Peace of Westphalia), but add that, in their view, "the time has come to take the proposal forward and make it a force for global action."[252]

By now, the appeal in the ICISS report to the international community was a very general one. There is an appeal to "common humanity."[253] This leaves the international community – in Tan's words – "with an 'imperfect duty'"[254] to protect. This ambiguity has several potential effects.

When responsibility is diffuse, it can be easier for states and international organizations to avoid their obligations. This would achieve the opposite result of what so many critics of *R2P* have worried about: No unrestrained interventionism, but inaction on the part of outside states.[255] Moreover, an imperfect duty offers suffering citizens within a state no real claim on the international community. While there is a duty to protect, there is no way to enforce fulfillment of the duty.[256] And a responsibility to protect without direct addressees misses a potentially positive deterrent effect.[257]

In the case of small island States, the State in question is, from the beginning, unable to tackle the question of climate change-induced infringements of human rights on their own. By its very nature, such infringement cannot be prevented by any State on its own. As Mary Robinson, president of the Mary Robinson Foundation – Climate Justice said: "No country could alone protect its citizens from the impacts of climate change," which means, according to her, "that the international community must work together to address the challenges that climate change posed for the realization of human rights [...]."[258] Later, the sinking State is not only unable to do so, but does not even exist anymore. The international community needs to address the legal vacuum that would arise as a result of States disappearing due to consequences associated with climate change.[259]

The idea of the *Responsibility to Protect* is "that sovereign states have a responsibility to protect their own citizens from avoidable catastrophe [...], but that when they are unwilling or unable to do so, that responsibility must be borne by the broader community of states."[260] Then UN Secretary-General Pérez de Guéllar pointed cautiously at the difference: It "is not the right of intervention but the collective obligation of states to bring relief and redress in human rights emergencies."[261] This shift from discretionary right to responsibility to ensure the protection of populations is an important one.[262] Javier Pérez de Cuéllar believed that "the protection of human rights has now become one of the keystones in the arch of peace" and that it now involves more international influence "than what was regarded as permissible under traditional international law."[263] Resisting that shift of the "heightened international interest in universalizing a regime of human rights" would be "politically as unwise as it is morally indefensible."[264]

During the aforementioned time of the Carter administration (1977–81), the shift to a cooperating society was already noticeable, even though it was still about a right to intervene: While it was emphasized that it was the prime responsibility of governments to protect the human rights of their citizens, the United States had a right and a responsibility to act (in the form of diplomatic intercessions or even military and economic aid cutoffs) when they failed to do so.[265]

> There is a growing recognition that the issue is not the "right to intervene" of any State, but the "responsibility to protect" of *every* State when it comes to people suffering from avoidable catastrophe [...]. And there is a growing acceptance that while sovereign Governments have the primary responsibility to protect their own citizens from such catastrophes, when they are unable or unwilling to do so that responsibility should be taken up by the wider international community – with it spanning a continuum involving prevention, response to violence, if necessary, and rebuilding shattered societies.[266]

Thus, the humanization of international law led to a dilemma around the interpretation of the sovereignty concept on the one hand and the international protection of human rights on the other hand.[267]

The "guiding light for the inception of the ICISS in 2000 was the concept of human security which put people, rather than state structures, at the centre of foreign policy."[268] It was hoped to ensure that whenever mass atrocities of human rights again erupted, "there would be a reflex international reaction: not that this was nobody's business, but that it was everybody's, with the only issue being not whether, but how, to respond."[269] The proclaimed aim of the commission was "a new emphasis on people rather than power."[270] The concept was feared by many for its potential threat towards the sovereignty of *States*:

> The maximum caution needs to be exercised lest the defense of human rights becomes a platform for encroaching on the essential domestic jurisdiction of States and eroding their sovereignty.[271]

While "[i]t seems to be beyond question that violations of human rights imperil peace," one was very cautious about the fact, that "disregard of the sovereignty of States would spell chaos."[272] Jean Ping, the Chairperson of the African Union Commission describes the process leading to the final adoption of the Concept of Responsibility to protect:

> I recall that most countries of the South at the level of the Non-aligned Movement were strongly opposed to the proposal of the Secretary-General. It would be true to say that they were frightened by the proposal, and with the Iraki syndrome what happened in Iraq at the back of their minds, they

> saw it as an instrument that could be used by the powerful countries against the weaker ones. Some talked of their fear of abuse and double standards. In particular, the Permanent Representative of an African Country made acerbic comments on the Report of the Secretary-General by suggesting that it was difficult to distinguish responsibility to protect from intervention. Further, he expressed the view that it had not been the object of international negotiations and had no legal basis in the Charter or in International law. Indeed, it was generally believed that the proposal would never sail through and would be defeated or postponed.[273]
>
> Finally, after having discussed the issue with the Ambassador of Pakistan, H.E. Akram Mounir, who was one of the Ambassadors most opposed to the concept, an amendment proposed by him enabled us to reach an agreement. His proposal was to link the responsibility to protect populations to specific crimes, namely, genocide, war crimes, ethnic cleansing and crimes against humanity. This is what was finally adopted in the Outcome document during the Plenary meeting of the General Assembly in September 2005.[274]

That way, the *R2P* principle was embraced unanimously by more than 150 heads of State and government attending the 2005 World Summit and sitting as the UN General Assembly within just four years since its initial articulation, an extraordinarily short timeframe given how long it usually takes new norms of international behavior to move to formal institutional embrace.[275] This was possible because "[t]he traditional principle that each state has jurisdiction over its territory [was] reinforced in the World Summit Outcome."[276]

There was a general acceptance and commitment to holding States to account for the performance of their sovereign responsibilities because the obligation upon States to protect their populations is clear.[277] This is the "bedrock" principle of the responsibility to protect.[278]

> The World Summit Outcome thus reaffirms that the world is divided into spatially defined units, within which politics takes place. The responsibility to protect concept takes as a given that physical space exists as a series of defined and bounded territories. Each territory can be "associated or identified with a sovereign.[279]

The sovereign State entity is holding the primary control over, and responsibility for, the inhabitants of its territory. It is a manifestation of the failure of the State to meet this responsibility when people are not protected or at risk.[280] The language agreed upon is clear and compelling:[281]

> Each individual State has the responsibility to protect its populations from genocide, war crimes, ethnic cleansing and crimes against humanity. This responsibility entails the prevention of such crimes, including their incitement, through appropriate and necessary means. We accept that responsibility

> and will act in accordance with it. The international community should, as appropriate, encourage and help States to exercise this responsibility and support the UN in establishing an early warning capability.
>
> The international community, through the UN, also has the responsibility to use appropriate diplomatic, humanitarian and other peaceful means, in accordance with Chapters VI and VIII of the Charter, to help to protect populations from genocide, war crimes, ethnic cleansing and crimes against humanity. In this context, we are prepared to take collective action, in a timely and decisive manner, through the Security Council, in accordance with the Charter, including Chapter VII, on a case-by-case basis and in cooperation with relevant regional organizations as appropriate, should peaceful means be inadequate and national authorities are manifestly failing to protect their populations from genocide, war crimes, ethnic cleansing and crimes against humanity. We stress the need for the General Assembly to continue consideration of the responsibility to protect populations from genocide, war crimes, ethnic cleansing and crimes against humanity and its implications, bearing in mind the principles of the Charter and international law. We also intend to commit ourselves, as necessary and appropriate, to helping States build capacity to protect their populations from genocide, war crimes, ethnic cleansing and crimes against humanity and to assisting those which are under stress before crises and conflicts break out.[282]

Thus, the first pillar is the responsibility of individual sovereign States to protect their people from such crimes, the second is that of other States to assist them to do so, and the third is the responsibility of States to take appropriate collective action – including, as necessary, forcible action under Chapter VII of the Charter when a State is "manifestly failing" to fulfill its own responsibility.[283]

While being a big step forward towards international cooperation,[284] the version of the World Summit Outcome is not a step forward for people affected by climate change, not only because the focus remains on the State instead of on the individuals, but also because climate change is explicitly excluded from the concept of the *R2P*: The *R2P* is not meant "to cover other calamities, such as HIV/AIDS, climate change or the response to natural disasters."[285]

Hence, while "linking the responsibility to protect to specific crimes was designed to address the fears of those who viewed the principle 'as an instrument that could be used by the powerful countries against the weaker ones',"[286] this now prevents the people affected from climate change to profit from the rules of the *R2P* principle. It is said that stretching the concept beyond its agreed terms fuels suspicions held by weaker States of a hidden interventionist agenda, which will ultimately harm the utility of *R2P*.[287]

However, intervention in order to protect the population is enforceable without the consent of the State when (and only then) the State misused its power of sovereignty (in the four listed crimes the respective State's sovereignty becomes suspended). Yet, intervention in order to protect the populations *with* the consent of the affected State does not need such limitation.

The less limited version of ICISS was opposed by States "which were either strongly attached to a traditional concept of sovereignty or had a bad human rights record (or both)."[288] which clearly shows that the problem lies in finding the balance between human rights and sovereignty, not in protecting individuals. Cohen adds that "[i]n identifying the four major crimes, *R2P* establishes the point at which international intervention becomes legitimate."[289] Yet, against whom is the responsibility to be legitimized? It seems like it is to be legitimized with respect to the committing government or possibly the intervening government. It is surely not illegitimate with respect to the victims.

International support for the islanders (from the point of view of the islanders) is certainly legitimate. Their case is, moreover, particular because it is truly global: While mass violations of human rights "normally" occur in the course of internal or international conflicts, the source of the entrenchments of the human rights discussed above is climate change. Thus, even if there is no responsibility according to the *R2P* principle, the particularity of the situation might give room for a responsibility *sui generis*.

Causal responsibility

All States have contributed to anthropogenic climate change. Humphrey says: "The activities that give rise to climate change have been known for at least a quarter of a century – during which time they have actually increased in most States. The harms are concrete. The causal chain, though complex, is uncontroversial. This looks like an open space for judicial activism."[290] Indeed, according to the IPCC, it can be shown that human activities *cause* climate change, and in particular cause rising surface temperatures globally ("Human influence on the climate system is clear.").[291] This anthropogenic force arises from territorially-bounded conduct, while not being territorially-limited in its impact.[292] However, while States "with lower levels of human development, especially small island developing states, generally have the lowest emissions" (but are often the most vulnerable to climate change), States with very high human development "are the biggest contributors to climate change, with average carbon dioxide emissions per capita of 10.7 tonnes, compared with 0.3 tonnes in low human development countries."[293] The International Council for Human Rights gave this metaphor in 2008:

> If my neighbour decided to convert his bungalow into a palace, and in the process directed a channel of toxic sludge through my garden, killing off the livestock and crops upon which I depend for food and income and effectively leaving me and my family destitute, I would have a strong case against her in a court of law. The case would remain strong even if my neighbour could show the splendour of her new life and the difficulty of returning to the cramped space of her original bungalow. It would probably be good enough to ensure that my neighbour took steps to rectify or avoid the situation rather than let it go to court. The questions of justice in this hypothetical example look fairly clear-cut.[294]

Consequently, more and more legal cases are being brought before various courts. Often the causal connection between the concrete damage and the emissions is difficult to prove and thus, in the end, accountability is sometimes rejected. However, in the case of greenhouse gas emissions, *all* States add their share. And, while the failure of one State "to reduce carbon dioxide emissions in line with its international obligations may not be sufficient on its own to cause adverse global warming, but the combined failure to reduce carbon dioxide emissions of many states can result in such an indivisible injury."[295] Hence, it seems just to construct a "Shared responsibility," as Nollkaemper and others point out in Principle 2 of their "Guiding Principles on Shared Responsibility in International Law."[296] On this basis, it can be argued that, far from adopting a lenient stance in assessing the adequacy of States' mitigation efforts, judges should resolve the ambiguity inherent in the fair share question in favor of injured parties.[297] If no obligation to make full reparation arises because the contribution to the injury is negligible, the international person concerned may nevertheless[298] be required to make partial reparation[299] for the indivisible injury caused, which would be apportioned on the basis of an estimate of its contribution to the injury.[300]

Indeed, to stay in the metaphor of the Human Rights Council, not all States "convert their bungalow into a palace." "[T]here is a strong correlation between a country's wealth and its current and past levels of greenhouse gas emissions."[301] Estimates indicate that between 1950 and 2000, the wealthiest ten percent of people in developed countries emitted 7.5 times more CO^2 than the poorest ten percent and 155 times more CO^2 than the poorest ten percent of people in developing countries.[302] And the societies that are most responsible for greenhouse gas emissions are those who are least vulnerable because of their adaptive capacity conferred upon them by the wealth that they have generated through dirty industrial production.[303]

With this in mind, could States be held responsible for emitting greenhouse gases at least to the extent of their percentage share? This would mean the strongest accountability for those States that emitted the most greenhouse gases. Holding them responsible seems just. Members of the Group of 77 stated in the "Caracas Declaration" of 1989:

> Since developed countries account for the bulk of the production and consumption of environmentally damaging substances, they should bear the main responsibility in the search for long-term remedies for global environment protection and should make the major contribution to international efforts to reduce consumption of such substances. The Group reiterates that measures taken at the international level should take full account of the existing asymmetry in global production and consumption patterns and should consciously seek to redress it.[304]

Yet, "no provision recognising the 'main responsibility' of developed states or their obligation to 'compensate' the most vulnerable nations" followed.[305]

Climate Justice requires States to look beyond their responsibility to their own people and accept responsibility for all those who are particularly vulnerable to climate change, including future generations.[306] However, in order to hold a State responsible, there needs to be a rule establishing such responsibility. Is there such a rule in international law? Principle No. 7 of the Rio Declaration on Environment and Development declares:

> States shall cooperate in a spirit of global partnership to conserve, protect and restore the health and integrity of the Earth's ecosystem. In view of the different contributions to global environmental degradation, States have common but differentiated responsibilities.[307]

The concept of common but differentiated responsibility is also set out in Art. 3(1) UNFCCC.[308] This principle, however, is rather vague and heavily contested.[309] But it is indeed necessary to refrain from insisting on formally equal treatment because such a behavior would prevent development without even being fair.[310] Yet, deep disagreements "over the appropriate burden-sharing principle" were "at the root of the difficulties parties have encountered in negotiating a comprehensive post-2012 commitment regime."[311] It has been argued that in the context of climate change, industrialized countries are both responsible for preventing further greenhouse gas emissions as well as for any damage caused to the economies and peoples of other States. Thus, they must compensate for past and present damages and prevent future damage.[312] It remains unclear, though, what these responsibilities look like.

According to the ILC – Draft Articles on State Responsibility (DASR),[313] a State is responsible for an injury if there is a breach (Arts. 12–15 DASR) of an international obligation (a legal rule that is either customary international law or that the State had ratified at the time of the violation)[314], this breach is attributable to the State (Art. 4 DASR), the breach is the State's fault (negligence in connection with the no harm rule is sufficient), and the injury is caused by the breach of the specific rule (Art. 31(2) DASR).[315]

Art. 2 UNFCCC imposes the duty of prevention regarding climate change on the contracting parties. In connection with Art. 4(2) UNFCCC, which sets forth the duty of conduct to reverse the long-term trend of ever-increasing greenhouse gas emissions, States (at least Annex I Parties) can be seen as breaching a primary rule that when breached establishes a wrongful act in the sense of Arts. 12–15 DASR.[316] Yet, up to now, "no consensus exists on the interpretation of Article 2 of the UNFCCC in conjunction with Article 4.2."[317]

There are many more hard- and soft-law obligations: such as the Trail Smelter principle[318] (States have a duty to prevent activities occurring within their jurisdiction from harming other States), Principle 21 of the Stockholm Declaration,[319] the UN Convention on the Law of the Sea (UNCLOS),[320] the Convention on Biological Diversity (CBD),[321] the Bali Road Map,[322] and the Copenhagen Accord.[323] All these rules are breached in the context of emissions that cause global warming.[324]

Establishing causation with regard to the islanders and their sunken States is difficult, though, if not impossible.[325] As climate events are not considered to be the "fault" of any particular nation, liability for harm cannot be attached easily to particular nations.[326]

It is virtually impossible to disentangle the complex causal relationships linking historical greenhouse gas emissions with a specific climate change-related effect, let alone with the range of direct and indirect implications for human rights.[327] With a view to Art. 13 DASR that codifies the prohibition of any retrospective assumption of responsibility, this becomes problematic. One would need a concept of joint and several liability. Yet, in absence of State practice and ignorance in international law literature on this issue, Brownlie concludes that such a concept does not exist in international law. Art. 47 DASR only applies to instances where several States are responsible for "the same wrongful act" and not to instances where several States independently commit acts that contribute to a (possibly indivisible) harm.[328]

It could still be possible, to hold States responsible because of violations of general rules of customary international law (such as the no harm rule).[329] Taking a customary rule (such as the no harm rule) as a primary obligation has the advantage, that it is applicable to all States. Yet, it also has the disadvantage that the rule is rather vague, which makes it difficult to determine its exact content.[330]

Moreover, global warming is often one of several contributing factors to climate change-related effects, such as hurricanes, environmental degradation, and water stress, which again makes it impossible to establish the extent to which a concrete climate change-related event with implications for human rights is attributable to global warming.[331]

Last, but not least, adverse effects of global warming are often projections about future impacts, whereas human rights violations are normally established after the harm has occurred.[332]

All in all, Fitzmaurice and Voigt conclude that "in light of all these unresolved issues [...] the classical rules on state responsibility" are not particularly "helpful in relation to climate change, even though they are not completely without relevance."[333] Thus, "[t]he mere fact, that climate change leads to the infringement of human rights does not necessarily mean that one state is responsible for the damage."[334]

In order to resolve these issues, affected States should try to bring climate cases to courts. "The more States become willing to invoke responsibility in court, the more jurisprudence will be available and the more clarity will develop with regard to the existing gaps."[335]

As such, the possibility of advancing an inter-state claim was mooted in 2002, when former Tuvaluan Prime Minister Talake announced that Tuvalu, joined by Kiribati and the Maldives, planned to sue the US and Australia. In the end, this claim was not pursued, but the possibility of advancing claims against those "responsible" is open.[336]

It is interesting to note the considerations of Keely Boom, who thought through two hypothetical scenarios in which Tuvalu files a case against Australia. Australia was thereby chosen because of its close geographical, social, and political relationship to Tuvalu and its historical failure to mitigate greenhouse emissions. The first is a case before the ICJ under the UNFCCC. The second is a case before the International Tribunal for the Law of the Sea under the UNCLOS (alleging a breach of Art. 194 UNCLOS).[337]

She points out that in order to file a successful claim, various obstacles (attribution, indispensable party principle, *lex specialis* principle, etc.)[338] have to be overcome. However, according to her, this could be possible. In the end, she sees better chances under UNCLOS than under UNFCCC:

> UNCLOS is likely to become a major focus for future disputes over the failure of industrialized states to mitigate GHG emissions.[339]

These are, until now, solely hypothetical cases though.[340] In contrast, the (previously mentioned) Inuit Petition was a "real" case before the Inter-American Commission on Human Rights in 2005,[341] where a group of Inuit in the Canadian and Alaskan Arctic were seeking compensation for alleged violations of their human rights resulting from climate change caused by greenhouse gas emissions from the United States of America.[342] It was directed against the US because of its withdrawal from the Kyoto Protocol and because of its high levels of emissions of greenhouse gases and resulting violation of the UNFCCC and international customary law ("no harm rule").[343]

Indeed, the United States, the world's largest economy, was responsible for 30.3 percent of the CO^2 emitted between 1900 and 1999.[344] While the case drew international attention to the threats posed by climate change to indigenous peoples, the Inter-American Commission deemed it inadmissible.[345] Other cases followed. However,

> "t]he current legal framework is clearly inadequate to accommodate claims by victims of climate change; causation, multiple actors, multiple victims, remedies and damage to future generations remain problematic. In the meantime, victims go uncompensated while perpetrators escape scot-free. This raises serious justice issues for the victims of climate change.[346]

Even if no single State can be made responsible, maybe all States together can? The human rights infringements of the islanders are ascribable to anthropogenic climate-change-induced rising sea levels. The extinction of the States is due to historic emissions of all States together, even the small island States themselves (although to a very limited extent).[347] While there are great variations regarding the amount of emissions, emissions are completely mixed in the atmosphere within two weeks, regardless of their location where they were emitted.[348] It is therefore naturally a common responsibility. Thus, "[c]limate change is a global phenomenon for which the entire community of states bears responsibility."[349]

Michael Gerrard said,

> that the big emitter nations could then be found liable under the international law principles of transboundary harm, when physical activities in one country impact adversely upon another, and the preservation of statehood something that becomes exceedingly difficult if a country is submerged between the rising oceans.[350]

Johnson Toribiong, then President of Palau, had formed an expert advisory committee in 2012 to bring the issue before the UN General Assembly (as individual States do not have the authority to request Advisory Opinions, the General Assembly would have had to approve the proposal to seek an Advisory opinion).[351] The General Assembly could have asked the court in The Hague to determine the legal ramifications of climate change under international law.[352] The question,[353] that was established by the initiative of Palau and the Republic of the Marshall Islands and was announced to be brought to the ICJ, asked whether States have a responsibility to ensure that activities carried out under their jurisdiction or control that emit greenhouse gases do not damage other States.[354] Thereby, it does not attempt to point out any State that is responsible for climate change, but tackles the issue that every State is responsible for climate change. Thus, if every State is responsible for climate change, the *international community* is responsible for climate change. Unfortunately, the initiative was taken back before it reached the General Assembly, so the court did not (yet) have a chance to give an advisory opinion on the issue.

Another interesting initiative of Micronesia that has not reached the respective courts requested the Czech Republic to initiate a transboundary environmental impact assessment with regard to the extension of the Czech Prunéřov II coal-fired power plant, "the largest single source of carbon dioxide (CO^2) emissions in the Czech Republic."[355] This is particularly remarkable because

> [w]hile transboundary [Environmental Impact Assessments] are common between neighbouring countries, this is the first time that a State from the opposite side of the world, which is threatened by climate change, has used the transboundary process to ensure its concerns are taken into consideration.[356]

Micronesia thereby "virtually introduced a new understanding of the concept of neighbourliness,"[357] which clearly mirrors how States globally moved closer together in a visible manner, particularly in the field of climate change.

Such direct accusations might be useful in another regard too. As such Torres Camprubí mentions three separate applications of the Republic of the Marshall Islands against the United Kingdom, Pakistan, and India with regard to their nuclear arms and the respective obligations to disarm and to negotiate the cessation.[358] These applications are interesting due to their content because the Republic of the Marshall Islands (RMI) explicitly associated its decision to institute proceedings on the obligation to nuclear disarmament with the obligations to combat climate change:

> It is obvious that the RMI's participation in the common struggle against climate change needs to lead to firm commitments by all States, which must include not only moral, but also legal obligations aimed at realising concrete, clear-cut goals in order to remove the threat of devastation caused by continued reliance on the use of fossil fuel energy sources. It is from this perspective of striving to reach agreement on such commitments in the struggle against climate change that the RMI has concluded that it is no longer acceptable simply to be a Party to the NPT while total nuclear disarmament pursuant to Article VI and customary law remains at best a distant prospect.[359]

Thereby, the Republic of the Marshall Islands "has conceptualized climate change as akin to the nuclear threat, in the sense that it has with the potential to result in the State's absolute destruction and ultimate disappearance."[360] The Paris Agreement that went into force on 4 November 2016 and "provides the most specific authoritative statement of a global mitigation objective"[361] can be the respective legal basis to the Non-Proliferation Treaty (NPT) in the above-mentioned cases.

And there, these applications also become interesting as to the procedure because in all three of them the court decided (in very close-run decisions) on 5 October 2016 to uphold

> the (first preliminary) objection to jurisdiction raised by [United Kingdom of Great Britain and Northern Ireland/Pakistan/India], based on the absence of a dispute between the Parties.[362]

The Court elaborates in its decisions that

> the question whether there is a dispute in a particular contentious case turns on the evidence of opposition of views [...]. In this regard, the conduct of a respondent can contribute to a finding by the Court that the views of the parties are in opposition [...]. However, [...], in the present case neither of the statements that were made in a multilateral context by the Marshall Islands offered any particulars regarding India's conduct. On the basis of such statements, it cannot be said that India was aware, or could not have been unaware, that the Marshall Islands was making an allegation that India was in breach of its obligations. In this context, the conduct of India does not provide a basis for finding a dispute between the two States before the Court.[363]

Seeing this, a previously admitted "real case" as the one between Micronesia and the Czech Republic or at least more concrete statements would have likely led to different findings in this regard. Such concrete cases would also circumvent the Monetary Gold principle[364] that was called the "most plausible of the other objections to jurisdiction and admissibility made by the Respondent" by Judge James Crawford in his dissenting opinion.[365] This should be kept in mind when filing future cases with regard to climate change.

Another idea would be to qualify the reduction of greenhouse gas emissions as an *erga omnes* obligation. Indeed, "by their very nature" the protection of the climate is "the concern of all States."[366] The category of *erga omnes* obligations was invented in order to make the violation of certain norms a concern for all States and not just for those directly affected (as in classical international law of coexistence).[367] The protection and improvement of the environment is at least since the UN conference on the Human Environment in Stockholm in 1972[368] internationally accepted and by now a "common concern" of the international community.[369]

Thus, with regard to the climate, all States do have an interest in protecting the world climate because all States will feel the effects. Due to the vague reasoning of the ICJ as to the effects of a violation of *erga omnes* obligations,[370] it remains unclear whether a State affected due to climate change would thereby get standing before the court. Moreover, the question of the respondent would be open (could it be the international community?). Last but not least, such a case would maybe tackle the causes but not directly lead to subsidiary protection for the individual victims. As this is what we are looking for here, the search for responsibility shall not come to an end at this point.

Nevertheless, this causal responsibility is important and should definitely be taken seriously, a lot more seriously than it had been up to now. Filing climate-based petitions or complaints advances innovative arguments and pushes international law in new directions,[371] which is urgently needed for a necessary evolution of international law in addressing climate change.

In combination with the Paris Agreement that provides, according to the Executive Secretary of the UNFCCC Patricia Espinosa, "a very comprehensive framework for action,"[372] this responsibility might even become stronger and more concrete, as mentioned before. However, "[c]limate change is really about the wellbeing of people"[373] and it seems like this causal responsibility is not really a responsibility to protect people.

Put differently, is it at all necessary to find a breach of a particular State? If climate change was not man-made, would there be no responsibility to protect the individuals that are suffering from the attached human rights infringements? This does not seem like the answer that we would expect with a view to what has been established above regarding the humanization of international law. But, as pointed out above, also the human rights approach did not lead to a more concrete international responsibility.

Responsibility of the one able to respond

In the context of climate change, States have acknowledged not only in the text of the UNFCCC itself,[374] but also in various Human Rights Council resolutions (e.g., 26/27,[375] 29/15,[376] and 32/33[377]) that "the global nature of climate change calls for the widest possible cooperation by all countries and their participation in an effective and appropriate international response."[378] No State can institute an effective response to climate change.[379] It is

> a problem with international origins and impacts; therefore, it would require an international solution. States must recognize their extraterritorial obligations, as enunciated in the Maastricht Principles on Extraterritorial Obligations of States in the Area of Economic, Social and Cultural Rights.[380]

Moreover, the UN Millennium Declaration stated explicitly that global challenges were to "be managed in a way that distributes the costs and burdens fairly in accordance with basic principles of equity and social justice. Those who suffer or who benefit least deserve help from those who benefit most." As such "[n]o individual and no nation must be denied the opportunity to *benefit* from globalization."[381]

Indeed, climate change is truly global,[382] unimpressed by the territorial borders of the world.[383] By its very nature, it is "the most all-encompassing and complex problem that countries have ever addressed"[384] and thereby "inherently extra-territorial [...] with solutions that will require intra- and inter-state action, as well as action by non state actors both within and outside of state institutions."[385] It "calls for collaborative global and local solutions. [...] It requires [...] sustained co-operation."[386] While international environmental law was marked from its very beginning by concern for common objectives and consideration for neighboring states,[387] the increasing importance of common global concerns such as the climate necessitate a further step in this regard.

This global nature brings with it several peculiarities that have been tackled above: First, making any particular State responsible for a globally caused problem is difficult, if not impossible. Second, every State is responsible. Third, it cannot be fought by any one State on its own.

This peculiarity should not be forgotten when searching for a responsible party. Etymologically, responsibility is a combination of "response" and "able," i.e., it means "the ability to respond."[388] The States in question lack (at least to some extent) the ability to respond to the needs of their population. The international community as a whole is the only "body"[389] that might be able to respond (collectively), hence it is the actual responsible party in this situation. It bears a responsibility to protect the populations in question from infringements on their human rights through climate-change-induced changing conditions.

This responsibility has to be, as previously mentioned, differentiated from the concept of *R2P*: The situation of the small island States is fundamentally different from those where the intervention is to be done against the will of the government in question. It is not comparable to the situation in Myanmar which is often recalled when speaking about the *R2P* in the context of natural disasters. There, the military junta governing Myanmar imposed restrictions on foreign assistance, so France's foreign minister Bernard Kouchner called upon the Security Council to authorize delivery of aid without Myanmar's consent.[390] Moreover, it is certainly not about a military intervention, which is the most sensible but by far not the only possible option regarding an action in the context of *R2P*. Evans argued in this respect that

> if an environmental emergency in the future raised the same sorts of concerns about the inadequacy of a government response being on such a scale that it could be characterized as involving the reckless infliction of great suffering, the "responsibility to protect" argument would be very relevant indeed.[391]

In the case of the sinking islands, it is recklessness on the part of the international community to not take action even though it sees the human rights aspects and the danger of the State disappearing. Those States are today asking for international support in their struggle to protect their citizens: As the president of the Republic of the Maldives already said in 1990:

> There is, however, a limit to what the small low-lying States can do. We need international help. In this multipolar world, where interdependency has become a key element, we believe that it is not just the responsibility of the nations threatened by sea-level rise to take preventive measures. We remain convinced that it is also the duty of those States whose race for development over many years had contributed to global warming, ozone depletion, acid rain and tropical deforestation to reverse the existing situation. We cannot accept that economic development has to be achieved at the expense of our environment. The Maldives calls upon the industrialized nations to take urgent measures to reduce the emission of greenhouse gases into the atmosphere and to adopt environmentally compatible technology. We urge them to assist the developing countries to implement similar measures. It is our earnest hope that the world community will heed our voice – that of low-lying States – and save us from the ignominy of becoming environmental refugees.[392]

25 years later, in 2015, Mr Tong from Kiribati said:

> that the Government had taken steps to protect its people and plan for the future. It had bought land in Fiji and aimed to prepare its people so they could migrate with dignity. However, he said, Kiribati could not address the problem or protect its people alone. Therefore, the President urgently appealed for assistance from the international community and for an immediate call to action from the Council as the voice of the vulnerable and the moral authority of the international community.[393]

Some day in the future, they will not even be able to ask for help anymore, once they cease to exist. The international community's inaction is reckless.

While the Inuit Circumpolar Conference calls what is happening to indigenous people in the Arctic "cultural genocide,"[394] it is not even necessary to bring the sufferings of the people thereby under the concept of the *R2P*.

The situations are just two different kinds. What then Secretary-General Pérez de Cuéllar said in 1991 seems to be as true today: Human rights situations where populations are "torn by war or oppression" raise sensitive political issues, whereas "[i]nternational relief efforts in emergencies [...] are mounted at the request of the affected State or States and generally create no legal or political problems."[395] Thus "[i]t would be unwise to put the two kinds of emergencies in the same conceptual basket."[396] The latter is exactly the situation here: There are no legal or political problems regarding the relief efforts. There is solely a lack of such efforts; and, thus, a need to find a way to encourage the international community to act according to its responsibility.

Deng articulated how he had dealt with the sensitive issue of sovereignty:

> Sovereignty is not a way of closing doors against the international community. In this world of intense interaction and interdependence, sovereignty is to me a positive concept, which stipulates state responsibility to provide protection and assistance for its people [...]. [T]he best way to protect sovereignty is to discharge the responsibilities of sovereignty and to call on the international community to assist in carrying out these responsibilities.[397]

He adds, "if the magnitude of the problem exceeds its capabilities, it will call on the international community to perform these humanitarian functions."[398] That is exactly what the island States are doing today. They are calling on the international community to assist them, but the international community does not answer.

Apparently, the possibility that the international community would not respond did not come to Deng's mind, nor does it seem to be a possibility in academic literature. Yet, it is a problem in practice.

A duty to offer assistance is discussed in the context of the protection of persons in the event of disasters. In 2011, the ILC asked whether the duty to cooperate with the affected State in disaster relief matters "does include a duty on States to provide assistance when requested by the affected State."[399]

Back then, the Hungarian delegation was at least "sympathetic to the idea that the duty of States to cooperate with the affected State in disaster relief matters included a duty to provide assistance when requested by the latter."[400] The Thai delegation even suggested that

> the word "duty" should replace the word "right" in draft Art. 12 (Right to offer assistance), as reproduced in Footnote 549 of the Commission's report (A/66/10), in that offers of assistance from the International Community were part of international cooperation, as opposed to an assertion of rights.[401]

This is in line with the shift that the ICISS report underwent:

> The traditional language of the sovereignty-intervention debate – in terms of "the right of humanitarian intervention" or the "right to intervene" – is unhelpful in [that] it necessarily focuses attention on the claims, rights and

> prerogatives of the potentially intervening states much more so than on the urgent needs of the potential beneficiaries of the action.[402]

While this "shifting the terms of the debate"[403] was regarded as the big advantage of the ICISS report,[404] the *R2P* concept of the World Summit Outcome seems to have gone a step backward in this regard, as – again – the focus is laid on the intervening States (and the danger of them intervening too quickly and disregarding the sovereignty of their weaker co-members of the international community). Unfortunately, the shift towards the victims has thus not made it into contemporary international law (yet).

In reply to the question of the ILC, States were "mainly arguing that such a duty had no basis in existing international law, customary law or practice, and that the creation of such a new duty would not only be controversial but would give rise to numerous legal and practical problems."[405] In any case, "a binding obligation on States to provide assistance upon request could be deemed unacceptable interference in a State's sovereign decision-making."[406] Thus, the focus, again, was not on the individuals, suffering, but on the sovereignty of the States. In order to make sure this sovereignty is not touched, there is solely a *right* for third States, not an *obligation*, to offer assistance.[407]

The Special Rapporteur observes that the use of the word "right" in draft Art. 16 [12] serves to emphasize that there exists no "duty" on the part of any assisting actor to provide assistance to an affected State. No duty exists for States either when it is a question of simply making an offer of assistance, which is the proper subject matter of draft Art. 16 [12].[408]

In the eighth report of 2016, the formulation was watered down even more: The current draft Art. 16 reads:

> Offers of external assistance: In responding to disasters, States, the UN and other potential assisting actors may address an offer of assistance to the affected State.[409]

Thereby, the advice of the United States

> to structure [the Commission's] work in such a way as to avoid the need for a definitive pronouncement on those issues [a right to offer assistance was likely to attract a wide range of divergent views], in the interest of facilitating the development of a product that would be of the most practical use to the international community,[410]

seems to be followed. However, the advantage of such a paragraph is questionable. As pointed out by the United Kingdom, as a matter of sovereignty, States could always offer whatever they wanted. Thus, the provision is superfluous by restating the obvious.[411]

This is bad for the credibility of the international community, the universal human rights system, and the Security Council, which has the prime responsibility for international peace and security and is knowingly[412] going into the very insecure situation of endangering entire States (member States of the UN) and their respective populations. This does not fit together with what Kofi Annan said in 2000:

> The UN has committed itself to the idea that no individual [...] shall have his or her human rights abused or ignored.[413]

Such reckless "inability of the international legal order to prevent blameless victims from suffering significantly negative consequences raises persistent questions about the effectiveness and legitimacy of that system."[414] Moreover, with regard to the fear, that "inventing" such a duty "would give rise to numerous legal and practical problems,"[415] the current situation is definitely also giving rise to numerous legal and practical problems. Thus, closing the eyes is not bringing the Community anywhere, not even economically as has been pointed out in the Stern Review and elsewhere.[416]

Some doubts regarding the duty are understandable, though. As such, the representative of Malaysia wanted to make sure with regard to the duty to offer assistance that it should not "be categorically imposed on a State without taking into account its resources and capabilities, as well as its domestic priorities and national interests,"[417] an argument restated in 2016.[418]

In addition, the fact that the neighboring countries would most likely be requested to offer assistance more than other States is a reason to be against the duty to offer assistance when requested. New Zealand,[419] and, in particular, Australia, for example, have shown resistance to relocating people in the Pacific region who are affected by climate change.[420] As such, when Tuvalu sought assistance from Australia in 2001, Australia "flatly refused."[421]

Françoise Hampson stated in her paper on the human rights situation of indigenous peoples in States and other territories threatened with extinction for environmental reasons that "there would seem to be no reason, in law or morality, why the closest States should shoulder the whole of the burden."[422] Moreover, as has been pointed out above,

> no state is obliged to admit into its territory anyone other than its own nationals. This basic sovereign right, together with the full discretion as to nationality and asylum, creates a difficult barrier for the guarantee of full protection for the human rights of the individuals concerned.[423]

Thus, such a duty would be better imposed on the international community as a whole which would then be responsible to coordinate the assistance.

A central coordination shall not be misunderstood, though, as an equal distribution of the "burden" in a sense that the displaced population would have to scatter evenly across the globe, for example. This would not only be unrealistic, but also potentially severely infringe upon the human rights of the people concerned (while admittedly being the easiest option to agree to by the receiving States: "No single receiving state faces a more significant compromise than another").[424]

The responsibility is common but differentiated. A differentiation between the duty of States and the duty of intergovernmental organizations has also been made in an earlier report (fifth from 2012): "[A]lthough a duty to provide assistance may exist for intergovernmental organizations when their mandates so provide, no such duty exists for States. In this respect, States remain free to decide whether or not to provide assistance, even if requested to do so by an affected State."[425]

The idea, to hold the international community responsible has been expressed by several States: In particular Sri Lanka, Thailand, and Poland which proposed reformulating the draft article to state that it was a duty of the international community to provide assistance.[426] This is exactly what would be needed in order to actually act according to the contemporary world order of humanized international law and in order to put the real focus on the victims.

Unfortunately, the international community does not seem to be brave enough to look further into such constructive suggestions, but prefers to follow Ireland, Slovenia, Germany, Greece, the Netherlands, Spain, and Belgium which expressed their view that, under contemporary international law, there existed no legal obligation to provide assistance.[427] This is a view that does not bring any improvement at all. It solely leads to the continuance of the fact that the general duty to cooperate (which could – if applied differently[428] – be a way of expanding human rights obligations so that they apply extraterritorially)[429] does not include a duty to offer assistance even when requested.[430]

Hungary suggested a compromise in this regard: Generally supporting the notion that the duty of cooperation with the affected State should include a duty to provide assistance, they suggested (at least) to "formulate such an obligation as a strong recommendation" because that was considered to be "wiser."[431]

The new draft reads, as has been mentioned above, "may address an offer of assistance to the affected State,"[432] which is certainly not a "strong recommendation." The perspective for a change in a more constructive way is not very promising, though. With regard to the *R2P* concept, powerful States (including the US) were already very reluctant concerning any legal obligations on them and/or on the Security Council including a curtail of the use of the veto:[433] As such, the representative of the United States in the discussions of the outcome document of 2005 declared:

> We do not accept that either the UN as a whole, or the Security Council, or individual States, have an obligation to intervene under international law.[434]

This is miserable with a view to the international community and stands in blatant contrast to what the international community sees itself.[435] Moreover, it is closing one's eye to the "humanization of sovereignty" which "has shifted the focus from rights of states to the needs of humans and has thus promoted a significant evolution of international law in the direction of a legal obligation of the Security Council to take humanitarian action."[436] To use the words of another representative of the US, Ms Rice, (in the context of placing climate change squarely on the global security agenda) in reply to a letter dated 1 July 2011 from the Permanent Representative of Germany to the UN on the Impact of climate change:

> Yet, this week *we have been unable* to reach consensus on even a simple draft presidential statement that climate change has the potential to impact peace and security in the face of the manifest evidence that it does. We have dozens of *countries* represented in this body and in this very Chamber *whose very existence is threatened.* They have asked the Council to demonstrate our understanding that their security is profoundly threatened. Instead, because of the refusal of a few to accept our responsibility, by its silence the Council is saying in effect "tough luck." That is *more than disappointing; it is pathetic, short-sighted and, frankly, a dereliction of duty.*[437]

In the meantime, "the inhabitants of the sinking States are suffering a fate that international law has not foreseen."[438] Despite the obvious developments, "the international response to the issue of people displaced [or otherwise affected] by the effects of climate change has so far been somewhere between slow and non-existent."[439] "[A]ll that can be done at present is to stretch existing definitions to include this almost unreal situation. Common sense and humanity will have to lead the way as the incompleteness of the international legal system becomes very apparent."[440]

This passivity has to change immediately, and it has to be changed by the international community. It cannot merely be the sum of national individual interests, but rather a community committed to the common good with a legal personality and its own purpose that can, if necessary, be held up against a resisting individual State.[441] Andreas Paulus says in this regard:

> [G]lobal challenges from nuclear weapons via famine and the habitual violation of core human rights to global warming demonstrate global interdependence and the need for a law beyond the State. Waiting for the consent of every State appears as a luxury the world cannot afford. Thus, the international community seems to have to act before a complete consensus is established. In this perception, the globe has become a single community of fate, which requires a respective community of laws that are effectively implemented and, if necessary, enforced.[442]

Conclusion

To come to a conclusion regarding, so to say, the global dimension of a State ceasing to exist and the question of a responsibility of the international community, several things become apparent.

First, despite the humanization of international law, there is no direct right of the individuals that have lost their State against the international community.

Second, despite the fact that there are developments with regard to holding the international community responsible in cases of human rights violations, there is no norm in contemporary international law imposing such responsibility as a duty to act.

Third, despite the fact that climate change is anthropogenic, making particular States responsible because of them having caused (or at least contributed to) the fate of the individuals is problematic.

Yet, there is a global responsibility of the international community as a whole, whereas there is no established way to claim compensation for a violation of such a responsibility from the international community.

This leads to the problematical situation that people are already suffering, today as well as foreseeably in the future. The State which is the prime protector of its people is unable to respond and the international community, the sole "institution" that would be able to lower the pain, is not responding.

Thus, there is a need for a concept of action. The "conceptual basket of *R2P*" from the World Summit Outcome offers some kind of legal guidance, yet it is only for the explicitly named four crimes. Moreover, whether it is indeed an emerging norm is highly debated. Its legal character is often negated.[443] Nevertheless upon this basis, a new concept could be developed upon which to hold those responsible accountable in their responsibility.

Up to now, in the case of sinking island States there is neither a legal obligation to offer assistance in the case of human rights violations (except those mentioned in the *R2P* concept),[444] nor – which is even worse – an obligation to answer requests calling for assistance. However, the idea behind the *R2P*[445] being the duty to protect people when the prime protector is unable or unwilling to help, could (and should) be applied easily. The rationale behind *R2P* fits well. The concept as such does not fit because of the clear wording in the outcome document. Yet, the concept is a vision of the recent developments (increasing importance of individuals, change towards responsible sovereignty, etc.) put into words. Thus, the international responsibility to protect the people of those island States does exist, even if there is no concept at hand naming it properly. Against this background, the international community must not absolve itself from its responsibility to the people.

It is necessary to build such a concept immediately, in order to overcome the "storm that is upon us:"[446] Concretely, that means that immediate action is needed. Action by whom? As climate change is not only caused globally, but also felt globally[447] and in particular only fightable globally,[448] it should be dealt with by the international community as a whole. Regarding a human rights approach to climate change, the international community even seems "broadly supportive:" As such, "88 UN member states supported Human Rights Council Resolution 10/4, which called for greater involvement by expert human rights bodies in the UNFCCC process."[449] But the term "International Community" is vague and "without policy edge."[450] Weiss criticizes:

> Using it [the term "International Community"] allows analysts to avoid pointing the finger at which specific entities are responsible when the so-called

> international community fails to respond or makes a mess of things. It also permits everyone to claim responsibility for successes. Because, as the old adage goes, "success has many parents, but failure is an orphan," greater clarity is required about criticisms and praise.[451]

When searching for an institution capable of representing the global community, it is appropriate to focus on the UN.[452] It is the "institutional expression" of the developments of globalization and humanization.[453] Within the UN, it is open for discussion regarding which organ should bear the prime responsibility.[454] Heiko Maas stated, as the German Foreign Minister, in 2019:

> The Arctic is an early warning system for climate change. The Security Council must become an early warning system for international policy. This is our shared responsibility.[455]

Also following the reasoning of the ICISS report (and later the World Summit Outcome),[456] the Security Council seems to be the right organ:[457]

> "The international community, through the UN, also has the responsibility to [...] protect populations [...]. In this context, we are prepared to take collective action, [...], through the Security Council, [...]."[458]

Even though the Security Council has often been criticized so far for neither being very consistent nor very effective in dealing with these [*R2P*] cases, very often acting too late, too hesitantly, or not at all,[459] this "cannot be cited as an argument, legal or moral, against the necessary corrective action, especially where peace is also threatened."[460] When the authors of the report were using the word "responsibility" instead of "obligations," the idea was to link the new concept to Art. 24 of the Charter.[461] Member States did transfer the "primary responsibility for the maintenance of international peace and security [to the Security Council], and agree[d] that in carrying out its duties under this responsibility the Security Council acts on their behalf."[462] Thus, the council is empowered to act and must act in a case of a threat to international peace and security. And, while security was originally understood primarily as the absence of international armed conflict,[463] in more general terms, it comprises the absence of human rights atrocities:[464]

> Any event or process that leads to large-scale death or lessening of life chances and undermines States as the basic unit of the international system is a threat to international security.[465]

In this concrete case, climate change is definitely a threat to peace and security ("perhaps the most extreme security challenge of the twenty-first century").[466] The consensual adaptation of the Paris Agreement on 12 December 2015 by representatives of 195 countries at the 21st Conference of the Parties of the UNFCCC in

Paris and its astonishingly quick ratification shows, moreover, that the community of States is aware of the dangerous situation.[467]

Thus, the international community needs to act. Action can and should be taken now, even "before a complete consensus is established. In this perception, the globe has become a single community of fate, which requires a respective community of laws that are effectively implemented and, if necessary, enforced."[468] In order to prepare for the challenge of having large numbers of people displaced by climate change, and in order to avoid large-scale humanitarian catastrophes, the international community must act now and deal with those issues comprehensively by protecting the human rights of those affected.[469] Precautionary[470] planning now would be prudent, rather than reacting after it is too late.[471] Responsibility to prevent is preferable to a responsibility to react:[472]

First, because of moral reasons, as taking over such a responsibility would actually place the people at the center of attention.

Second, because of financial reasons: As such, many States (including France and Germany) stated explicitly that the cost of action would be lower than the cost of inaction.[473] According to the Stern Review, a lot of money could indeed be saved.[474] As such, conferring to the Carnegie Commission on preventing deadly conflict, the international community has spent approximately US$200 billion on conflict management in seven major interventions in the 1990s, but could have saved US$130 billion through a more effective preventive approach.[475]

Last, but not least, while preventive action/intervention in the context of conflicts can be seen as problematic with regard to the sovereignty of the involved State,[476] preventive action with regard to those States threatened by the rising seas does not even present an obstacle in this regard, because the affected States are actually asking for assistance.

Thus, what should preventive action look like? According to Roeben it is a function of the institution of responsibility to concretize norms into doctrine and to link this doctrine with enforcement machinery.[477] The members of the Security Council, as delegates of all members of the organization and "trustees of the international community,"[478] should at least have a coordinating role in that battle against climate change. However, Pattison criticizes the authorization of the Security Council in general because it only identifies a procedure and not the particular agent.[479] Moreover, economically, "it is hardly comprehensible that Governments impose far-reaching and costly responsibilities on the Organization, as they judge they must, but are themselves unwilling to fulfill corresponding financial obligations."[480]

States have to absolutely become engaged in the process.[481] "[E]very member state [has] a responsibility form the Charter [Art. 2(5)] to support the UN Security Council in fulfilling its responsibility to prevent threats to the peace."[482] Hence, the Security Council needs to work on the coordinating framework, from which States must act together to maintain international peace and security in accordance with the Charter. The management of risks and threats that affect all the world's peoples should be considered multilaterally.[483] States must act according to the global coordination. They need to recognize "that the response to a fundamentally extra-territorial problem should not be constrained by an excessively narrow understanding of sovereign territoriality."[484]

Therefore, not all States will have to act in the same way. In this sense, it is a common but differentiated responsibility.[485] One component of this principle is that a State's obligations should be dependent upon its ability to act,[486] hence differentiated. The other component is common. Yet, while the consequences of climate change are commonly felt, the effects and risks of climate change are significantly higher in low-income countries.[487] Small island States whose contribution to climate change is negligible, and will continue to be so, will be at the front line of the consequences of climate change;[488] and at the mercy of those States that caused the problem in the first place.[489] Thus, generally, it is clear that the States most affected will lack the necessary resources to take sustainable adaptation measures, organize mass relocation, buy or build new land, pay reparation to dislocated populations, etc.

Therefore,

> the international community, particularly developed countries, must step in. Small island States are among the poorest nations in the world. They lack the necessary resources to take adaptation measures to protect their people from the adverse impacts of climate change. Developed countries (particularly the major emitters) must step in and help these vulnerable peoples to adapt to climate change and, when the time comes, help them relocate, including providing them with physical land for relocation,[490]

coordinated by the Security Council and not left with the island States nor (alone) with their neighbors. Certainly, richer countries have somehow gained their fortune through greenhouse gas emissions. However, it is not even necessary to determine which individual countries have the world's largest greenhouse gas emissions[491] and who is responsible for which historical or present emissions that would not be clearly assignable anyway. As De Vattel already observed in 1758 "those who have provisions to spare should assist nations suffering from famine [or other human rights infringements] as an instinctive 'act of humanity'."[492]

Interestingly, the options examined for responsibilities mirror globalization and humanization. In the end, however, it looks like, the focus is again on the State: "the predominant ordering logic in the world" "rests on a 'pure states system,' based on equality of all states and nonintervention by 'imperial actors serving as global enforcers'."[493] "[T]he naturalistic logic, connotes the idea that certain rights inhere in human nature, and that these rights should be respected by all organized societies."[494] "The world needs a public order system free from the constraints of notions of nonintervention in the 'internal affairs' of sovereign nation-states if these involve violations of human rights."[495] – or if human rights are violated with no national State to help. "At its highest level of abstraction the naturalistic logic posits human dignity as the highest value, whose pursuit does not even require the consent of a sovereign state authority."[496]

While the ILC articles on the responsibility of States logically focus on the State breaching international law, the *R2P* concept does, not eventually really focus on those that should be protected, but rather focuses on the intervening States and the States where intervention should take place. However, "international cooperation is not merely a matter of the obligations of a State towards other States, but also of the obligations towards individuals,"[497] that demand not to be left alone and "becoming 'a football to be kicked around' in 50 to 60 years," as President Tong of Kiribati has presaged.[498]

Then Secretary-General Kofi Annan stated in the beginning of the twenty-first century:

> I placed the individual at the heart of my efforts to advance our understanding of what it means to be a community of nations. Whether it means advancing development, improving the environment, or emphasizing the importance of preventative action, [...], the individual has been the focus of our concerns.[499]

If there is now no focus on the protection of the individuals, all key development issues identified beforehand could be invalidated again: The State seems to be the sole subject. Territory and particularly the foreclosure of a territory becomes vital again when individuals try to overcome borders. The international community appears to be no supplementary actor in addition to States that are focused on themselves. In this regard, Fassbender warned in 2003 of the danger that a refocus on the sovereign interests of States might become more prominent, with States trying to push the common interest aside at a time in which the experience of the two world wars and decolonization is fading.[500]

Unfortunately, today, various States tend to refocus on themselves. Even the benevolent intentions of countries leave them torn between the desire to preserve the greatest possible legal independence, and the insight that mankind urgently needs a more effective international organization.[501]

Fortunately, with regard to the small island States, many States do, at least in theory, not seem to agree to such a closed and self-focused vision of the world order but call for an urgently needed response instead. That "global rhetoric" should

> be increasingly translated into concrete action, of maintaining that rights inhere inalienably in the individuals and peoples of the world and that governments and multilateral institutions of the world community lose their legitimacy and effectiveness to the extent that they fail to uphold and promote these rights.[502]

This section closes with the exemplary words of the former Minister for Foreign Affairs of Ukraine, Mr Klimkin:

> An S.O.S. call is being sent right now from the small island developing States (SIDS) that are losing their territories, populations and resources, and thus their very existence, due to the grave impacts of climate change. It is our

> common obligation to hear their call and to respond to it without any further delay.[503]

Concluding thoughts on what it means not to be a State anymore

Thus, solidarity in the fight against the impacts of climate change is not only badly needed, but also just, as has been stated by the parties to the Paris Agreement:

> We call for strong solidarity with those countries most vulnerable to the impacts of climate change, and underscore the need to support efforts aimed to enhance their adaptive capacity, strengthen resilience and reduce vulnerability.[504]

Thereby, States should focus less on possibilities to circumvent their respective (causal) responsibilities, and more on the global need to work together in order to save the planet from global problems and protect individuals. While virtually any individual State could be seen as being at least somewhat responsible for the violations of human rights inflicted by climate change due to its greenhouse gas emissions, it seems neither possible nor useful "to disentangle the complex causal relationships" linking emissions from a particular country to a specific effect.[505] There are too many practical obstacles to such an undertaking:

> Greenhouse gases emitted anywhere contribute to global warming everywhere. Billions of people contribute to climate change and will experience its effects, and the causal chains linking individual contributions with specific effects may be impossible to discern with certainty.[506]

Thus, "[c]limate change is probably not best understood as a set of simultaneously occurring transboundary harms that should be addressed by each State trying to take into account its individual contribution to the effects of climate change in every other State in the world,"[507] but rather as a global matter that should be dealt with globally. As such, "it would seem obvious that this is a matter for international law."[508] The problem there is that

> the world order as portrayed by international law initially did not readily allow for organizing collective action. Rather international law traditionally suggested a view of the globe as divided into sovereign territorial States, which coexist and interact only in those (few) situations where the matters at hand require it.[509]

This coexistence paradigm is fundamentally ill-suited for dealing with climate change being "a paradigmatic example of a global threat that is impossible to address effectively without coordinated international action."[510]

Indeed, in "a world in which global warming connects the long-term fate of many Pacific islands to the actions of tens of millions of private motorists across the globe, the conventional territorial conception of political community appears profoundly inadequate."[511] Although small island States are at particular risk from the negative effects of climate change, climate change is "a common concern of humankind" and therefore a global problem requiring global cooperation.[512] While small island developing States are among those that contribute least to global climate change and sea-level rise, they are also among those that suffer the most from the negative impacts of these phenomena, and in some cases could become uninhabitable. As such, they are entitled to assistance under the UNFCCC, including adaptation and mitigation measures.[513]

> [G]lobalisation requires nothing short of a concomitant "globalisation of accountability"[514]

– accountability also towards individuals. The challenge on the global and on the local level is however different: The challenge for affected States is to adapt in order to protect themselves. The challenge for the international community is to reduce emissions to the extent that such adaptation can be effective, and to help affected States adapt as they see fit. "This is possible, and anything less is unacceptable."[515]

In any case, there must be a focus on human beings. Their dignity and wellbeing

> are the values that should be at the heart of any collective security system for the twenty-first century, but too often States have failed to respect and promote them. The collective security we seek to build today asserts a shared responsibility on the part of all States and international institutions, and those who lead them, to do just that.[516]

Indeed, State practice shows that all States are actually involved. The global treatment of the issue started in 1988 with the creation of the Intergovernmental Panel on Climate Change, the adoption of the UNFCCC in 1992, and the Paris Agreement that entered into force in 2016.[517] Notably, the UNFCCC was the first agreement to be negotiated by virtually all member States of the international community. Its preamble describes the global stratosphere as the "common concern of mankind."[518] To protect this global stratosphere, a meaningful reduction of greenhouse gas emissions is necessary. This does require substantial international coordination (to assure broad adoption and compliance) and cooperation (to support compliance-monitoring as well as mitigation and adaptation in less developed countries).[519]

Since the Peace of Westphalia, there was a focus on territoriality.[520] Today, there is a "need for 'de-territorialized' action."[521] Climate change

> penetrates every part of every state. Yet the human conduct helping to drive climate change takes place within sovereign states. The problem thus defies territorial limits, while the solution must arise from within territorial boundaries. This begs the question of how territorially-bound regimes respond to an extra-territorial – perhaps a-territorial – threat.[522]

Deterritorialized statehood or internationalized territories are suggested on various occasions as an alternative future for endangered States.[523] This requires international law to reconceptualize the law of statehood and to accept such "new" forms of statehood. As noted by Österdahl:

> We talk about states and non-state actors, we do not talk about full-states, half-states, quarter states, and "entities formally known as states"... [t]he question is for how long this conceptual system can remain in international law. For how long will international law be able to continue using the fiction of the uniform concept of the state?[524]

Crawford and Rayfuse state concretely that

> [i]t will be incumbent on the international community to react to the altered circumstances of states forced to "recreate" themselves in response to climate change.[525]

While new categories might become inevitable at some point, the focus should be on the individuals and their protection. Only if it becomes necessary in order to protect individuals, new categories should be built. Probably an improvement of the international refugee system might be the preferable option.

The fight against climate change and the fight for international protection of human rights go hand in hand in this regard. Dannenmaier compares both regimes in their "degree of universality and domestic policy penetration."[526] Both global regimes must be mutually reinforced in the fight against climate change.[527] The International Council on Human Rights Policy gives several reasons as to why human rights would not assist the creation of policies to deal with climate change. Namely, those reasons are that climate change generally (if not exclusively) affects categories of human rights that have notoriously weak enforcement mechanisms under international law, extraterritorial responsibility and local accountability is hard to establish, emergency conditions limit the application of human rights law and rights might conflict, as human rights protect others besides those who are potentially harmed by climate change.[528] This should not lead to a lack of consideration the human rights regime in the fight against climate change. While, for example the UNFCCC requirement on wealthy States to provide "new and additional" funding for adaptation is arguably stronger than the duty of international assistance under human rights law, and is applicable to broadly similar activities,[529] this does not prevent the duty of international assistance under human rights law from getting applied.

Currently, there is not actually a legal obligation to actively provide assistance. State sovereignty is a constant obstacle to the vague concept of support from the world community. States fear any changes to the principle of state sovereignty, as such could jeopardize the stability of international law.[530] Thereby, the attitude in the international arena becomes "to each his own." Thus, the approach that initially led States into crisis could ultimately deny them the bailout they need.[531] Matthews pointed out 20 years ago:

> States feel they need more capable international organizations to deal with a lengthening list of transnational challenges, but at the same time fear competitors. Thus they vote for new forms of international intervention while reasserting sovereignty's first principle: no interference in the domestic affairs of states. They hand international organizations sweeping new responsibilities and then rein them in with circumscribed mandates or inadequate funding. With states ambivalent about intervention, a host of new problems demanding attention, and NGOs bursting with energy, ideas, and calls for a larger role, international organizations are lurching toward an unpredictable, but certainly different, future.[532]

Against this background, international law will have to change in order to meet the new challenges of changing circumstances and achieve the overall objectives of facilitating stability and peace. Thereby it seems that sea-level rise presents only a very vivid example:

> The prospects of sea-level rise introduce a general dilemma that international law may need to face in the foreseeable future. To put it briefly: *If the Earth is entering the Anthropocene, will international law stay in the Holocene*?[533]

The answer must be negative. Hence, the transformation of international law must embrace the fundamental principles of this legal system in which geography is firmly and deeply embedded.[534] The needs of human beings must be, as Anne Peters points out, the "starting point of analysis."[535] Humankind will have to organize society differently, in line with its actual needs and purposes, and not primarily on the basis of assertion of sovereign rights over territory.[536]

> Therefore, the examination of the rules on intervention should not begin, as in the traditional public international law perspective, with an eventual exceptional right of states to intervene in extreme cases, but with the need of human beings for help.[537]

The concept of the *R2P* grounds authority – both of States and the international community – in the capacity to provide effective protection to populations at risk.[538] This could be useful here. In the case of sinking States, the State in question cannot protect the population (on its own), thus the international community bears authority. However, with regard to the *R2P* concept, States seem very afraid of it being used as "a Trojan Horse for bad old imperial, colonial and militarist habits."[539] Hence, the principle is construed very narrowly.[540]

A balance needs to be found between the importance of sovereignty and the importance of individuals. This balance is hard to establish because it would include a change in the current system of international law. While tendencies of a shift towards the individual have been visible for several years already, major changes are difficult to achieve. They depend on political entrepreneurs and social groups. Those would have to form new coalitions which can unseat the dominant ones. Political elites in power have few incentives to alter existing institutions and experiment with new systems of rule. Given that the State system has also been produced by mutual empowerment, there are barriers for any non-sovereign form of organization that wishes to be recognized as a legitimate participant in international relations.[541] Once a particular form of organization is established, political actors and social groups are reluctant to surrender their positions. Change will only occur if the contenders' relative position becomes strong enough to allow the formation of new political coalitions that can effectively challenge the old order[542] or if the older order becomes too weak or too ineffective to uphold the order. As such, progressive action of (international and subnational) non-State actors is needed. Possible actors in that regard are already present, but up to now often too hesitant in their actions.

A well-established organ of international law that should orient itself more towards the protection of individuals is the ICJ. Jennings pointed out in this regard in 1997 that

> The new kind of international law which directly concerns individuals [...] is, [...] a rapidly growing part of the whole system of international law. There is accordingly a considerable and growing area of international law which does not find its way to the World Court other than almost by accident as an ancillary item in an orthodox case between States.[543]

This has not changed yet, even though humanization has advanced considerably. Human rights can only come via States to the ICJ. The Court is still in its developmental stages concerning its role in matters of human rights. It would also be well equipped to tackle the issue of climate change from a human rights perspective.[544] As such, asking the Court to clarify in an advisory opinion about the effects of climate change on human rights and possible responsibilities resulting therefrom for States and the international community would be a good option, bringing in the human rights perspective where it belongs. The Court has already

> accepted and developed what might be called "international legal vehicles" which have been put to use to give human rights obligations even greater legal authority; in the first instance the category of jus cogens, and, doctrinally connected to such higher law, that of obligations erga omnes.[545]

If obligations arising from climate change were to be seen as *erga omnes* obligations,[546] which they should be due to their very nature, the question of climate change-related obligations also with respect to their effects on human rights is well placed at the ICJ, "the only court of a universal character with general jurisdiction."[547]

Climate change could, as suggested by the Special Rapporteur on the issue of human rights obligations relating to the enjoyment of a safe, clean, healthy, and sustainable environment, be addressed "as a matter of extraterritoriality – that is, to conclude that it implicates the obligation of each State to protect the human rights of those outside, as well as those within, its own jurisdiction."[548] This is controversial. The ICJ stated in its wall opinion:[549]

> The Court would observe that, while the jurisdiction of States is primarily territorial, it may sometimes be exercised outside the national territory. Considering the object and purpose of the International Covenant on Civil and Political Rights, it would seem natural that, even when such is the case, States parties to the Covenant should be bound to comply with its provisions.[550]

Thereby, the

> primary human rights obligations continue to rest with the domestic state. Each state is therefore still fully accountable for the human rights situation in its own territory, if and to the extent that the lack of implementation of human rights obligations results from the unwillingness of that country to give them effect. In the case of genuine inability, the primary responsibility of the domestic state remains, but the complementary obligations of other duty-bearers, in particular also obligations to "fulfill," gain importance.[551]

Hence,

> [m]aybe the time has come for us to stop thinking of human rights and human needs as "internal affairs." "Human needs" are coming to be regarded as first charge on the world's resources. And "human rights" are becoming a first charge on the public conscience of people (if not governments) everywhere.[552]

This certainly challenges the traditional concept of State sovereignty. Through the increasing importance of individuals, the States' abilities to act freely and in an unrestricted manner however they like towards their nationals and towards the globe is restricted. Such restriction must be accompanied by an active enrollment of the international community in the field of human rights and in the (partly related) field of climate change.

Notes

1 D. Wong, "Sovereignty Sunk? The Position of 'Sinking States' at International Law," *14 Melbourne Journal of International Law* (2013), p. 350.
2 M. A. Burkett, "The Nations Ex-Situ: On Climate Change, Deterritorialized Nationhood and the Post-Climate Era," *2 Climate Law* (2011), p. 354.
3 See generally I. Österdahl, "Relatively Failed. Troubled Statehood and International Law' "*14 Finnish Yearbook of International Law* (2003); M. Gerrard and G. E. Wannier, "Disappearing States: Harnessing International Law to Preserve Cultures and Society" in O. C. Ruppel (ed.), *Climate Change: International Law and Global Governance* (2013), p. 619.

4 D. Wong, "Sovereignty Sunk? The Position of 'Sinking States' at International Law," *14 Melbourne Journal of International Law* (2013), p. 349.

5 Cf. L. Yamamoto and M. Esteban, *Atoll Island States and International Law: Climate Change Displacement and Sovereignty* (2014), p. 183; cf. C. J. Tams, "Article 6" in B. Simma, H. Mosler, A. Paulus, E. Chaitidou (eds), *The Charter of the UN: A Commentary* (2012).

6 L. Yamamoto and M. Esteban, *Atoll Island States and International Law: Climate Change Displacement and Sovereignty* (2014), p. 177, citing A. Maas and A. Carius, "Territorial Integrity and Sovereignty: Climate Change and Security in the Pacific and Beyond" in J. Scheffran, M. Brzoska, H. G. Brauch, P. M. Link, J. Schilling (eds), *Climate Change, Human Security and Violent Conflict. Challenges for Societal Stability* (2012), p. 658.

7 D. Wong, "Sovereignty Sunk? The Position of 'Sinking States' at International Law," *14 Melbourne Journal of International Law* (2013), p. 349; L. Yamamoto and M. Esteban, *Atoll Island States and International Law: Climate Change Displacement and Sovereignty* (2014), p. 177, citing A. Maas and A. Carius, "Territorial Integrity and Sovereignty: Climate Change and Security in the Pacific and Beyond" in J. Scheffran, M. Brzoska, H. G. Brauch, P. M. Link, J. Schilling (eds), *Climate Change, Human Security and Violent Conflict. Challenges for Societal Stability* (2012), p. 658.

8 A. G. Jain, "The 21st Century Atlantis: The International Law of Statehood and Climate Change-Induced Loss of Territory," *50 Stanford Journal of International Law* (2014), p. 10.

9 Ibid., p. 9.

10 Ibid., p. 7.

11 D. Wong, "Sovereignty Sunk? The Position of 'Sinking States' at International Law," *14 Melbourne Journal of International Law* (2013), p. 350.

12 S. Caney, "Climate Change, human rights and moral thresholds" in S. Humphreys, M. Robinson (eds), *Human Rights and Climate Change* (2010), p. 90; N. Tuana, "Climate change and human rights" in T. Cushman (ed.), *Handbook of Human Rights* (2012), p. 410 et seq.; J. H. Knox, "Human Rights Principles and Climate Change" in C. P. Carlarne, K. R. Gray, R. G. Tarasofsky (eds), *The Oxford Handbook of International Climate Change Law* (2016), p. 215 et seq.; UN Human Rights Council, *Human Rights and Climate Change*, 28 March 2008, p. 1; UN Human Rights Council, *Summary report of the Office of the UN High Commissioner for Human Rights on the outcome of the full-day discussion on specific themes relating to human rights and climate change*, 1 May 2015, p. 3, para. 1; UN Human Rights Council, *Report of the Special Rapporteur on the issue of human rights obligations relating to the enjoyment of a safe, clean, healthy and sustainable environment*, 1 February 2016; UN Human Rights Council, *Report of the Office of the UN High Commissioner for Human Rights on the relationship between climate change and human rights*, 15 January 2009; UN Human Rights Council Res. 18/22 of 17 October 2011, p. 2.

13 https://www.ohchr.org/EN/Issues/HRAndClimateChange/Pages/HRCAction.aspx (last visited 29 August 2019).

14 S. Humphreys, "The Covenants in the Light of Antropogenic Climate Change" in D. Moeckli, H. Keller, C. Heri (eds), *The Human Rights Covenants at 50: Their Past, Present, and Future* (2018), p. 298.

15 Ibid.

16 Cf. ILC, *Sea-level rise in relation to international law, Second issues paper by Patrícia Galvão Teles and Juan José Ruda Santolaria* (73rd session of the ILC (2022)), # 246 et seq.

17 D. Vidas, "Sea-Level Rise and International Law," *4 Climate Law* (2014), p. 84.

18 S. Humphreys, "The Covenants in the Light of Anthropogenic Climate Change" in D. Moeckli, H. Keller, C. Heri (eds), *The Human Rights Covenants at 50: Their Past, Present, and Future* (2018), p. 286.

19 UNHCR, *Summary of Deliberations on Climate Change and Displacement* (2011), p. 7.
20 S. Park, *Climate Change and the Risk of Statelessness: The Situation of Low-lying Island States* (2011), p. 15.
21 Submission of the Republic of the Maldives, *Submission of the Maldives to the Office of the UN High Commissioner for Human Rights under Resolution HRC 7/23*, 25 September 2008, p. 39.
22 P. Weis, *Nationality and Statelessness in International Law* (1979), p. 239.
23 J. Klabbers, *International Law* (2013), p. 83; on the notion "nationality," its origins and its territorial/personal focus, s. P. Weis, *Nationality and Statelessness in International Law* (1979), p. 4.
24 UNHCR, *Climate Change and Statelessness: An Overview* (2009), p. 2; cf. S. Park, *Climate Change and the Risk of Statelessness: The Situation of Low-lying Island States* (2011), p. 15.
25 UNHCR, *Climate Change and Statelessness: An Overview* (2009), p. 1; cf. UNFCCC Ad hoc Working Group on long-term cooperative action under the convention, *Ideas and proposals on the elements contained in paragraph 1 of the Bali Action Plan*, 25 May 2009, p. 11 (Paper No. 3A: Office of the UNHCR).
26 Arguing for de facto statelessness in the case of climate refugees: J. L. Noto, "Creating a Modern Atlantis: Recognizing Submerging States and Their People," *62 Buffalo Law Review* (2014), p. 778; s. on a definition of both: UN Department of Social Affairs, *A Study of Statelessness*, August 1949, p. 7; cf. L. Yamamoto and M. Esteban, *Atoll Island States and International Law: Climate Change Displacement and Sovereignty* (2014), p. 254 et seq.
27 S. Park, *Climate Change and the Risk of Statelessness: The Situation of Low-lying Island States* (2011), p. 15; UNHCR, *Climate Change and Statelessness: An Overview* (2009), p. 2.
28 L. Yamamoto and M. Esteban, *Atoll Island States and International Law: Climate Change Displacement and Sovereignty* (2014), p. 210. For Tibetans, their "exile-passports" can even have negative consequences in some cases: They can be persecuted by Chinese authorities if they return to Tibet carrying a Tibetan passport. (F. McConnell, *Rehearsing the State: The Political Practices of the Tibetan Government-in-Exile* (2016), p. 140).
29 UNHCR, *Climate Change and Statelessness: An Overview* (2009), p. 2.
30 A. Edwards, "The Meaning of Nationality in International Law in an Era of Human Rights: Procedural and Substantive Aspects" in A. Edwards, L. van Waas (eds), *Nationality and Statelessness under International Law* (2014), p. 12.
31 S. L. Yamamoto and M. Esteban, *Atoll Island States and International Law: Climate Change Displacement and Sovereignty* (2014), p. 259 with further references.
32 Permanent Court of International Justice, *Nationality Decrees Issued in Tunis and Morocco* – Advisory Opinion (7 February 1923), p. 24; UN Department of Social Affairs, *A Study of Statelessness*, August 1949, p. 4; cf. R. Y. Jennings and A. Watts, Oppenheim's International Law (1992), p. 852: "It is not for international law but for the internal law of each State to determine who is, and who is not, to be considered its national;" cf. Art. 1 and 2 "Convention on Certain Questions relating to the Conflict of Nationality Laws: 1930 Hague Convention" (1930); C. d. Visscher, *Theory and Reality in Public International Law* (1968), p. 183; I. Brownlie, "The Relations of Nationality in Public International Law," *39 British Yearbook of International Law* (1963), p. 287.
33 Supreme Court of the United States, *Trop v. Dulles* – No. 70 (31 March 1958), p. 101.
34 L. van Waas, *Nationality Matters – Statelessness under International Law* (2008), p. 415, citing Supreme Court of the United States, *Trop v. Dulles* – No. 70 (31 March 1958).
35 L. van Waas, *Nationality Matters – Statelessness under International Law* (2008), p. 221.

36 D. Weissbrodt; C. Collins, "The Human Rights of Stateless Persons" *28 Human Rights Quarterly 1* (2006), p. 248, cited after L. van Waas, *Nationality Matters – Statelessness under International Law* (2008), p. 221.

37 L. van Waas, *Nationality Matters – Statelessness under International Law* (2008), p. 220.

38 Ibid., p. 221.

39 Ibid, p. 223.

40 Ibid, p. 221.

41 Cf. S. Forlati, "Nationality as a human right" in S. Forlati, A. Annoni (eds), *The Changing Role of Nationality in International Law* (2013), p. 19; cf. A. Peters, "Extraterritorial Naturalizations: Between the Human Right to Nationality, State Sovereignty and Fair Principles of Jurisdiction," *53 German Yearbook of International Law* (2010), p. 659–60 in more detail; K. Hailbronner, "Nationality in public international law and european law" in R. Bauböck, H. Waldrauch, E. Ersbøll, K. Groenendijk (eds), *Acquisition and loss of nationality: Policies and trends in 15 European states* (2006), p. 37; D. Corlett, *Stormy Weather: The Challenge of Climate Change and Displacement (Briefings)* (2009), p. 54; L. Yamamoto and M. Esteban, *Atoll Island States and International Law: Climate Change Displacement and Sovereignty* (2014), p. 258.

42 Art. 15 "Universal Declaration of Human Rights: UDHR" (1948).

43 L. van Waas, *Nationality Matters – Statelessness under International Law* (2008), p. 415.

44 H. Arendt, *Imperialism: Part Two of The Origins of Totalitarianism* (1968), p. 279; cited by F. Costamagna, "Statelessness in the context of state succession: An appraisal under international law" in S. Forlati, A. Annoni (eds), *The Changing Role of Nationality in International Law* (2013), p. 37.

45 L. van Waas, *Nationality Matters – Statelessness under International Law* (2008), p. 415.

46 'American Convention on Human Rights' (1969); cf. J. L. Blackman, "State Successions and Statelessness: The Emerging Right to an Effective Nationality Under International Law," *19 Michigan Journal of International Law* (1998), p. 1173.

47 Inter-American Court of Human Rights, *Case of Ivcher Bronstein v. Peru* – Judgment (5 February 2001), para. 87; Inter-American Court of Human Rights, *Case of Castillo Petruzzi et al. v. Peru* – Judgment (30 May 1999), para. 100; Inter-American Court of Human Rights, *Proposed Amendment to the Naturalization Provision of the Constitution of Costa Rica* – Advisory Opinion (19 January 1984), para. 34. On nationality and political rights, s.: D. Rudan, "Nationality and political rights" in S. Forlati, A. Annoni (eds), *The Changing Role of Nationality in International Law* (2013), p. 113–34; on nationality and social rights, s.: A. Annoni, "Nationality and social rights" in S. Forlati, A. Annoni (eds), *The Changing Role of Nationality in International Law* (2013), p. 135–52.

48 G. Jellinek, *System der subjektiven öffentlichen Rechte*, 2nd. edn. (1905), p. 116 (status civitatis).

49 A. Edwards, "The Meaning of Nationality in International Law in an Era of Human Rights: Procedural and Substantive Aspects" in A. Edwards, L. van Waas (eds), *Nationality and Statelessness under International Law* (2014), p. 40, 12; cf. K. Hailbronner, "Nationality in public international law and European law" in R. Bauböck, H. Waldrauch, E. Ersbøll, K. Groenendijk (eds), *Acquisition and loss of nationality: Policies and trends in 15 European states* (2006), p. 71; 78 et seq.; P. Weis, *Nationality and Statelessness in International Law* (1979), p. 239; cf. ICJ – The Hague, *Nottebohm case (Liechtenstein v. Guatemala)* – Judgment (6 April 1955), p. 23.

50 L. van Waas, *Nationality Matters – Statelessness under International Law* (2008), p. 219.

51 D. Rudan, "Nationality and political rights" in S. Forlati, A. Annoni (eds), *The Changing Role of Nationality in International Law* (2013), p. 113–34; on nationality and social rights, s.: A. Annoni, "Nationality and social rights" in S. Forlati, A. Annoni (eds), *The Changing Role of Nationality in International Law* (2013), p. 117.
52 D. Rudan, "Nationality and political rights" in S. Forlati, A. Annoni (eds), *The Changing Role of Nationality in International Law* (2013), p. 126.
53 A. Annoni, "Nationality and social rights" in S. Forlati, A. Annoni (eds), *The Changing Role of Nationality in International Law* (2013), p. 144.
54 A. Edwards, "The Meaning of Nationality in International Law in an Era of Human Rights: Procedural and Substantive Aspects" in A. Edwards, L. van Waas (eds), *Nationality and Statelessness under International Law* (2014), p. 39.
55 L. van Waas, *Nationality Matters – Statelessness under International Law* (2008), p. 219.
56 UN Committee on the Elimination of Discrimination Against Women (CEDAW), *CEDAW General Recommendation No. 21: Equality in Marriage and Family Relations*, 1994, p. 2.
57 L. van Waas, *Nationality Matters – Statelessness under International Law* (2008), p. 219.
58 Inter-American Court of Human Rights, *Case of the Girls Yean and Bosico v. Dominican Republic* – Judgment (8 September 2005), para. 137.
59 K. Hailbronner, "Nationality in public international law and european law" in R. Bauböck, H. Waldrauch, E. Ersbøll, K. Groenendijk (eds), *Acquisition and loss of nationality: Policies and trends in 15 European states* (2006), p. 71; cf. J. L. Blackman, "State Successions and Statelessness: The Emerging Right to an Effective Nationality Under International Law," *19 Michigan Journal of International Law* (1998), p. 1150.
60 L. van Waas, *Nationality Matters – Statelessness under International Law* (2008), p. 219.
61 Ibid., p. 219–20.
62 A. Kesby, *The Right to Have Rights: Citizenship, Humanity, and International Law* (2012), p. 53–4.
63 ILC, *Documents of the fifty-second session – First report on diplomatic protection, by Mr. John R. Dugard, Special Rapporteur*, Yearbook of the ILC 2000 Volume II, Part One, 2009, p. 213 et seq., para. 17, 22–32.
64 Ibid., p. 215, para. 32.
65 A. Kesby, *The Right to Have Rights: Citizenship, Humanity, and International Law* (2012), p. 55.
66 F. Costamagna, "Statelessness in the context of state succession: An appraisal under international law" in S. Forlati, A. Annoni (eds), *The Changing Role of Nationality in International Law* (2013), p. 37.
67 I. A. Shearer, *Starke's International Law* (2003), p. 307.
68 A. Edwards, "The Meaning of Nationality in International Law in an Era of Human Rights: Procedural and Substantive Aspects" in A. Edwards, L. van Waas (eds), *Nationality and Statelessness under International Law* (2014), p. 13; cf. A. Boll, "Nationality and Obligations of Loyalty in International and Municipal Law," *24 Australian Year Book of International Law* (2005), p. 37; J. L. Blackman, "State Successions and Statelessness: The Emerging Right to an Effective Nationality Under International Law," *19 Michigan Journal of International Law* (1998), p. 1149.
69 A. Kesby, *The Right to Have Rights: Citizenship, Humanity, and International Law* (2012), p. 53–4.
70 S. Oliver, "A New Challenge to International Law: The Disappearance of the Entire Territory of a State," *16 International Journal on Minority and Group Rights* (2009), p. 234.
71 L. van Waas, *Nationality Matters – Statelessness under International Law* (2008), p. 223.

72 R. Hansen, "State Controls: Borders, Refugees, and Citizenship" in E. Fiddian-Qasmiyeh, G. Loescher, K. Long, N. Sigona (eds), *The Oxford Handbook of Refugee and Forced Migration Studies* (2014), p. 253; R. Hansen, "The poverty of postnationalism: citizenship, immigration, and the new Europe," *38 Theory and Society* (2009), p. 5 in much more detail.

73 S. Oliver, "A New Challenge to International Law: The Disappearance of the Entire Territory of a State," *16 International Journal on Minority and Group Rights* (2009), p. 216; citing E.-I. A. Daes, *Status of the Individual and Contemporary International Law: Promotion, Protection and Restoration of Human Rights at National, Regional and International Levels* (1992), p. 35.

74 F. Costamagna, "Statelessness in the context of state succession: An appraisal under international law" in S. Forlati, A. Annoni (eds), *The Changing Role of Nationality in International Law* (2013), p. 47; J. L. Blackman, "State Successions and Statelessness: The Emerging Right to an Effective Nationality Under International Law," *19 Michigan Journal of International Law* (1998), p. 1150.

75 A. Edwards, "The Meaning of Nationality in International Law in an Era of Human Rights: Procedural and Substantive Aspects" in A. Edwards, L. van Waas (eds), *Nationality and Statelessness under International Law* (2014), p. 40.

76 A. Branthwaite, "The Psychological Basis of Independent Statehood" in R. H. Jackson, A. James (eds), *States in a Changing World: A Contemporary Analysis* (1993), p. 51.

77 Ibid., p. 51.

78 Ibid., p. 51; J. Mack, "Nationalism and the self," *11 Psychohistory Review* (1983), 55.

79 A. Branthwaite, "The Psychological Basis of Independent Statehood" in R. H. Jackson, A. James (eds), *States in a Changing World: A Contemporary Analysis* (1993), p. 52.

80 Ibid., p. 51.

81 J. L. Blackman, "State Successions and Statelessness: The Emerging Right to an Effective Nationality Under International Law," *19 Michigan Journal of International Law* (1998), p. 1176.

82 Art. 1 "Convention Relating to the Status of Stateless Persons" (1954).

83 "Convention on the Reduction of Statelessness" (1961); cf. Art. 15 "Universal Declaration of Human Rights: UDHR" (1948), Art. 20 "American Convention on Human Rights" (1969), Art. 4 "European Convention on Nationality" (1997).

84 Cf. F. Costamagna, "Statelessness in the context of state succession: An appraisal under international law" in S. Forlati, A. Annoni (eds), *The Changing Role of Nationality in International Law* (2013), p. 38 with further references; cf. L. van Waas, "The UN Statelessness Conventions" in A. Edwards, L. van Waas (eds), *Nationality and Statelessness under International Law* (2014), p. 72.

85 Ibid., p. 75 (emphasis added); s. Draft Convention on the Elimination of Future Statelessness in ILC, *Documents of the sixth session including the report of the Commission to the General Assembly*, Yearbook of the ILC 1954 Volume II, 1954, p. 143; cf. ILC, *Report of the ILC Covering the Work of its Fifth Session, 1 June–14 August 1953*, Official Records of the General Assembly, Eighth Session, Supplement No. 9 (Extract from the Yearbook of the ILC 1953 Volume II), 1953, p. 221 et seq., para. 123 et seq.

86 Cf. "Convention on the Reduction of Statelessness" (1961), which sets forth principles which bear on the right to a nationality. Art. 1(1); cf. L. van Waas, "The UN Statelessness Conventions" in A. Edwards, L. van Waas (eds), *Nationality and Statelessness under International Law* (2014), p. 70, cf. p. 75 where van Waas mentions a draft on the elimination of statelessness, that again would not tackle people who lose their statehood later.

87 S. Forlati, "Nationality as a human right" in S. Forlati, A. Annoni (eds), *The Changing Role of Nationality in International Law* (2013), p. 28.
88 S. Oliver, "A New Challenge to International Law: The Disappearance of the Entire Territory of a State," *16 International Journal on Minority and Group Rights* (2009), p. 234.
89 J. Klabbers, *International Law* (2013), p. 83.
90 In the case of the Islanders, the *non-refoulement principle* could well be applicable. This principle, saying that "[n]o refugee shall be returned in any manner whatsoever to any country where he or she would be at risk of persecution," is today an integral part of human rights protection, not limited to the "refugee" in the sense of the refugee convention anymore. (G. S. Goodwin-Gill, "The International Law of Refugee Protection" in E. Fiddian-Qasmiyeh, G. Loescher, K. Long, N. Sigona (eds), *The Oxford Handbook of Refugee and Forced Migration Studies* (2014), p. 39–40.) While the scope of this principle is not clearly defined, particularly with regard to climate change, improved understanding is visible in a sense that the focus is not laid on the "risk of persecution" but more on "risk." (V. Türk and R. Dowd, "Protection Gaps" in E. Fiddian-Qasmiyeh, G. Loescher, K. Long, N. Sigona (eds), *The Oxford Handbook of Refugee and Forced Migration Studies* (2014), p. 283.) Thus, islanders explicitly under risk with regard to their human rights should, on the basis of this principle, (probably) not be allowed to be sent back.
91 I. A. Shearer, *Starke's International Law* (2003), p. 316; C. d. Visscher, *Theory and Reality in Public International Law* (1968), p. 189.
92 I. A. Shearer, *Starke's International Law* (2003), p. 314 with further references; cf. J. L. Blackman, "State Successions and Statelessness: The Emerging Right to an Effective Nationality Under International Law," *19 Michigan Journal of International Law* (1998), p. 1151; House of Lords, Privy Council, *Musgrove v. Chung Teeong Toy* (18 March 1891); Supreme Court of the United States, *Nishimura Ekiu v. United States et al.* (18 January 1892); Supreme Court of the United States, *Fong Yue Ting v. United States et al., Wong Quan v. Same, Lee Joe v. Same* (15 May 1893); G. S. Goodwin-Gill, "The International Law of Refugee Protection" in E. Fiddian-Qasmiyeh, G. Loescher, K. Long, N. Sigona (eds), *The Oxford Handbook of Refugee and Forced Migration Studies* (2014), p. 36.
93 I. A. Shearer, *Starke's International Law* (2003), p. 314.
94 L. van Waas, *Nationality Matters – Statelessness under International Law* (2008), p. 398.
95 H. Arendt, *Imperialism: Part Two of The Origins of Totalitarianism* (1968), p. 171–2.
96 World Bank, *Indigenous Peoples – Operational Directive*, September 1991, p. 1; cf. T. Meron, *The Humanization of International Law* (2006), p. 349–51.
97 R. Tsosie, "Climate change and indigenous peoples: comparative models of sovereignty" in R. Abate, E. A. Kronk (eds), *Climate Change and Indigenous Peoples: The Search for Legal Remedies* (2013), p. 94.
98 UN Permanent Forum on Indigenous Issues – 14th Session: *Concept Note for Discussion* (2015), p. 1–2.
99 Ibid., p. 2.
100 C. Binder, *Die Landrechte indigener Völker unter besonderer Bezugnahme auf Mexiko und Nicaragua* (2004), p. 7 with further references, 120, 198.
101 "Indigenous and Tribal Peoples Convention (No. 169)" (1989).
102 "UN Declaration on the Rights of Indigenous Peoples" (2007); similarly: "American Declaration on the Rights of Indigenous Peoples" (2016).
103 Cf. L. Bennett, *Rising Sea Levels and Indigenous Communities* (2017), p. 7.
104 B. Kingsbury, "Indigenous Peoples' in International Law: A Constructivist Approach to the Asian Controversy," *92 AJIL* (1998), p. 437.

105 F. Francioni, O. Quirico, "Untying the Gordian Knot: towards the human right to a climatically sustainable environment?" in O. Quirico, M. Boumghar (eds), *Climate Change and Human Rights: An international and comparative law perspective* (2016), p. 155.
106 J. Donnelly, "Human Rights, Individual Rights and Collective Rights" in J. Berting et al. (eds), *Human Rights in a Pluralist World: Individuals and Collectivities* (1990), p. 52.
107 "UN Declaration on the Rights of Indigenous Peoples" (2007).
108 "American Declaration on the Rights of Indigenous Peoples" (2016).
109 Cf. in much detail: N. J. Ross, *Low-lying states, climate change-induced relocation, and the collective right to self-determination* (2019), https://nathanrossconz.files.wordpress.com/2020/02/nathan-jon-ross-phd-thesis-final.pdf (last visited 29 May 2022).
110 J. McAdam, B. Burson, W. Kälin, and S. Weerasinghe, "International Law and Sea-Level Rise: Forced Migration and Human Rights," *FNI Report 1/2016* (2016), p. 16.
111 J. Donnelly, "Human Rights, Individual Rights and Collective Rights" in J. Berting et al. (eds), *Human Rights in a Pluralist World: Individuals and Collectivities* (1990), p. 55.
112 UN Commission on Human Rights, *Expanded working paper by Françoise Hampson on the human rights situation of indigenous peoples in States and other territories threatened with extinction for environmental reasons*, 16 June 2005, para. 17.
113 D. Ingram, "Group rights: A defense" in T. Cushman (ed.), *Handbook of Human Rights, Routledge International Handbooks* (2012), p. 277.
114 UN Commission on Human Rights, *Expanded working paper by Françoise Hampson on the human rights situation of indigenous peoples in States and other territories threatened with extinction for environmental reasons*, 16 June 2005, para. 17.
115 UN Department of Social Affairs, *A Study of Statelessness*, August 1949, p. 8.
116 J. H. Burgers, "The Functions of Human Rights as Individual and Collective Rights" in J. Berting et al. (eds), *Human Rights in a Pluralist World: Individuals and Collectivities* (1990), p. 73.
117 F. Francioni, "International Human Rights in an Environmental Horizon," *21 The EJIL 1* (2010), p. 53. The case of the Human Rights Committee, *Lubicon Lake Band v. Canada*, Communication No. 167/1984 (26 March 1990) is an exception in this regard, because "Committee accepted the applicants' argument that the term 'family' ought to be interpreted in light of the customary traditions of the island's autochthonous population to include the entire indigenous community whose life was affected by the construction project" (F. Francioni, "International Human Rights in an Environmental Horizon," *21 The EJIL 1* (2010), p. 54).
118 F. Francioni, "International Human Rights in an Environmental Horizon," *21 The EJIL 1* (2010), p. 43.
119 Ibid., p. 44.
120 K. Buchanan, *New Zealand: "Climate Change Refugee" Case Overview* (2015).
121 Court of Appeal of New Zealand, *Teitiota v. Chief Executive of Ministry of Business, Innovation, and Employment* 8 May 2014), para. 40.
122 Ibid., para. 24.
123 Berlin Climate and Security Conference, *Conference summary*, 4 June 2019 (https://berlin-climate-security-conference.de/sites/berlin-climate-security-conference.de/files/documents/summary_berlin_climate_and_security_conference.pdf) (last visited 29 August 2019).
124 J. von Doussa, "Human Rights and Climate Change: A Tragedy in the Making," *31 UNSW Law Journal 3* (2008), p. 958.
125 Human Rights Committee, *Ioane Teitiota v. New Zealand*, Communication No. 2728/2016 (24 October 2019), para. 9.14.

126 G. Citroni, "Human Rights Committee's decision on the case Ieoane Teitiota v. New Zealand: Landmark or will-o'-the-wisp for climate refugees?," *QIL, Zoom-in 75* (2020), p. 3; Human Rights Committee, *Ioane Teitiota v. New Zealand*, Communication No. 2728/2016 (24 October 2019), para. 9.14–10.
127 G. Citroni, "Human Rights Committee's decision on the case Ieoane Teitiota v. New Zealand: Landmark or will-o'-the-wisp for climate refugees?," *QIL, Zoom-in 75* (2020), p. 5.
128 F. Francioni, O. Quirico, "Untying the Gordian Knot: towards the human right to a climatically sustainable environment?" in O. Quirico, M. Boumghar (eds), *Climate Change and Human Rights: An international and comparative law perspective* (2016), p. 151–2.
129 Human Rights Committee, *Ioane Teitiota v. New Zealand*, Communication No. 2728/2016 (24 October 2019), Annex I, Individual opinion of Committee member Duncan Laki Muhumuza (dissenting), p. 14, para. 6.
130 F. Francioni, "International Human Rights in an Environmental Horizon," *21 The EJIL 1* (2010), p. 44.
131 Ibid, p. 51.
132 M. Talbot, "Collective Rights in the Inter-American and African Human Rights Systems," *49 Georgetown Journal of International Law* (2018), p. 165.
133 F. Francioni, "International Human Rights in an Environmental Horizon," *21 The EJIL 1* (2010), p. 52.
134 Ibid., p. 44.
135 Ibid., p. 41.
136 J. Barnett, "Human rights and vulnerability to climate change" in S. Humphreys, M. Robinson (eds), *Human Rights and Climate Change* (2010), p. 266.
137 D. Vidas, "Sea-Level Rise and International Law," *4 Climate Law* (2014), p. 84, with further references.
138 E. Crawford and R. G. Rayfuse, "Climate Change, Sovereignty and Statehood," *11/59 Legal Studies Research Paper* (2011), p. 12.
139 "Paris Agreement" (2016).
140 J. L. Noto, "Creating a Modern Atlantis: Recognizing Submerging States and Their People," *62 Buffalo Law Review* (2014), p. 783.
141 J. M. Welsh, "Who should act? Collective responsibility and the Responsibility to Protect" in W. A. Knight, F. Egerton (eds), *The Routledge Handbook of the Responsibility to Protect* (2012), p. 103, with further references.
142 B. G. Ramcharan, "The National Responsibility to Protect Human Rights," *39 Hong Kong Law Journal* (2009), p. 363.
143 UNHCR, *Summary of Deliberations on Climate Change and Displacement* (2011), p. 9, para. 42.
144 J. McAdam, B. Burson, W. Kälin, and S. Weerasinghe, "International Law and Sea-Level Rise: Forced Migration and Human Rights," *FNI Report 1/2016* (2016), p. 43
145 O. d. Schutter, *International Human Rights Law: Cases, Materials, Commentary* (2014), p. 427.
146 UN Human Rights Council, *Report of the Special Rapporteur on the issue of human rights obligations relating to the enjoyment of a safe, clean, healthy and sustainable environment*, 1 February 2016, p. 9, para. 33.
147 UNHCR, *Summary of Deliberations on Climate Change and Displacement* (2011), p. 9, para. 42.
148 European Court of Human Rights, *Budayeva and others v. Russia* – Judgment (20 March 2008), para. 131, cf. UN Human Rights Council, *Report of the Office of the UN High Commissioner for Human Rights on the relationship between climate change and human rights*, 15 January 2009, para. 74.
149 Ibid., para. 38; cf. UNHCR, *Handbook on Housing and Property Restitution for Refugees and Displaced Persons – Implementing the "Pinheiro Principles"* (2007),

p. 72, 106 (cited in UN Human Rights Council, *Report of the Office of the UN High Commissioner for Human Rights on the relationship between climate change and human rights*, 15 January 2009, p. 28).

150 S. Atapattu, *Human Rights Approaches to Climate Change: Challenges and Opportunities* (2015), p. 80.

151 M. A. Burkett, "The Nation Ex-Situ" in M. Gerrard, G. E. Wannier (eds), *Threatened Island Nations: Legal Implications of Rising Seas and a Changing Climate* (2013), p. 103; cf. J. Campbell, "Climate-Induced Community Relocation in the Pacific: The Meaning and Importance of Land" in J. McAdam (ed.), *Climate change and displacement: Multidisciplinary perspectives* (2010), p. 60; UNHCR, *Summary of Deliberations on Climate Change and Displacement* (2011), p. 7–8; cf. in detail: M. E. Vaha, "Hosting the Small Island Developing States: two scenarios," *10 (2) International Journal of Climate Change Strategies and Management* (2018), p. 229 et seq.

152 S. Park, *Climate Change and the Risk of Statelessness: The Situation of Low-lying Island States* (2011), p. 20; cf. I. Kelman, "Island evacuation," *31 Forced Migration Review* (2008), p. 20–1.

153 UN Human Rights Council, *Report of the Office of the UN High Commissioner for Human Rights on the relationship between climate change and human rights*, 15 January 2009, para. 39.

154 J. D. Hestetune, *The Invading Waters: Climate Change Dispossession, State Extinction, and International Law* (2013), p. 54.

155 UNHCR, *Climate Change and Statelessness: An Overview* (2009), p. 3.

156 UNGA, *Rights and Duties of States – Draft Declaration submitted by the delegation of Panama*, 15 January 1947, Art. 1 and 9; cf. UNGA, *Preparatory Study Concerning a Draft Declaration on the Rights and Duties of States – Memorandum submitted by the Secretary-General*, 15 December 1948, p. 45 et seq., p. 78 et seq.

157 Ibid., p. 78.

158 American Society of International Law, "UN: Report of the ILC: Covering its first session, April 12–June 9, 1949," *44 AJIL* (1950), p. 15–18 (text of the draft declaration).

159 Ibid., p. 19–20.

160 'Draft Declaration on Rights and Duties of States' (1949), p. 289, para. 49 (Observations concerning the draft declaration).

161 A. El Ouali, *Territorial Integrity in a Globalizing World: International Law and States' Quest for Survival* (2012), p. xvi, with further explanations.

162 J. Delbrück, "The International Obligation to Cooperate – An Empty Shell or a Hard Law Principle of International Law? – A Critical Look at a Much Debated Paradigm of Modern International Law" in H. Hestermeyer, R. Wolfrum (eds), *Coexistence, Cooperation and Solidarity: Liber Amicorum Rüdiger Wolfrum* (2012), p. 5; cf. UNGA Res. 25/2625 of 24 October 1970, Annex: "the development of friendly relations and co-operation between nations are among the fundamental purposes of the UN."

163 L. Glanville, "The Responsibility to Protect Beyond Borders," *12 Human Rights Law Review* (2012), p. 6, mentioning Grotius and Pufendorf.

164 D. Thürer, "Failing States," (last updated October 2009) in R. Wolfrum (ed.), *The Max Planck Encyclopedia of Public International Law: opil.ouplaw.com.home/EPIL* (2012), para. 12.

165 A. Branthwaite, "The Psychological Basis of Independent Statehood" in R. H. Jackson, A. James (eds), *States in a Changing World: A Contemporary Analysis* (1993), p. 57.

166 S. Oliver, "A New Challenge to International Law: The Disappearance of the Entire Territory of a State," *16 International Journal on Minority and Group Rights* (2009), p. 213: "citizens should relocate somewhere as close to their original habitat as possible."

167 The idea of burden-sharing came up, however the future of burden-sharing in the people movement context in Europe looks unpromising. (F. Thornton, *Climate Change and People on the Move* (2018), p. 176).

168 A. Boyle, "Human Rights and the Environment: Where Next?" in B. Boer (ed.), *Environmental Law Dimensions of Human Rights* (2015), p. 236–7, subsequently arguing that it may be better to accept that existing human rights law is not the right medium for addressing the shared problem of climate change.

169 Ibid., p. 238.

170 UN Human Rights Council, *Report of the Special Rapporteur on the issue of human rights obligations relating to the enjoyment of a safe, clean, healthy and sustainable environment*, 1 February 2016, p. 10–11, para. 40, 44.

171 Cf. A. Boyle, "Human Rights and the Environment: Where Next?" in B. Boer (ed.), *Environmental Law Dimensions of Human Rights* (2015), p. 236–7, who subsequently argues that it may be better to accept that existing human rights law is nor the right medium for addressing the shared problem of climate change.

172 C. Apodaca, "The right to food" in T. Cushman (ed.), *Handbook of Human Rights* (2012), p. 349.

173 ICJ – The Hague, *Legal Consequences cf the Construction of a Wall in the Occupied Palestinian Territory* – Advisory Opinion (9 July 2004), para. 155–9; cf. A. Seibert-Fohr, "The International Covenant on Civil and Political Rights: Moving from Coexistence to Cooperation and Solidarity" in H. Hestermeyer, R. Wolfrum (eds), *Coexistence, Cooperation and Solidarity: Liber Amicorum Rüdiger Wolfrum* (2012), p. 533–4.

174 ICJ – The Hague, *Legal Consequences cf the Construction of a Wall in the Occupied Palestinian Territory* — Separate Opinion of Judge Higgins (9 July 2004), para. 37; ICJ – The Hague, *Legal Consequences cf the Construction of a Wall in the Occupied Palestinian Territory* – Separate Opinion of Judge Kooijmans (9 July 2004), para. 40; cf. A. Seibert-Fohr, "The International Covenant on Civil and Political Rights: Moving from Coexistence to Cooperation and Solidarity" in H. Hestermeyer, R. Wolfrum (eds), *Coexistence, Cooperation and Solidarity: Liber Amicorum Rüdiger Wolfrum* (2012), p. 534.

175 UN High Commissioner for Human Rights, *Frequently Asked Questions on a Human Rights-based Approach to Development Cooperation* (2006), p. 15.

176 Br. Lewis, *Environmental Human Rights and Climate Change: Current Status and Future Prospects* (2018), p. 193.

177 J. von Doussa, "Human Rights and Climate Change: A Tragedy in the Making," *31 UNSW Law Journal 3* (2008), p. 960 giving the example that Indigenous people would have to be "considered as a major stakeholder in an emissions trading scheme, and that their custodial role over traditional lands, flow on impacts for environmental protection and caring for country, are fully taken into account when developing strategies for mitigation and adaptation."

178 S. Oliver, "A New Challenge to International Law: The Disappearance of the Entire Territory of a State," *16 International Journal on Minority and Group Rights* (2009), p. 228.

179 M. J. Aznar-Gómez, "The Extinction of States" in K. Wellens, E. R. Rieter, H. C. F. J. A. d. Waele (eds), *Evolving principles of international law: Studies in honour of Karel C. Wellens* (2012), p. 43, 51 (focusing on "failed states").

180 Cf. T. Meron, *The Humanization of International Law* (2006), p. 339–41.

181 A. Peters, *Jenseits der Menschenrechte: Die Rechtsstellung des Individuums im Völkerrecht* (2014), p. 232.

182 Ibid., p. 218 with further references.

183 Cf. D. Wong, "Sovereignty Sunk? The Position of 'Sinking States' at International Law," *14 Melbourne Journal of International Law* (2013), p. 391.

184 A. Peters, *Jenseits der Menschenrechte: Die Rechtsstellung des Individuums im Völkerrecht* (2014), p. 224 ("treffen jedenfalls den Territorialstaat").
185 "Maastricht Principles on Extraterritorial Obligations of States in the Area of Economic, Social and Cultural Rights," 2013.
186 A. Peters, *Jenseits der Menschenrechte: Die Rechtsstellung des Individuums im Völkerrecht* (2014), p. 229 with further references.
187 Ibid., p. 231.
188 Cf. K. Wellens, "Revisiting Solidarity as a (Re-)Emerging Constitutional Principle: Some Further Reflections" in C. Kojima, R. Wolfrum (eds), *Solidarity: A Structural Principle of International Law* (2010), p. 17; who earlier had thought that there would be such a right: K. Wellens, "Solidarity as a Constitutional Principle" in R. J. St. MacDonald, D. M. Johnston (eds), *Towards World Constitutionalism: Issues in the Legal Ordering of the World Community* (2005), p. 785.
189 K. Newland, E. Patrick. and M. Zard, *No refuge: the challenge of internal displacement* (2003), p. 68; cf. R. Cohen, "From Sovereign Responsibility to R2P" in W. A. Knight, F. Egerton (eds), *The Routledge Handbook of the Responsibility to Protect* (2012), p. 11–12.
190 S. C. Breau, *The Responsibility to Protect in International Law: An Emerging Paradigm Shift* (2016), p. 121; cf. Art. 2(1) ICESCR.
191 Art. 2(1) "International Covenant on Economic, Social and Cultural Rights: ICESCR" (1966): "Each State Party to the present Covenant undertakes to take steps, *individually and through international assistance and cooperation*, especially economic and technical, to the maximum of its available resources, with a view to achieving progressively the full realization of the rights recognized in the present Covenant by all appropriate means, including particularly the adoption of legislative measures" (emphasis added).
192 Art. 2(1) "International Covenant on Civil and Political Rights: ICCPR" (1966): 1. "Each State Party to the present Covenant undertakes to respect and to ensure to all individuals within its territory and subject to its jurisdiction the rights recognized in the present Covenant," cf. T. Meron, *The Humanization of International Law* (2006), p. 462 et seq.
193 UN Human Rights Council, *Report of the Office of the UN High Commissioner for Human Rights on the relationship between climate change and human rights*, 15 January 2009, para. 86; S. Atapattu, *Human Rights Approaches to Climate Change: Challenges and Opportunities* (2015), p. 62; W. Vandenhole, "EU and Development: Extraterritorial Obligations under the ICESCR" in M. E. Salomon, A. Tostensen, W. Vandenhole (eds), *Casting the Net Wider: Human Rights, Development and New Duty-Bearers* (2007), p. 85 et seq.
194 S. Atapattu, *Human Rights Approaches to Climate Change: Challenges and Opportunities* (2015), p. 63, with further references; M. Ammer, *Climate Change and Human Rights: The Status of Climate Refugees in Europe* (2009), p. 36 et seq.
195 Ibid., p. 37; citing UN Committee on Economic Social and Cultural Rights, *The nature of States parties' obligations,* General Comment 3, Fifth session, 1990, para. 13–14.
196 M. Ammer, *Climate Change and Human Rights: The Status of Climate Refugees in Europe* (2009), p. 38.
197 Ibid., p. 38; cf. W. Vandenhole, "EU and Development: Extraterritorial Obligations under the ICESCR" in M. E. Salomon, A. Tostensen, W. Vandenhole (eds), *Casting the Net Wider: Human Rights, Development and New Duty-Bearers* (2007), p. 97, 105.
198 Ibid., p. 87, 95.
199 Cf. M. Ammer, *Climate Change and Human Rights: The Status of Climate Refugees in Europe* (2009), p. 39.

200 S. Humphreys, "The Covenants in the Light of Antropogenic Climate Change" in D. Moeckli, H. Keller, C. Heri (eds), *The Human Rights Covenants at 50: Their Past, Present, and Future* (2018), p. 296.
201 M. Gerrard and G. E. Wannier, "Overview" in M. Gerrard, G. E. Wannier (eds), *Threatened Island Nations: Legal Implications of Rising Seas and a Changing Climate* (2013), p. 6; citing K. M. Wyman, "The National Immigration Policy Option: Limits and Potential" in M. Gerrard, G. E. Wannier (eds), *Threatened Island Nations: Legal Implications of Rising Seas and a Changing Climate* (2013), p. 337 et seq.
202 J. McAdam, B. Burson, W. Kälin, and S. Weerasinghe, "International Law and Sea-Level Rise: Forced Migration and Human Rights," *FNI Report 1/2016* (2016), p. 44.
203 U. Scheuner, "Solidaritat unter den Nationen als Grundsatz in der gegenwärtigen internationalen Gemeinschaft" in J. Delbrück, K. Ipsen, D. Rauschning (eds), *Recht im Dienst des Friedens: Festschrift für Eberhard Menzel zum 65. Geburtstag am 21. Januar 1976* (1975), p. 273, 251 et seq.
204 S. Atapattu, *Human Rights Approaches to Climate Change: Challenges and Opportunities* (2015), p. 175.
205 UNGA Res. 45/100 of 14 December 1990 and UNGA Res. 43/131 of 8 December 1988.
206 K. Watkins et al., *UNDP Human Development Report 2007/2008 – Fighting Climate Change: Human Solidarity in a Divided World* (2007), p. 198.
207 D. Wallace, "Introduction: security and global climate change" in D. Wallace, D. Silander (eds), *Climate Change, Policy and Security: State and Human Impacts* (2018), p. 2; cf. K. Watkins et al., *UNDP Human Development Report 2007/2008 – Fighting Climate Change: Human Solidarity in a Divided World* (2007), p. 12.
208 UN Human Rights Council, *Summary report of the Office of the UN High Commissioner for Human Rights on the outcome of the full-day discussion on specific themes relating to human rights and climate change*, 1 May 2015, p. 5, para. 15.
209 Art. 1(3) "Charter of the UN" (1945); cf. R. Wolfrum, "Article 1" in B. Simma, H. Mosler, A. Paulus, E. Chaitidou (eds), *The Charter of the UN: A Commentary* (2012), para. 26 ("much more explicit than the corresponding Dumbarton Oaks text").
210 UN Human Rights Council, *Report of the Office of the UN High Commissioner for Human Rights on the relationship between climate change and human rights*, 15 January 2009, p. 30.
211 J. L. Brierly, H. Lauterpacht and C. H. M. Waldock, *The Basis of Obligation in International Law, and Other Papers* (1958), p. 357.
212 Cf. B. Fassbender, *The UN Charter as the Constitution of the International Community* (2009), p. 52.
213 Ibid., p. 7; cf. p. 73, fn. 305
214 B. Fassbender, "Article 2(1)" in B. Simma, H. Mosler, A. Paulus, E. Chaitidou (eds), *The Charter of the UN: A Commentary* (2012), p. 157, para. 53.
215 A. L. Paulus, "International Community," (last updated March 2013) in R. Wolfrum (ed.), *The Max Planck Encyclopedia of Public International Law: opil.ouplaw.com .home/EPIL* (2012), para. 12.
216 A. L. Paulus, *Die internationale Gemeinschaft im Völkerrecht: Eine Untersuchung zur Entwicklung des Völkerrechts im Zeitalter der Globalisierung* (2001), p. 435.
217 Ibid., p. 439; A. L. Paulus, "International Community," (last updated March 2013) in R. Wolfrum (ed.), *The Max Planck Encyclopedia of Public International Law: opil .ouplaw.com.home/EPIL* (2012), para. 3.
218 J. L. Noto, "Creating a Modern Atlantis: Recognizing Submerging States and Their People," *62 Buffalo Law Review* (2014), p. 785.
219 K. Wellens, "Revisiting Solidarity as a (Re-)Emerging Constitutional Principle: Some Further Reflections" in C. Kojima, R. Wolfrum (eds), *Solidarity: A Structural*

Principle of International Law (2010), p. 5; A. Bianchi, "Human Rights and the Magic of Jus Cogens," *19 EJIL* (2008), p. 495.

220 G. I. Hernández, "A Reluctant Guardian: the International Court of Justice and the Concept of 'International Community'," *83 British Yearbook of International Law* (2013), p. 14.

221 A. L. Paulus, "International Community," (last updated March 2013) in R. Wolfrum (ed.), *The Max Planck Encyclopedia of Public International Law: opil.ouplaw.com .home/EPIL* (2012), para. 8; cf. on the International Community: S. C. Breau, *The Responsibility to Protect in International Law: An Emerging Paradigm Shift* (2016), p. 33 et seq.

222 Ibid., p. 114–15.

223 R. C. Thakur, *The UN, Peace and Security: From Collective Security to the Responsibility to Protect* (2006), p. 11.

224 A. L. Paulus, *Die internationale Gemeinschaft im Völkerrecht: Eine Untersuchung zur Entwicklung des Völkerrechts im Zeitalter der Globalisierung* (2001), p. 3; cf. C. Tomuschat, "Obligations Arising for States Without or Against Their Will," *241 Recueil Des Cours* (1993), p. 209 et seq.; B. Simma, "From bilateralism to community interest in international law," *250 Recueil Des Cours* (1994), p. 243 et seq.

225 B. Fassbender, *The UN Charter as the Constitution of the International Community* (2009), p. 73.

226 Ibid.

227 B. Fassbender, "Der Schutz der Menschenrechte als zentraler Inhalt des völkerrechtlichen Gemeinwohls," *30 Europäische Grundrechte-Zeitschrift* (2003), p. 11; cf. K. A. Annan, "The Legitimacy to Intervene," *Financial Times*, 10 January 2000, p. 19: "What is clear is that the rights of the individual are now central to the 'common interest'."

228 B. Fassbender, *The UN Charter as the Constitution of the International Community* (2009), p. 73.

229 International Tribunal for the Prosecution of Persons Responsible for Serious Violations of International Humanitarian Law Committed in the Territory of the Former Yugoslavia since 1991, *Prosecutor v. Anto Furundžija* (10 December 1998), para. 153.

230 Cf. B. Fassbender, "Der Schutz der Menschenrechte als zentraler Inhalt des völkerrechtlichen Gemeinwohls," *30 Europäische Grundrechte-Zeitschrift* (2003), p. 5–6.

231 ICJ – The Hague, *Questions relating to the Obligation to Prosecute or Extradite (Belgium v. Senegal)* – Separate opinion of Judge Cançado Trindade (20 July 2012), para. 182.

232 While there is no universal agreement on which norms have attained the status of *jus cogens* norms, generally the prohibition of genocide, piracy, slavery, and torture are seen as such.

233 A. L. Paulus, *Die internationale Gemeinschaft im Völkerrecht: Eine Untersuchung zur Entwicklung des Völkerrechts im Zeitalter der Globalisierung* (2001), p. 358; C. Tomuschat, "International Law: Ensuring the Survival of Mankind on the Eve of a New Century," *281 Recueil Des Cours* (1999), p. 81; cf. B. Fassbender, "Der Schutz der Menschenrechte als zentraler Inhalt des völkerrechtlichen Gemeinwohls," *30 Europäische Grundrechte-Zeitschrift* (2003), p. 6.

234 S. Kadelbach, *Zwingendes Völkerrecht* (1992), p. 320; cf. B. Fassbender, "Der Schutz der Menschenrechte als zentraler Inhalt des völkerrechtlichen Gemeinwohls," *30 Europäische Grundrechte-Zeitschrift* (2003), p. 6.

235 A. Maguire, J. McGee, "A Universal Human Right to Shape Responses to a Global Problem? The Role of Self-Determination in Guiding the International Legal Response to Climate Change" *26 Review of European Community & International Environmental Law 1* (2017), p. 61 (footnotes omitted).

236 UNGA, *A more secure world: our shared responsibility,* Report of the High-level Panel on Threats, Challenges and Change, 2 December 2004, p. 22, para. 30.
237 UN Human Rights Council, *Report of the Special Rapporteur on the issue of human rights obligations relating to the enjoyment of a safe, clean, healthy and sustainable environment*, 1 February 2016, p. 9–11.
238 Institut de droit international, "The Protection of Human Rights and the Principle of Non-intervention in Internal Affairs of States," *63 Institut de Droit International Annuaire 338* (1989).
239 K. Wellens, "Revisiting Solidarity as a (Re-)Emerging Constitutional Principle: Some Further Reflections" in C. Kojima, R. Wolfrum (eds), *Solidarity: A Structural Principle of International Law* (2010), p. 5; citing A. Peters, "Compensatory Constitutionalism: The Function and Potential of Fundamental International Norms and Structures," *19 Leiden Journal of International Law* (2006), p. 601; E. de Wet, "The Emergence of International and Regional Value Systems as a Manifestation of the Emerging International Constitutional Order," *19 Leiden Journal of International Law* (2006), p. 612.
240 H. P. Hestermeyer, "Reality or Aspiration? – Solidarity in International Environmental and World Trade Law" in H. Hestermeyer, R. Wolfrum (eds), *Coexistence, Cooperation and Solidarity: Liber Amicorum Rüdiger Wolfrum* (2012), p. 63; cf. K. Wellens, "Revisiting Solidarity as a (Re-)Emerging Constitutional Principle: Some Further Reflections" in C. Kojima, R. Wolfrum (eds), *Solidarity: A Structural Principle of International Law* (2010), p. 9.
241 A. L. Paulus, *Die internationale Gemeinschaft im Völkerrecht: Eine Untersuchung zur Entwicklung des Völkerrechts im Zeitalter der Globalisierung* (2001), p. VII.
242 D. Wallace, "Introduction: security and global climate change" in D. Wallace, D. Silander (eds), *Climate Change, Policy and Security: State and Human Impacts* (2018), p. 2; cf. K. Watkins et al., *UNDP Human Development Report 2007/2008 – Fighting Climate Change: Human Solidarity in a Divided World* (2007), p. 12.
243 I. Österdahl, "Relatively Failed. Troubled Statehood and International Law," *14 Finnish Yearbook of International Law* (2003), p. 64.
244 S. M. Byers, "International law and the responsibility to protect" in C. M. Chinkin, F. Baetens (eds), *Sovereignty, Statehood and State Responsibility: Essays in Honour of James Crawford* (2015), p. 24 et seq. on the development of R2P; cf. D. Wallace, "The UN regime on global climate change" in D. Wallace, D. Silander (eds), *Climate Change, Policy and Security: State and Human Impacts* (2018), p. 56 et seq.
245 B. Fassbender, "Article 2(1)" in B. Simma, H. Mosler, A. Paulus, E. Chaitidou (eds), *The Charter of the UN: A Commentary* (2012), p. 155–6, para. 52.
246 L. Glanville, *Sovereignty and the Responsibility to Protect: A New History* (2014), p. 205.
247 A. Peters, *Jenseits der Menschenrechte: Die Rechtsstellung des Individuums im Völkerrecht* (2014), p. 219.
248 S. on the different options to intervene: N. Aloupi, "The Right to Non-intervention and Non-interference," *4 Cambridge Journal of International and Comparative Law* (2015), p. 570 et seq.
249 A. Peters, *Jenseits der Menschenrechte: Die Rechtsstellung des Individuums im Völkerrecht* (2014), p. 218; S. C. Breau, *The Responsibility to Protect in International Law: An Emerging Paradigm Shift* (2016), p. 17 et seq. in much detail.
250 G. J. Evans and M. Sahnoun, *The Responsibility to Protect. Report of the International Commission on Intervention and State Sovereignty* (2001), p. 17, para. 2.31.
251 F. M. Deng, S. Kimaro, T. Lyons and D. Rothchild, *Sovereignty as Responsibility: Conflict Management in Africa* (1996), p. xii–xiii; cf. L. Glanville, "The Responsibility to Protect Beyond Borders," *12 Human Rights Law Review* (2012), p. 9.

252 L. Axworthy and A. Rock, "R2P: A New and Unfinished Agenda," *1 Global Responsibility to Protect* (2009), p. 68–9.
253 J. M. Welsh, "Who should act? Collective responsibility and the Responsibility to Protect" in W. A. Knight, F. Egerton (eds), *The Routledge Handbook of the Responsibility to Protect* (2012), p. 105.
254 K.-C. Tan, "The Duty to Protect" in T. Nardin, M. S. Williams (eds), *Humanitarian intervention* (2006), p. 95.
255 J. M. Welsh, "Who should act? Collective responsibility and the Responsibility to Protect" in W. A. Knight, F. Egerton (eds), *The Routledge Handbook of the Responsibility to Protect* (2012), p. 106.
256 Ibid., p. 106.
257 Ibid., p. 106, citing J. Pattison, *Humanitarian Intervention and the Responsibility to Protect: Who Should Intervene?* (2010), p. 10–11.
258 UN Human Rights Council, *Summary report of the Office of the UN High Commissioner for Human Rights on the outcome of the full-day discussion on specific themes relating to human rights and climate change*, 1 May 2015, p. 6, para. 21; cf. UNGA, *A more secure world: our shared responsibility,* Report of the High-level Panel on Threats, Challenges and Change, 2 December 2004, p. 11; p. 21, para. 24.
259 S. Atapattu, *Human Rights Approaches to Climate Change: Challenges and Opportunities* (2015), p. 235.
260 G. J. Evans and M. Sahnoun, *The Responsibility to Protect. Report of the International Commission on Intervention and State Sovereignty* (2001), p. VIII.
261 J. Pérez de Cuéllar, "Report of the Secretary-General on the work of the Organization," *45 Yearbook of the UN* (1991), p. 8.
262 L. Glanville, *Sovereignty and the Responsibility to Protect: A New History* (2014), p. 225; A. Peters, "The Responsibility to Protect: Spelling out the Hard Legal Consequences for the UNSC and its Members" in U. Fastenrath, R. Geiger, D.-E. Khan, A. Paulus, S. von Schorlemer, C. Vedder (eds), *From Bilateralism to Community Interest: Essays in Honour of Judge Bruno Simma* (2011), p. 299.
263 J. Pérez de Cuéllar, "Report of the Secretary-General on the work of the Organization," *45 Yearbook of the UN* (1991), p. 7.
264 Ibid., p. 7.
265 R. Cohen, "From Sovereign Responsibility to R2P" in W. A. Knight, F. Egerton (eds), *The Routledge Handbook of the Responsibility to Protect* (2012), p. 10.
266 UNGA, *A more secure world: our shared responsibility,* Report of the High-level Panel on Threats, Challenges and Change, 2 December 2004, p. 56–7, para. 201; cf. C. Stahn, "Responsibility to Protect: Political Rhetoric or Emerging Legal Norm?," *101 AJIL* (2007), p. 99–100.
267 Cf. P. Hilpold, "From Humanitarian Intervention to Responsibility to Protect: Making Utopia True?" in U. Fastenrath, R. Geiger, D.-E. Khan, A. Paulus, S. von Schorlemer, C. Vedder (eds), *From Bilateralism to Community Interest: Essays in Honour of Judge Bruno Simma* (2011), p. 467.
268 L. Axworthy and A. Rock, "R2P: A New and Unfinished Agenda," *1 Global Responsibility to Protect* (2009), p. 67–8.
269 G. J. Evans, "The Responsibility to Protect in Environmental Emergencies," *103 Proceedings of the Annual Meeting (American Society of International Law)* (2009), p. 27.
270 L. Axworthy and A. Rock, "R2P: A New and Unfinished Agenda," *1 Global Responsibility to Protect* (2009), p. 67–8.
271 J. Pérez de Cuéllar, "Report of the Secretary-General on the work of the Organization," *45 Yearbook of the UN* (1991), p. 8.
272 Ibid., p. 8.

273 J. Ping, *Keynote Address at the Round-Table High-Level Meeting of Experts on "The Responsibility to Protect in Africa"* (2008).

274 Ibid.; cf. E. C. Luck, "Environmental Emergencies and the Responsibility to Protect: A Bridge Too Far?," *103 Proceedings of the Annual Meeting (American Society of International Law)* (2009), p. 37–8; G. J. Evans, "The Responsibility to Protect in Environmental Emergencies," *103 Proceedings of the Annual Meeting (American Society of International Law)* (2009), p. 28; A. El Ouali, *Territorial Integrity in a Globalizing World: International Law and States' Quest for Survival* (2012), p. 196 et seq., 219 et seq.

275 G. J. Evans, "The Responsibility 'to Protect in Environmental Emergencies," *103 Proceedings of the Annual Meeting (American Society of International Law)* (2009), p. 28.

276 A. Orford, *International Authority and the Responsibility to Protect* (2011), p. 181.

277 L. Glanville, *Sovereignty and the Responsibility to Protect: A New History* (2014), p. 205; A. Orford, *International Authority and the Responsibility to Protect* (2011), p. 181.

278 UN Secretary General B. Ki-moon, *Secretary-General defends, clarifies "Responsibility to Protect" at Berlin even on "Responsible Sovereignty:"* International Cooperation for a changed World, 15 July 2008.

279 S. Dorsett, "Mapping Territories" in S. McVeigh (ed.), *Jurisprudence of Jurisdiction* (2007), p. 138; cf. A. Orford, *International Authority and the Responsibility to Protect* (2011), p. 181.

280 Ibid., p. 181.

281 G. J. Evans, "The Responsibility to Protect in Environmental Emergencies," *103 Proceedings of the Annual Meeting (American Society of International Law)* (2009), p. 28.

282 UNGA Res. 60/1 of 24 October 2005, para. 138, 139.

283 G. J. Evans, "The Responsibility to Protect in Environmental Emergencies," *103 Proceedings of the Annual Meeting (American Society of International Law)* (2009), p. 28.

284 It is often said that "R2P shifts the debate from the right of the International Community 'to intervene' to the responsibility of states to protect while invoking 'collective action' when a state manifestly fails to provide protection for people threatened by the most grave human rights crimes." G. J. Evans and M. Sahnoun, *The Responsibility to Protect. Report of the International Commission on Intervention and State Sovereignty* (2001), p. 16; cf. R. Cohen, "From Sovereign Responsibility to R2P" in W. A. Knight, F. Egerton (eds), *The Routledge Handbook of the Responsibility to Protect* (2012), p. 15.

285 UN Secretary General, *Implementing the responsibility to protect, Report of the Secretary-General*, 12 January 2009, para. 10b; cf. P. Hilpold, "From Humanitarian Intervention to Responsibility to Protect: Making Utopia True?" in U. Fastenrath, R. Geiger, D.-E. Khan, A. Paulus, S. von Schorlemer, C. Vedder (eds), *From Bilateralism to Community Interest: Essays in Honour of Judge Bruno Simma* (2011), p. 475.

286 A. Orford, *International Authority and the Responsibility to Protect* (2011), p. 180; cf. p. 179; cf. H.-J. Heintze, "Responsibility to Protect and the Protection of Persons in the Event of Disasters" in P. Hilpold (ed.), *The Responsibility to Protect (R2P): A New Paradigm of International Law?* (2014), p. 320; A. Peters, *Jenseits der Menschenrechte: Die Rechtsstellung des Individuums im Völkerrecht* (2014), p. 219; L. Glanville, "The Responsibility to Protect Beyond Borders," *12 Human Rights Law Review* (2012), p. 11–12; E. C. Luck, "Environmental Emergencies and the Responsibility to Protect: A Bridge Too Far?," *103 Proceedings of the Annual Meeting (American Society of International Law)* (2009), p. 33.

287 J. Harrington, "R2P and Natural Disasters" in W. A. Knight, F. Egerton (eds), *The Routledge Handbook of the Responsibility to Protect* (2012), p. 141; G. J. Evans, "The Responsibility to Protect in Environmental Emergencies," *103 Proceedings of the Annual Meeting (American Society of International Law)* (2009), p. 29.

288 P. Hilpold, "R2P and Humanitarian Intervention in a Historical Perspective" in P. Hilpold (ed.), *The Responsibility to Protect (R2P): A New Paradigm of International Law?* (2014), p. 60; cf. on suspicion towards community-based values: M. Koskenniemi, *From Apology to Utopia: The Structure of International Legal Argument* (2015), p. 480 et seq.

289 R. Cohen, "From Sovereign Responsibility to R2P" in W. A. Knight, F. Egerton (eds), *The Routledge Handbook of the Responsibility to Protect* (2012), p. 16.

290 S. Humphreys, "The Covenants in the Light of Antropogenic Climate Change" in D. Moeckli, H. Keller, C. Heri (eds), *The Human Rights Covenants at 50: Their Past, Present, and Future* (2018), p. 294.

291 IPCC 2022: *Chapter 1, Summary of IPCC AR5 and Special Report findings*, IPCC WGII Sixth Assessment Report, #26.

292 E. Dannenmaier, "Constructing Transnational Climate Regimes" in G. Handl, J. Zekoll, P. Zumbanse (eds), *Beyond Territoriality: Transnational Legal Authority in an Age of Globalization* (2012), p. 524; cf. A. Zahar, "The climate change regime" in S. Alam (ed.), *Routledge Handbook of International Environmental Law* (2013), p. 349, pointing out that "[e]ach person contributes to increasing the concentration of greenhouse gases in the atmosphere simply by being alive."

293 S. Jahan et al., *UNDP Human Development Indicators and Indices: 2018 Statistical Update* (2018), p. 11.

294 S. Humphreys, *Climate Change and Human Rights: A Rough Guide* (2008), p. 64.

295 A. Nollkaemper, J. d'Aspremont, C. Ahlborn, B. Boutin, N. Nedeski, I. Plakokefalos, with the collaboration of D. Jacobs, "Guiding Principles on Shared Responsibility in International Law," *31 EJIL 1* (2020), p. 28.

296 Ibid, p. 16: "Principle 2: Shared responsibility of international persons: 1. The commission by multiple international persons of one or more internationally wrongful acts that contribute to an indivisible injury entails shared responsibility. 2. Contribution to an indivisible injury may be individual, concurrent or cumulative."

297 G. Liston, "Enhancing the efficacy of climate change litigation: how to resolve the 'fair share question' in the context of international human rights law," *Cambridge International Law Journal, Vol. 9 No. 2* (2020), p. 263.

298 Cf. Hoge Raad der Nederlanden, *De Staat der Nederlanden tegen Stichting Urgenda*, ECLI:NL:HR:2019:2006, 20 December 2019, where the State's argument that it should have no responsibility at all with regard to climate change because of its small contribution to climate change was rejected.

299 Cf. Oberlandesgericht Hamm, *Rechtsstreit Lliuya./.RWE* (Az. 5 U 15/17 OLG Hamm), 30 November 2017, where the farmer demanded 0.47 percent of the costs needed for a protective dam for his village.

300 A. Nollkaemper, J. d'Aspremont, C. Ahlborn, B. Boutin, N. Nedeski, I. Plakokefalos, with the collaboration of D. Jacobs, "Guiding Principles on Shared Responsibility in International Law," *31 EJIL 1* (2020), pp. 58, 59.

301 J. Barnett, "Titanic states? Impacts and responses to climate change in the Pacific islands," *59 Journal of International Affairs* (2005), p. 205.

302 Ibid., p. 205.

303 Ibid., p. 205; cf. UN Human Rights Council, *Report of the Office of the UN High Commissioner for Human Rights on the relationship between climate change and human rights*, 15 January 2009, p. 5, para. 10–11; N. Bergmann, *Versinkende Inselstaaten: Auswirkungen des Klimawandels auf die Staatlichkeit leiner Inselstaaten* (2016), p. 160; P. Hunt and R. Khosla, "Climate change and the right to the highest

attainable standard of health" in S. Humphreys, M. Robinson (eds), *Human Rights and Climate Change* (2010), p. 252.

304 "Caracas Declaration" (1989), para. 34.

305 F. Simlinger, B. Mayer, "Legal Responses to Climate Change Induced Loss and Damage" in R. Mechler, L. M. Bouwer et al. (eds), Loss and Damage from Climate Change: Concepts, Methods and Policy Options (2019), p. 193. Art. 3 and 4(4) ("UNFCCC" (1992) go in the right direction, however not far enough.

306 UN Human Rights Council, *Summary report of the Office of the UN High Commissioner for Human Rights on the outcome of the full-day discussion on specific themes relating to human rights and climate change*, 1 May 2015, p. 17, para. 78; cf. "Barbados Declaration" (1994), Sec. III, 2.

307 "Rio Declaration on Environment and Development: Rio Declaration" (1992); cf. V. Roeben, "Responsibility in International Law," *16 Max Planck Yearbook of UN Law* (2012), p. 157; P. Sands, J. Peel, A. Fabra Aguilar, and R. Mackenzie, *Principles of International Environmental Law* (2012), p. 233–6; S. C. Breau, *The Responsibility to Protect in International Law: An Emerging Paradigm Shift* (2016), p. 160 et seq.; UN Human Rights Council, *Report of the Special Rapporteur on the issue of human rights obligations relating to the enjoyment of a safe, clean, healthy and sustainable environment*, 1 February 2016, p. 12–13.

308 "UNFCCC" (1992). Cf. R. Verheyen, *Climate Change Damage and International Law: Prevention Duties and State Responsibility* (2005), p. 227; UNFCCC Ad hoc Working Group on long-term cooperative action under the convention, *Ideas and proposals on the elements contained in paragraph 1 of the Bali Action Plan*, 25 May 2009.

309 G. Liston, "Enhancing the efficacy of climate change litigation: how to resolve the 'fair share question' in the context of international human rights law," *Cambridge International Law Journal, Vol. 9 No. 2* (2020), p. 244, with more references.

310 Cf. H. P. Hestermeyer, "Reality or Aspiration? – Solidarity in International Environmental and World Trade Law" in H. Hestermeyer, R. Wolfrum (eds), *Coexistence, Cooperation and Solidarity: Liber Amicorum Rüdiger Wolfrum* (2012), p. 53.

311 J. Brunnée, "The Global Climate Regime: Wither Common Concern?" in H. Hestermeyer, R. Wolfrum (eds), *Coexistence, Cooperation and Solidarity: Liber Amicorum Rüdiger Wolfrum* (2012), p. 736.

312 R. Verheyen, *Climate Change Damage and International Law: Prevention Duties and State Responsibility* (2005), p. 227.

313 "Draft articles on Responsibility of States for Internationally Wrongful Acts" (2001).

314 R. Verheyen, *Climate Change Damage and International Law: Prevention Duties and State Responsibility* (2005), p. 235, pointing out in this regard that the US and Australia cannot be held responsible for non-compliance with the Kyoto Protocol's ("Kyoto Protocol to the UNFCCC" 1997) reduction targets, even after its entry into force because they have not ratified it. Cf. M. Fitzmaurice, "Responsibility and Climate Change," *53 German Yearbook of International Law* (2010), p. 112 et seq.

315 R. Verheyen, *Climate Change Damage and International Law: Prevention Duties and State Responsibility* (2005), p. 235 et seq.; 238 et seq.; 240 et seq.; 248 et seq.; F. Simlinger, B. Mayer, "Legal Responses to Climate Change Induced Loss and Damage" in R. Mechler, L. M. Bouwer et al. (eds), *Loss and Damage from Climate Change: Concepts, Methods and Policy Options* (2019), p. 187.

316 Cf. C. Voigt, "State Responsibility for Climate Change Damages," *77 Nordic Journal of International Law* (2008), p. 6–7; cf. M. Fitzmaurice, "Responsibility and Climate Change," *53 German Yearbook of International Law* (2010), p. 107.

317 C. Voigt, "State Responsibility for Climate Change Damages," *77 Nordic Journal of International Law* (2008), p. 7.

318 Warren, Charles; Greenshields, Robert A. E; Hostie, Jan Frans, *Trail smelter case (USA, Canada)* - Arbitration Award (16 April 1938 and 11 March 1941); J. E. Read, "The Trail Smelter Dispute," *1 Canadian Journal of International Law* (1963), p. 213.

319 "Declaration of the UN Conference on the Human Environment: Stockholm Declaration" (1972). Cf. S. Atapattu, *Human Rights Approaches to Climate Change: Challenges and Opportunities* (2015), p. 63 "States have, in accordance with the Charter of the UN and The Principles of International Law, the sovereign right to exploit their own resources pursuant to their own environmental policies, and the responsibility to ensure that activities within their jurisdiction or control *do not cause damage* to the environment of other States or of areas beyond the limits of national jurisdiction" (emphasis added).

320 "UN Convention on the Law of the Sea (UNCLOS)" (1982).

321 "Convention on Biological Diversity: CBD" (1992).

322 "Bali Road Map" (2007); cf. M. Fitzmaurice, "Responsibility and Climate Change," *53 German Yearbook of International Law* (2010), p. 108, 136–7.

323 "Copenhagen Accord" (2009); cf. M. Fitzmaurice, "Responsibility and Climate Change," *53 German Yearbook of International Law* (2010), p. 108 et seq., 136.

324 A. G. Jain, "The 21st Century Atlantis: The International Law of Statehood and Climate Change-Induced Loss of Territory," *50 Stanford Journal of International Law* (2014), p. 65; cf. A. Strauss, "Climate Change Litigation: Opening the Door to the International Court of Justice" in W. C. G. Burns, H. M. Osofsky (eds), *Adjudicating Climate Change: State, National, and International Approaches* (2009), p. 352–3; cf. M. Fitzmaurice, "Responsibility and Climate Change," *53 German Yearbook of International Law* (2010), p. 103 et seq.; C. Voigt, "State Responsibility for Climate Change Damages," *77 Nordic Journal of International Law* (2008), p. 5 et seq.

325 Cf. ibid., p. 15. Causation could be established either on the sole basis of contribution to the problem of climate change or by the fact that any emission of greenhouse gases has increased the risk of a specific damage by contributing to the increased concentrations of greenhouse gases in the atmosphere (p. 16).

326 R. Tsosie, "Climate change and indigenous peoples: comparative models of sovereignty" in R. Abate, E. A. Kronk (eds), *Climate Change and Indigenous Peoples: The Search for Legal Remedies* (2013), p. 92; M. Rosso Grossman, "Climate Change and the Individual," *66 The American Journal of Comparative Law* (2018), p. 360.

327 UN Human Rights Council, *Report of the Office of the UN High Commissioner for Human Rights on the relationship between climate change and human rights*, 15 January 2009, p. 23, para. 70; cf. M. Ammer, *Climate Change and Human Rights: The Status of Climate Refugees in Europe* (2009), p. 35; E. Dannenmaier, "Constructing Transnational Climate Regimes" in G. Handl, J. Zekoll, P. Zumbanse (eds), *Beyond Territoriality: Transnational Legal Authority in an Age of Globalization* (2012), p. 524.

328 R. Verheyen, *Climate Change Damage and International Law: Prevention Duties and State Responsibility* (2005), p. 269, citing I. Brownlie, *State Responsibility* (1983), p. 189. One could argue though that emitting green-house gases is "the same wrongful act."

329 C. Voigt, "State Responsibility for Climate Change Damages," *77 Nordic Journal of International Law* (2008), p. 7; R. Verheyen, *Climate Change Damage and International Law: Prevention Duties and State Responsibility* (2005), p. 235.

330 C. Voigt, "State Responsibility for Climate Change Damages," *77 Nordic Journal of International Law* (2008), p. 7–8, 17; criticizing the ILC in this regard, as the no-harm rule "is not about whether the relevant activity as such is unlawful but whether the home State has done everything in its means to avoid causing transboundary harm." Thus, Voigt argues, the approach by the ILC in its "Draft Articles on Prevention of

Transboundary Harm from Hazardous Activities" (2001) "seems to be fundamentally misconceived and, to a certain extent, superfluous" (p. 8).

331 UN Human Rights Council, *Report of the Office of the UN High Commissioner for Human Rights on the relationship between climate change and human rights*, 15 January 2009, p. 23, para. 70.

332 Ibid., p. 23, para. 70.

333 M. Fitzmaurice, "Responsibility and Climate Change," *53 German Yearbook of International Law* (2010), p. 129–30; cf. C. Voigt, "State Responsibility for Climate Change Damages," *77 Nordic Journal of International Law* (2008), p. 21.

334 J. H. Knox, "Climate Change and Human Rights Law," *50 Virginia Journal of International Law* (2009), p. 163.

335 C. Voigt, "State Responsibility for Climate Change Damages," *77 Nordic Journal of International Law* (2008), p. 21.

336 D. Wong, "Sovereignty Sunk? The Position of 'Sinking States' at International Law," *14 Melbourne Journal of International Law* (2013), p. 388 with further references. Wong also points out that the issue of having standing before the ICJ according to Art. 34(1) of the Statute of the ICJ (only States have standing) could be sidestepped by the sinking island States by commencing the proceedings before inundation, because jurisdiction is determined at the time that the act instituting proceedings is filed and will continue regardless of subsequent events. Cf. A. Strauss, "Climate Change Litigation: Opening the Door to the International Court of Justice" in W. C. G. Burns, H. M. Osofsky (eds), *Adjudicating Climate Change: State, National, and International Approaches* (2009), p. 339

337 K. Boom, "The rising tide of international climate litigation: an illustrative hypothetical of Tuvalu v. Australia" in R. Abate, E. A. Kronk (eds), *Climate Change and Indigenous Peoples: The Search for Legal Remedies* (2013), p. 412.

338 Ibid., p. 424 et seq.

339 Ibid., p. 438.

340 Cf. A. Strauss, "Climate Change Litigation: Opening the Door to the International Court of Justice" in W. C. G. Burns, H. M. Osofsky (eds), *Adjudicating Climate Change: State, National, and International Approaches* (2009), p. 335.

341 S. Watt-Cloutier, S., *Petition to The Inter-American Commission on Human Rights Seeking Relief From Violations Resulting from Global Warming Caused By Acts and Omissions of the United States: Inuit Petition* (7 December 2005).

342 UN Human Rights Council, *Report of the Office of the UN High Commissioner for Human Rights on the relationship between climate change and human rights*, 15 January 2009, p. 8–22; cf. H. M. Osofsky, "The Inuit Petition as a Bridge? Beyond Dialectics of Climate Change and Indigenous Peoples' Rights," *31 American Indian Law Review* (2007), p. 675 et seq.; R. Tsosie, "Climate change and indigenous peoples: comparative models of sovereignty" in R. Abate, E. A. Kronk (eds), *Climate Change and Indigenous Peoples: The Search for Legal Remedies* (2013), p. 92.

343 Cf. H. M. Osofsky, "The Inuit Petition as a Bridge? Beyond Dialectics of Climate Change and Indigenous Peoples' Rights," *31 American Indian Law Review* (2007), p. 680; M. Ammer, *Climate Change and Human Rights: The Status of Climate Refugees in Europe* (2009), p. 36.

344 Over the same period, EU countries were responsible for 22.1 percent. In 2002, the five largest polluters in terms of total CO^2 emissions were the United States (24 percent of global emissions), China, Russia, India, and Japan. However, on a per capita basis, Australia, the United States, Germany, Russia, and the United Kingdom are the world's largest CO^2 emitters (Cf. J. Barnett, "Titanic states? Impacts and responses to climate change in the Pacific islands," *59 Journal of International Affairs* (2005), p. 205 with the respective references).

345 UN Human Rights Council, *Report of the Office of the UN High Commissioner for Human Rights on the relationship between climate change and human rights*, 15 January 2009, p. 8–22; S. McInerney-Lankford, M. Darrow, and L. Rajamani, *Human Rights and Climate Change: A Review of the International Legal Dimensions* (2011), p. 8.
346 S. Atapattu, *Human Rights Approaches to Climate Change: Challenges and Opportunities* (2015), p. 290.
347 A. G. Jain, "The 21st Century Atlantis: The International Law of Statehood and Climate Change-Induced Loss of Territory," *50 Stanford Journal of International Law* (2014), p. 66; S. Atapattu, *Human Rights Approaches to Climate Change: Challenges and Opportunities* (2015), p. 241.
348 F. Soltau, "Common Concern of Humankind" in C. P. Carlarne, K. R. Gray, R. G. Tarasofsky (eds), *The Oxford Handbook of International Climate Change Law* (2016), p. 209.
349 A. G. Jain, "The 21st Century Atlantis: The International Law of Statehood and Climate Change-Induced Loss of Territory," *50 Stanford Journal of International Law* (2014), p. 66.
350 Pacific Islands News Association, *Island nations want climate change in world court* (2012).
351 K. Boom, "The rising tide of international climate litigation: an illustrative hypothetical of Tuvalu v. Australia" in R. Abate, E. A. Kronk (eds), *Climate Change and Indigenous Peoples: The Search for Legal Remedies* (2013), p. 416; A. Strauss, "Climate Change Litigation: Opening the Door to the International Court of Justice" in W. C. G. Burns, H. M. Osofsky (eds), *Adjudicating Climate Change: State, National, and International Approaches* (2009), p. 348ff; cf. Yale Center for Environmental Law & Policy, *Climate Change and the International Court of Justice: Seeking an Advisory Opinion on Transboundary Harm from the Court* (2014), p. 8 et seq. with further references in much detail.
352 Pacific Islands News Association, *Island nations want climate change in world court* (2012).
353 Cf. Yale Center for Environmental Law & Policy, *Climate Change and the International Court of Justice: Seeking an Advisory Opinion on Transboundary Harm from the Court* (2014), p. 13.
354 K. Boom, "The rising tide of international climate litigation: an illustrative hypothetical of Tuvalu v. Australia" in R. Abate, E. A. Kronk (eds), *Climate Change and Indigenous Peoples: The Search for Legal Remedies* (2013), p. 416; S. Atapattu, *Human Rights Approaches to Climate Change: Challenges and Opportunities* (2015), p. 227 (UN News Service Section, *UN News – Palau seeks UN World Court opinion on damage caused by greenhouse gases* (2011)); cf. Yale Center for Environmental Law & Policy, *Climate Change and the International Court of Justice: Seeking an Advisory Opinion on Transboundary Harm from the Court* (2014), p. 17: "What are the obligations under international law of a State for ensuring that activities under its jurisdiction or control that emit greenhouse gases do not cause, or substantially contribute to, serious damage to another State or States?"
355 Greenpeace, *Legal Steps taken by the Federated States of Micronesia against the Prunéřov II coal-fired power plant, Czech Republic* (2010), p. 1–3.
356 Ibid., p. 5.
357 A. Torres Camprubí, *Statehood under Water: Challenges of Sea-Level Rise to the Continuity of Pacific Island States* (2016), p. 254.
358 Cf. ibid., p. 255.
359 ICJ – The Hague, *Obligations concerning Negotiations relating to Cessation of the Nuclear Arms Race and to Nuclear Disarmament (Marshall Islands v. United Kingdom)* – Application instituting proceedings against the United Kingdom of Great

Britain and Northern Ireland (24 April 2014), para. 10; ICJ – The Hague, *Obligations concerning Negotiations relating to Cessation of the Nuclear Arms Race and to Nuclear Disarmament (Marshall Islands v. Pakistan)* – Application instituting proceedings against the Islamic Republic of Pakistan (24 April 2014), para. 9; ICJ – The Hague, *Obligations concerning Negotiations relating to Cessation of the Nuclear Arms Race and to Nuclear Disarmament (Marshall Islands v. India)* – Application instituting proceedings against the Republic of India (24 April 2014), para. 9.

360 A. Torres Camprubí, *Statehood under Water: Challenges of Sea-Level Rise to the Continuity of Pacific Island States* (2016), p. 256.

361 B. Mayer, "Interpreting States' general obligations on climate change mitigation: A methodological review," *Review of European Community & International Environmental Law* (2019), p. 4.

362 ICJ – The Hague, *Obligations concerning Negotiations relating to Cessation of the Nuclear Arms Race and to Nuclear Disarmament (Marshall Islands v. United Kingdom)* – Judgment (Preliminary objections) (5 October 2016), para. 59; ICJ – The Hague, *Obligations concerning Negotiations relating to Cessation of the Nuclear Arms Race and to Nuclear Disarmament (Marshall Islands v. Pakistan)* – Judgment (Jurisdiction of the Court and admissibility of the application) (5 October 2016), para. 56; ICJ - The Hague, *Obligations concerning Negotiations relating to Cessation of the Nuclear Arms Race and to Nuclear Disarmament (Marshall Islands v. India)* – Judgment (Jurisdiction of the Court and admissibility of the application) (5 October 2016), para. 56.

363 Ibid., para. 52; similarly for Pakistan: ICJ – The Hague, *Obligations concerning Negotiations relating to Cessation of the Nuclear Arms Race and to Nuclear Disarmament (Marshall Islands v. Pakistan)* – Judgment (Jurisdiction of the Court and admissibility of the application) (5 October 2016), para. 52 and for the UK: ICJ – The Hague, *Obligations concerning Negotiations relating to Cessation of the Nuclear Arms Race and to Nuclear Disarmament (Marshall Islands v. United Kingdom)* – Judgment (Preliminary objections) (5 October 2016), para. 57.

364 S. T. Thienel, "Third States and the Jurisdiction of the International Court of Justice: The Monetary Gold Principle," *57 German Yearbook of International Law* (2014), p. 321 et seq. ("The Monetary Gold principle is widely recognised as preventing the International Court of Justice from deciding a case between two parties where the legal interests of a third State take centre stage.").

365 ICJ – The Hague, *Obligations concerning Negotiations relating to Cessation of the Nuclear Arms Race and to Nuclear Disarmament (Marshall Islands v. United Kingdom)* – Dissenting opinion of Judge Crawford (5 October 2016), para. 32.

366 Cf. ICJ – The Hague, *Barcelona Traction, Light and Power Company, Limited* – Judgment (5 February 1970), p. 32, para. 33.

367 B. Fassbender, "Der Schutz der Menschenrechte als zentraler Inhalt des völkerrechtlichen Gemeinwohls," *30 Europäische Grundrechte-Zeitschrift* (2003), p. 7.

368 "Declaration of the UN Conference on the Human Environment: Stockholm Declaration" (1972).

369 Cf. B. Fassbender, "Der Schutz der Menschenrechte als zentraler Inhalt des völkerrechtlichen Gemeinwohls," *30 Europäische Grundrechte-Zeitschrift* (2003), p. 11 with further references.

370 Cf. ibid., p. 7.

371 D. Hunter, "The Implications of Climate Change Litigations: Litigation for International Environmental Law Making" in W. C. G. Burns, H. M. Osofsky (eds), *Adjudicating Climate Change: State, National, and International Approaches* (2009), p. 367.

372 Pacific Islands News Association, *Climate change is really about the wellbeing of people* (2016).

373 Ibid.
374 As such, the Parties to the UNFCCC were "acknowledging that change in the Earth's climate and its adverse effects are a *common concern* of humankind" ("UNFCCC" (1992), preamble) – emphasis added.
375 UN Human Rights Council, *Human Rights and Climate Change*, 25 June 2014.
376 UN Human Rights Council, *Human Rights and Climate Change*, 30 June 2015.
377 UN Human Rights Council, *Human Rights and Climate Change*, 28 June 2016.
378 UN Human Rights Council, *Report of the Special Rapporteur on the issue of human rights obligations relating to the enjoyment of a safe, clean, healthy and sustainable environment*, 1 February 2016, p. 9–11.
379 Cf. R. Tsosie, "Climate change and indigenous peoples: comparative models of sovereignty" in R. Abate, E. A. Kronk (eds), *Climate Change and Indigenous Peoples: The Search for Legal Remedies* (2013), p. 90 (cf. Green Climate Fund, explaining that a response requires the collective action from all countries – https://www.greenclimate.fund/about-gcf/global-context#response-description (last visited 30 June 2019)).
380 UN Human Rights Council, *Summary report of the Office of the UN High Commissioner for Human Rights on the outcome of the full-day discussion on specific themes relating to human rights and climate change*, 1 May 2015, p. 15.
381 UNGA,Res. 55/2 of 18 September 2000, para. 6; K. A. Annan, *We the Peoples: The Role of the UN in the Twenty-first Century* (2000), p. 77 (emphasis added).
382 Cf. A. Zahar, "The climate change regime" in S. Alam (ed.), *Routledge Handbook of International Environmental Law* (2013), p. 349, speaking of "a 'global-global' problem."
383 S. Humphreys, "The Covenants in the Light of Antropogenic Climate Change" in D. Moeckli, H. Keller, C. Heri (eds), *The Human Rights Covenants at 50: Their Past, Present, and Future* (2018), p. 282.
384 E. Brown Weiss, "Strengthening Compliance with Climate Change Commitments" in H. Hestermeyer, R. Wolfrum (eds), *Coexistence, Cooperation and Solidarity: Liber Amicorum Rüdiger Wolfrum* (2012), p. 701.
385 E. Dannenmaier, "Constructing Transnational Climate Regimes" in G. Handl, J. Zekoll, P. Zumbanse (eds), *Beyond Territoriality: Transnational Legal Authority in an Age of Globalization* (2012), p. 521.
386 Ibid., p. 545
387 H. P. Hestermeyer, "Reality or Aspiration? – Solidarity in International Environmental and World Trade Law" in H. Hestermeyer, R. Wolfrum (eds), *Coexistence, Cooperation and Solidarity: Liber Amicorum Rüdiger Wolfrum* (2012), p. 52, mentioning the Trail Smelter Arbitration, principle 21 of the "Declaration of the UN Conference on the Human Environment: Stockholm Declaration" (1972) and principle 2 of the "Rio Declaration on Environment and Development: Rio Declaration" (1992).
388 R. Verheyen, *Climate Change Damage and International Law: Prevention Duties and State Responsibility* (2005), p. 227; cf. V. Roeben, "Responsibility in International Law," *16 Max Planck Yearbook of UN Law* (2012), p. 106.
389 On its nebulous character, s. C. Tomuschat, "Die internationale Gemeinschaft," *33 Archiv des Völkerrechts* (1995), p. 1 et seq.
390 J. Harrington, "R2P and Natural Disasters" in W. A. Knight, F. Egerton (eds), *The Routledge Handbook of the Responsibility to Protect* (2012), p. 144 et seq.; cf. L. Viikari, "Responsibility to Protect and Environmental Considerations: A Fundamental Mismatch or the Way Forward?" in P. Hilpold (ed.), *The Responsibility to Protect (R2P): A New Paradigm of International Law?* (2014), p. 375 et seq.; N. Matz-Lück, "Solidarität, Souveränität und Völkerrecht: Grundzüge einer internationalen Solidargemeinschaft zur Hilfe bei Naturkatastrophen" in H. Hestermeyer, R. Wolfrum (eds), *Coexistence, Cooperation and Solidarity: Liber Amicorum Rüdiger Wolfrum* (2012), p. 144–5 (cf. North Korea).

391 G. J. Evans, "The Responsibility to Protect in Environmental Emergencies," *103 Proceedings of the Annual Meeting (American Society of International Law)* (2009), p. 31.
392 UNGA, *Provisional verbatim record of the tenth meeting*, 27 September 1990 (Mr Maumoon Abdul Gayoom, President of the Republic of Maldives), p. 9–10.
393 UN Human Rights Council, *Summary report of the Office of the UN High Commissioner for Human Rights on the outcome of the full-day discussion on specific themes relating to human rights and climate change*, 1 May 2015, p. 5, para. 17.
394 L. Axworthy and A. Rock, "R2P: A New and Unfinished Agenda," *1 Global Responsibility to Protect* 2009), p. 65–6.
395 J. Pérez de Cuéllar, 'Report of the Secretary-General on the work of the Organization," *45 Yearbook of the UN* (1991), p. 11.
396 Ibid., p. 11.
397 Cited after T. G. Weiss and D. A. Korn, *Internal Displacement: Conceptualization and its Consequences* (2006), p. 45; cf. R. Cohen, "From Sovereign Responsibility to R2P" in W. A. Knight, F. Egerton (eds), *The Routledge Handbook of the Responsibility to Protect* (2012), p. 14.
398 Cited after ibid., p. 14.
399 UNGA, *Report of the ILC*, 5 October 2011, para. 43–4; cf. J. Harrington, "R2P and Natural Disasters" in W. A. Knight, F. Egerton (eds), *The Routledge Handbook of the Responsibility to Protect* (2012), p. 147 on the efforts of the ILC.
400 UNGA, *Sixth Committee – Summary record of the 24th meeting*, 1 December 2011, para. 59 – Mr Horváth (Hungary).
401 Ibid., para. 92 – Mr Kittichaisaree (Thailand).
402 G. J. Evans and M. Sahnoun, *The Responsibility to Protect. Report of the International Commission on Intervention and State Sovereignty* (2001), p. 16.
403 Ibid., p. 16.
404 However, ICISS was also mainly dealing with the issue of state sovereignty and was as such heavily influenced by Deng's report F. M. Deng, S. Kimaro, T. Lyons, and D. Rothchild, *Sovereignty as Responsibility: Conflict Management in Africa* (1996); cf. S. C. Breau, *The Responsibility to Protect in International Law: An Emerging Paradigm Shift* (2016), p. 19.
405 ILC, *Fifth report on the protection of persons in the event of disasters by Eduardo Valencia-Ospina, Special Rapporteur*, 9 April 2012, para. 52.
406 Ibid., para. 53.
407 A. Peters, *Jenseits der Menschenrechte: Die Rechtsstellung des Individuums im Völkerrecht* (2014), p. 225.
408 ILC, *Eighth report on the protection of persons in the event of disasters by Eduardo Valencia-Ospina, Special Rapporteur*, 17 March 2016, para. 314.
409 Ibid., para. 316.
410 UNGA, *Agenda item 81: Report of the ILC on the work of its sixty-third session (continued)*, 2 December 2011, para. 69; ILC, *Eighth report on the protection of persons in the event of disasters by Eduardo Valencia-Ospina, Special Rapporteur*, 17 March 2016, para. 302.
411 Ibid., para. 302; UNGA, *Agenda item 81: Report of the ILC on the work of its sixty-third session (continued)*, 14 November 2011, para. 45; UNGA, *Agenda item 81: Report of the ILC on the work of its sixty-third and sixty-fifth sessions (continued)*, 2 December 2013, para. 39 (view shared by the UK and the Russian Federation).
412 UNSC, *Security Council holds first-ever debate on impact of climate change on peace, security*, 17 April 2007; UN Economic and Social Council, *Study on the relationship between indigenous peoples and the Pacific Ocean*, 19 February 2016, p. 7, para. 25 (precast of the world bank).

413 K. A. Annan, "The Legitimacy to Intervene," *Financial Times*, 10 January 2000, p. 19.
414 A. G. Jain, "The 21st Century Atlantis: The International Law of Statehood and Climate Change-Induced Loss of Territory," *50 Stanford Journal of International Law* (2014), p. 10.
415 ILC, *Fifth report on the protection of persons in the event of disasters by Eduardo Valencia-Ospina, Special Rapporteur*, 9 April 2012, para. 52.
416 N. Stern, *Stern Review: The Economics of Climate Change* (2006); p. vi; cf. Yale Center for Environmental Law & Policy, *Climate Change and the International Court of Justice: Seeking an Advisory Opinion on Transboundary Harm from the Court* (2014), p. 95–9 (The economic costs of inaction); D. Anthoff, R. J. Nicholls and R. S. J. Tol, "The Economic Impact of Substantial Sea-level Rise," *15 Mitigation and Adaptation Strategies for Global Change* (2010), p. 325 et seq.
417 UNGA, *Sixth Committee – Summary record of the 24th meeting*, 1 December 2011, para. 120 – Ms Abdul Rahman (Malaysia).
418 ILC, *Eighth report on the protection of persons in the event of disasters by Eduardo Valencia-Ospina, Special Rapporteur*, 17 March 2016, para. 304, UNGA, *Sixth Committee – Summary record of the 24th meeting*, 1 December 2011, para. 120.
419 S. Park, *Climate Change and the Risk of Statelessness: The Situation of Low-lying Island States* (2011), p. 22: The Pacific Access Category is intended for labour migration purposes and is subject to conditions including being between 18 and 45 years of age, having an existing "acceptable offer of employment" meeting minimum income requirements, as well as requirements for English, good health, and character. As such it is based on employment, not environmental factors. Moreover, per year, only up to 75 citizens of Kiribati, 75 citizens of Tuvalu, and 250 citizens of Tonga are being granted residence in New Zealand. See the New Zealand Department of Labour, Pacific Access Category, available online at: https://www.immigration.govt.nz/new-zealand-visas/apply-for-a-visa/about-visa/pacific-access-category-resident-visa (last visited 21 May 2022); cf. K. M. Wyman, "The National Immigration Policy Option: Limits and Potential" in M. Gerrard, G. E. Wannier (eds), *Threatened Island Nations: Legal Implications of Rising Seas and a Changing Climate* (2013), p. 353; J. McAdam, *Climate Change, Forced Migration, and International Law* (2012), p. 115–17; D. Wong, "Sovereignty Sunk? The Position of 'Sinking States' at International Law," *14 Melbourne Journal of International Law* (2013), p. 351, fn. 33; S. F. Martin, *Climate Change and International Migration* (2010), p. 5.
420 UN Economic and Social Council, *Study on the relationship between indigenous peoples and the Pacific Ocean*, 19 February 2016, p. 7, para. 25 (which does not mean that they are very welcoming with regard to other refugees); cf. UN Commission on Human Rights, *Expanded working paper by Françoise Hampson on the human rights situation of indigenous peoples in States and other territories threatened with extinction for environmental reasons*, 16 June 2005, para. 32. The Green Party's initiative of establishing a "climate refugee visa" in immigration law was defeated in 2007 (cf. S. F. Martin, *Climate Change and International Migration* (2010), p. 5).
421 Cf. R. G. Rayfuse, "International Law and Disappearing States – Maritime Zones and the Criteria for Statehood," *41 Environmental Policy and Law* (2011), p. 285.
422 UN Commission on Human Rights, *Expanded working paper by Françoise Hampson on the human rights situation of indigenous peoples in States and other territories threatened with extinction for environmental reasons*, 16 June 2005, para. 17, 27; disagreeing: S. Oliver, "A New Challenge to International Law: The Disappearance of the Entire Territory of a State," *16 International Journal on Minority and Group Rights* (2009), p. 213–14 (mentioning the unlikelihood of displaced populations scattering evenly across the globe).
423 Ibid., p. 217.

424 S. Oliver, "A New Challenge to International Law: The Disappearance of the Entire Territory of a State," *16 International Journal on Minority and Group Rights* (2009), p.213–14.

425 ILC, *Fifth report on the protection of persons in the event of disasters by Eduardo Valencia-Ospina, Special Rapporteur*, 9 April 2012, para. 59.

426 ILC, *Eighth report on the protection of persons in the event of disasters by Eduardo Valencia-Ospina, Special Rapporteur*, 17 March 2016, para. 304; cf. UNGA, *Agenda item 81: Report of the ILC on the work of its sixty-third session (continued)*, 8 December 2011, para. 20; UNGA, *Agenda item 79: Report of the ILC on the work of its sixty-third and sixty-fourth sessions (continued)*, 4 December 2012, para. 40; UNGA, *Agenda item 81: Report of the ILC on the work of its sixty-third session (continued)*, 2 December 2011, para. 86.

427 ILC, *Eighth report on the protection of persons in the event of disasters by Eduardo Valencia-Ospina, Special Rapporteur*, 17 March 2016, para. 305.

428 J. McAdam, B. Burson, W. Kälin, and S. Weerasinghe, "International Law and Sea-Level Rise: Forced Migration and Human Rights," *FNI Report 1/2016* (2016), p. 45 et seq.

429 Br. Lewis, *Environmental Human Rights and Climate Change: Current Status and Future Prospects* (2018), p. 181.

430 A. Peters, *Jenseits der Menschenrechte: Die Rechtsstellung des Individuums im Völkerrecht* (2014), p. 225; s.a ILC, *Fifth report on the protection of persons in the event of disasters by Eduardo Valencia-Ospina, Special Rapporteur*, 9 April 2012, para. 68.

431 ILC, *Eighth report on the protection of persons in the event of disasters by Eduardo Valencia-Ospina, Special Rapporteur*, 17 March 2016, para. 304; UNGA, *Sixth Committee – Summary record of the 24th meeting*, 1 December 2011, para. 59.

432 ILC, *Eighth report on the protection of persons in the event of disasters by Eduardo Valencia-Ospina, Special Rapporteur*, 17 March 2016, para. 316.

433 J. M. Welsh, "Who should act? Collective responsibility and the Responsibility to Protect" in W. A. Knight, F. Egerton (eds), *The Routledge Handbook of the Responsibility to Protect* (2012), p. 108.

434 A. Peters, *Jenseits der Menschenrechte: Die Rechtsstellung des Individuums im Völkerrecht* (2014), p. 220, fn. 14, citing a letter of John Bolton from August 30, 2005.

435 Cf. Chapter D; cf. ICJ – The Hague, *Conditions of Admission of a State to Membership in the UN (Article 4 of the Charter)* – Advisory Opinion – Individual Opinion by M. Alvarez (28 May 1948), p. 68; cf. M. Koskenniemi, *From Apology to Utopia: The Structure of International Legal Argument* (2015), p. 213; K. Wellens, "Revisiting Solidarity as a (Re-)Emerging Constitutional Principle: Some Further Reflections" in C. Kojima, R. Wolfrum (eds), *Solidarity: A Structural Principle of International Law* (2010), p. 9.

436 A. Peters, "Humanity as the A and Ω of Sovereignty," *20 EJIL* (2009), p. 540.

437 UNSC, *Maintenance of international peace and security: Impact of climate change: Letter dated 1 July 2011 from the Permanent Representative of Germany to the UN addressed to the Secretary-General (S/2011/408)*, 20 July 2011, p. 7 (emphasis added).

438 S. Oliver, "A New Challenge to International Law: The Disappearance of the Entire Territory of a State," *16 International Journal on Minority and Group Rights* (2009), p. 210.

439 S. Gruber, "Human Displacement and Climate Change in the Asia-Pacific" in B. Boer (ed.), *Environmental Law Dimensions of Human Rights* (2015), p. 192.

440 S. Oliver, "A New Challenge to International Law: The Disappearance of the Entire Territory of a State," *16 International Journal on Minority and Group Rights* (2009), p. 210.

441 B. Fassbender, "Der Schutz der Menschenrechte als zentraler Inhalt des völkerrechtlichen Gemeinwohls," *30 Europäische Grundrechte-Zeitschrift* (2003), p. 5.

442 A. L. Paulus, "International Community," (last updated March 2013) in R. Wolfrum (ed.), *The Max Planck Encyclopedia of Public International Law: opil.ouplaw.com.home/EPIL* (2012), para. 15.

443 V. Roeben, "Responsibility in International Law," *16 Max Planck Yearbook of UN Law* (2012), p. 155 (no legally binding human rights norm); L. Glanville, *Sovereignty and the Responsibility to Protect: A New History* (2014), p. 204 (political pressure); L. Glanville, "The Responsibility to Protect Beyond Borders," *12 Human Rights Law Review* (2012), p. 12; C. Stahn, "Responsibility to Protect: Political Rhetoric or Emerging Legal Norm?," *101 AJIL* (2007), p. 118, 116 (probably no positive duty to cooperate; Art. 41(1) DARS "may reflect the progressive development of international law;" A. Peters, "The Responsibility to Protect: Spelling out the Hard Legal Consequences for the UNSC and its Members" in U. Fastenrath, R. Geiger, D.-E. Khan, A. Paulus, S. von Schorlemer, C. Vedder (eds), *From Bilateralism to Community Interest: Essays in Honour of Judge Bruno Simma* (2011), p. 303, 324 on the limits of R2P as a legal concept; cf. J. M. Welsh, "Who should act? Collective responsibility and the Responsibility to Protect" in W. A. Knight, F. Egerton (eds), *The Routledge Handbook of the Responsibility to Protect* (2012), p. 105, 109; E. C. Luck, "Environmental Emergencies and the Responsibility to Protect: A Bridge Too Far?," *103 Proceedings of the Annual Meeting (American Society of International Law)* (2009), p. 32; A. Zimmermann, "The Obligation to Prevent Genocide: Towards a General Responsibility to Protect?" in U. Fastenrath, R. Geiger, D.-E. Khan, A. Paulus, S. von Schorlemer, C. Vedder (eds), *From Bilateralism to Community Interest: Essays in Honour of Judge Bruno Simma* (2011), p. 631; J. Pattison, *Humanitarian Intervention and the Responsibility to Protect: Who Should Intervene?* (2010), p. 15 et seq.; I. Winkelmann, "Responsibility to Protect," (last updated October 2010) in R. Wolfrum (ed.), *The Max Planck Encyclopedia of Public International Law: opil.ouplaw.com.home/EPIL* (2012), para. 22.

444 A. Peters, *Jenseits der Menschenrechte: Die Rechtsstellung des Individuums im Völkerrecht* (2014), p. 225; cf. ILC, *Fifth report on the protection of persons in the event of disasters by Eduardo Valencia-Ospina, Special Rapporteur*, 9 April 2012, para. 68.

445 Similarly: S. C. Breau, *The Responsibility to Protect in International Law: An Emerging Paradigm Shift* (2016), p. 179; cf. L. Axworthy and A. Rock, "R2P: A New and Unfinished Agenda," *1 Global Responsibility to Protect* (2009), p. 64; cf. G. J. Evans, "The Responsibility to Protect in Environmental Emergencies," *103 Proceedings of the Annual Meeting (American Society of International Law)* (2009), p. 32. I do not disagree with Evans as to his reasoning and his fear of watering down the R2P (undermining the utility of "responsibility to protect," serious risk of diluting its capacity) (s. ibid., p. 32). Yet, I see a decisive difference in the treatment of small island States.

446 L. Axworthy and A. Rock, "R2P: A New and Unfinished Agenda," *1 Global Responsibility to Protect* (2009), p. 68.

447 While here only small island States are dealt with, a recent US analysis forecasted that as sea levels rise, nearly 1.9 million US homes could be underwater by 2100 (B. Dennis, *As sea levels rise, nearly 1.9 million US homes could be underwater by 2100* (2016)). The number of climate refugees from small island States is rather small in comparison to the total number of climate refugees. (N. Myers, "Environmental Refugees in a Globally Warmed World," *43 BioScience* (1993), p. 757.). The estimated number of displaced worldwide vary from 20 million to 200 million by 2050 (S. Atapattu, "Climate Change: Disappearing States, Migration, and Challenges for international law," *4 Washington Journal of Environmental Law & Policy* (2014), p. 28.).

448 Global warming can only be dealt with through cooperation by all members of the International Community. UN Human Rights Council, *Report of the Office of the UN High Commissioner for Human Rights on the relationship between climate change and human rights*, 15 January 2009, p. 30, para. 84; cf. UNHCR, *Summary of Deliberations on Climate Change and Displacement* (2011), p. 9, para. 43; P. J. Sands and I. Millar, "Climate, International Protection," (last updated March 2012) in R. Wolfrum (ed.), *The Max Planck Encyclopedia of Public International Law: opil .ouplaw.com.home/EPIL* (2012), para. 65.
449 Willcox, S., "A Rising Tide: The Implications of Climate Change Inundation for Human Rights and State Sovereignty," *9 Essex Human Rights Review 1* (2012), p. 13, citing S. McInerney-Lankford, M. Darrow, and L. Rajamani, *Human Rights and Climate Change: A Review of the International Legal Dimensions* (2011), p. 9.
450 J. Pattison, *Humanitarian Intervention and the Responsibility to Protect: Who Should Intervene?* (2010), p. 4; citing T. G. Weiss, "Researching Humanitarian Intervention: Some Lessons," *38 Journal of Peace Research* (2001), p. 424.
451 Ibid., p. 424.
452 Cf. B. Fassbender, *The UN Charter as the Constitution of the International Community* (2009), p. 75; A. Orford, *International Authority and the Responsibility to Protect* (2011), p. 181; cf. J. Pattison, *Humanitarian Intervention and the Responsibility to Protect: Who Should Intervene?* (2010), p. 5.
453 R. C. Thakur, *The UN, Peace and Security: From Collective Security to the Responsibility to Protect* (2006), p. 11.
454 A. Orford, *International Authority and the Responsibility to Protect* (2011), p. 183.
455 Maas, H., *Statement by Foreign Minister Heiko Maas at the open debate of the UNSC Addressing the Impacts of Climate-related Disasters on International Peace and Security*, 25 January 2019 – https://new-york-un.diplo.de/un-en/news-corner/190125 -maas-climate-security/2182018 (last visited 29 August 2019).
456 UNGA Res. 60/1 of 24 October 2005, para. 138, 139; cf. J. M. Welsh, "Who should act? Collective responsibility and the Responsibility to Protect" in W. A. Knight, F. Egerton (eds), *The Routledge Handbook of the Responsibility to Protect* (2012), p. 103.
457 On the role of the Security Council addressing the threat to small island States, s. K. Conca, J. Thwaites, G. Lee, *Climate Change and Global Security: What Role for the UNSC?* (2017), p. 5.
458 UNGA Res. 60/1 of 24 October 2005, para. 139.
459 UNGA, *A more secure world: our shared responsibility,* Report of the High-level Panel on Threats, Challenges and Change, 2 December 2004, p. 57, para. 202; s. J. Pattison, *Humanitarian Intervention and the Responsibility to Protect: Who Should Intervene?* (2010), p. 5 for critics with regard to UN interventions.
460 J. Pérez de Cuéllar, "Report of the Secretary-General on the work of the Organization," *45 Yearbook of the UN* (1991), p. 7.
461 A. Peters, "The Responsibility to Protect: Spelling out the Hard Legal Consequences for the UNSC and its Members" in U. Fastenrath, R. Geiger, D.-E. Khan, A. Paulus, S. von Schorlemer, C. Vedder (eds), *From Bilateralism to Community Interest: Essays in Honour of Judge Bruno Simma* (2011), p. 305.
462 Art. 24 "Charter of the UN" (1945).
463 M. Nowak, "The three pillars of the UN: Security, Development and Human Rights" in M. E. Salomon, A. Tostensen, W. Vandenhole (eds), *Casting the Net Wider: Human Rights, Development and New Duty-Bearers* (2007), p. 39.
464 A. Peters, "The Responsibility to Protect: Spelling out the Hard Legal Consequences for the UNSC and its Members" in U. Fastenrath, R. Geiger, D.-E. Khan, A. Paulus, S. von Schorlemer, C. Vedder (eds), *From Bilateralism to Community Interest: Essays in Honour of Judge Bruno Simma* (2011), p. 311.

465 UNGA, *A more secure world: our shared responsibility,* Report of the High-level Panel on Threats, Challenges and Change, 2 December 2004, p. 12.

466 L. Axworthy and A. Rock, "R2P: A New and Unfinished Agenda," *1 Global Responsibility to Protect* (2009), p. 68.

467 Concerning the ratifications: While no State can be forced to ratify a particular treaty, a State that does not ratify the Paris Agreement might be considered as failing to display the cooperative behavior required to achieve the aims of the FCCC (paragraph 6 of the preamble to the FCCC acknowledges that "the global nature of climate change calls for the widest possible cooperation by all countries and their participation in an effective and appropriate international response ..."). (cf. R. Verheyen, *Climate Change Damage and International Law: Prevention Duties and State Responsibility* (2005), p. 285.)

468 A. L. Paulus, "International Community," (last updated March 2013) in R. Wolfrum (ed.), *The Max Planck Encyclopedia of Public International Law: opil.ouplaw.com .home/EPIL* (2012), para. 15.

469 S. Gruber, "Human Displacement and Climate Change in the Asia-Pacific" in B. Boer (ed.), *Environmental Law Dimensions of Human Rights* (2015), p. 200.

470 On the precautionary principle: P. Sands, J. Peel, A. Fabra Aguilar, and R. Mackenzie, *Principles of International Environmental Law* (2012), p. 217–28; S. C. Breau, *The Responsibility to Protect in International Law: An Emerging Paradigm Shift* (2016), p. 156 et seq.

471 I. Kelman, "Island evacuation," *31 Forced Migration Review* (2008), p. 21; cf. S. Atapattu, *Human Rights Approaches to Climate Change: Challenges and Opportunities* (2015), p. 230.

472 Cf. L. Woocher, "The Responsibility to Prevent: Towards a Strategy" in W. A. Knight, F. Egerton (eds), *The Routledge Handbook of the Responsibility to Protect* (2012), p. 22–3.

473 UNSC, *Security Council holds first-ever debate on impact of climate change on peace, security,* 17 April 2007; cf. S. Atapattu, *Human Rights Approaches to Climate Change: Challenges and Opportunities* (2015), p. 258; D. Anthoff, R. J. Nicholls and R. S. J. Tol, "The Economic Impact of Substantial Sea-level Rise," *15 Mitigation and Adaptation Strategies for Global Change* (2010), p. 330, cf. N. Stern, *Stern Review: The Economics of Climate Change* (2006), p. vi.

474 Ibid., p. vi: "If a wider range of risks and impacts is taken into account, the estimates of damage could rise to 20% of GDP or more. In contrast, the costs of action – reducing greenhouse gas emissions to avoid the worst impacts of climate change – can be limited to around 1% of global GDP each year."

475 G. J. Evans and M. Sahnoun, *The Responsibility to Protect. Report of the International Commission on Intervention and State Sovereignty* (2001), p. 20.

476 Cf. ibid., p. 25.

477 V. Roeben, "Responsibility in International Law," *16 Max Planck Yearbook of UN Law* (2012), p. 156.

478 A. Peters, "The Responsibility to Protect: Spelling out the Hard Legal Consequences for the UNSC and its Members" in U. Fastenrath, R. Geiger, D.-E. Khan, A. Paulus, S. von Schorlemer, C. Vedder (eds), *From Bilateralism to Community Interest: Essays in Honour of Judge Bruno Simma* (2011), p. 314.

479 J. Pattison, *Humanitarian Intervention and the Responsibility to Protect: Who Should Intervene?* (2010), p. 4

480 J. Pérez de Cuéllar, "Report of the Secretary-General on the work of the Organization," *45 Yearbook of the UN* (1991), p. 12.

481 V. Roeben, "Responsibility in International Law," *16 Max Planck Yearbook of UN Law* (2012), p. 158.

482 L. Woocher, "The Responsibility to Prevent: Towards a Strategy" in W. A. Knight, F. Egerton (eds), *The Routledge Handbook of the Responsibility to Protect* (2012), p. 23.

483 K. A. Annan, *We the Peoples: The Role of the UN in the Twenty-first Century* (2000), p. 77.
484 E. Dannenmaier, "Constructing Transnational Climate Regimes" in G. Handl, J. Zekoll, P. Zumbanse (eds), *Beyond Territoriality: Transnational Legal Authority in an Age of Globalization* (2012), p. 547.
485 Following the principle contained in the UNFCCC.
486 R. Verheyen, *Climate Change Damage and International Law: Prevention Duties and State Responsibility* (2005), p. 277.
487 UN Human Rights Council, *Report of the Office of the UN High Commissioner for Human Rights on the relationship between climate change and human rights*, 15 January 2009, para. 84.
488 D. Wilson, *Interview: Climate Change ... Nobody is immune – Anote Tong (President of Kiribati)* (2009), p. 1 "we are first on the line;" cf. Yale Center for Environmental Law & Policy, *Climate Change and the International Court of Justice: Seeking an Advisory Opinion on Transboundary Harm from the Court* (2014), p. 5; cf. P. Rudiak-Gould, *Climate Change and Tradition in a Small Island State: The Rising Tide* (2013), p. 117; I. de Águeda Corneloup and A. P. J. Mol, "Small island developing states and international climate change negotiations: the power of moral 'leadership,'" *14 International Environmental Agreements: Politics, Law and Economics* (2014), p. 282.
489 S. Atapattu, *Human Rights Approaches to Climate Change: Challenges and Opportunities* (2015), p. 235.
490 Ibid., p. 241.
491 M. Gerrard and G. E. Wannier, "Overview" in M. Gerrard, G. E. Wannier (eds), *Threatened Island Nations: Legal Implications of Rising Seas and a Changing Climate* (2013), p. 14.
492 H.-J. Heintze, "Responsibility to Protect and the Protection of Persons in the Event of Disasters" in P. Hilpold (ed.), *The Responsibility to Protect (R2P): A New Paradigm of International Law?* (2014), p. 310; citing E. d. Vattel, *Le droit des gens ou Principes de la loi naturelle appliqués à la conduite et aux affaires des nations et des souverains* (1758).
493 S. O. Gyandoh, Jr, "Human Rights and the Acquistion of National Sovereignty" in J. Berting et al. (eds), *Human Rights in a Pluralist World: Individuals and Collectivities* (1990), p. 174.
494 Ibid., p. 174.
495 Ibid., p. 180.
496 Ibid., p. 174.
497 UN Human Rights Council, *Report of the Office of the UN High Commissioner for Human Rights on the relationship between climate change and human rights*, 15 January 2009, para. 87.
498 D. Wilson, *Interview: Climate Change ... Nobody is immune – Anote Tong (President of Kiribati)* (2009), p. 2.
499 K. A. Annan, "The Legitimacy to Intervene," *Financial Times*, 10 January 2000, p. 19; cited by B. Fassbender, "Der Schutz der Menschenrechte als zentraler Inhalt des völkerrechtlichen Gemeinwohls," *30 Europäische Grundrechte-Zeitschrift* (2003), p. 11.
500 Ibid., p. 16.
501 Ibid., p. 16.
502 S. O. Gyandoh, Jr, "Human Rights and the Acquisition of National Sovereignty" in J. Berting et al. (eds), *Human Rights in a Pluralist World: Individuals and Collectivities* (1990), p. 181.
503 UNSC, *Peace and security challenges facing small island developing States*, 30 July 2015, p. 40.

504 "Marrakech Action Proclamation for our climate and sustainable development" (2016).
505 UN Human Rights Council, *Report of the Office of the UN High Commissioner for Human Rights on the relationship between climate change and human rights*, 15 January 2009, p. 20, para. 70; Br. Lewis, *Environmental Human Rights and Climate Change: Current Status and Future Prospects* (2018), p. 186 et seq.
506 UN Human Rights Council, *Report of the Special Rapporteur on the issue of human rights obligations relating to the enjoyment of a safe, clean, healthy and sustainable environment*, 1 February 2016, p. 9, para. 34.
507 Ibid., p. 11, para. 41.
508 P.-T. Stoll, "The Climate as a Global Common" in D. A. Farber, M. Peeters (eds), *Elgar Encyclopedia of Environmental Law, vol 1: Climate Change Law* (2016), p. 132.
509 Ibid., p. 132.
510 UN Human Rights Council, *Report of the Special Rapporteur on the issue of human rights obligations relating to the enjoyment of a safe, clean, healthy and sustainable environment*, 1 February 2016, para. 44.
511 D. Held and A. G. McGrew, *Globalization/Anti-Globalization: Beyond the Great Divide* (2007), p. 215.
512 Yale Center for Environmental Law & Policy, *Climate Change and the International Court of Justice: Seeking an Advisory Opinion on Transboundary Harm from the Court* (2014), p. 95 (footnotes omitted); cf. M. Fitzmaurice, "Responsibility and Climate Change," *53 German Yearbook of International Law* (2010), p. 103 et seq.
513 "Barbados Declaration" (1994), Sec. III, 2.
514 H. Hazelzet, M. E. Salomon, A. Tostensen, and W. Vandenhole, "Conclusions New Human Rights Duty-Bearers: A conversation on Policy Implications" in M. E. Salomon, A. Tostensen, W. Vandenhole (eds), *Casting the Net Wider: Human Rights, Development and New Duty-Bearers* (2007), p. 398.
515 J. Barnett and J. Campbell, *Climate Change and Small Island States: Power, Knowledge and the South Pacific* (2010), p. 184.
516 UNGA, *A more secure world: our shared responsibility,* Report of the High-level Panel on Threats, Challenges and Change, 2 December 2004, p. 22, para. 30.
517 UN Human Rights Council, *Report of the Special Rapporteur on the issue of human rights obligations relating to the enjoyment of a safe, clean, healthy and sustainable environment*, 1 February 2016, para. 42–4.
518 S. C. Breau, *The Responsibility to Protect in International Law: An Emerging Paradigm Shift* (2016), p. 164; P. Sands, J. Peel, A. Fabra Aguilar, and R. Mackenzie, *Principles of International Environmental Law* (2012), p. 276.
519 E. Dannenmaier, "Constructing Transnational Climate Regimes" in G. Handl, J. Zekoll, P. Zumbanse (eds), *Beyond Territoriality: Transnational Legal Authority in an Age of Globalization* (2012), p. 525; on mitigation and adaptation strategies, see D. Wallace, "Introduction: security and global climate change" in D. Wallace, D. Silander (eds), *Climate Change, Policy and Security: State and Human Impacts* (2018), p. 15 et seq.
520 P. Hilpold, "R2P and Humanitarian Intervention in a Historical Perspective" in P. Hilpold (ed), *The Responsibility to Protect (R2P): A New Paradigm of International Law?* (2014), p.79–80.
521 E. Dannenmaier, "Constructing Transnational Climate Regimes" in G. Handl, J. Zekoll, P. Zumbanse (eds), *Beyond Territoriality: Transnational Legal Authority in an Age of Globalization* (2012), p. 521.
522 Ibid., p. 526.
523 M. A. Burkett, "The Nations Ex-Situ: On Climate Change, Deterritorialized Nationhood and the Post-Climate Era," *2 Climate Law* (2011), p. 356ff; R. Rayfuse, "Sea Level Rise and Maritime Zones: Preserving the Maritime Entitlements of

'Disappearing' States" in M. Gerrard, G. E. Wannier (eds), *Threatened Island Nations: Legal Implications of Rising Seas and a Changing Climate* (2013), p. 179; J. R. Crawford, The Creation of States in International Law (2006), p. 233 et seq.

524 I. Österdahl, "Relatively Failed. Troubled Statehood and International Law," *14 Finnish Yearbook of International Law* (2003), p. 49.

525 E. Crawford and R. G. Rayfuse, "Climate Change, Sovereignty and Statehood," *11/59 Legal Studies Research Paper* (2011), p. 12.

526 E. Dannenmaier, "Constructing Transnational Climate Regimes" in G. Handl, J. Zekoll, P. Zumbanse (eds), *Beyond Territoriality: Transnational Legal Authority in an Age of Globalization* (2012), p. 525.

527 S. Humphreys, *Climate Change and Human Rights: A Rough Guide* (2008), p. 14.

528 Ibid., p. 4–5; cf. L. Yamamoto and M. Esteban, *Atoll Island States and International Law: Climate Change Displacement and Sovereignty* (2014), p. 268–9.

529 S. Humphreys, *Climate Change and Human Rights: A Rough Guide* (2008), p. 14.

530 S. Oliver, "A New Challenge to International Law: The Disappearance of the Entire Territory of a State," *16 International Journal on Minority and Group Rights* (2009), p. 243.

531 Ibid.

532 J. T. Mathews, "Power Shift," *76 Foreign Affairs* (1997), p. 58.

533 D. Vidas, "Sea-Level Rise and International Law," *4 Climate Law* (2014), p. 83.

534 Ibid., p. 83 (footnotes omitted).

535 A. Peters, "Humanity as the A and Ω of Sovereignty," *20 EJIL* (2009), p. 535.

536 D. Vidas, "Sea-Level Rise and International Law," *4 Climate Law* (2014), p. 83 (footnotes omitted).

537 A. Peters, "Humanity as the A and Ω of Sovereignty," *20 EJIL* (2009), p. 535.

538 A. Orford, *International Authority and the Responsibility to Protect* (2011), p. 16.

539 G. J. Evans, "The Responsibility to Protect: An Idea Whose Time Has Come … and Gone?," *22 International Relations* (2008), p. 289; cf. A. Peters, "Humanity as the A and Ω of Sovereignty," *20 EJIL* (2009), p. 523.

540 Ibid., p. 523.

541 H. Spruyt, *The Sovereign State and Its Competitors: An Analysis of Systems Change* (1996), p. 192.

542 Ibid., p. 187.

543 R. Y. Jennings, "The Role of the International Court of Justice," *68 British Yearbook of International Law* (1997), p. 58.

544 Cf. B. Simma, "Human Rights Before the International Court of Justice: Community Interests Coming to Life?" in C. J. Tams (ed.), *The Development of International Law by the International Court of Justice* (2013), p. 323–4.

545 Ibid., p. 325 with further references.

546 Cf. M. Fitzmaurice, "Responsibility and Climate Change," *53 German Yearbook of International Law* (2010), p. 98 et seq.

547 ICJ – The Hague, *Questions relating to the Obligation to Prosecute or Extradite* (16 July 2012), p. 5; cited after G. I. Hernández, "A Reluctant Guardian: the International Court of Justice and the Concept of 'International Community'," *83 British Yearbook of International Law* (2013), p. 57.

548 UN Human Rights Council, *Report of the Special Rapporteur on the issue of human rights obligations relating to the enjoyment of a safe, clean, healthy and sustainable environment*, 1 February 2016, p. 11, para. 41.

549 Cf. A. Boyle, "Human Rights and the Environment: Where Next?" in B. Boer (ed.), *Environmental Law Dimensions of Human Rights* (2015), p. 231 et seq., examining different case law.

550 ICJ – The Hague, *Legal Consequences cf the Construction of a Wall in the Occupied Palestinian Territory* – Advisory Opinion (9 July 2004), p. 179, para. 109.

551 H. Hazelzet, M. E. Salomon, A. Tostensen, and W. Vandenhole, “Conclusions New Human Rights Duty-Bearers: A conversation on Policy Implications” in M. E. Salomon, A. Tostensen, W. Vandenhole (eds), *Casting the Net Wider: Human Rights, Development and New Duty-Bearers* (2007), p. 399–400.

552 H. Cleveland, “The Internationalization of internal affairs” in A. H. Henkin (ed.), *Human Dignity: The Internationalization of Human Rights: with Selected International Human Rights Documents: Essays Based on an Aspen Institute Workshop* (1978), p. 46.

6 Closing remarks

The State criteria according to the Montevideo Convention turn out to be all rather flexible, so quite different entities do qualify as States all the same. Particularly the criteria territory and population are endangered by climate change-induced rising seas. It will be difficult for States to remain States under current international law when permanently losing State criteria to the rising seas.

It was demonstrated why it is at all useful to be a State and how the concept of the State and State's sovereignty became transformed. Globalization and humanization led to the growing importance of the individual (and with it the State's *population*) and the diminishing importance of *territory*. New subjects of international law appeared next to the State. One could presume that the territorial State lost some of its importance in this transformation. Against this background, it was explored how territorial States are (still) essential for their populations and the international system.

With all of these findings in mind, it becomes clear that despite a strengthened international human rights protection and despite a supposedly dwindling importance of the State as such, in the end people will be left alone when their State is sinking. It becomes apparent that the State still plays an (too) important role in the international protection of human rights. It is therefore necessary to further adapt human rights protection measures accordingly, not only for those affected, but for the international human rights system in general. In addition to an even stronger commitment against climate change, this is the urgent task of the international community. One must realize that the action taken by key actors of this international system to prevent the rising seas from existentially threatening some States has been insufficient. Whereas international law has almost always successfully prevented the involuntary extinction of States, "[i]n painful contrast, in this instance [of the dangers by the rising sea], international law *de lege lata* seems incapable of honouring its reciprocal obligations under the international social contract."[1]

Climate change is only one of a number of challenges for the current world order, but it stands out as a very interesting and significant one in that it is a truly *global* problem and a problem that endangers *individuals*. It currently shows a dramatic change that is more rapid and more destabilizing than ever before. Thereby, it mirrors the trends of humanization and globalization in modern international

DOI: 10.4324/9781003263593-6

law. While the former is challenging the (small island) State in particular, the latter is challenging the State in general. Not only is the pace of change of the international system "more rapid today and its consequences more destabilizing than ever;"[2] but it also decreases the importance of territory and increases the importance of individuals/human rights and can be seen in international law in general. The case of small island States is the dramatic miniature version of this bigger picture.

Hence, while it remains questionable as to whether the State as such is a declining actor in international law, the sinking island State is clearly a declining actor in international law. Nasheed said in this regard in 2009 as then president of the Maldives: "The Maldives is the canary in the world's carbon coal mine."[3] He thereby used Al Gore's image of the Arctic and Antarctica as early warning signs of the effects of climate change.[4] And indeed, "Small islands offer sites where the great global narratives of climate change can be comprehended, interpreted and made tangible and visible, and where 'proof' of the reality of climate change can supposedly be constructed from indigenous testimonials."[5] Thus, if people from the Maldives are left alone in their fight for their human rights, the international human rights system in general will suffer. If, however, those people from sinking States are provided with the aid they need, the international human rights system will gain from such precedence. Thus, the endangered States may be small, but "[a] dwarf is as much a man as a giant is; a small Republic is no less a sovereign State than the most powerful Kingdom."[6] And if a "small Republic" sinks and thereby loses its ability to protect its people, the danger for the international community is big – if it does not come into play as a fill in. Al Gore said in this regard:

> We, the human species, are confronting a planetary emergency – a threat to the survival of our civilization that is gathering ominous and destructive potential even as we gather here. But there is hopeful news as well: we have the ability to solve this crisis and avoid the worst – though not all – of its consequences, if we act boldly, decisively and quickly.[7]

While States generally might have lost power and influence through the trends of humanization and globalization, for sinking States, this "loss" is even worse: These States are (becoming) factually powerless. While States in general "may simply no longer be the natural problem-solving unit,"[8] they clearly cannot be a problem-solving unit anymore once they become submerged by the sea. Hence, when protection through the States does not appear promising (like in the fight against climate change where global action is needed); attention shifts – rightly – to the international community.

As the international community can most likely not offer territory for populations from sinking States, it should focus on the protection of the human rights of these people. In any case, the main goal of the State and, subsidiarily, of the international community is to protect the individual (also collectively), ideally without regard to territory.

Thereby, "[t]he absolutes of the Westphalian system [...] are all dissolving."[9] As such, Burkett points out that "[i]n the postclimate era, our legal systems will not be immune to dramatic change."[10] Both subjects (the States and the international community) seem to be uneasy with this situation. This uneasiness comes at the expense of the individual which is ironic because the individual is the one that is supposed to be protected by both – the State and the international community.

The international community is certainly not a "super-State." But there seems to be a need for such a "super-State." Schiffer suggested a World State for "matters of general concern for the global community."[11] Climate change is a matter of general concern for the global community, but there is no world State. However, the UN hosts State characteristic institutions, like the General Assembly as its parliament, the Security Council as its executive organ, the ICJ as its judicial organ, and the UN Charter as its constitution.[12] Marquardt compares the "level" of statehood of the UN with the statehood of the States up to the sixteenth and seventeenth century.[13] Thus, there is an entity which could and should be taken as a starting point for dealing with global matters.

According to Nowak, this entity does already do its global job in the "'war on terror,' as if terrorism was the root cause of contemporary world problems, not simply another symptom."[14] Yet, it is "still far from being dominated by concerns as to how to achieve effectively the ambitious Millennium Development Goals," such as the combat of "global poverty, global violence, global environmental destruction and global human rights violations."[15] In the fight against climate change, the international community might have to be reminded that it actually became an *actor* under international law and can and should *act*. States, however, are torn between the wish to preserve as much independence as possible, and the realization that mankind desperately needs a more effective international organization.[16]

On the one hand, States expect the UN to act:

> My people want to know what *the UN* will *do to save* the Maldives and other small island nations from being engulfed by the sea. Indeed, the small island nations are most susceptible to the dangers of environmental crises as well, especially those due to climate change and sea-level rise. Unless the industrialized countries drastically cut down the emission of greenhouse gases, with immediate effect, the small island States and other low-lying areas will face an environmental catastrophe of unprecedented proportions.[17]

On the other hand, they do not actually empower the UN to do so. This reflects the state of a society which is extremely contradictory. The States are "both desperately clinging to the legal and political symbols of national sovereignty and being pushed towards the pursuit of common needs and goals that can be achieved only by a steadily intensifying degree of international organisation."[18] This was a statement made by Friedmann in 1964. Now, more than 50 years later, it is still valid. Perhaps it is time to overcome this contradiction – for the benefit of individuals.

When States fail to act, the "new subject" on the global stage needs to come into play. The UN organization is such a (new) actor on the international scene. Hence, today's globalized world does have an actor for global matters. This actor should act.

It should act, in particular, when the solution is by its very nature "global," since individual States cannot act as efficiently as a global actor (as in the case of the fight against climate change where "the (natural) borderlessness of the world is especially invidious").[19] Moreover it should certainly act when States cannot protect their own individuals anymore, as in the case of sinking States. It should also act in situations where States are dropping out of an international system. In this regard, Ms Heine, then president of the Marshall Islands said months before the United States announced its (now reversed) withdrawal from the Paris Agreement:

> If we do not peak global emissions by 2020 and keep global temperature increases within 1.5 degrees Celsius the survival of my island home is at stake. We expect the continued leadership and engagement from all who led the way to Paris, including the United States.[20]

This "expectation" should be backed up by the UN, if only because global problems that cannot be dealt with by any State on its own should be dealt with by global institutions on a global level. Being dependent on its State parties, such back-up is without a question difficult without the support of (particularly powerful) member States. Nevertheless, the UN must become more independent in global matters.

Actions that should be taken are various. First of all, greenhouse gases should be stabilized. Only the global reduction of greenhouse gas emissions can address the root causes of climate change.[21] The UN must do more to make sure that such reduction takes place. Moreover, technical adaptation facilities should be provided for the States in need, and money for such adaptation should be given to the respective States (e.g., via the Green Climate Fund).[22] Additionally, protection mechanisms for the individuals that suffer from the effects of climate change should be established on a global level. In this regard, in 1991 Vanuatu proposed, as the Chair of the Alliance of Small Island States (AOSIS), an insurance scheme as part of the UNFCCC to address the consequences of sea-level rise. Although this was not taken up entirely under the 1992 agreement, reference to insurance is made in Art. 4(8) of the Convention.[23] Such rules and their enforceability are important because the State level will not be the effective level for the protection of affected individuals (at least in this particular case of sinking island States).

As the first two "action-complexes" are mainly technical or scientific measures that are better dealt with by technicians and scientists, this text shall take a closer look at the third complex of "action:"

Human rights should be truly internationalized. Since the end of WWII, human rights have stopped being an internal State matter. However, they are not yet truly internationalized, nor are they really decoupled from the nation State.

Taking human rights seriously would lead to actually caring about human rights with a focus on the rightsholders and with corresponding international duty-bearers, at least when the national State is either unable or unwilling to offer the necessary protection. According to Nowak this is also necessary not least because anything else contributes "to the credibility deficit and loss of reputation of the UN."[24]

While various human rights are endangered by the rising seas, the particular situation when people have to leave their homeland seems massively in need of some legal framework that guides this process in a manner that conforms with human rights expectations. There is no major destination country that has a proactive or welcoming policy for people to resettle in case of climate change-induced displacement.[25] Most developed States even desire to restrict rather than improve the existing refugee system. Thus, hoping for an automatic improvement of the situation of endangered populations is unrealistic.[26]

The aforementioned case where a man from Kiribati (unsuccessfully) applied for asylum in New Zealand highlighted the legal void on climate refugees.[27] Section 129 of the New Zealand Immigration Act 2009[28]

> only permits recognition as a refugee if the requirements of the Convention are met. It is the legal conception which applies, not the sociological one [...]. The legal conception requires that the applicant establish that he is at risk of "being persecuted," and that status be linked to one of the five Convention grounds.[29]

Art. 1 of the Refugee Convention[30] defines such persons eligible for this status as someone who

> owing to well-founded fear of being persecuted for reasons of race, religion, nationality, membership of a particular social group or political opinion, is outside the country of his nationality and is unable or, owing to such fear, is unwilling to avail himself of the protection of that country; or who, not having a nationality and being outside the country of his former habitual residence as a result of such events, is unable or, owing to such fear, is unwilling to return to it.

Thus, it is clear that the convention does not apply to climate change-displaced people.[31] The root causes of a person's displacement would have to be of political nature. Therefore, the rights and protection options for victims of natural disasters are uncertain under international law, with no agency having a mandate to protect them.[32] Interestingly, the judgment of the New Zealand Court of Appeal in 2014 ended with a conclusion where it was explicitly stated that

> No-one should read this judgment as downplaying the importance of climate change. It is a major and growing concern for the international community. The point this judgment makes is that climate change and its effect

> on countries like Kiribati is not appropriately addressed under the Refugee Convention.[33]

This legal vacuum needs to be closed and this should happen now – before the numbers of people displaced increase.[34] The established human rights system does mainly focus on blaming States that actively violate human rights.[35] In the context of climate change, any State or no State is normally determined to be blameworthy. The focus should therefore be placed elsewhere: On individuals in need of help and States, institutions, or organizations that are *able* to help. People should be enabled to get protection and States should be supported to offer protection and this should be coordinated globally (as the protection of climate refugees should be seen as a global problem and a global responsibility).[36] But powerful States might not want such a change of focus. Yamamoto and Esteban argue in this regard that the typical "saviors" would need to see themselves realistically as the "savages" in the situation of climate change (because of their emissions). Such a switch will not happily be accepted.[37]

Nevertheless, such a switch is necessary.[38] Any new legislation[39] should pave the way in such a direction. The *R2P* (Responsibility to Protect) principle (which is not directly relevant in this case but shows a shift in thinking) entails not only the responsibility of sovereign States to protect their populations but also the responsibility of the international community to act to ensure that populations are protected.[40] Today, there is an ongoing debate about whether individuals can only be given rights by (their) States or whether they are indeed (already) subjects of international law themselves.[41] Meron points out how Jennings and Watts, on the one hand, grant individuals limited international personality based on their direct rights and duties, while Prosper Weil, on the other hand, emphasizes that these developments result from the operation of inter-State rules of conventional and customary law.[42] Indeed international law seems to hang in the balance. While individuals gained personality in regional systems, this step has not (yet) been fully carried out globally. But there is a "growing consensus that the status of the individual in international law is being transformed from a mere object to a subject, a subject whose rights are different and lesser, but a subject nonetheless."[43] Thus, people who cannot be protected in their rights through the operation of their respective States could (and should) be granted a limited personality internationally in order not to be left un-protected.

Although the idea of some Bangladeshi NGOs that proposed the creation of a new status, a "Universal Natural Person," seems appealing,[44] it is very unlikely to find international acceptance (particularly with a view not only to the millions of people affected in Bangladesh,[45] but also for the several thousands of the affected island States).

The "Declaration of a Roma Nation" points in a similar direction:

> We have a dream, the political concrete dream of the rule of law being the rule for each and everybody, in the frame and thanks to a juridical system able to assure democracy, freedom, liberty to each and everybody, being

> adequate to the changing world, the changing society, the changing economy. We have a dream, the one of the rule of law being a method, and not a value. A pragmatic, concrete, way how individuals agree on rules, institutions, juridical norms, adequate to the new needs. A transnational Nation as the Roma one needs a transnational rule of law: this is evident; we do believe that such a need is shared by any individual, independently of the Nation he or she belongs to.[46]

This indeed is still a dream. Neither will States cease to exist anytime soon, nor will people be granted a right to go anywhere wherever they want to. People who cannot be protected by their States should have some (subsidiary) right to get protection from some State. They should be able to apply for a "*climate refugee visa*"[47] (which would be permanent, not temporary like a normal visa).[48] As climate change is a global problem and the neighboring States should not be left alone to deal with this problem, the respondent for such an application would be an institution of the international community. This institution would have to find a solution that is acceptable for the people (also with regard to their human rights) as well as for the receiving States. The requirement for access to this institution would be that the national State is unwilling or unable to protect its people (similar to the *R2P* concept, but clearly not limited to the four crimes). This institution would then, probably by financial means (so the new host State would not have to fear the financial burden), make sure that some other State takes over. Not only should individuals be entitled to file such a claim, but also communities that used to live together.

This would certainly be a huge step. As there is a necessity to find a solution for these people, maybe this idea could be a start. The world is globalized and humanized enough to be able to take such a step. Why not start[49] with the climate refugees?

Moreover, it would seem beneficial to establish an International Court for Human Rights[50] or create an extra chamber at the ICJ which, despite showing some signs of humanization[51] and despite human rights being a big part of international law, is "not a specialized human rights institution, either in terms of its mandate, its jurisdiction, its procedures, or its personnel."[52] This could give assistance against the problem of non-enforcement of UN treaty norms by the UN machinery.[53] Also, advisory opinions could help pave the way towards truly internationalized human rights.

In any case, arguably, it would have been even worse for individuals to lose a State's territory in the time of the peace of Westphalia because the territorial delimitations of the State were even more impermeable, territory was more important, and the individual was less important on the international level at that time. Today, there are some internationalized protection facilities for individuals regardless of their home State. In an ideal humanized and globalized world, national borders would not matter. We are closer to such a system than back in 1648, but we are still undoubtedly far away from such a world.

However, as Eyffinger pointed out in 1998:

> [a]round 1600, when the Pope and Emperor ignored the call for just change, they unleashed forces beyond their control – and were simply swept away. Today, in their turn, their successors are challenged. Around 1650, the nascent states, [...], claimed absolute sovereignty and unrestricted freedom of policy. They had to experience the destructive effects of their conflicting independent policies before identifying cooperation as self-interest. At about 1900, still in the learning process, they came to understand the profits to be gained from intergovernmental organization, even if this implied some restriction of sovereignty. Only recently, the European nations, [...], delegated significant authority to a Union which will shortly operate independently from their stringent control. As it is, on the global scale, the majority of nations still envy the UN the resources and authority to grow beyond a mere debating club of nations. However, irrevocably, social processes well beyond their control will keep stretching their willingness to comply to the outer limits. Increasing interconnectedness imposes interdependence. Transnational issues require multilateral action. Already, environmental policies are being globalized; terrorists have challenged the state's exclusive claim to force, [...]. Prompted by non-governmental organization, human rights issues infringe [upon] the public sphere. [...] In short, the international regime imposes itself — and not necessarily at the expense of state entities. If these latter are open to just change and willing to share, a bright future will lay ahead. To those who so far have ignored the writing on the wall, we may advise: remember Westphalia![54]

Thus, cooperation between States has to and will remain increasingly important. The "good" point about the search for unified action in the case of climate change is that such cooperation is "an example of self-centered solidarity:"[55]

> The analogy is to a ship, which has a big hole in it. The ship will sink unless those on board can work together to repair it and to ensure that it continues its voyage, regardless of who caused the hole.[56]

As Tomuschat pointed out, the planet Earth is the home of all people from which there is no escape route to other places. The future of mankind can therefore only be secured if, on the basis of common fundamental values, the ever more complex problems of an industrialized [globalized] world are solved by mutual cooperation.[57] As such, then Minister of Climate Change, Adaptation, Geo-Hazard, Environment, and Energy, Ham Lini Vanuaroroa, from Vanuatu said in 2016:

> I stand before you today from the world's most vulnerable country on the planet [...]. But it is not just my country that is at stake; no nation – large or small, wealthy or poor – is immune to climate change.[58]

Indeed, the changes in the Pacific might accelerate climate change's "cascading effect" all over the world. "We're engaged in an epic battle to save planet Earth," said Toribiong during the Press Conference on the request for the ICJ's Advisory Opinion on Climate Change.[59]

States seem to be aware of the direct impact of global warming on each of them. "Even though cooperation to tackle it leaves much to be desired [...], it is obviously in the interest of all cooperating states."[60]

Thus, all States should

> agree on measures to slow down the rate at which the hole grows bigger and ultimately to keep it from exceeding a tipping point. [...] At the same time, [they] need to initiate measures to assist those affected by the hole to adjust to the changes.[61]

This fits together very well with the Statement by Ban Ki-moon, then Secretary-General of the UN, delivered on 15 November 2016 at the 22nd Conference of the Parties to the UNFCCC in Marrakech:

> This is a new dawn for global cooperation on climate change. The Paris Agreement is one of the most complex international accords ever reached. It entered into force years ahead of expectations. Countries have strongly supported the Agreement because they realize their own national interest is best secured by pursuing the common good. Now we have to translate words into effective policies and actions. This is critical to protect our planet, safeguard the most vulnerable and drive shared prosperity. Low-emission development and climate resilience will advance all the Sustainable Development Goals. The UN will help countries implement this Agreement. The quicker we act, the more we gain.[62]

Even though it is said that "[c]urrent commitments are simply not enough to avoid climate catastrophe,"[63] "the planet is on the verge of dramatic climate change. It is still possible to avoid the most deleterious effects, but only if prompt actions are taken to stabilize global temperature close to its present value."[64] Plans to do so must be made immediately, closely followed by action regardless of whether one opts for one of the following courses of action: try to avoid risking the statehood of at-risk island States by radically lowering emissions, help out with protecting territory, or providing alternative territory, or even eventually resettle the populations somewhere in a manner that conforms with human rights expectations. The situations should not be ignored until it is too late. "If we fail to plan, we plan to fail," was stated by José Riera.[65] Indeed, the

> business-as-usual model for adaptation is indefensible and unsustainable. Putting in place large-scale adaptation investments in rich countries while leaving the world's poor to sink or swim is not just a prescription for human development reversals. It is a prescription for a more divided, less prosperous, and more insecure 21st Century.[66]

Ban Ki-moon ended his statement at the abovementioned Conference of the Parties to the UNFCCC in Marrakech, his last COP as Secretary-General of the UN with the words:

> I leave you with the hope that we will have the courage, tenacity and wisdom to live up to our responsibility to future generations by protecting our only home: this beautiful planet Earth.[67]

Indeed, if courage, tenacity, and wisdom are used in that fight, climate change as the "greatest collective challenge facing humankind today" could be turned "into the greatest opportunity for common progress towards a sustainable future."[68] For the sake of the people, the international community should take this opportunity!

Notes

1 A. G. Jain, "The 21st Century Atlantis: The International Law of Statehood and Climate Change-Induced Loss of Territory," *50 Stanford Journal of International Law* (2014), p. 11.
2 C. W. Kegley, G. A. Raymond, *Exorcising the Ghost of Westphalia: Building World Order in the New Millennium* (2002), p. 155, citing J. N. Rosenau, *Turbulence in World Politics: A Theory of Change and Continuity* (1990); cf. J. N. Rosenau, "Turbulence in World Politics: A Theory of Change and Continuity" in R. W. Mansbach, E. J. Rhodes (eds), *Global Politics in a Changing World: A Reader* (2008), p. 13 et seq.
3 C. Toomey, *The Maldives: Trouble in paradise* (2009).
4 Cf. M. Nissani, *Al Gore's Inconvenient Truth – An Interpretive Synopsis of the Film* (2007).
5 J. Connell, "Nothing There Atoll? 'Farewell to the Carteret Islands'" in T. Crook; P. Rudiak-Gould (eds), *Pacific Climate Cultures: Living Climate Change in Oceania* (2018), p. 83 (footnote omitted).
6 E. d. Vattel, *The Law of Nations: Or, Principles of the Law of Nature Applied to the Conduct and Affairs of Nations and Sovereigns* (1797), p. lxiii.
7 A. A. Gore, *Nobel Lecture, Oslo* (2007).
8 J. T. Mathews, "Power Shift," *76 Foreign Affairs* (1997), p. 65–6.
9 Ibid., p. 50.
10 M. A. Burkett, "The Nation Ex-Situ" in M. Gerrard, G. E. Wannier (eds), *Threatened Island Nations: Legal Implications of Rising Seas and a Changing Climate* (2013), p. 120.
11 W. Schiffer, *The Legal Community of Mankind: A Critical Analysis of the Modern Concept of World Organization* (1972), p. 291.
12 Cf. B. Fassbender, *UNSC Reform and the Right of Veto. A Constitutional Perspective* (1998), p. 58; B. Marquardt, *Universalgeschichte des Staates: Von der vorstaatlichen Gesellschaft zum Staat der Industriegesellschaft* (2009), p. 629; B. Simma, "From bilateralism to community interest in international law," *250 Recueil Des Cours* (1994), p. 258 et seq.; P. M. Kennedy, *The Parliament of Man: The Past, Present, and Future of the UN* (2007), p. xi; 274.
13 B. Marquardt, *Universalgeschichte des Staates: Von der vorstaatlichen Gesellschaft zum Staat der Industriegesellschaft* (2009), p. 632.
14 M. Nowak, "The three pillars of the UN: Security, Development and Human Rights" in M. E. Salomon, A. Tostensen, W. Vandenhole (eds), *Casting the Net Wider: Human Rights, Development and New Duty-Bearers* (2007), p. 40.
15 Ibid., p. 40.

16 B. Fassbender, "Die Souveränität des Staates als Autonomie im Rahmen der völkerrechtlichen Verfassung" in H.-P. Mansel (ed.), *Festschrift für Erik Jayme* (2004), p. 1101.

17 UNGA, *50th Session, 40th Plenary meeting*, 24 October 1995 (Mr. Maumoon Abdul Gayoom, President of the Republic of Maldives), p. 18 (emphasis added).

18 W. G. Friedmann, *The Changing Structure of International Law* (1964), p. 293–4; cf. B. Fassbender, "Der Schutz der Menschenrechte als zentraler Inhalt des völkerrechtlichen Gemeinwohls," *30 Europäische Grundrechte-Zeitschrift* (2003), p. 16.

19 S. Humphreys, "The Covenants in the Light of Anthropogenic Climate Change" in D. Moeckli, H. Keller, C. Heri (eds), *The Human Rights Covenants at 50: Their Past, Present, and Future* (2018), p. 282.

20 H. Heine, *Statement of Her Excellency Ms Hilda Heine, President of the Marshall Islands, delivered on 15 November 2016 at the 22nd Conference of the Parties to the UNFCCC in Marrakech* (2016).

21 J. Barnett, "Human rights and vulnerability to climate change" in S. Humphreys, M. Robinson (eds), *Human Rights and Climate Change* (2010), p. 266.

22 http://www.greenclimate.fund/home (last visited 30 June 2019). It is intended to be the centerpiece of long-term financing under the UNFCCC, which has set itself a goal of raising US$100 billion per year by 2020.

23 M. Talakai, "Loss and damage gap analysis from climate change," *Kiribati country report for the Secretariat of the Pacific Environmental Programme (SPREP) and GIZ, June 2015* (2015), p. 5.

24 M. Nowak, "The three pillars of the UN: Security, Development and Human Rights" in M. E. Salomon, A. Tostensen, W. Vandenhole (eds), *Casting the Net Wider: Human Rights, Development and New Duty-Bearers* (2007), p. 40.

25 L. Yamamoto and M. Esteban, *Atoll Island States and International Law: Climate Change Displacement and Sovereignty* (2014), p. 276 with further references.

26 Cf. ibid., p. 241.

27 Court of Appeal of New Zealand, *Teitiota v. Chief Executive of Ministry of Business, Innovation, and Employment* (8 May 2014); A. Leslie, *Kiribati asylum case highlights legal void on "climate refugees"* (2013).

28 "Immigration Act 2009: Public Act 2009 No 51" (2009), section 129 Recognition as refugee:

> (1) A person must be recognised as a refugee in accordance with this Act if he or she is a refugee within the meaning of the Refugee Convention.
> (2) A person who has been recognised as a refugee under subsection (1) cannot be deported from New Zealand except in the circumstances set out in section 164(3).

29 Cf. Court of Appeal of New Zealand, *Teitiota v. Chief Executive of Ministry of Business, Innovation, and Employment* (8 May 2014), para. 17.

30 "Convention Relating to the Status of Refugees" (1951).

31 http://www.unhcr.org/climate-change-and-disasters.html (last visited 30 June 2019); cf. L. Yamamoto and M. Esteban, *Atoll Island States and International Law: Climate Change Displacement and Sovereignty* (2014), p. 230 et seq.

32 Ibid., p. 230, 233. Sweden and Finland are positive exceptions from that rule in that they have included environmental migrants in their immigration policies. Within its asylum system, Sweden includes persons who do not qualify for refugee status but have a need for protection. Such a person in need of protection "has left his native country and does not wish to return there because he: – has a fear of the death penalty or torture – is in need of protection as a result of war or other serious conflicts in the country – is unable to return to his native country because of an environmental disaster." The decision is made on an individual, not group, basis. Although many recipients of this status are presumed to be in temporary need of protection, the Swedish rules foresee that some persons may be in need of permanent solutions. Similarly, in the Finnish Aliens Act,

"aliens residing in the country are issued with a residence permit on the basis of a need for protection if [...] they cannot return because of an armed conflict or environmental disaster" (S. F. Martin, *Climate Change and International Migration* (2010), p. 4.).

33 Court of Appeal of New Zealand, *Teitiota v. Chief Executive of Ministry of Business, Innovation, and Employment* (8 May 2014), para. 41; cf. Supreme Court of New Zealand, *Teitiota v. Ministry of Business Innovation, and Employment* (20 July 2015) for the Supreme Court Decision in 2015.

34 L. Yamamoto and M. Esteban, *Atoll Island States and International Law: Climate Change Displacement and Sovereignty* (2014), p. 276; J. von Doussa, "Human Rights and Climate Change: A Tragedy in the Making," *31 UNSW Law Journal 3* (2008), p. 963.

35 Cf. ibid., p. 242.

36 M. Shamsuddoha and R. K. Chowdhury, *Climate Change Induced Forced Migrants: in need of dignified recognition under a new Protocol* (2009), p. 5.

37 L. Yamamoto and M. Esteban, *Atoll Island States and International Law: Climate Change Displacement and Sovereignty* (2014), p. 243–4.

38 Cf. B. Docherty and T. Giannini, "Confronting a Rising Tide: A Proposal for a Convention on Climate Change Refugees," *33 Harvard Environmental Law Review* (2009), p. 349 et seq.; L. Yamamoto and M. Esteban, *Atoll Island States and International Law: Climate Change Displacement and Sovereignty* (2014), p. 234 et seq. on a convention to protect climate-change-displaced people.

39 Critically with respect to such a convention: J. McAdam, "Swimming Against the Tide: Why a Climate Change Displacement Treaty is Not the Answer," *23 International Journal of Refugee Law* (2011).

40 Cf. L. Glanville, *Sovereignty and the Responsibility to Protect: A New History* (2014), p. 204.

41 Cf. T. Meron, *The Humanization of International Law* (2006), p. 253.

42 Ibid., p. 253–4 with further references.

43 Ibid., p. 254.

44 M. Shamsuddoha and R. K. Chowdhury, *Climate Change Induced Forced Migrants: in need of dignified recognition under a new Protocol* (2009); cf. L. Yamamoto and M. Esteban, *Atoll Island States and International Law: Climate Change Displacement and Sovereignty* (2014), p. 276.

45 "[J]ust a 1 to 2 degree increase in temperature would force physical dislocation of more than 35 million people in Bangladesh" (M. Shamsuddoha and R. K. Chowdhury, *Climate Change Induced Forced Migrants: in need of dignified recognition under a new Protocol* (2009), p. 4).

46 "Declaration of a Roma Nation (IRU)" (2001).

47 S. F. Martin, *Climate Change and International Migration* (2010), p. 5.

48 S. L. Yamamoto and M. Esteban, *Atoll Island States and International Law: Climate Change Displacement and Sovereignty* (2014), p. 277.

49 This would be an option for refugees in general and could thus be enlarged gradually.

50 Cf. M. Nowak, "The Need for a World Court of Human Rights," *7 Human Rights Law Review* (2007), p. 251 et seq. See also (more critically): F. D. Gaer, "The Institutional Future of the Covenants: A World Court for Human Rights?" in D. Moeckli, H. Keller, C. Heri (eds), *The Human Rights Covenants at 50: Their Past, Present, and Future* (2018), p. 346 et seq.

51 Cf. B. Simma, "Human Rights Before the International Court of Justice: Community Interests Coming to Life?" in C. J. Tams (ed.), *The Development of International Law by the International Court of Justice* (2013), p. 325.

52 J. R. Crook, "The International Court of Justice and Human Rights," *1 Northwestern Journal of International Human Rights* (2004), p. 2.

53 F. D. Gaer, "The Institutional Future of the Covenants: A World Court for Human Rights?" in D. Moeckli, H. Keller, C. Heri (eds), *The Human Rights Covenants at 50:*

Their Past, Present, and Future (2018), p. 336, referring to Manfred Nowak and Martin Scheinin.

54 A. Eyffinger, "Europe in the Balance: An Appraisal of the Westphalian System," *45 Netherlands international law review* (1998), p. 186–7.

55 H. P. Hestermeyer, "Reality or Aspiration? – Solidarity in International Environmental and World Trade Law" in H. Hestermeyer, R. Wolfrum (eds), *Coexistence, Cooperation and Solidarity: Liber Amicorum Rüdiger Wolfrum* (2012), p. 51, pointing out that self-centered solidarity should be implementable (and implemented) even easier than "altruistic solidarity" (p. 63); cf. R. Wolfrum, "Means of Ensuring Compliance with and Enforcement of International Environmental Law," *272 Recueil Des Cours* (1998), p. 139.

56 E. Brown Weiss, "Strengthening Compliance with Climate Change Commitments" in H. Hestermeyer, R. Wolfrum (eds), *Coexistence, Cooperation and Solidarity: Liber Amicorum Rüdiger Wolfrum* (2012), p. 701.

57 C. Tomuschat, "Die internationale Gemeinschaft," *33 Archiv des Völkerrechts* (1995), p. 20 [instead of becoming the trigger for (military) conflicts].

58 H. L. Vanuaroroa, *Statement by the Minister of Climate Change, Adaptation, Geo-Hazard, Environment and Energy, the Honorable Ham Lini Vunuaroroa delivered on 15 November 2016 at the 22nd Conference of the Parties to the UNFCCC in Marrakech* (2016).

59 UN Department of Public Information, *Press Conference on request for International Court of Justice Advisory Opinion on Climate Change.*

60 H. P. Hestermeyer, "Reality or Aspiration? – Solidarity in International Environmental and World Trade Law" in H. Hestermeyer, R. Wolfrum (eds), *Coexistence, Cooperation and Solidarity: Liber Amicorum Rüdiger Wolfrum* (2012), p. 51.

61 E. Brown Weiss, "Strengthening Compliance with Climate Change Commitments" in H. Hestermeyer, R. Wolfrum (eds), *Coexistence, Cooperation and Solidarity: Liber Amicorum Rüdiger Wolfrum* (2012), p. 720.

62 http://unfccc.int/meetings/marrakech_nov_2016/items/10041.php (last visited 20 November 2019).

63 T. E. Remengesau, *Remarks of His Excellency Tommy E. Remengesau, Jr, President of the Republic of Palau, delivered on 15 November 2016 at the 22nd Conference of the Parties to the UNFCCC in Marrakech* (2016).

64 W. C. G. Burns and H. M. Osofsky, "Overview: The Exigencies That Drive Potential Causes of Action for Climate Change" in W. C. G. Burns, H. M. Osofsky (eds), *Adjudicating Climate Change: State, National, and International Approaches* (2009), p. 1; citing J. E. Hansen, *Dangerous Human-Made Interference with Climate* (2007), p. 5.

65 Green Cross International, *Climate change is a human rights issue: 26th session of the UN Human Rights Council in Geneva* (2014).

66 K. Watkins et al., *UNDP Human Development Report 2007/2008 – Fighting Climate Change: Human Solidarity in a Divided World* (2007), p. 198. "For human development to become truly sustainable, the world needs to break with business-as-usual approaches and adopt sustainable production and consumption patterns." (S. Jahan et al., *UNDP Human Development Indicators and Indices: 2018 Statistical Update* (2018), p. 12–13.)

67 http://unfccc.int/meetings/marrakech_nov_2016/items/10041.php (last visited 20 November 2019).

68 UN Habitat, *How the UN System Supports Ambitious Action on Climate Change: UN System Chief Executives Board for Coordination* (2014); cf. A. Proelß, "International Environmental Law and the Challenge of Climate Change," *53 German Yearbook of International Law* (2010), p. 65: "Climate change represents a turning point [...] for the development of international law."

Index

"1Point5 to stay alive" 11

ability to response, responsibility 191–8
absolute sovereignty 110–11
accountability 250; *see also* responsibility
acknowledging climate change 169
Act of Chapultepec 123
action, concept of 199–201, 203, 245–6
actors 113
adaptation 7, 15n11; mechanisms 4; strategies 8
"al Qaeda's global ummah" 48
allegiance 43
Alliance of Small Island States (AOSIS) 10
Alliance of Small Island States Leaders' Declaration 60
ambulatory baselines 35
American Declaration on the Rights of Indigenous Peoples 166
American Law Institute 25
annexation 52
Anthropocene 9
aquitorial sovereignty 35
archipelagic States, baselines 34
Argentina 39
"Armed Activities on the Territory of the Congo" 39
artificial adaptation 7
Australia 35, 187, 196
Austria 52
Avena Case 55

Bahamas 7
Bali Road Map 186
Baltic States 52
Bangladesh 5
Banjul Charter 168
Barbados declaration 11, 60
baselines 33–5
Boers case 63, 66
borders 124–5
boundaries 124–5
Brexit 124
burden-sharing 219n167

Canal Zone (Panama) 39–40
Caracas Declaration (1989) 185
Carteret Islands 8–9
case law: Argoud, A. 39; Avena Case 55; *Coulson v Government of the Canal Zone* 40; Eichmann, Adolf 39; *Juliana v US* 117; LaGrand Case 55; League of Nations control over the Saar 42; *Lliuya v. RWE* 118–19; *People's Climate Case* 118; *Re Burriel* 40; *Re Cia. de Transportes des Gelabert* 40; *Re Kenneth Robert Bartlett* 40; Reparation for injuries case 113; "Sovereignty over Pedra Branca/Pulau Batu Puteh, Middle Rocks and South Ledge" 43 *Teitiota Case* 167–8; *Urgenda Foundation v. State of the Netherlands* 116–17
Catholic Church 51
causal responsibility 184–91
causation 228n325
China 34, 59–60
Christianity 51
church 46–8
citizenship: international citizenship 129; Maastricht Treaty 112; of the Union 112; Virtual States 53–4; Wirtland 53–4
Citizenship Act, New Zealand 167
City Leagues 47
Climate Change Convention 131
Climate change metaphors 184–5
climate change migrants 64
climate justice 186

climate refugee visa 249
climate refugees 236n447, 247, 249
climate-change induced rising sea levels *see* sea-level rise
climate-induced displacement 7
coexistence of two sovereigns 63
coexistence paradigm 204
Committee on International Law and Sea Level Rise 1
common but differentiated responsibility 186, 197
common heritage of mankind 122
common humanity 180
contemporary concept of State 102–5; globalization 114–28; humanization 105–14
contemporary international legal system 41
Convention on Biological Diversity (CBD) 186
Convention on the Law of the Sea (UNCLOS) 186, 188
cooperation 174, 176, 192, 197, 250–1; *see also* international cooperation
Copenhagen Accord 186
Coulson v Government of the Canal Zone 40
Covenant of the League of Nations 102
criterion population 64, 67
Cuba, Guantanamo Bay 40
cultural genocide 193
Czech Prunéřoy II 189
Czech Republic 189

DASR (Draft Articles on State Responsibility) 186–7
"Declaration of a Roma Nation" 248–9
Declaration on Principles of International Law concerning Friendly Relations and Cooperation among States 101–2
Declaration on Rights and Duties of States 24, 171
Declaration on Rights of Indigenous Peoples 165
decline of sovereignty 128–9
defined territory 33–8
denationalisation of protection 160
deterritorialisation 124
de-territorialized action 205
deterritorialized statehood 45, 70, 206
deterritorialized States 70
dethronement of religion 48
diasporas 42
diplomatic envoys 38
diplomatic protection 55, 162
diplomatic relations 102
disappearance of State 8, 14, 36, 64, 71, 159, 190
displaced people 196, 247–8; legal status 169
Draft Articles on State Responsibility (DASR) 186–7
Draft Declaration on Rights and Duties of States 100–1, 108
Dutch State, GHG emissions 116–17
duties: of conduct 186; to intervene 179; to offer assistance 194; of prevention 186; of the State 101

economy, globalization 130
elimination of statelessness 164
environmental migrants 253n32
environmental policy 115
equal rights 132
e-residency 53–4
erga omnes 173, 178, 191, 208
Estonia 52, 54
Ethiopia 52
Ethnic movements 49
European Coal and Steel Community 122
European Convention on Human Rights 107
European Court of Human Rights 107, 127, 170
European General Court 118
European Union 124; borders 124–5; sovereignty 122
exiled government 40
ex-situ nationhood 53
extinction of a State 14, 31, 32, 61, 69, 158–9; *see also* loss of statehood
extraterritorial obligations 174–5

Falkland Islands/Malvinas 42
feudalism 46
Fiji 64
financial obligations 201
Finland 40, 253n32
fixed personalized loyalty 113
Fongafale Island 8
foreign territory, sovereignty 39–42
fresh water 36
fulfill-facilitate 175
fulfill-provide 175
functional sovereignty 42, 51

General Assembly (UN) 2, 9–10, 59, 102, 106–7, 112, 158, 164, 182–3, 189, 245
Geneva Refugee Convention 167

GHG emissions 116–17
global action 176
global warming 8–9, 187, 251
globalization 104, 129–30
governments in exile 40
greenhouse effect 3–4, 57
greenhouse gases 246
Greenpeace Southeast Asia 119
Group of 77 59–60, 185
Guantanamo Bay 40, 162
guest States 40–1

habitable territory 35
Hansa 47
Hay-Bunau Varilla treaty 39
Hezbollah 48
Holy Roman Empire 46–7
Holy See 50–1
Hong Kong 40
host States 38, 40–1, 66–8, 169, 249
human rights 106–14, 130, 246–7; importance of nationality 160–5; infringements on 165–9; nationality 161; protection of 132
human rights approach 172–5
human rights atrocities 200
Human Rights Council 111
human security 181
human settlement 34
humanization 14, 104–14, 131–2
Hungary 197

ice sheets 5
Immigration Act, New Zealand 167, 247
impermeable borders 124
India 171
Indigenous and Tribal Peoples Convention (1989) 165
indigenous peoples: infringements on human rights 165–9; relocation 196
individualism 112, 132
individuals 107, 112–13, 245, 248; nationality 160–5; Universal Natural Person 248
infrared radiation 3
infringements on human rights 165–9
insurance 246
Inter-American Commission on Human Rights 188
Inter-American Conference 123
Inter-American Convention on Human Rights 161, 188
Inter-American Court of Human Rights 161
Inter-American States 123
interconnectivity 115, 250
Intergovernmental Panel on Climate Change (IPCC) 4, 6, 10, 57, 184
international citizenship 129
International Commission on Intervention and State Sovereignty (ICISS) 179
international community 41, 112, 126, 173, 199, 244; solidarity 175–9
international cooperation 126, 174, 176; *see also* cooperation
International Council on Human Rights Policy 206
International Court for Human Rights 249
International Court of Justice (ICJ) 112, 158, 208–9
International Covenant on Civil and Political Rights (ICCPR) 44, 167, 168, 174
International Covenant on Economic, Social and Cultural Rights (ICESCR) 44, 174, 178
International Law Association, Committee on International Law and Sea Level Rise 1
International Law Commission (ILC) 101, 195, 203; Declaration on Rights and Duties of States (1947) 171; Draft Articles on State Responsibility (DASR) 186; Draft Declaration on Rights and Duties of States 108
international person 102
international security 111–12
internet-based sovereign country, Wirtland 53
inter-state claims 187–8
interventions 179–80, 182–3, 201; *see also* preventative action/intervention
Inuit Circumpolar Conference 193
Inuit Petition 188
Iran 48
Islamic State 48
Israel 39
Israeli and Palestinian Declarations of Independence 65–6

Jerusalem 42
Jewish diaspora 65
joint sovereignty 42
Juliana v US 117
jurisdiction 45–6, 54–6; universal jurisdiction 178
jurisdictional conflicts 127
jus cogens 178
jus cosmopoliticum (providing rules for the relationships between individuals and foreign States) 112

jus gentium (providing something like a constitutional order among States) 112

Kanton Island 8
Kiribati 7–8, 58, 67, 168, 193
Kyoto Protocol (1997) 11, 131, 172, 188

labour migrants 234n419
LaGrand Case 55
landlines 33
Latvia 52
law, concept of 26
Law of the Sea Convention 34–5
League of Nations 42
lease agreements 40
legal characteristics of States 100
legal status, displaced people 169
legitimacy 26
Libya 40, 110
limitations on action on foreign territory 41–2
Lithuania 52
litigation, climate change 116–19
livelihood 170
Lliuya v. RWE 118–19
loss of population 64–8
loss of statehood 159, 204–9; nationality 160–5
loss of territory 32–3, 69; considerations with regard to potential loss 56–62; defined territory 33–8
low-tide elevation 33–4
loyalty 113

Maastricht Principles on Extraterritorial Obligations of States in the Area of Economic, Social and Cultural Rights 174
Maastricht Treaty 112
Malaysia 43
Maldives 7, 35, 41, 56–7, 67, 193, 244
Malta *see* Sovereign Military Order of Malta
maritime entitlements 35
maritime zones 35
Marshall Islands *see* Republic of Marshall Islands
membership in international organizations 102
Micronesia 189–90
migrants 64, 234n419; environmental migrants 253n32
migration 31
Millennium Declaration 192
Millennium Development Goals 245
modern State, rights of 100–2
Monetary Gold principle 190–1
Montevideo Convention on the Rights and Duties of States 25, 28n17, 53–4
Muslims 48
Myanmar 192

national sovereignty 121, 131
nationalism 124
nationality 160–5, 171
natural adaptation 7
Nauru 7, 58
Netherlands 116–17
new world order 130
New Zealand 35, 196; Citizenship Act 167; Immigration Act 247–8
Non-Proliferation Treaty (NPT) 190
non-refoulement principle 215n90
non-State transnational actors 119
non-territorial unions 46–50
NPT (Non-Proliferation Treaty) 190

obligation: ensure enjoyment of human rights 178; financial obligations 201; to fulfill 175; to protect, human rights approach 172–5; of State 169–71
Operation Lifeline Sudan 174
opinio juris 61
Order of Malta *see* Sovereign Military Order of Malta

Pacific Access Category 234n419
Pacific Islands Forum 35
Palau 1, 58–9, 189
Panama 171; Canal Zone 39–40
Papua New Guinea, Carteret Islands 8–9
Paris Agreement 11, 116, 169, 172, 204
Peace of Westphalia 36, 47, 105, 113, 123, 160, 205
Pedra Branca/Pulau Batu Puteh 43
People, territory, and power ("Drei-Elemente-Lehre") 25
People's Climate Case 118
permeable boundaries 124–5
personal allegiance 36, 43
personal sovereignty 43
Philippine Human Rights Commission 119
Philippines 34
Phoenix Islands group 8
Pliocene Epoch 4
population: criterion 64; displacement 36; loss of 64–8; right to protect 182–3

post-Westphalian system 122, 126, 130
potential loss of territory 56–62
preventative action/intervention 201
Prevention of Discrimination and Protection of Minorities 68
"Principality of Sealand" 65
Prohibition of retrospective assumption of responsibility 187
protection of human rights 132
Protection of Human Rights and the Principle of Non-intervention in Internal Affairs of States 107

Rangzen Lag-Teb (Green Book) 66
Re Burriel 40
Re Cia. de Transportes des Gelabert 40
Re Kenneth Robert Bartlett 40
reciprocity 55
reduction of statelessness 164
Refugee Convention 247
refugee crisis 124, 172
refugee law 167–9
refugee status 167
refugees, climate refugees 236n447, 247, 249
religion 44, 47–8; Catholic Church 51
relocating populations 65, 67, 169–70
Republic of Marshall Islands (RMI) 7–8, 58, 189–90
Republic of Nauru 7
Resolution 43/53 9
responsibility 106, 199–203; causal responsibility 184–91; common but differentiated responsibility 186, 197; human rights approach 172–5; of individuals 106; of the one able to respond 191–8; to prevent 201; R2P *see* Responsibility to Protect; solidarity 175–9
responsibility *sui generis* 184
Responsibility to Protect (R2P) 14, 110, 179–84, 192–3, 195, 197, 199, 203, 207, 248
responsible sovereignty 111
reterritorialized 125
Rhodesia 114
right: to existence 63, 69, 171; to enter the State 161; to international assistance 174; to intervene 179, 181; to protect citizens against violation by another State 162; to sovereignty 38–9; to vote 161–2
rights gap 164
rights of a Modern State 100–2
Rio Declaration on Environment and Development 115, 131, 186
rocks 33–4
Roma Nation 49
Rome Statute of the International Criminal Court (ICC) (1998) 122

Saar 42
Saint Vincent and the Grenadines, potential loss of territory 60
scattered people 65–7
sea-level rise 1–6, 11, 35, 57, 59, 61, 159, 175, 193, 205, 207, 245
Security Council 61, 111, 200–2
self-centered solidarity 250
self-determination 44, 48, 50, 68, 103, 113–14, 132
shared responsibility 185
Sharia 48
SIDS (small island developing States) 61
Singapore 43
small island developing States (SIDS) 61
solidarity 110, 122; responsibility 175–9; self-centered solidarity 250
South China Sea Arbitration 34
sovereign authority 110
sovereign equality 62
Sovereign Military Order of Malta 50–1
sovereign right 131
sovereign subjects of international law without territory 50–1
sovereignty 37–8, 62, 103–4, 109, 127, 194, 206; absolute sovereignty 110–11; aquitorial sovereignty 35; decline of 128–9; foreign territory 39–42; functional sovereignty 42; globalization 120–2; human rights 108–9; as international social function 127; joint sovereignty 42; national sovereignty 131; personal sovereignty 43; redefining 109–10; responsible sovereignty 111; rights and duties 38–9; territorial sovereignty 42, 45–6; unlimited sovereignty 108
"Sovereignty over Pedra Branca/Pulau Batu Puteh, Middle Rocks and South Ledge" 43
Soviet Union 40, 52
State: definition 24–6, 37, 99; legal characteristics of 100; role of 13, 114; thin State 120
statehood 13, 24–7, 45, 99; deterritorialized statehood 45;

endangered by loss of defined territory 36–8; extinction of a State 32; importance of 158; Westphalian notion of statehood 46
statehood without territory: non-territorial unions 46–50; sovereign subjects of international law without territory 50–1; States that temporarily lost their territory 52; Virtual States 52–6
stateless nations 50
statelessness 163–4
States that temporarily lost their territory 52
Statism 108
steric sea level rise 5
Stockholm Declaration 186
subsidiarity 175
succession of States 45
super-State 245
supranationality 122
supra-territorial issues 127–8
supremacy of international law 108
Sweden 253n32

tax transparency, Virtual States 54
Teitiota Case 167–8
temporary loss of territory 52
territorial integrity 63
territorial jurisdiction, citizenship 54
territorial sea 33–4
territorial sovereignty 42, 45–6
territoriality 37, 62, 125
territory 26, 32–3, 62–3, 70, 244
thermal expansion 5
thin State 120
Thirty Years War 48
Tibetans 66
tolerated action on foreign territory 39–41
Trail Smelter principle 186
Tulele Peisa 8–9
Tuvalu 7–8, 57–8, 187

UNCLOS (UN Convention on the Law of the Sea) 186, 188
UNEP (UN Environment Programme) 10
UNFCCC (Framework Convention on Climate Change) 10–11, 131, 175, 186, 205–6
United Kingdom 40
United Nations 123, 245–6; Charter 106, 121–2, 131; Commission on Human Rights 111; Convention on the Law of the Sea (UNCLOS) 186, 188; Convention to Combat Desertification 116; Covenants 166; Declaration on the Rights of Indigenous Peoples 165; Environment Programme (UNEP) 10; Framework Convention on Climate Change (UNFCCC) 10–11, 131, 175, 186, 205–6; General Assembly 102, 189; Human Rights Committee 167–8; Human Rights Council 111; Millennium Declaration 192; Responsibility to Protect 14; Security Council 61, 111, 200–2; Universal Declaration of Human Rights 107, 131, 161; World Summit Agreement 110
United States 188; greenhouse gas emissions 188; Guantanamo Bay 40; Panama Canal Zone 39–40; potential loss of territory 59; Supreme Court 160
Universal Declaration of Human Rights 107, 131, 161
universal jurisdiction 178
Universal Natural Person 248
unlimited sovereignty 108
unsuitable for human settlement 34
Urgenda Foundation v. State of the Netherlands 116–17

Vanuatu 246
Vatican City 51
Vienna Convention on Succession of States in Respect of States Property, Archives, and Debts 45
Vienna Convention on Succession of States in Respect of Treaties 45
Vienna Convention on the Law of Treaties 24
Virtual States 52–6

Wesphalian system 103
Western Sahara Advisory opinion 65
Westphalia 44, 47, 126; *see also* Peace of Westphalia
Westphalian notion of statehood 46
Westphalian system 130
Wirtland 53, 56
WMO (World Meteorological Organization) 10
World Bank 107
world citizens 112–13
World Meteorological Organization (WMO) 10
World State 245
World Summit Agreement (UN) 110
World Summit Outcome 182
World Trade Organization (WTO) 122